FERTILIZATION IN HIGHER PLANTS

LIVERPOOL UNIVERSITY LIBRARY

FERTILIZATION IN HIGHER PLANTS

Proceedings of the International Symposium on Fertilization in Higher Plants
Nijmegen, the Netherlands, August 28-30, 1974

Editor:
H. F. Linskens

1974

NORTH-HOLLAND PUBLISHING COMPANY – AMSTERDAM • OXFORD
AMERICAN ELSEVIER PUBLISHING COMPANY, INC. – NEW YORK

Library of Congress Catalog Card Number: 74–83732

North-Holland ISBN: 0 7204 45078
American Elsevier ISBN: 0 444 107487

PUBLISHERS:
NORTH-HOLLAND PUBLISHING COMPANY – AMSTERDAM
NORTH-HOLLAND PUBLISHING COMPANY, LTD. – OXFORD

SOLE DISTRIBUTORS FOR THE U.S.A. AND CANADA:
AMERICAN ELSEVIER PUBLISHING COMPANY, INC.
52 VANDERBILT AVENUE, NEW YORK, N.Y. 10017

PRINTED IN THE NETHERLANDS

TO THE MEMORY OF OUR FRIENDS

G. Erdtman († February 18, 1973)
E.A. Britikov († December 26, 1973)
R.G. Stanley († April 15, 1974)

This volume is dedicated to the memory of three eminent scientists, who attended the previous meetings and are no longer among us:

Gerd Erdtman, the famous Swedish palynologist and great old man of pollen research, whose humorous and witty speech at the London symposium will be remembered by many colleagues. He died last year at the age of 83,

Zhenja Britikov, the Russian pioneer in fertilization physiology, a good man and a dear fried for many years, who died in December 1973, a few days after my last visit to Moscow, and

Bob Stanley, a stimulating personality who fascinated many young scientists – and artists – for more than 20 years. He was suddenly taken away a few weeks after our last trip together through Central America, and after his last work, a book on the biochemistry of pollen, was taken into print. He was killed on April 15, 1974.

May they stand for all others working in our common field of interest, who passionately wanted to join us but were not permitted to attend through adverse circumstances.

PREFACE

This volume contains papers presented at the International Symposium "Fertilization in Higher Plants", held at the Department of Botany, University of Nijmegen, August 28–30, 1974.

The conference was the fourth meeting of plant embryologists (previous meetings were held in Paris in 1968, Reims in 1970, and Siena in 1972) and the third meeting of pollen physiologists (previous meetings were held in Nijmegen in 1963 and in Pullman, Washinton in 1969). The purpose of these conferences is to bring together scientists specialising in fundamental processes of the starting phase of seed production in higher plants, from the maturation of the gametes to the formation of the diploid zygote. This has been approached experimentally and theoretically through the biochemical, cytological and phylogenetic disciplines.

The following people acted as chairmen during the various sessions: M. Favre-Duchartre, W.A. Jensen, J.P. Mascarenhas, D.L. Mulcahy, P. Pfahler, G. Sarfatti, J. Tupý, J.F.G.M. Wintermans and M.T.M. Willems. Their help, was greatly appreciated.

It is a pleasure to acknowledge the help of Michael Favre-Duchartre (Reims), Giaccomo Sarfatti (Siena), J. Heslop-Harrison (Kew Gardens), B.M. Johri (Dehli) and the late Robert G. Stanley in preparing this conference. The lectures are reproduced in full, including references, in this volume, and formed the base of discussions.

Special thanks are due to the staff of the Faculty of Science of the University of Nijmegen for perparing and organising the meeting: in particular to Dr. C.J.M. Aarts, director of the faculty, his assistant Mr. P.J.M. Toll, my secretary Mrs. E.R. Tummers-Moesker and all who collaborated to create a suitable environment for the exchange of scientific results and ideas.

The rapid publication of this volume was possible thanks to the excellent work of ASP Biological and Medical Press, Amsterdam and the cooperation of Drs. J. Geelen. Mr. N. Kirby and Miss A.M. Jo Kiem Tioe are gratefully acknowledged for their assistance in preparing the manuscripts for publication.

The contributions have not been reviewed before printing. The authors therefore take full responsibility for the contents of their papers.

University of Nijmegen
(The Netherlands)
November 1974

H.F. Linskens

CONTENTS

THE PROGAMIC PHASE

THE FUSION

WHY FERTILIZATION RESEARCH?
In place of an introduction

The fact that most of the food products used by man are derived from fertilization products of higher plants has not yet penetrated the public conscience, nor attracted the general attention to the scientific community. Not only wheat, rice and oil delivering seeds, but also the majority of vegetables, spices, fruits and flowers are produced by application of the fertilization process to members of the plant kingdom.

The process of fertilization, which can be defined as the transition from the haploid to the diploid phase during development, has, as its complementary event, meiosis. Sexuality has, therefore, to be seen in the light of rearrangement of genetic material among individuals to ensure variability. In higher plants this regenerating aspect of fertilization to guarantee genetic homoeostatis has become combined with aspects of multiplication and dispersal.

The special situation in phanerogamic plants is their strong tendency to reduce the gametophyte and thus give up their autonomy. In researching fertilization of the higher plants, we are therefore confronted with special physiological problems. These problems arise in connection with the metabolic exchange between the surrounding sporophytic tissue and the ripening microgametophytes (pollen) and the macro(mega)gametophytes (eggs). However, these processes are preceded by a phase of intensive interaction between the male gametophyte and the sporophyte, which can be called the progamic phase (Linskens, 1967).

Putting this meeting in a wider context, we are anxious to find out the scientific basis of world food production. For, aside from trial-and-error methods, future food production requires not only insight into the fertilization processes of higher plants, but also the creation of prerequisites for the handling and directing of fertilization processes.

At the present time we are moving away from descriptive embryology and phylogenetic speculations about fertilization towards a more experimental, biochemical approach. The ultimate target will be to break through the intergeneric and intrageneric fertilization barriers in order to achieve fertilization engineering. This will make an important contribution towards ensuring that food production matches the population increase on earth and at the same time it may provide a weapon to bring about world peace (Stanley, 1973).

It is a fact that, up until now, granting and subsidizing agencies in many countries have not realized the importance of reinforcing basic research in fertilization processes in higher plants. The basic and practical problems of reproductive physiology in corn and crop plants have still to be solved. Problems of the quantitative and qualitative control of fertility will become the central topic of a comparative gametology and syngamy in the near future (Tyler, 1967). All modern means and methods, including ultrastructural research (Jensen, 1972) and biochemical approaches, have to be concentrated on these fundamental questions. All people with new ideas are called upon to join plant embryologists, pollen physiologists and reproduction biochemists. We should bot be afraid to seek publicity. The ultimate goal is: Food for Peace.

H.F. Linskens

REFERENCES

W.A. Jensen, *The embryo sac and fertilization in angiosperms.* Harold L. Lyon Arboretum, Hawaii, 1972.

H.F. Linskens, *Reproduction, sexuality and fertilization. A general concept.* Encl. Pl. Physiol. 18, 1–4, 1967.

R.G. Stanley, *Food for Piece*, Gordon and Beach, New York, 1973.

A. Tyler, *Problems and procedures of comparative gametology and syngamy.* Fertilization (eds. C.B. Metz, A. Monroy) I, 1–26 (1967), Academic Press, New York–London.

POLLEN GENETICS

Fertilization in Higher Plants, ed. H.F. Linskens.

POLLEN GENOTYPE STUDIES IN MAIZE (ZEA MAYS L.)

P. L. Pfahler

Department of Agronomy
University of Florida
Gainesville, Florida 32611, U.S.A.

1. Introduction

Limited information is available concerning the influence of the genes contained in the pollen grain on the composition and function of the pollen grain. A unique example is the waxy locus in maize which is known to alter both aspects. Pollen grains containing the dominant (Wx) allele possess amylose while those containing the recessive (wx) allele have no amylose[1]. In relation to function, wx pollen grains are less efficient in fertilizing when in competition with Wx pollen grains[2,3,4]. Probably a relationship between amylose content and fertilization exists but the mechanism is not known at this time. This example indicates that the composition and function of the pollen grain can be altered by the pollen genotype.

Maize is ideally adapted to research relating pollen genotype to the composition and function of pollen grains because of the large numbers of pollen grains produced, the ease in pollinating and crossing, the large numbers of inbreds and hybrids available and the wealth of genetic information present. The existence of many endosperm mutants is also a distinct advantage since many of their biochemical effects in the endosperm are known and their use makes possible the classification of very large populations.

This report summarizes the major results found in my maize pollen research program. Many important aspects were done in close cooperation with Professor Dr. H.F. Linskens of Nijmegen University. The studies include both aspects mentioned above. The composition studies included free amino acid content, ash percentage and mineral element content. The functions included both fertilization ability and *in vitro* germination studies.

2. Materials and methods

In all tests, large quantities of pollen grains were collected by the method of Pfahler[5]. This method involved cutting the tassels in the late afternoon (1500 to 1800 hours) on one day and immediately placing the cut ends in water. The tassels were then placed in a closed room overnight. The next morning (800 to 1000 hours) the anthers dehisced and the pollen released. The advantage of this method was that since the environmental conditions associated with collection were standardized, the pollen collected over various dates and years would be more uniform.

COMPOSITION

Free amino acid content. The effect of the alleles at the waxy (*wx*), sugary (su_1) and shrunken (sh_2) loci on the content during various pollen storage periods at 2°C was examined. Comparisons between the dominant and recessive alleles at each locus were in the same average genetic background. Additional details are given in Linskens and Pfahler[6].

Ash percentage and mineral element content. The ash percentage and mineral element content of the pollen grains from two inbred lines (Oh43,H55) and three single cross hybrids (Wf9x55,Ky49xKy27,K64xK55) were determined. Additional details are given in Pfahler and Linskens[7].

FUNCTIONS

Fertilization ability. The dominant (*Y*) and recessive (*y*) alleles at the yellow endosperm locus were used as a genetic marker. Pollen grains (*Y*) from each of four yellow (*YY*) single cross hybrids (Wf9xH55,Wf9xH50,H49xH55,H49xH50) were mechanically mixed on an equal volume basis with pollen grains (*y*) from each of two white (*yy*) single cross hybrids (Ky49xKy27,K64xK55). The mixtures were then used to pollinate each of two white (*yy*) female sporophytes (single cross hybrids, Ky49xKy27,K64xK55) in all possible combinations. The percent yellow (*Yyy*) kernels on each ear obtained from the pollination were then classified. Based on pollen diameter, the percent yellow kernels was adjusted so that theoretically a value of 50 would represent equal fertilization ability between the *Y* and *y* pollen grains in the mixture. Further details are given in Pfahler[8].

In vitro germination tests. The medium consisted of 15% sucrose and 0.6% bacto-agar supplemented with all possible combinations of two levels (0 and 0.03%) of calcium nitrate, $Ca(NO_3)_2 \cdot 4H_2O$ and two levels (0 and 0.01%) of boric acid, H_3BO_3. The preparation of this medium and the procedure for classifying percent germination and measuring pollen tube length are presented in Pfahler[9].

To test the effect of pollen source, the pollen grains from six single cross hybrids (Wf9xH55,Wf9xH50,H49xH55,H49xH50,Ky49xKy27,K64x K55) were used. Additional details are given in Pfahler[10].

To test the effect of heterozygosity level of the pollen source, the pollen grains of three inbred lines (H49,H55,H50) and two of their single cross hybrids (H49xH55,H49xH50) were used. Further details are given in Pfahler[11].

To test the effect of the $\underline{Rf}_1$ and $\underline{rf}_1$ alleles, pollen grains from $\underline{Rf}_1\underline{Rf}_1$ and $\underline{rf}_1\underline{rf}_1$ in two inbred isogenic backgrounds (Oh43,106) were used. Additional details are given in Pfahler[12].

The relationship between pollen storage at 2°C and the alleles at the waxy (wx), sugary ($\underline{su}_1$) and shrunken ($\underline{sh}_2$) loci was tested. Comparisons between the dominant and recessive alleles at each locus were in the same average genetic background. Further details are given in Pfahler and Linskens[13].

3. Results

COMPOSITION

Free amino acid content. The results are presented in Table 1.

Table 1

Storage effects of the free amino acid content (μ moles/mg dry pollen) of pollen grains containing the dominant and recessive alleles at three loci. Only those amino acids at each locus which showed a significant allele x storage interaction are presented[a]

Locus	Amino Acid	Allele	Storage (days at 2°C) 0	5
Waxy	Alanine	Wx	12.39	8.14
		wx	12.04	8.91
	Ethanolanine	Wx	2.95	11.17
		wx	2.16	5.88
	Aspartic acid	Wx	4.23	8.69
		wx	4.51	12.62
	Glycine	Wx	1.43	1.26
		wx	1.21	1.06
Sugary	Alanine	$\underline{Su}_1$	13.33	7.34
		$\underline{su}_1$	12.26	10.37
	Ethanolanine	$\underline{Su}_1$	2.96	11.08
		$\underline{su}_1$	2.61	5.98
	Aspartic acid	$\underline{Su}_1$	4.13	12.01
		$\underline{su}_1$	3.25	7.98

	Aminobutyric acid	Su_1	3.02	5.42
		su_1	1.70	8.00
Shrunken	Alanine	Sh_2	13.13	9.28
		sh_2	12.35	9.50
	Ethanolanine	Sh_2	2.72	8.99
		sh_2	2.00	4.70
	Aspartic acid	Sh_2	4.57	12.80
		sh_2	3.75	8.65
	Valine	Sh_2	1.23	1.34
		sh_2	0.84	1.10
	Leucine	Sh_2	0.44	0.82
		sh_2	0.34	0.65

[a]Adapted from Linskens and Pfahler[6]

Of the 15 amino acids tested, only 7 were associated with a significant allele x storage interaction at one or more loci. Alanine, ethanolanine and aspartic acid were influenced by the alleles at all loci. Glycine was only influenced by the alleles at the waxy locus, aminobutyric acid by those at the sugary locus and valine and leucine by those at the shrunken locus. Apparently, three amino acids are altered by all loci while four amino acids are locus-specific.

Ash percentage and mineral element content. The ash percentage results are given in Table 2. A distinct difference was found between

Table 2

Ash percentage of pollen grains from various pollen sources[a]

Pollen source	Percentage
Wf9xH55	2.93
Ky49xKy27	2.94
K64xK55	2.83
Oh43	3.70
H55	3.77

[a]Adapted from Pfahler and Linskens[7]

the hybrids and inbreds with no difference occurring within each group. Apparently, ash percentage is primarily associated with heterozygosity level with the hybrids having a substantially lower ash percentage than the inbreds.

A broad range in element content was found (Table 3). Based on

Table 3

Mineral element content of pollen grains[a]

Element	Content	
	Micrograms/gram dry weight	Micrograms/gram ash weight
Al	0.46[c]	13.83[b]
Ca	9.20[c]	288.39[c]
Cu	0.20	6.43
Fe	0.48[c]	15.06[c]
K	105.09[c]	3287.58[c]
Mg	11.58	370.27[c]
Mn	0.24	7.48[b]
Na	5.93	185.55
P	69.57	2176.65
Zn	1.90	58.65

[a] Adapted from Pfahler and Linskens[7]
[b,c] Significant differences (F values) at the 5 and 1% level respectively between pollen source means that were averaged to obtain this value.

either dry weight or ash weight, K was the major element followed by P, Mg, Ca and Na. The Mg content was considerably higher than the Ca content. Based on dry weight, significant differences resulting from pollen sources were obtained for Al, Ca, Fe and K. Based on ash weight, the same elements were significant but significant pollen source differences were found for Mn and Mg also. Apparently, pollen source can alter the mineral element content of the pollen grains.

FUNCTIONS

Fertilization ability. The results are presented in Table 4.

Table 4

Fertilization ability (percent yellow kernels) of pollen grains from various yellow pollen sources to fertilize two female sporophytes in competition with pollen grains from two white pollen sources. A value of 50 indicates equal fertilization ability of the yellow and white pollen grains in the mechanical mixture[a]

Yellow pollen source	White pollen source			
	Ky49xKy27		K64xK55	
	Female sporophyte		Female sporophyte	
	Ky49xKy27	K64xK55	Ky49xKy27	K64xK55
Wf9xH55	57	62	40	44
Wf9xH50	52	55	39	40

H49xH55	48	53	34	38
H49xH50	53	54	37	41

[a]Adapted from Pfahler[8]

Distinct differences were found between the yellow pollen sources in their ability to compete in fertilization. As an example, with Ky49x Ky27 as the white pollen source and female sporophyte, a range of 57 to 48% was found between the yellow pollen sources. Differences were also found between the white pollen sources. As an example, with Wf9 xH55 pollen mixed with Ky49xKy27 pollen used to pollinate Ky49xKy27, a value of 57% was obtained. When Wf9xH55 pollen was mixed with K64x K55 pollen and this mixture was used to pollinate Ky49xKy27, a value of 40% was found. Differences were also found between female sporophytes. A (Wf9xH55)+(Ky49xKy27) mixture used to pollinate Ky49xKy27 had a value of 57% but when used to pollinate K64xK55, a value of 62% was obtained. Apparently, fertilization ability is a very complex process depending not only on the pollen source and female sporophyte but also on their interaction.

In vitro germination tests. Distinct differences were found between the pollen grains of various single cross hybrids when placed on a medium supplemented with two levels of calcium nitrate and boric acid (Table 5). Maximum germination and pollen tube length was obtained when both compounds were present in the medium. However, the response to the presence of calcium nitrate or boric acid or both varied greatly depending on the hybrid involved.

Table 5

In vitro germination characteristics of the pollen grains from various single cross hybrids with different concentrations of calcium nitrate (Ca) and boric acid (B) in the basal medium (15% sucrose + 0.6% bacto-agar)[a]

Character	Hybrid	Medium supplement			
		0%Ca+0%B	0%Ca+0.01B	0.03%Ca+0%B	0.03%Ca+00.01%B
Percent germination	Wf9xH55	33	11	26	42
	Wf9xH50	26	5	37	39
	H49xH55	42	13	37	54
	H49xH50	31	7	42	42
	Ky49xKy27	27	9	17	20
	K64xK55	58	30	27	46

Pollen tube length (μ)	Wf9xH55	320	254	322	414
	Wf9xH50	257	225	310	393
	H49xH55	300	262	334	435
	H49xH50	253	222	314	340
	Ky49xKy27	311	254	340	412
	K64xK55	277	261	289	399

[a]Adapted from Pfahler[10]

The same situation occurred when pollen grains from various inbred lines and their hybrid combinations were placed on a medium supplemented with various levels of calcium nitrate and boric acid (Table 6). A distinct source effect was indicated with the hybrids in general within the parental range.

Table 6

In vitro germination characteristics of the pollen from three inbred lines and two of their hybrid combinations with different concentrations of calcium nitrate (Ca) and boric acid (B) in the basal medium (15% sucrose + 0.6% bacto-agar)[a]

Character	Pollen source	Medium supplement			
		0%Ca+0%B	0%Ca+0.01%B	0.03%Ca+0%B	0.03%Ca+0.01%B
Percent germination	H55	50	10	53	74
	H49xH55	39	30	41	48
	H49	46	30	44	55
	H49xH50	23	13	28	35
	H50	7	3	14	16
Pollen tube length (μ)	H55	305	304	346	460
	H49xH55	300	330	317	372
	H49	297	267	310	425
	H49xH50	227	248	279	369
	H50	223	207	321	359

[a]Adapted from Pfahler[11]

The effect of the $\underline{Rf_1}$ and $\underline{rf_1}$ alleles appeared to be conditioned by genetic background (Table 7). In the Oh43 background, the germination percentage was quite high and the pollen tube length quite long. In the 106 background, the reverse was found. Very few differences were found between the $\underline{Rf_1}$ and $\underline{rf_1}$ pollen grains in an Oh43 background

Table 7

In vitro germination characteristics of pollen grains containing the $\underline{Rf}_1$ and $\underline{rf}_1$ alleles with different concentrations of calcium nitrate (Ca) and boric acid (B) in the basal medium (15% sucrose + 0.6% bacto-agar)[a]

Character	Pollen source	Medium supplement			
		0%Ca+o%B	o%Ca+0.01%B	0.03%Ca+0%B	0.03%Ca+0.01%B
Percent germination	Oh43$\underline{Rf}_1\underline{Rf}_1$	57	56	28	50
	Oh43$\underline{rf}_1\underline{rf}_1$	57	54	32	55
	106$\underline{Rf}_1\underline{Rf}_1$	16	16	8	23
	106$\underline{rf}_1\underline{rf}_1$	30	20	16	44
Pollen tube length (μ)	Oh43$\underline{Rf}_1\underline{Rf}_1$	363	372	393	513
	Oh43$\underline{rf}_1\underline{rf}_1$	373	364	410	578
	106$\underline{Rf}_1\underline{Rf}_1$	328	302	279	408
	106$\underline{rf}_1\underline{rf}_1$	339	312	326	426

[a]Adapted from Pfahler[12]

but considerable differences were found in a 106 background.

The alleles at the waxy, sugary and shrunken loci altered germination percentage and pollen tube length at various storage periods (Table8). In all cases, a substantial increase in both germination percentage and pollen tube length occurred with 1 day of storage with a decrease observed thereafter. Interactions with the alleles at each locus was obtained with storage periods. The most pronounced example was at the waxy locus. At 3 days of storage, no germination of *Wx* pollen grains was observed while considerable germination was obtained with *wx* pollen grains. Apparently, alleles at some endosperm loci will alter germination characteristics.

Table 8

Storage effects on the *in vitro* germination characteristics of pollen grains containing the dominant and recessive alleles at three endosperm mutant loci. Medium contained 15% sucrose, 0.6% bacto-agar 0.03% calcium nitrate and 0.01% boric acid[a]

Character	Locus	Allele	Storage (days at 2° C)				
			0	1	2	3	4
Percent germination	Waxy	*Wx*	45	69	41	0	
		wx	35	70	66	31	0
	Sugary	$\underline{Su}_1$	30	57	36	23	0
		$\underline{su}_1$	34	60	57	34	0

	Shrunken	$\underline{Sh}_2$	35	64	64	40	0
		$\underline{sh}_2$	46	70	63	36	0
Pollen tube length (μ)	Waxy	Wx	437	463	447		
		wx	406	437	435	376	
	Sugary	$\underline{Su}_1$	420	453	422	400	
		$\underline{su}_1$	429	464	450	357	
	Shrunken	$\underline{Sh}_2$	472	524	495	439	
		$\underline{sh}_2$	472	512	500	429	

[a]Adapted from Pfahler and Linskens[13]

4. Discussion

Male gametes offer unique advantages to study many aspects of higher plants and animals. Male gametes are free-living, independent single cells that are active metabolically and are capable of growth in higher plants and movement in higher animals. Their simplicity relative to the sporophyte in both structure, physiology and function allows for intensive analysis without the confounding effect of differentiation. Their haploid genetic condition allows for critical examination of the effects of specific alleles without the confounding effect of dominance or epistasis.

The major problem associated with male gamete research is separating the effect of the male gamete genotype from that of its diploid source. The effect of the diploid source is equalized in a situation where the male gametes from one individual differ either in composition or function or both. Only a few instances are known. As indicated earlier[1], one example in higher plants is the waxy locus in maize. In this case, Wx and wx pollen grains from a heterozygous (Wx wx) plant can be distinguished both by composition (amylose content) and function (fertilization ability). In crosses of diploid x triploid plants of *Spinacia oleracea*, transmission differences between n+1 gametes associated with different chromosomes were pronounced[14]. In mammals, size differences between X and Y-bearing sperm from individual males have been reported and partially successful attempts have been made to control the sex ratio of progeny by selecting either type using various treatments[15,16]. In mice, aberrant ratios at the "tailless" locus as a result of differential transmission have been reported although no morphological or biochemical differences between sperm containing the T or t alleles have been observed[17,18]. However, for most studies, the use of male gametes derived from only one individual is impractical or impossible.

Another approach in which the effect of the male gamete genotype can be separated from its diploid source is to develop isogenic lines differing only in the locus under study. The development of isogenic lines is difficult and time consuming and complete isogenicity is never assured. This method was used in comparing $\underline{Rf_1Rf_1}$ and $\underline{rf_1rf_1}$ in two presumably isogenic inbred backgrounds (Table 7).

A third method to reduce or minimize the relationship between the male gamete genotype and its diploid source is to develop a common genetic background for the locus under study by appropriate crossing and selection procedures. In this method, the alleles are compared not in identical genetic backgrounds but in the same average genetic background. In the studies reported here, this type of comparison was involved in the free amino acid content (Table 1) and the *in vitro* storage effect (Table 8) studies.

The most common approach is to compare male gametes from various lines and assume differences are genetic. The effect of the source genotype cannot be separated from the genotype of the male gamete it produces. This approach was used in the studies reported here for ash content (Table 2), mineral element content (Table 3), fertilization ability (Table 4), and *in vitro* germination characteristics of hybrids and inbred lines (Tables 5 and 6). Differences between maize pollen isozymes were reported by testing the pollen grains from various inbred lines[19]. This approach was also used in determining differences between sperm from various mammalian species[15]. Strain differences were found for size, shape, fertility, melanizing ability, DNA content and antigenic properties.

The information derived from the studies reported here and in fact from all similar studies, is based on the approach used and this factor should be considered in the interpretation and conclusions. It is apparent from these results that differences between pollen genotype or pollen source genotype as reflected by the pollen grains exist. These differences were associated with many aspects of the composition and functions of the pollen grains.

The theoretical and practical implications of this research are broad and far reaching. In a theoretical sense, the results obtained from male gamete studies, in this case pollen grains from a highly differentiated organism, should make significant contributions to our understanding of molecular, biochemical and physiological genetics of higher organisms. In a practical sense, information linking pollen genotype to pollen structure, physiology and function may be used to select gametes to produce more desirable progeny. The control of sex ratio in humans and domesticated animals by sperm treatments is a well-known example. Another is the selection against aneuploid gametes by sperm treatment so as to eliminate aneuploid progeny which may possess undesirable qualities. Most predictive models used in both qualitative and quantitative genetics are based on the assumption that the ability of the male gamete to fertilize is completely independent of the genes it contains. No major difficulties are encountered in qualitative genetics since deviations from simple ratios would readily indicate those loci in which this assumption would be invalid. However, in quantitative genetics a major problem would exist. Because of the complexity of the segregation patterns, any deviations resulting from male transmission rates would be almost impossible to detect and thus predictions made as a result of using the models would be incorrect and misleading.

5. Acknowledgements

Many persons made significant contributions to the studies reported here. Thanks and appreciation for their assistance and cooperation are extended to Professor Dr. H.F. Linskens and his staff at Nijmegen University and to Carol H. Davis, Marketta M. Mount, H.S. Anspach, J.C. Harper and W.T. Mixon at the University of Florida. The skill of Patricia Cotton in the typing and organization of this manuscript is acknowledged and appreciated.

References

1. Neuffer, M.G., Jones, L. and Zuber, M.S., 1968, The mutants of maize (Crop Science Soc. Amer., Madison, Wisconsin).
2. Jones, D.F., 1922, Biol. Bull. 43, 1967.
3. Jones, D.F., 1924, Proc. Natl. Acad. Sci. U.S. 10, 218.
4. Sprague, G.F., 1933, Proc. Natl. Acad. Sci. U.S. 19, 838.
5. Pfahler, P.L., 1965, Genetics 52, 513.
6. Linskens, H.F. and Pfahler, P.L., 1973, Theor. Appl. Genet. 43, 49.
7. Pfahler, P.L. and Linskens, H.F., 1974, Theor, Appl. Genet. 44 (in press).
8. Pfahler, P.L., 1967, Genetics 57, 513.
9. Pfahler, P.L., 1967, Can. J. Bot. 45, 839.
10. Pfahler, P.L., 1968, Can. J. Bot. 46, 235.

11. Pfahler, P.L., 1970, Can. J. Bot. 48, 111.
12. Pfahler, P.L., 1971, Can. J. Bot. 49, 55.
13. Pfahler, P.L. and Linskens, H.F., 1972, Theor. Appl. Genet. 42, 136.
14. Janick, J., Mahoney, D.L. and Pfahler, P.L., 1959, J. Hered, L, 47.
15. Béatty, R.A., 1961, Animal Breeding Abstr. 29, 243.
16. Westoff, C.F. and Rindfuss, R.R., 1974, Science 184, 633.
17. Braden, A.W.H., 1958, Nature 181, 786.
18. Dunn, L.C., 1960, Amer. Nat. 94, 385.
19. Makinen, Y. and Macdonald, T., 1968, Physiol. Plant. 21, 477.

Fertilization in Higher Plants, ed. H.F. Linskens.

FERTILIZATION ABILITY OF MAIZE (ZEA MAYS L.) POLLEN GRAINS IV. INFLUENCE OF STORAGE AND THE ALLELES AT THE SHRUNKEN, SUGARY AND WAXY LOCI

P. L. Pfahler

Department of Agronomy
University of Florida
Gainesville, Florida 32611, U.S.A.

1. Introduction

The fertilization ability of pollen grains is an important and highly complex phenomenon. The effect of pollen genotype on fertilization ability varies widely depending on the species involved. In self-incompatible species, the allele contained in the pollen grain determines whether the pollen grain can effect fertilization through the style of a certain genotype[1,2,3]. In self-compatible species, no relationship between pollen genotype and fertilization ability is assumed. However, at a few loci within self-compatible species, exceptions have been reported. At the waxy locus in maize, pollen grains containing the wx allele are generally less competitive than Wx pollen grains but large environmental variations were noted[4,5,6]. Therefore, in plants, the effect of pollen genotype on fertilization ability covers the whole spectrum ranging from complete dependence to total independence depending on the species, locus and environment.

In maize which is classified as a self-compatible species, the percentage of pollen grains actually participating in fertilization is extremely small because of the millions released compared to the relatively small number of ovules available for fertilization. Since many pollen grains fall and germinate on an individual style, the competition as to which pollen grain will succeed in fertilizing the ovule is intense. In this situation, any relationship between pollen genotype and fertilization ability would influence the transmission of the allele to the next generation and as a result, would have great genetic and evolutionary significance.

The purpose of this study was to determine the effect of the dominant and recessive alleles at the shrunken (sh_2), sugary (su_1) and waxy (wx) loci on the fertilization or competitive ability of the pollen grains in which they are contained. Four collection dates were included to determine environmental effects.

2. Materials and methods

Three populations which were heterozygous ($\underline{Sh_2sh_2}$, $\underline{Su_1su_1}$, $\underline{Wxwx}$) for each locus were used. On each of four dates in 1973, large quantities of pollen from at least 40 plants in each population were collected by the method of Pfahler[7]. The collection dates were 30 May, 2 June, 6 June and 13 June and hereafter are designated A, B, C, and D respectively. Immediately after collection, a portion of the pollen from each population was used to pollinate 10 ears of the appropriate population. The remainder was placed in an open container at 2°C with no humidity control. At 1,2,3,4,5, and 6 days after storage initiation, a portion of the pollen was removed from each container and used to pollinate 10 ears in each corresponding population. Therefore, from the pollen collected from three populations on each of four collection dates, 10 ears were pollinated with pollen stored at 2°C for 0,1,2,3,4,5, and 6 days.

To reduce contamination, an excess of pollen was used for each pollination and the plants pollinated had been previously detasselled.

After maturity, each ear was harvested and classified for the mutant involved.

Heterogeneity chi square values (Table 1) between the 10 ears in the same locus, collection date and storage day were determined using no expected ratio[8]. At the shrunken locus, degrees of freedom were 9 except day 0 date C and day 6 date C which were 8,and day 6 date D which were 6. At the sugary locus, degrees of freedom were 9 except day 2 date C, day 2 date D, day 3 date B, day 5 date A, day 5 date C and day 6 date C which were 8. At the waxy locus, degrees of freedom were 9 except day 0 date C and day 4 date B which were 8.

The fertilization percentage (Table 2, Fig. 1) or the percentage of kernels fertilized by pollen grains containing the recessive allele at each locus was determined by multiplying the % recessive kernels by 2.

Chi square determinations were made to compare dates at day 0 within each locus (Table 3). A 3:1 ratio was used to determine significance assuming no differences between the fertilization ability of the dominant and recessive pollen grains. Also the observed ratio obtained at one date was used to test a second date.

Chi square tests were used to compare successive days within each locus, date and the total (Table 4). In this case, the observed ratio obtained in one day was used to test a second day.

3. Results

The total number of kernels classified and the % recessive kernels found are presented in Table 1. A distinct loss of pollen viability

Table 1

The total number of kernels classified and the % recessive kernels found for each locus

Locus	Day		Date A	B	C	D	Total
Shrunken	0	Number	4491	4873	4589	3869	17822
		% shrunken	22.11[b]	23.50	21.94	21.35[b]	22.28
	1	Number	4949	4251	4388	2482	16070
		% shrunken	23.28	23.95	23.86	24.78	23.85
	2	Number	3625	4056	4760	3960	16401
		% shrunken	23.26	24.85	22.69	23.43	23.53
	3	Number	3006	3571	4789	2987	14353
		% shrunken	24.22	24.28	22.97	23.30	23.63
	4	Number	2712	2112	3514	2617	10955
		% shrunken	23.53	25.24	22.03	23.08	23.27
	5	Number	1912	2074	2288	2783	9057
		% shrunken	23.59	22.52	21.63	23.25	22.74
	6	Number	352	1140	874	501	2867
		% shrunken	29.83	21.32[a]	26.20	22.16	24.00
	Total	Number	21047	22077	25202	19199	87525
		%shrunken	23.33	23.92	22.74	23.06	23.25
Sugary	0	Number	4609	3788	4293	3867	16557
		% sugary	26.27[b]	24.89	24.69	24.72	25.19
	1	Number	5178	4523	4908	3519	18128
		% sugary	25.80	23.52	25.00	23.10[b]	24.49
	2	Number	4529	3910	4661	2162	15262
		% sugary	25.77	23.91	24.07	22.66	24.33
	3	Number	4220	3541	4100	4007	15868
		% sugary	26.28	24.85	25.66	23.58	25.12
	4	Number	3271	3178	3232	2404	12085
		% sugary	26.05	23.66	23.95	21.88	24.02
	5	Number	2405	2098	1396	3387	9286
		% sugary	24.07	24.59	20.92	23.35	23.45
	6	Number	850	515	258	2031	3654
		% sugary	22.71	22.72	25.97	22.35[b]	22.74

	Total	Number	25062	21553	22848	21377	90840
		% sugary	25.72	24.16	24.48	23.27	24.46
Waxy	0	Number	4347	4890	4622	5942	19801
		% waxy	24.32	22.25	21.90	24.05[b]	23.16
	1	Number	5343	6175	5924	5758	23200
		% waxy	22.33	22.30[a]	22.60	23.08	22.58
	2	Number	4433	5148	5162	4991	19734
		% waxy	21.41	21.60	24.82[b]	22.58	22.65
	3	Number	4035	4839	4405	4320	17599
		% waxy	19.80	19.94	22.66	19.33	20.44
	4	Number	2894	3774	3409	2864	12941
		% waxy	19.11	18.39	21.82	18.92[b]	19.57
	5	Number	2826	2203	2940	2606	10575
		% waxy	19.89	19.02	20.27	16.81[a]	19.05
	6	Number	783	1233	794	1216	4026
		% waxy	17.88	14.84	18.01	18.01	17.01
	Total	Number	24661	28262	27256	27697	107876
		% waxy	21.30	20.66	22.43	21.37	21.43

[a,b] Significant heterogeneity values between the ears within each locus, day and date at the 5 and 1% level respectively

was apparent with increasing storage but since an excess of pollen was applied on each day, no reliable estimate of viability loss is possible. The percentage of significant heterogeneity values is within expected limits.

To simplify comparisons, the % recessive kernels was converted to fertilization percentage of the recessive pollen grains and these values are presented in Table 2.

Table 2

The fertilization percentage of the recessive pollen grains. A value of 50% would indicate equal fertilization ability between the dominant and recessive grains at each locus. A value below 50% would indicate that the recessive grains had less fertilization ability than the dominant grains, while a value above 50% would indicate the recessive grains had greater fertilization ability

Locus	Day	Date				Total
		A	B	C	D	
Shrunken	0	44.22	47.00	43.88	42.70	44.56
	1	46.56	47.90	47.72	49.56	47.70
	2	46.52	49.70	45.38	46.86	47.06
	3	48.44	48.56	45.94	46.60	47.26

	4	47.06	50.48	44.06	46.16	46.54
	5	47.18	45.04	43.26	46.50	45.48
	6	59.66	42.64	52.40	44.32	48.00
	Total	46.66	47.84	45.48	46.12	46.50
Sugary	0	52.54	49.78	49.38	49.44	50.38
	1	51.60	47.04	50.00	46.20	48.98
	2	51.54	47.82	48.14	45.32	48.66
	3	52.56	49.70	51.32	47.16	50.24
	4	52.10	47.32	47.90	43.76	48.04
	5	48.14	49.18	41.84	46.70	46.90
	6	45.42	45.44	51.94	44.70	45.48
	Total	51.44	48.32	48.96	46.54	48.92
Waxy	0	48.64	44.50	43.80	48.10	46.32
	1	44.66	44.60	45.20	46.16	45.16
	2	42.82	43.20	49.64	45.16	45.30
	3	39.60	39.88	45.32	38.66	40.88
	4	38.22	36.78	43.64	37.84	39.14
	5	39.78	38.04	40.54	33.62	38.10
	6	35.76	29.68	36.02	36.02	34.02
	Total	42.60	41.32	44.86	42.74	42.86

At the shrunken locus on day 0, the fertilization percentages of the $\underline{sh}_2$ grains was less than that of the $\underline{Sh}_2$ grains on all dates as indicated by the significant deviations from a 3:1 ratio (Table 3).

Table 3

Chi square values from comparisons between collection dates at storage day 0

Locus	Comparison[a]		Chi square value
	Column 1	Column 2	
Shrunken	3:1	A	19.99[c]
	3:1	B	5.87[b]
	3:1	C	22.86[c]
	3:1	D	27.50[c]
	A	B	5.43[b]
	A	C	0.07
	A	D	1.30
	B	C	6.15[b]
	B	D	9.93[c]
	C	D	0.80

Sugary	3:1	A	3.99[b]
	3:1	B	0.02
	3:1	C	0.22
	3:1	D	0.16
	A	B	3.73
	A	C	5.56[b]
	A	D	4.81[b]
	B	C	0.09
	B	D	0.06
	C	D	0.00
Waxy	3:1	A	1.09
	3:1	B	19.73[c]
	3:1	C	23.76[c]
	3:1	D	2.87
	A	B	11.34[c]
	A	C	14.71[c]
	A	D	0.23
	B	C	0.34
	B	D	11.12[c]
	C	D	16.12[c]

[a] A 3:1 ratio or the observed ratio of the date in column 1 was used as the expected ratio to test the date in column 2

[b,c] Significant from the expected ratio at the 5 and 1% level respectively with 1 degree of freedom

Ratio differences between dates at day 0 were present but not pronounced. Dates greatly influenced the reponse to storage (Table 4).

Table 4

Chi square values from comparisons between successive storage days within collection dates and the total

Locus	Comparison[a]		Date				
	Day	Day	A	B	C	D	Total
Shrunken	0	1	3.91[b]	0.48	9.41[c]	17.38[c]	22.71[c]
	1	2	0.00	1.82	3.60	3.83	0.91
	2	3	1.56	0.63	0.21	0.03	0.07
	3	4	0.71	1.05	1.77	0.07	0.78
	4	5	0.00	8.13[c]	0.20	0.04	1.39
	5	6	7.61[c]	0.94	10.75[c]	0.34	2.56
Sugary	0	1	0.60	4.54[b]	0.25	4.96[b]	4.62[b]
	1	2	0.00	0.33	2.14	0.23	0.20

	2	3	0.06	1.72	5.65[b]	1.93	5.31[b]
	3	4	0.09	2.41	4.96[b]	3.87[b]	7.63[c]
	4	5	4.86[b]	1.01	7.04[c]	4.30[b]	1.68
	5	6	0.87	0.98	3.98[b]	1.14	1.03
Waxy	0	1	11.44[c]	0.01	1.73	2.95	4.43[b]
	1	2	2.17	1.45	14.45[c]	0.70	0.05
	2	3	6.18[c]	7.86[c]	11.01[c]	26.13[c]	48.96[c]
	3	4	0.88	5.70[b]	1.35	0.30	5.96[b]
	4	5	1.11	0.58	4.15[b]	7.61	1.81
	5	6	1.98	13.97[c]	2.51	1.26	10.86[c]

[a] The observed ratio of the day in the first column was used as the expected ratio to test the day in the second column

[b,c] Significant from the expected ratio at the 5 and 1% level respectively with 1 degree of freedom

Between day 0 and 1, a significant increase in the fertilization ability of the $\underline{sh_2}$ grains was obtained in all dates and the total except date B. With increased storage beyond day 1, no change occurred in date D or the total. However, a significant increase occurred between day 5 and 6 in dates A and C and a significant decrease was found between day 4 and 5 in date B.

At the sugary locus, a different reponse was observed. At day 0, only one date (A) out of the four significantly differed from a fertilization percentage of 50 or a 3:1 ratio (Table 3). At date A, the $\underline{su_1}$ grains exceeded the $\underline{Su_1}$ grains in fertilization percentage. Ratio differences between dates at day 0 involved only date A. Changes in the fertilization percentage of $\underline{su_1}$ grains with storage depended to a large extent on date (Table 4). Between day 0 and 1, a significant decrease in the fertilization percentage of $\underline{su_1}$ grains occurred at dates B, D and the total. At date A, the only significant decrease occurred between day 4 and 5. The other dates and the total exhibited completely different patterns.

At the waxy locus, a third pattern emerged. At day 0, two out of four dates differed from a fertilization percentage of 50 or a 3:1 ratio with the Wx grains exceeding the wx grains in fertilization percentage at all dates (Table 3). Ratio differences between dates at day 0 were quite pronounced. The response to storage was quite unique (Table 4). With increasing storage, the fertilization percentage of the wx grains decreased consistently but the date altered both the rate and storage period in which the decrease occurred.

A graphical presentation of the storage effect on the fertilization percentage of the grains containing the recessive allele is presented in Fig. 1. In general, the fertilization percentage of

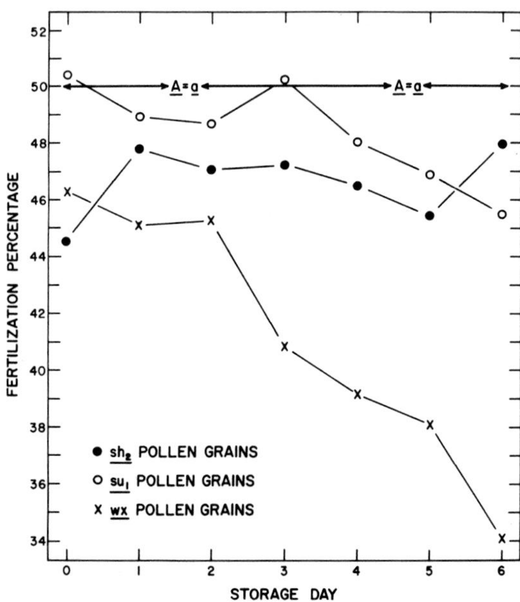

Fig. 1. The effect of storage on the fertilization percentage of pollen grains containing the recessive allele in competition with its dominant counterpart. 50% represents equal fertilization ability between the dominant and recessive pollen grains at the same locus.

$\underline{sh_2}$ grains was lowest (44.56%) at day 0 and increased slightly with storage but never reached 50%. The fertilization percentage of the $\underline{su_1}$ grains was above 50% at day 0 and decreased slightly with increasing storage. The fertilization percentage of wx grains was intermediate (46.32%) at day 0 and a major and consistent decrease was obtained with storage. It should be emphasized that these general conclusions are based on the totals over four dates and that the dates exerted a major and frequently inconsistent influence on the effect of storage on fertilization ability.

4. Discussion

The results of this study clearly indicate that at these three loci, the fertilization ability of the dominant and recessive-bearing grains differ. Very little information is available regarding the effect of allelomorphs at various loci on the fertilization ability of the male gametes containing them. Possibly this lack of information is because, in most experiments not designed to detect differential male transmission rates, unexpected or unusual ratios resulting from differential male transmission rates are not reported. One exception in plants is the waxy locus in maize in which slightly aberrant ratios were associated with differential male transmission.[4] Kempton[5] concluded that the fertilization ability of Wx and wx grains differed immediately after dehiscence. In mice, many alleles at the "tailless" locus are lethal when homozygous but in spite of this, the gene frequency of the t alleles is extraordinarily high in wild populations.[9] It was found that under normal mating conditions, a heterozygous (Tt) male transmitted t to about 95% of its progeny instead of the expected 50%. From the study reported here, the dominant and recessive alleles at the shrunken, sugary and waxy loci altered the fertilization ability of the grains. At day 0, the grains containing the recessive allele at 2 out of 3 loci possessed less fertilization ability than their dominant counterparts. The lower fertilization ability of the grains containing the recessive allele would be predicted if small deletions were associated with the recessive allele. In evolutionary terms, the effect of any new mutation on fertilization ability would largely determine its survival, rate and level of establishment in a new population.

Attempts to isolate the mechanism responsible for differential male transmission rates have been limited. At the waxy locus in maize, Sprague[10] concluded that the Wx grains were more competitive than the wx grains because of their higher rate of pollen tube establishment. Comparing Wx and wx grains, Kempton[6] found no differences in size, weight, specific gravity or maturity at dehiscence. He postulated that the chemical nature of the wx grains produced more moisture absorption or retention and thus the wx grains would adhere together in groups and as a result, be less effective in fertilization than the ungrouped Wx grains. In actuality, little is known about the morphology, physiology or biochemistry of pollen grains as effected by genotype so development of theories is difficult.

An irradiation study with mature pollen grains indicated that levels of irradiation sufficient to severely damage the chromosomes did not alter fertilization ability but did produce an aborted embryo after fertilization occurred.[11] Apparently, factors involved in fertilization ability are very complex and it appears as if the capacity to germinate and compete in fertilization is developed before pollen maturity since it seems independent of chromosomal activity after maturity.

The results of this study clearly indicate that extended pollen storage at 2°C distinctly altered the fertilization ability of the dominant and recessive grains at the shrunken, sugary and waxy locus. The effect of various treatments on male gametes to alter fertilization ability has not been studied extensively. Very limited studies with the waxy locus in maize have indicated that short (under 24 hours) storage, sunlight, artifical light and temperature treatments would alter the fertilization ability of wx grains relative to Wx grains.[6] At the "tailless" locus in mice, it was found that when a Tt male is mated at the normal time relative to oestrus, the sperm reside in the female tract for about 8 hours before fertilization take place.[12] When a mating late in oestrus is imposed however, only 1 hour elapses before fertilization. The transmission of the t sperm relative to the T sperm was not the same in the late-mated group as in the normal-mated group. Apparently, the period between the release of the mature male gametes and fertilization is an influencing factor. Contrary to the findings of Kempton[5,6], the results reported here indicate that the fertilization ability of the wx grains decreased with increasing storage. However, his storage periods were under 24 hours and thus were much shorter. Also, the postulation by Kempton[5,6] concerning the increase in fertilization ability of wx grains after short storage because of the drying and subsequent separation of the grouped wx grains would obviously not apply.

In all studies mentioned and the study reported here, general conclusions are difficult because of the large amount of variation present within treatments and between individual plants, collection dates and the female parent. Apparently, many environmental and genetic factors acting at the time of the production, release, pollination, germination and tube growth of pollengrains can influence the fertilization ability and pollen genotype effect. Under these circumstances, it is difficult to visualize how simple mendelian ratios would be determined with any accuracy.

The relationship between male gamete genotype and fertilization ability has not been studied in any detail. The results reported here indicate that simple pollen treatments such as storage can appreciably alter the fertilization ability of one pollen genotype relative to a second. This indicates that simple treatments may be effective in selecting male gametes that would produce more desirable progeny. This would represent a most important application in plant and animal improvement programs.

5. Acknowledgements

The skill and diligence of Patricia Cotton in the typing and organization of this manuscript is acknowledged with thanks. Appreciation is also expressed to H.S. Anspach and W.T. Mixon for technical assistance and to J.C. Harper for statistical computations.

References

1. Linskens, H.F., 1969, in: Fertilization, vol. 2, eds. C.B. Metz and A. Monroy (Academic Press, New York-London) p. 189.
2. Linskens, H.F., 1967, Encycl. Plant Physiol. 18, 368.
3. Nettancourt, D. de, 1972, Genet. Agr. 26, 163.
4. Brink, R.A., 1925, Genetics 10, 359.
5. Kempton, J.H., 1927, J. Agr. Res. 35, 39.
6. Kempton, J.H., 1936, J. Agr. Res. 52, 81.
7. Pfahler, P.L., 1965, Genetics 52, 513.
8. Snedecor, G.W., 1956, Statistical methods (Iowa State University Press, Ames, Iowa).
9. Dunn, L.C., 1960, Amer. Nat. 94, 385.
10. Sprague, G.F., 1933, Proc. Natl. Acad. Sci. U.S. 19, 838.
11. Pfahler, P.L., 1967, Genetics 57, 523.
12. Braden, A.W.H., 1958, Nature 181, 786.

Fertilization in Higher Plants, ed. H.F. Linskens.
© 1974, North-Holland Publishing Company – Amsterdam, the Netherlands.

ADAPTIVE SIGNIFICANCE OF GAMETIC COMPETITION

David L. Mulcahy
Department of Botany
University of Massachusetts
Amherst, Massachusetts

What is the function of a gametophyte in higher plants? Most obviously it bridges the gap between meiosis and fertilization, thus allowing resumption of the elaborated sporophytic condition. Also, the microgametophyte may provide a valuable mechanism for gene dispersal. But notice, in each of these capacities, the role of the gametophyte is completely passive. It is the purpose of this paper to present evidence that the gametophyte of angiosperms plays a far more active role in adaptive processes. The competitive ability of pollen tubes is determined, at least in part, by the genetic contents of the individual gametophytes. Furthermore, some of the genetic factors expressed in the gametophyte are expressed also in the sporophyte, a phenomenon I refer to as "genetic overlap." But what evidence indicates that the gametophyte actually plays this additional and active role?

Microspores showing gross chromosomal abnormalities exhibit, quite early in the meiotic process, a competitive inferiority[1, 2]. Similarly, genetic factors known as "sperm killers or pollen killers" illustrate competitive interactions between the microspores from one individual[3].

Once meiosis and pollination have been accomplished, the products of meiosis are then subject to certation, that is, competition between growing pollen tubes. Also this process is well known to allow selection between gametophytes from a single plant, either during germination of the pollen, as seems to be the case in waxy versus non-waxy pollen[4] or during the actual growth of the pollen tubes through the style. The latter may occur when meiotic products are distinguished by gross differences in chromosome complement, by differences in a single gene, and, most importantly, by differences based on polygene complement.

The chromosomal determination of competitive ability may reflect the elimination of unbalanced genomes[5], or an adaptive mechanism found in several dioecious species[6-9]. The basis of this mechanism is that pollen tubes bearing an X chromosome grow faster than do those bearing a Y chromosome.

Single gene differences determine the outcome of pollen tube competition in cases of the gametophytic system of incompatibility and also in the isolated but widespread examples of gametophytic factors. These are well illustrated in studies of *Zea mays* and *Phaseolus limensis*[10-13].

The above examples prove that the quality of the gametophyte can certainly be influenced by the actual genetic contents of that gametophyte. Nevertheless, this indicates very little about the generalized importance of gametophytic competition in evolutionary processes. It is not surprising that gross chromosomal differences could influence the functioning of a gametophyte. Similarly, although the significance of isolated gametophytic factors is unknown, adaptive processes are not usually based on single genetic factors. More often, generalizations about adaptation refer to qualities determined by polygenic inheritance. In vivo studies of polygenic inheritance in the angiosperm gametophyte have been infrequent because of technical difficulties inherent in working with so microscopic a system. Nonetheless, several such studies exist[6, 14-18].

An apparent contradiction between two of these studies[14, 15], has indicated polygenic inheritance in the gametophyte of Zea mays. To silks of Zea mays, Jones[14] applied mixtures of a plant's own pollen and pollen from another line. In 20 out of 21 mixtures, the pollen tubes from the plant's own pollen showed faster growth through the style than did those from pollen of the other line. When Pfahler[15] repeated this study, however, he found no consistent pattern in outcome of pollen tube competition. Self pollen was the better competitor in some cases, but certainly not as frequently as Jones[14] observed it. These two investigations differed principly in that Jones[14] employed only highly inbred lines and Pfahler[15] used only F_1 hybrids. It is this difference which could resolve the apparent contradiction. If the speed of pollen tube growth is determined by the genetic contents of the individual gametophyte, then in each generation of selfing, selection will favor those genotypes which can penetrate the stylar tissues with the greatest speed. After several generations of selfing, a plant's own pollen will be able to penetrate that stylar tissue with much greater speed than will the unselected pollen tubes from another line. This would explain Jones'[14] conclusion that self pollen nearly always wins. By using only F_1 plants, Pfahler[15] was comparing two unselected populations of pollen and that is why he found no consistent pattern. To test this hypothesis Claire Johnson, (Univ. of Massachusetts, unpublished) made a series of "self and other" pollen mixtures on the F_1 through F_8 generations of Zea mays. Her data show that the competitive ability of "self" pollen increases significantly in the inbred generations. This conclusion is important because it suggests 1) that speed of pollen tube growth is, at least in part, determined by the gametophytic genotype, 2) that the gametophytic genotype does respond to selective pressures, and 3) that gametophytic control is not limited to the few well known "gametophytic factors" reported in the literature.

Since the diploid phase of development is the dominant part of the life cycle, it is necessary to ask if this diploid phase is modified by the selective forces acting upon the haploid phase. Several studies, indicate that gametophytic competition can indeed modify the quality of the sporophyte in _Gossypium hirsutum_, _Vigna sinensis_, _Triticum aestivum_, and also in _Lepus cuniculus_, the common rabbit, _Lycoperisicum esculentum_ and _Zea mays_[17-22].

My most recent studies have demonstrated that in _Dianthus chinensis_, seeds produced under conditions of heavy gametic competition germinate faster and more uniformly than do seeds of equal size produced under conditions of little gametic competition.

The only explanation possible for the results observed in these seven studies is genetic overlap, that is, a significant portion of the genetic system is expressed in both phases of the life cycle. But can this actually be so? Basic mendelian concepts such as the 3:1 ratio require that fertilization is basically a random phenomenon and, by implication, that the speed of pollen tube growth is _not_ determined by the genetic contents of the pollen. There is thus a fundamental conflict between the concepts of genetic overlap and random fertilization, and rapidly accumulating evidence suggests that the randomness of fertilization has been overestimated. To understand how a nonrandom process could give the appearance of randomness it is necessary to consider once more the nature of the gametophyte. Because the gametophyte is so reduced in size minor differences in morphology, pigmentation, etc. are presently invisible to us. The meotic products from a single individual can be distinguished only if they exhibit markedly different growth rates, rates which are determined by a very large number of genetic factors. Consider then two alleles, A_1 and A_2 which, in the sporophyte, can be distinguished by some morphological feature. What is the probability that sporophytes which differ only at this locus will differ significantly in vigor? Although many investigators have searched for examples of single locus heterosis in the sporophytic generation, success has been minimal. Why then should we expect to find it in the gametophytic generation?

Single gene influences upon vigor are difficult to detect because a single allele represents only a miniscule fraction of the genotype. Thus alleles A_1 and A_2 may produce a nearly perfect 3:1 ratio, which implies random fertilization. This in turn implies that these alleles are not expressed in the gametophyte. However,it may instead mean that the influence of these alleles is virtually lost among those of the thousands of other loci. Significantly, it has been demonstrated that when the influence of genetic background is reduced, as in the case of isogenic lines, then examples of single gene heterosis are common[23]. Similar studies of the gametophyte will very likely reach similar conclusions. Gametic competition in plants, and perhaps also in animals, would then be seen as an extremely vital adaptive process.

References

1. Barber, H. N., 1941, J. Genet. 42: 223-257.

2. Gülcan, R. and Sybenga, J., 1967, Genetica 38: 163-170.

3. Hartl, D. L., 1972, Theor. and Appl. Genetics 42: 81-88.

4. Sprague, G. F., 1933, Proc. Natl. Acad. Sci., U.S.A. 19: 838-841.

5. Buchholz, J. T., 1932, Amer. Jour. Botany 19: 604-626.

6. Correns, C., 1928, Bestimmung, Vererbung and verteilung des geschlechtes bei den hoheren Pflanzen. Handbuch der Vererbungswissenschaft. Band II, 1-138.

7. Kihara, H. and Hirayoshi, I., 1932, Eighth Congr. Japan, Assoc. Advan. Sci., pp. 363-367.

8. Mulcahy, D. L., 1967a, Taxon 16: 280-283.

9. Mulcahy, D. L., 1967b, Heredity 22: 411-423.

10. Schwartz, D., 1950, Proc. Natl. Acad. Sci., U.S.A. 36: 719-724.

11. Nelson, O. E., 1952, Genetics 37: 101-124.

12. Jimenez, J. R. and Nelson, O. E., 1965, J. Heredity 56: 259.

13. Bemis, W. P., 1959, Genetics 44: 555-562.

14. Jones, D. F., 1928, Selective fertilization, Univ. of Chicago Press. Chicago.

15. Pfahler, P. L., 1967a, Genetics 57: 513-521.

16. Pfahler, P. L., 1967b, Genetics 57: 522-530.

17. Mulcahy, D. L., 1971, Science 171: 1155-1156.

18. Mulcahy, D. L., 1974, Nature 249: 491-493.

19. Ter-Avanesian, D. V., 1949, Bull. Appl. Botany Genet. Plant Breeding Leningrad 28: 119-133.

20. Ter-Avanesian, D. V., 1969, Genetika 5, No. 9: 168-170.

21. Ter-Avanesian, D. V. and Kameneva, E. I., 1969, Genetika 5, No. 10: 103-108.

22. Lewis, D., 1954, Annual Report of the Department of Genetics. Ann. Rep. John Innes Hort. Inst. 45: 12-17.

23. Wills, C. and Nichols, L., 1972, Proc. Nat. Acad. Sci. U.S.A. 69: 323-325.

Fertilization in Higher Plants, ed. H.F. Linskens.

GERMINATION IN VITRO OF POLLEN FROM DIPLOID AND TRISOMIC RYEGRASS

B.S. Ahloowalia
Plant Breeding Department, Agricultural Institute,
Oakpark Research Centre, Carlow, Eire

1. Introduction

Selective fertilization plays an important role in obtaining increased yields in several cultivated plant species. Induction and isolation of male sterile genotypes is a critical part of programmes aimed at the exploitation of hybrid vigour. Male sterility in conjunction with trisomy has been used in the production of hybrid barley varieties through the technique of 'balanced tertiary trisomics' (BTT)[1].

Perennial ryegrass (Lolium perenne L.) is a diploid (2n = 14) self-incompatible, cross-fertilizing species. Primary trisomics (2n + 1 = 15) of this species were obtained in order to develop BTT system and to search for male sterility[2]. Since then more primary trisomics have been isolated. It was, therefore, of interest to compare pollen fertility of some of these trisomics by in vitro germination and conventional staining procedure.

2. Materials and methods

Pollen from normal diploid Italian (L. multiflorum Lam.) or perennial ryegrass and primary trisomics of perennial ryegrass were germinated on 20% (w/w) sucrose solution with 10 ppm each of calcium chloride, boric acid and Na_2-EDTA as described in a previous communication[3]. Instead of the double cavity slides, however, microchambers were made from tops of 18 and 22 mm cover-slip boxes which slid into each other. A cover slip was attached to a box-top with a drop of the solution and another hanging drop was applied on its reverse side. Pollen grains from single anthers were dusted onto the drop and the 18 mm top was gently lowered into the 22 mm bottom part of the microchamber filled with the same solution: This avoided a change in concentration of the hanging drop. The solution was preheated to 30°C and the temperature was maintained by placing the microchambers on a hot plate. Pollen-tube growth was stopped by heating the hanging drop over a flame. Pollen was stained with 1% alcoholic safranin in glycerol and water (1:2:1). Most experiments were terminated after 10 minutes of pollen dusting. In each germination test, pollen from diploid and trisomic plants were cultured and sampled for staining simultaneously. In conventional staining, empty, partially filled and shrivelled pollen grains were counted as sterile. Each plant was tested six times, and in each test, no less than 150 grains were counted with a hand tally counter.

3. Results

Pollen germination tests showed that variation existed between different florets from the same plant. Duplicate samples from the same floret were, however, consistent in germination ability (see table 1).

Table 1

Germination and stainability of pollen from disomic and trisomic plants of ryegrass

Expt. No	Germination (%)		Stainability (%)	
	disomic	trisomic*	disomic	trisomic
1	63.9	15.3		
	69.6	10.2	85.7	59.3
2	73.9	24.1		
	74.9	22.9	78.3	57.7
3	31.1	1.1		
	42.1	2.4	50.8	60.2
Mean	60.1	12.1	72.4	58.9

*Tri-15

Pollen from disomics showed consistently higher germination and faster pollen tube growth than that from the trisomics (Figs. 1-2). The haploid pollen from disomic plants had an average pollen tube length of 165 μm as against that of 61 μm from tri-15. In disomics, germination reflected the stainability index of the sampled pollen. Most pollen from the disomics showed well filled normal grains (Fig. 3) while collapsed and shrivelled pollen varying from 18 to 97% was present in the trisomics. Pollen germination and stainability showed that trisomics differed from each other in their fertility (see table 2).

Table 2

Pollen germination and stainability of disomic and trisomic ryegrass

Plant genotype	No. of pollen grains	Germination (%)	No. of pollen grains	Stainability (%)
disomic	1464	60.1	537	72.4
tri-15	1611	12.1	517	58.9
disomic	990	55.0	540	95.7
tri-38	1241	2.5	705	21.3
disomic	689	26.2	644	81.2
tri-68	596	0.2	755	3.2
tri-19	301	32.8	912	46.3
tri-63	225	25.0	620	64.4
tri-25	-	-	610	71.8

Tri-68 was almost completely male sterile (Fig. 4). In some trisomics, although pollen stainability was high, pollen germination was poor. Some trisomics formed pollen of varying size.

Trisomic plants had different extra chromosomes, as shown by their meiotic behaviour in microsporogenesis (see table 3). In tri-15, the extra chromosome is a large one with a median centromere (likely chromosome No. 1), while in tri-38, the extra chromosome has a secondary constriction and can be identified from its association with thenucleolusat diakinesis (Figs. 5-6). The two trisomics also differ in their frequency of univalent and trivalent association at the first meiotic metaphase (see table 3).

Table 3

Chromosome association at meiotic metaphase I in trisomics of ryegrass

Plant No.	No. of PMC'S	Mean chromosome assoc./cell		
		I	II	III
tri-15	30	0.97	6.27	0.50
tri-38	20	0.35	6.35	0.65
tri-68	20	0.35	6.20	0.75
tri-19	20	1.70	6.20	0.30
tri-63	20	0.75	6.60	0.35
tri-25	20	1.40	6.20	0.40

4. Discussion

The results clearly show that trisomics of perennial ryegrass differ from each other in their pollen fertility as indicated by both germination and staining tests. In other words, presence of different extra chromosomes produces mild to extreme effects on both pollen development and germination. Such chromosomal effects strongly suggest that the genetic information concerning pollen formation and function in ryegrass is carried by a number of different chromosomes within the genome rather than by a single chromosome. Since tri-68 is associated with complete pollen abortion, the extra chromosome in this trisomic has perhaps the most vital genetic message for pollen development, while that in tri-38 which is a nucleolar chromosome, carries genes affecting pollen germination as well.

Pollen sterility has been reported in trisomics of a number of different plants, e.g. Datura, tobacco, barley, spinach, rye etc., however, pollen abortion in trisomics is not very high, the average for all species being about 15 per cent[4]. The drastic effects on pollen development in ryegrass trisomic-68 and -38 are unique in contrast to those reported. The slower rate of tube growth of tri-15 pollen is similar to that reported for Datura trisomics[5].

The behaviour of the extra chromosomes in meiosis may have considerable influence on pollen viability. Although trisomics investigated show differences in the extent of univalent and trivalent frequency, pollen viability and germination do not seem to be related to the meiotic behaviour of the extra chromosomes. For example, although tri-38 and tri-68 are different, and have similar univalent and trivalent numbers per cell, yet differ markedly in their pollen fertility. Once again, specific chromosomes rather than their meiotic behaviour appear to be more important in determining pollen fertility.

All trisomic plants may produce a certain number of haploid (n = 7) and aneuhaploid (n = 8,9) pollen depending upon the frequency of univalent formation, precocious division of univalents and their inclusion in sister chromatids. In the absence of specific chromosomal effects on pollen development and a 7:8 segregation, 50% or more viable haploid (n = 7) pollen would be expected from all trisomics. The results suggest to the contrary a highly reduced fertility.

In most plants, pollen grains with unbalanced chromosome numbers either fail to participate in fertilization or are eliminated in competition with the normal haploid pollen, thus transmission of trisomics via pollen is very low as has been shown in maize, Datura, tomato and several other species[4]. Since germination *in vitro* does not involve competition, estimates on reduced pollen fertility *per se* are more realistic than those obtained from seed set. From a practical viewpoint, however, effective male sterility of ryegrass trisomics would be high, and can be triggered by different trisomics. Since perennial ryegrass is self-incompatible, even 2-10% viable pollen would be non-effective due to elimination either in competition or selective cross-fertilization. Thus, trisomics of ryegrass may provide an important male sterile system for hybrid seed production.

Figs. 1-2. Pollen germination of (1) a disomic, and (2) a trisomic plant. Fig. 3. Fertile pollen of a disomic. Fig. 4. Sterile pollen of tri-68. Fig. 5. Diakinesis in tri-38; note two bivalents and a trivalent associated with the nucleolus. Fig. 6. Metaphase I; 6 II + 1 III in tri-38.

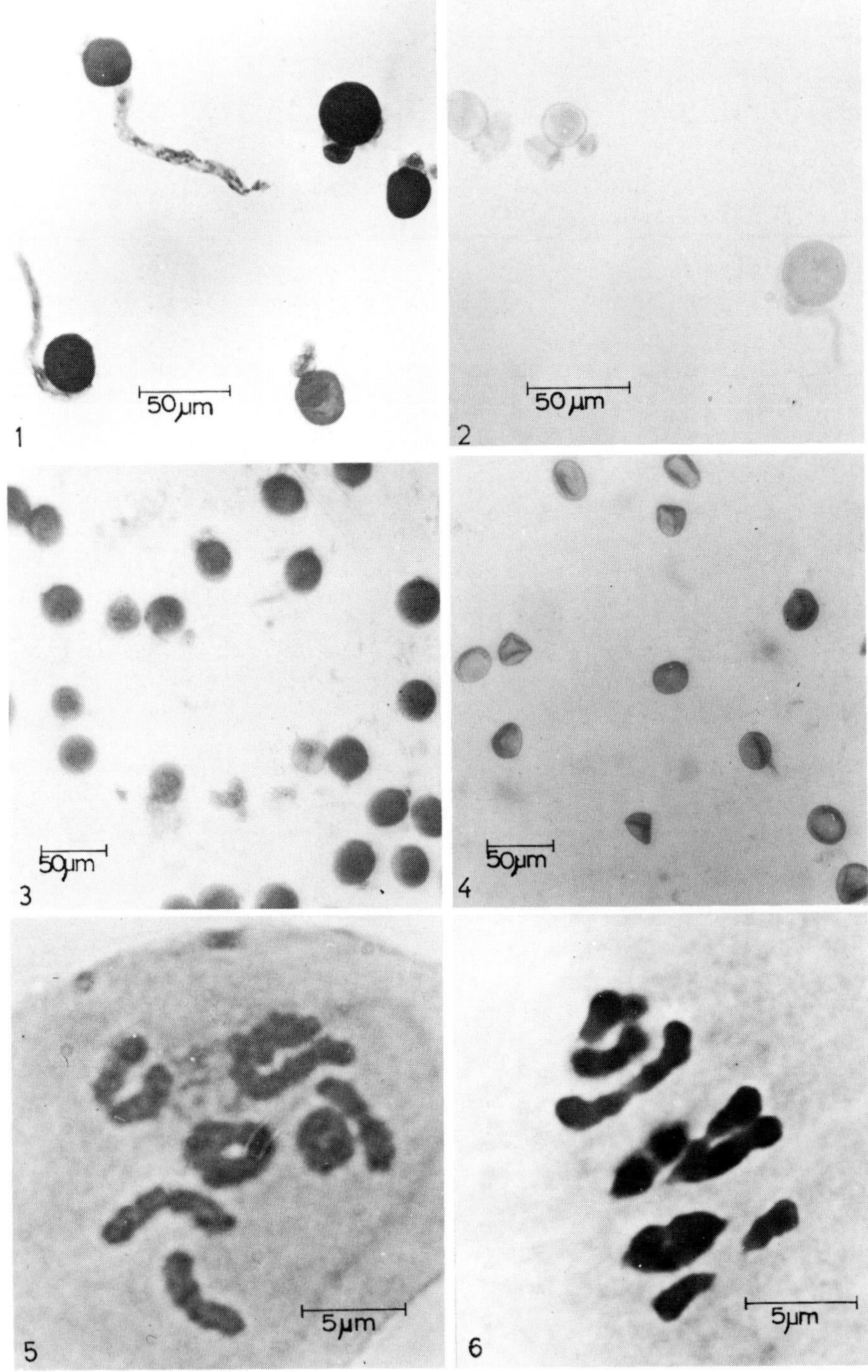

50 μm
1
50 μm
2
50μm
3
50μm
4
5μm
5
5μm
6

References

1. Ramage, R.T., 1965, Crop Sci. 5, 177.
2. Ahloowalia, B.S., 1972, Theoret. appl. Genetics, 42, 363.
3. Ahloowalia, B.S., 1973, Euphytica 22, 575.
4. Khush, G.S., 1973, Cytogenetics of aneuploids (Academic Press, London).
5. Buchholz, J.T. and Blakeslee, A.F., 1932, Amer. J. Bot. 19, 604.

Fertilization in Higher Plants, ed. H.F. Linskens.

ACCEPTANCE OF SELF-COMPATIBLE POLLEN FROM *SOLANUM VERRUCOSUM* IN DIHAPLOIDS FROM *S.TUBEROSUM*

J.G.Th. Hermsen, J. Olsder, P. Jansen en E. Hoving

Agricultural University, Department of Plant Breeding
Wageningen, The Netherlands

1. Introduction

Solanum verrucosum is a wild species, which is indigenous in Mexico. The species is diploid (2n = 2x = 24) and self-compatible. *S.tuberosum* is an autotetraploid species (2n = 4x = 48). It is cultivated and consists of two sub-species (Hawkes[3]). Sub-species *tuberosum* is cultivated all over the world and sub-species *andigena* is cultivated in Central and Southern America.

Dihaploids originate from unfertilized egg cells of *S.tuberosum* and therefore have the diploid chromosome number. Such female parthenogenesis can easily be induced in *S.tuberosum* using pollen from *S.phureja* (Hermsen and Verdenius[4]). Dihaploids as a rule are self-incompatible (one locus gametophytic), but self-compatible dihaploids are also found.

Acceptance of pollen refers to successful pollinations. With non-acceptance inhibition of pollen tube growth occurs somewhere in the pistil and no fertilization can take place. This inhibition may be caused either by the mechanism of incompatibility (mostly intra-specific) or by interspecific or intergeneric crossability barriers. For the latter case Hogenboom[6] introduced the term incongruity.

Crosses between species or genera may be successful in one direction only. This phenomenon is known as unilateral incompatibility (see review Lewis and Crowe[7] and Abdalla and Hermsen[1]) or unilateral incongruity (see review Hogenboom[6]). Crossing *S.verrucosum* as a female with dihaploid *S.tuberosum* is always successful. When using dihaploids of *S.tuberosum* as a female the pollen of *S.verrucosum* as a rule is rejected. The dihaploids involved are called non-acceptors (NA). Exceptionally dihaploids occur which as females cross readily with *S.verrucosum*. Such dihaploids are called acceptors (A). The terms acceptor/non-acceptor were introduced by Grun and Aubertin[2] in 1966. In this article experiments are described to elucidate the genetics of acceptance/non-acceptance in *S.tuberosum*.

2. Material and methods

In 1972 one of the authors (J.O.) discovered two acceptors of *S.verrucosum* pollen in a population of 22 F_1 plants from a cross between two NA-dihaploids of *S.tuberosum*. In another F_1 not one acceptor was found among 23 plants. Acceptors and non-acceptors were intercrossed and self-pollinated. The progenies AxA, AxNA and NAxNA were pollinated in 1973 with *S.verrucosum* in order to determine the ratios A:NA. In addition new test crosses were made for further studies in 1974.

The *S.verrucosum* used was a pollen mixture of a number of plants from the accession PI 195172. In 1974 different genotypes of *S.verrucosum* will be studied separately.

Apart from pollinations with *S.verrucosum* most acceptors and non-acceptors were tested for self-compatibility in order to investigate a possible genetic relation between (non)acceptance and (in)compatibility.

Pollen tube growth was studied using a slight modification of the method of Linskens and Esser[8].

3. Results

The results of testing for acceptance are presented in table 1. Furthermore the observed ratios are tested on the basis of two genetic models:

Model I: two independent genes, A_1 and A_2, only double recessives $a_1a_1a_2a_2$, being acceptor.

Model II: one dominant acceptor gene A and one dominant inhibitor gene I, only the genotypes iiAA and iiAa being acceptor.

It is apparent from table 1 that 12 out of 14 ratios fit model I, whereas all 14 ratios are in accordance with the expectation on the basis of model II.

From the tests of (in)compatibility of acceptors and non-acceptors it appeared, that acceptors and non-acceptors are equally distributed among self-compatible and self-incompatible plants.

Pollen tube growth studies revealed that in acceptor styles no inhibition of *S.verrucosum* pollen tubes occurred. In styles of non-acceptors a sudden inhibition of all tubes just below the stigma was most common. In some cases the type of inhibition resembled that of self-incompatibility: a thinning bundel of pollen tubes. In a few non-acceptors a number of pollen tubes even reached the ovary. These quantitative differences of inhibition may have a genetic basis as has been suggested before (Grun and Aubertin[2], Hogenboom[5]).

Table 1

Two genetic models to explain the observed ratios acceptor (A) : non-acceptor (NA)

Cross	Parents type	genotypes model I	genotypes model II	Ratios observed A	Ratios observed NA	Ratios expected Model I A : NA	Ratios expected Model II A : NA
GB39 selfed	A	$a_1a_1a_2a_2$	iiAA	6	0	1 : 0	1 : 0
GB53 selfed	A	$a_1a_1a_2a_2$	iiAa	14	5	1 : 0*	3 : 1
BG30 selfed	NA	$A_1a_1a_2a_2$	IiAA	4	13	1 : 3	1 : 3
BG47 selfed	NA	$A_1a_1a_2a_2$	IiAa	3	11	1 : 3	3 : 13
G254 selfed	NA	$A_1a_1A_2a_2$	IiAa	1	12	1 : 15	3 : 13
B16 selfed	NA	$A_1a_1a_2a_2$	IiAa	7	27	1 : 3	3 : 13
BG41 selfed	NA	A_1A_1. .	II..	0	52	0 : 1	0 : 1
G254 x B16	NAx	NA		10	51	1 : 7	3 : 13
GB47 x BG41	NAx	NA		0	11	0 : 1	0 : 1
GB53 x G254	Ax	NA		16	23	1 : 3*	3 : 5
GB39 x B16	Ax	NA		9	11	1 : 1	1 : 1
GB53 x B16	Ax	NA		8	9	11 : 1	3 : 5
GB47 x GB39	NAx	A		12	15	1 : 1	1 : 1
GB39 x BG41	Ax	NA		0	25	0 : 1	0 : 1

*observed ratios deviating significantly from expectation.

4. Discussion and conclusions

The genetic model I in this article is in agreement with the hypothesis put forward by Grun and Aubertin[2] who worked with different Solanum species. The size of most populations in this study is too small for decisive conclusions owing to the occurrence of lethal recessive genes. Therefore the experiments should be repeated on a larger scale. Also the occurrence of differences in degree of inhibition should be investigated carefully. Finally a research on the effect of different *S.verrucosum* genotypes on acceptance has to be carried out.

The following preliminary conclusions may be drawn. Acceptance of *S.verrucosum* pollen in pistils of dihaploid *S.tuberosum* has a genetic basis. There is more than one gene involved and acceptance appears recessive according to model I. Though strong inhibition is the rule, different degrees of inhibition in non-acceptor pistils occur. In the material investigated no relation was found between (in)compatibility in haploid *S.tuberosum* and its genotypes for (non)-acceptance of *S.verrucosum* pollen.

5. References

1. Abdalla, M.M.F. and Hermsen, J.G.T., 1972. Euphytica 21, 32.
2. Grun, P. and Aubertin, M., 1966, Heredity 21, 131.
3. Hawkes, J.G., 1963, Rec.Scott.Pl.Breed.Stat., 76.
4. Hermsen, J.G.T. and Verdenius, J., 1973, Euphytica 22, 244.
5. Hogenboom, N.G., 1972, Euphytica 21, 405.
6. Hogenboom, N.G., 1973, Euphytica 22, 219.
7. Lewis, D. and Crowe, L.K., 1958, Heredity 12, 233.
8. Linskens, H.F. and Esser, K.L., 1957, Naturwissenschaften 1, 16.

GAMETE MATURATION

Fertilization in Higher Plants, ed. H.F. Linskens.

THE NON-HISTONE CHROMOSOMAL PROTEINS FROM MEIOTIC AND SOMATIC CELLS OF LILIUM.

M.J.M.Martens and A.F.Croes

Department of Botany,
University, Nijmegen, the Netherlands.

1. Introduction.

A considerable contraction of the chromosomes occurs during both meiotic and mitotic prophase. Other changes in chromosome morphology which have been observed in meiotic chromosomes only, accompany the formation and breakdown of the synaptonemal complex. The latter events are clearly related to the process of recombination, which is thought to take place during early pachytene.

The chromatin, the constituent material of the chromosomes, is built up from DNA, RNA, histones, and non-histone chromosomal proteins (NHCP). Of these, the protein components are presumably responsible for the maintenance of chromosome integrity. Alterations in chromosome structure could, therefore, be brought about by changes in the amount or in the composition of the histones and the NHCP.

It is, at the moment, controversial if the amount of histones per unit mass of DNA fluctuates during early meiosis[1,2].

The behaviour of the NHCP during meiotic prophase has not been studied at all. Our attention was, therefore, mainly focused on the following two problems:

1. Are there differences in the amount and in the composition of the NHCP between meiotic and somatic cells?
2. Are there differences in the amount and in the composition of the NHCP between cells in different stages of meiotic prophase?

To attack these problems, we used microsporocytes and leaf cells of *Lilium henryi*. The microsporocytes develop in good synchrony within a single bud and large amounts of meiocytes in each stage of meiotic prophase can, therefore, be collected. Moreover, it is relatively easy to free the meiocytes from contaminating somatic tissue and specifically from tapetal nuclei[3].

2. Preparation of the NHCP.

The procedure to prepare the NHCP from the meiotic cells included the following steps: 1. Isolation of nuclei; 2. preparation of purified chromatin; 3. removal of histones; 4. removal of DNA and RNA; 5. solubilisation of NHCP in 8M urea supplemented with 1% sodium dodecyl sulphate (SDS) and 1% β-mercapto-ethanol. The NHCP fraction obtained was analysed by electrophoresis on SDS-polyacrylamide gels. NHCP from leaf cells was prepared and analysed in the same way.

3. Results.

We have examined 4 stages of the meiotic cycle: premeiotic interphase, leptotene, zygotene and pachytene. The changes in chromosome structure, visible in the cell as it progresses through these stages can be seen in figure 1.

The results of the determinations of DNA, total protein (histone + NHCP) and histone have been expressed as protein/DNA ratios and are shown in table 1. The total protein/DNA ratio in meiotic cells is markedly different from that in somatic tissue. A second point is, that at zygotene and pachytene much more protein is associated with the chromatin than during the earlier stages.

Table 1.
Protein/DNA ratios in chromatin.

Nature of protein	Cells	Protein/DNA ratio
total protein	leaf	1.9
	premeiotic interphase	3.5
	leptotene	3.3
	zygotene	5.3
	pachytene	4.9
histone	premeiotic interphase	1.16
	leptotene	1.05
	zygotene	1.33
	pachytene	1.42

Figure 1. Stages of early meiosis. a.-premeiotic interphase; b.-leptotene; c.-zygotene; d.-pachytene.

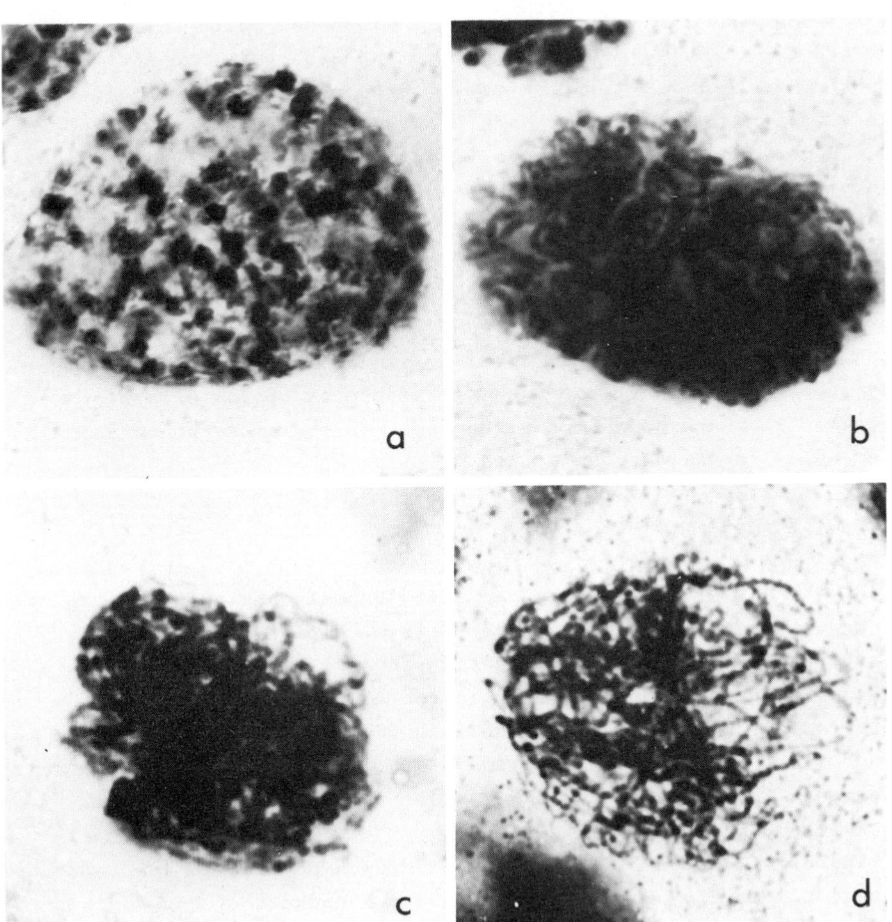
a
b
c
d

A third result is, that there is an increase in the histone of the order of 20-30% between leptotene and zygotene. The increase, however, is by far not great enough to account for the increase in the total protein/DNA ratio, which occurs at the same time. The conclusion should be that at late leptotene or early zygotene the protein content of the chromatin rises, and that this rise is most conspicuous in the NHCP.

The distribution of the NHCP in meiotic and somatic cells after gel electrophoresis is shown in figure 2. It should especially be noted, that in meiotic cells the NHCP of high molecular weight are much more prevalent than in somatic tissue. There is a great similarity, however, in the fast-running components of low molecular weight. There are no marked differences in the patterns obtained from cells in the various stages of meiosis.

4. Discussion.

At the onset of zygotene, the synaptonemal complex begins to be formed. The proteinaceous nature of this complex has been well established[4]. We find an increase in the protein components of the chromatin at the same stage. It is probably, therefore, that the new proteins, which become associated with the chromatin at this stage, take part in the formation of the synaptonemal complex. Our experiments also indicate, that these new components are mainly non-histone proteins.

The distribution patterns of the NHCP on polyacrylamide gels are more difficult to explain. The relative abundance of NHCP of high molecular weight in meiotic cells as compared with somatic cells may be related, in an unknown fashion, to meiosis. When the outcome of the electrophoresis experiments is considered in combination with the fact, that much more NHCP is present in meiotic than in somatic cells, one gets the impression, that the amount of the fast-moving NHCP components is relatively stable in cells of different type. The amount of slow-moving components, however, would greatly vary with the tissue.

Figure 2. Distribution of NHCP from different cell types on polyacrylamide gels. a.-premeiotic interphase; b.-leptotene; c.-zygotene d.-pachytene; e.-leaf cells.
The gels were scanned with a densitometer, after staining.

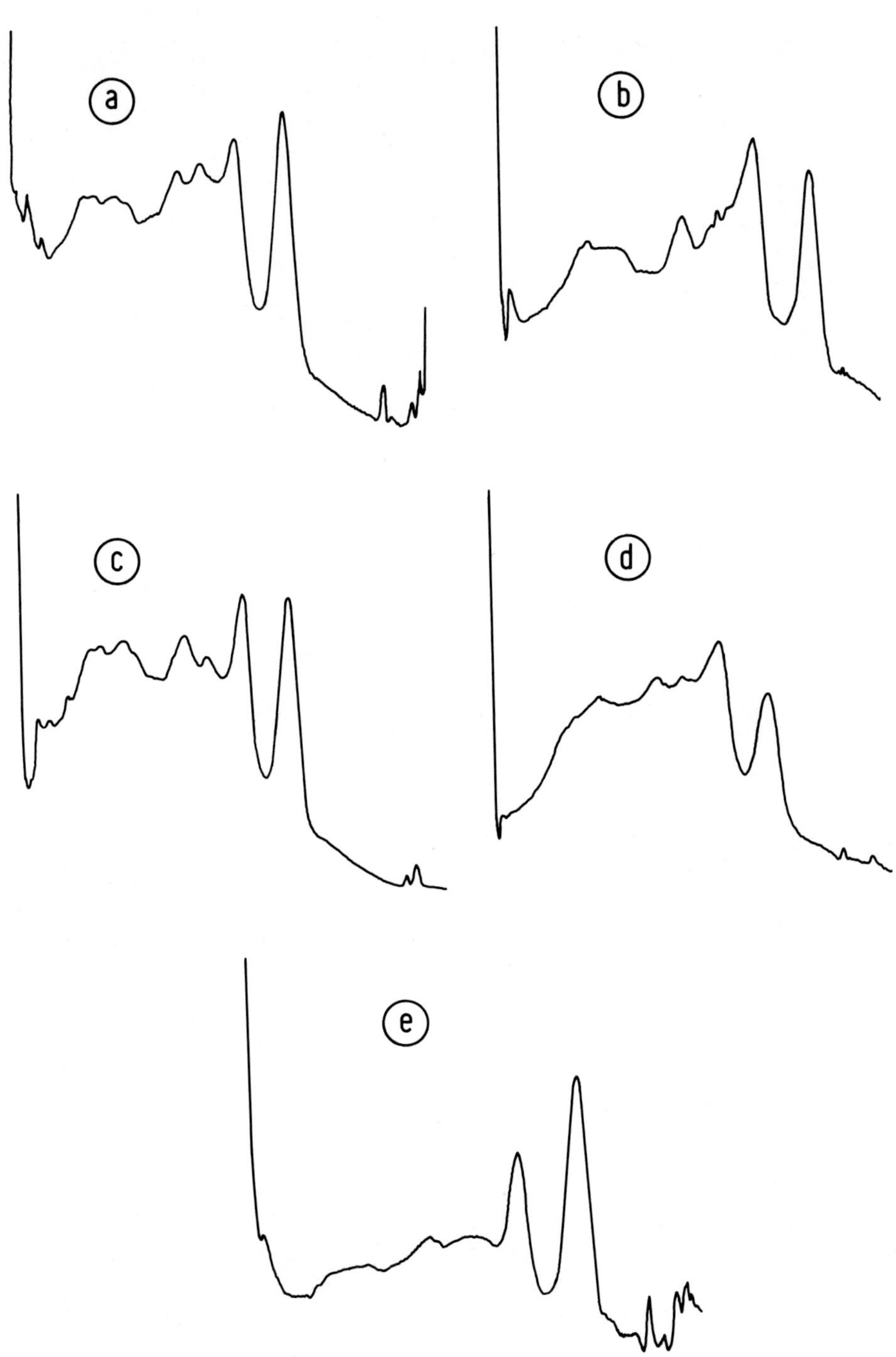
a
b
c
d
e

Qualitative differences in NHCP between meiotic cells at various stages of prophase, if present, do not show up very clearly in our gels.

References.

1. Bogdanov,Yu.F. and Antropova,E.N., 1971,: Delayed Termination of Nuclear Histone Doubling after Premeiotic DNA Synthesis in Triturus vulgaris Male Meiosis. Chromosoma 35,353-373.
2. Sheridan,W.F. and Stern,H., 1967,: Histones of Meiosis. Exptl. Cell Res. 45,323-335.
3. Linskens,H.F. and Schrauwen,J., 1968,: Quantitative nucleic acid determination in the microspore and tapetum fractions of Lily anthers. Proc. Kon. Nederl. Akad. Wetens. Ser. C. 71,267-279.
4. Comings,D.E. and Okada,T.A., 1972,: Architecture of meiotic cells and mechanisms of chromosomal pairing. Advan. Cell Mol. Biol. 2,310-384.

Fertilization in Higher Plants, ed. H.F. Linskens.

NON-HISTONE PROTEIN SYNTHESIS DURING MICROSPOROGENESIS IN THE RHOEO DISCOLOR HANCE

L. Albertini and A. Souvré

Laboratoire de Cytologie, E.N.S.Agronomique, Toulouse, France
Laboratoire de Biologie Végétale, Université P. Sabatier, Toulouse

1. Introduction

In an article published in 1971, one of us[1] studied the incorporation of ^{3}H-arginine into the proteins of Pollen Mother Cells (PMC), the microspores and the tapetum of the Rhœo discolor, a plant wich has the characteristics of showing a meiosis with a phenomenon of catenation and a tapetum of plasmodial type.

In the present article, our purpose is to study the synthesis of non-histone proteins, using the same plant. Indeed, these are worthy of particular notice for they are of considerable physiological importance. For example, chromatic acidic proteins partly cancel the duplication inhibitions of DNA and its transcription (syntheses of RNA) caused by histones (Wang[2], Kamiyama et al[3]) and according to Kostraba et al[4], they are involved in the stimulation of specific gene transcription and in the regulation of differential gene expression. That is why the precise study of the syntheses of non-histone proteins in Rhœo discolor microsporocytes and its tapetum became obvious to us.

We know that animal and plant nuclear histones contain little or no tryptophane (Tristram et al[5], Bonner[6], Vendrely et al[7], Autran et al[8]) and that basic cytoplasmic proteins, according to their physico-chemical characteristics (Horn[9]) and their amino-acid composition (Ts'o et al[10], Taleporos[11], Butler et al[12], Horn[9]), are very similar to nuclear histones. Therefore, like Cave[13] (Chironomus thummi) and Yonesawa et al[14], we have also chosen ^{3}H-tryptophane so as to specifically detect the synthesis of cellular non-histone proteins, in order to localise this synthesis and measure its extent.

The following points will be studied :

- Incorporation of ^{3}H-tryptophane into the proteins of the PMC, the microspores and the tapetum during microsprogenesis ; analysis of nuclear and cytoplasmic behaviour.
- Nucleolar activity in the PMC as well as in the tapetum.
- Relationship between tapetum-microsporocytes ; in particular the determination of transfers or non-transfers of non-histone proteins from the tapetum to meiocytes and to microspores.

2. Techniques

The different stages of the microsporogenesis of the Rhœo discolor have been previously described by one of us[15,1].

^{3}H-tryptophane (25 µ Ci/ml) has been supplied to anthers of Rhœo discolor excised at different stages of development according to a protocol previously described[1] (time of labelling : 10 mn, 30 mn or 2 h ; and 2 h of labelling either followed or not by an extra 2 hour's or 16 hour's incubation in a non-radioactive medium). The anthers fixed by ethanol-acetic acid 3/1, then embedded in paraffin have been sliced into sections 8 µ thick which have undergone Ficq's[16] autoradiographic treatment (nuclear emulsion K_2 type in gel form ; time of exposure in a dark room : 1 month ; developer : diaminophenol). Before mounting, the sections were stained with methyl green-pyronine.

The total activity of a cellular structure has been determined as being the total number of silver grains counted above a cellular structure observed, deduction made from background. Each result in fig. 1 and table 1 is the average obtained after counting the number of grains above 10-40 nucleoli, nuclei or cytoplasms at a given stage.

3. Results

The synthesis of non-histone proteins in Pollen Mother Cells (PMC) and in microspores

During the premeiotic rest (fig. 1,2), the incorporation level of ^{3}H-tryptophane is high in the nucleus and in the cytoplasm of the PMC ; the intensity of non-histone protein synthesis in the nucleus which is at its maximum during the period 2 of the premeiotic rest (part 1 of the premeiotic S stage) varies during periods 2 and 3 of the premeiotic rest (period 3 = part 2 of S stage) in a way which is fairly parallel to that of the euchromatic DNA synthesis (Albertini[1]).

As soon as the meiosis begins (synizesis) the nuclear (chromosomal) and cytoplasmic activities (fig. 1,4,5) decrease fairly distinctly. From the zygotene to stage 2 of the microspores, these activities remain low for incubation in ^{3}H-tryptophane of 30 mn and 2 h (fig. 1,8,9,12,14) ; chromatic activities are at their highest point at diakinesis (fig. 1) but they are slight.

Throughout the premeiotic resting stage, the nucleolus (table 1) and above all the perinucleolar chromatin (fig. 2) is the zone in the PMC nucleus where the incorporation of ^{3}H-tryptophane is the most intense. During the synizesis, nucleolar activity decreases distinctly until it becomes non-existent at the beginning of the zygotene.

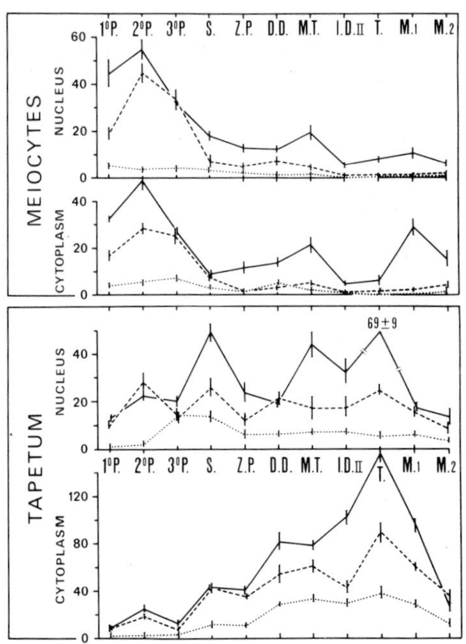

Fig. 1. Total activity of nucleus or cytoplasm expressed in number of silver grains (^{3}H-tryptophane supply (25 µ Ci/ml) to the excised anthers of the Rhœo discolor ; t : 19°C ± 1°C). Dotted line : 30 mn supply of ^{3}H-tryptophane ; broken line : 2 h supply of ^{3}H-tryptophane ; continuous line : 2 h supply of ^{3}H-tryptophane then 16 h incubation without radiotracer. Each average is accompanied by its confidence interval determined with a 95% safety factor. 1° P : period 1 of the premeiotic rest ; 2° P : period 2 = 1 st part of the S stage ; 3° P : period 3 = 2 nd part of the premeiotic S stage ; S : synizesis; Z.P. : zygotene-pachytene ; D.D. : diplotene-diakinesis ; M.T. : metaph. I - anaph. I - teloph. I ; I-D II : interphase I-II and division II ; T : tetrad stage ; M_1 : microspores at stage 1 ; M_2 : microspores at stage 2.

Table 1

Nucleolar activity during microsporogenesis (number 1 : total activity expressed in number of silver grains ; number 2 in brackets : ratio of the total nucleolar activity over the total activity of the corresponding cytoplasm.

		2°P	3°P	Syn.	T	M_2
Meiocytes	2 h*	6,3(0,22)	4,4(0,18)	2,4(0,34)	-	-
	2 h* + 16 h	3,2(0,06)	3,5(0,13)	2,3(0,26	-	-
Tapetum	2 h*	3,0(0,16)	2,1(0,25)	10,2(0,24)	6,3(0,07)	1,8(0,05)
	2 h* + 16 h	1,6(0,06)	1,7(0,14)	1,9(0,05)	8,5(0,05)	2,3(0,08)

2 h* : 2 h in ^{3}H-tryptophane (25 µ Ci/ml) ; 2 h* + 16 h : 2 h in ^{3}H-tryptophane (25 µ Ci/ml) then 16 h without radiotracer.

The synthesis of non-histone proteins in the tapetum

The tapetum nuclei incorporate ^{3}H-tryptophane very well throughout the premeiotic rest as well as during meiosis (fig. 1).

The cytoplasmic activity of the tapetum (fig. 1), low during the premeiotic rest, becomes clear at the synizesis and increases during meiosis to reach its maximum at the tetrad stage (fig. 4,5,9,12). This cytoplasmic labelling, which appears rapidly during meiosis (fig. 3) since, in 10 minute's time, it is of 10 grains per cellular unity at the zygotene and of 13 grains at the tetrad, is stable (fig. 1,10,13). The cytoplasmic activity of the tapetum becomes insignificant at stage 3 of the microspores.

From the synizesis to stage 2 of the microspores, a quick and intensive incorporation of ^{3}H-tryptophane takes place in the tapetum nucleoli (table 1). At first exclusively perinucleolar (fig. 6 ; 30 mn), the activity also becomes intranucleolar later on (fig. 7 ; 2 h).

4. Remarks and discussion

In the PMC nucleus, the evolution of the incorporation level of ^{3}H-tryptophane during the premeiotic rest (PR) differs from that concerning ^{3}H-arginine and ^{3}H-leucine ; whereas the nuclear incorporation level of arginine determined at the period 3 of the PR is twice as high as that measured during period 2 of the PR and level concerning ^{3}H-leucine does not significatively vary during the premeiotic S period (Albertini[1]), the incorporation of tryptophane which is maximum during period 2 of the PR (part 1 of S period) becomes distinctly lower (35 to 65 %) during period 3 of the PR (part 2 of S period). In fact, if during the S period, the nuclear incorporation level of arginine in the PMC váries in the same way as the intensity of eu- and heterochromatic DNA synthesis, the intensity of the synthesis of non-histone proteins, as shown by ^{3}H-tryptophane incorporation (fig. 1,2 and table 1) varies in a way which is fairly parallel to the euchromatic and perinucleolar DNA synthesis ; these DNA are known to constitute the loci of an extensive activity of RNA synthesis, essentially during period 3 of the premeiotic rest (Albertini[1]). Such a result fits in with the theory drawn

---

Supply of ^{3}H-tryptophane (25 µ Ci/ml) to excised anthers.

Fig. 2. Period 2 of the premeiotic rest ; time of supply : 2 h - The chromatin and the cytoplasm of PMC are active ; the perinucleolar chromatin (arrow) incorporates. Fig. 3. Synizesis ; time of supply : 10 mn. The cytoplasm of the tapetum (cy. t.) is clearly labelled ; the PMC (pmc) are exempt from labelling. Fig. 4. Synizesis ; 30 mn. The tapetum (at the top and on the right) is distinctly more labelled than the PMC (pmc). The chromatin (ch) and the nucleoli (arrows) of the tapetum are active. Fig. 5. Synizesis ; 2 h. Increase of the level of synthesis ; the tapetum (at the top) remains distinctly more active than the PMC (pmc). Fig. 6. Synizesis ; 30 mn. The labelling of the tapetal nucleolus (arrow) exclusively perinucleolar, is due to the activity of the perinucleolar chromatin. Fig. 7. Synizesis ; 2 h. In the tapetum, the labelling of the nucleolus (arrow) is not only perinucleolar but also intranucleolar. Fig. 8. PMC at the ring stage (diakinesis) ; time of supply : 30 mn. Distinct activity of periplasmodium (t).

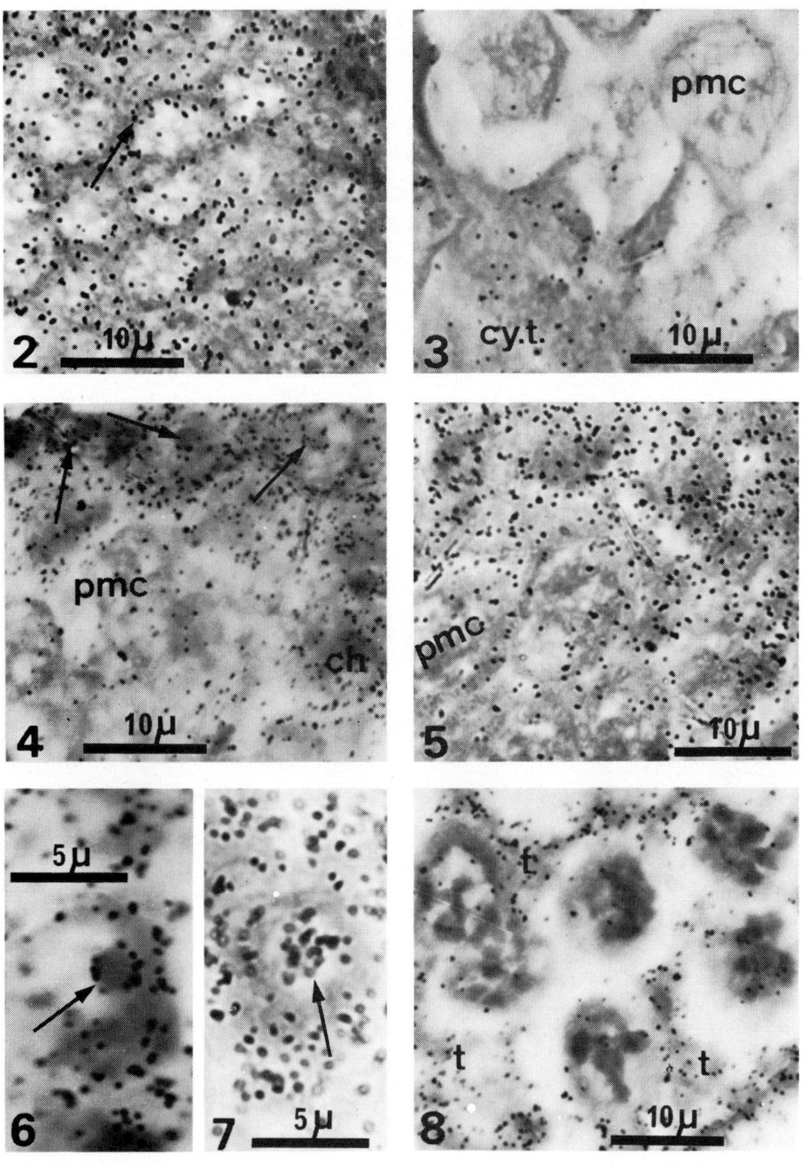
2
10µ
3
pmc
cy.t.
10µ
4
pmc
ch
10µ
5
pmc
10µ
6
5µ
7
5µ
8
t
t
t
10µ

from biochemical data (Kamiyama et al[3] ; Kostraba et al[4]) that we recalled in the introduction.

From the zygotene to the advanced stages of the microspores, the variation of ^{3}H-tryptophane cellular incorporation level (fig. 1) is fairly similar to that concerning ^{3}H-leucine (Albertini[1]). However, only tryptophane clearly reveals a peak in the synthesis of nuclear and cytoplasmic non-histone proteins at diakinesis ; given that proteins with a high -S-S- content are non-histone proteins (Tristram et al[5]), this result fits in with the histochemical data according to which the concentration of proteic -S-S- increases at this stage in the cytoplasm and in the chromatin of the Rhœo discolor PMC (Albertini[17]).

From the synizesis to stages 1 and 2 of the microspores, the syntheses of non-histone proteins are intensive in the plasmodial tapetum in the chromatin and perinucleolar zone as well as in the cytoplasm (fig. 1,6,12,14 ; table 1). Such a type of synthesis, the relative stability of the synthetized proteins (fig. 1 ; table 1) as well as cytochemical results (SH-proteins found by the reaction of Barrnett and Seligman[18]) go to prove that an intense building up of non-histone proteins is made progressively in the nucleolus and above all in the periplasmodium cytoplasm throughout this long period ; the cytoplasmic protein content of the tapetum seems to be at its maximum during period 2 of the microspores.

During microsporogenesis, the non-histone protein matter is transferred from the anther connective to the microsporocytes and to the microspores ; this transfer, increased at the beginning of the meiosis, during diakinesis-metaphase I and from the tetrad stage, is under domination of the tapetum which, it seems, acts as a filter, a reservoir and a transfer regulator adapted to each meiotic stage and this associated with its capacity of synthesis already stated. Such a conclusion is especially compatible with certain data of electronic microscopy (Rowley[19], Mepham et al[20] ; different Commelinaceae) according to which there is a continuity between the membrane systems of the tapetum and microspores allowing the transfer of macromolecules from the tapetum to the microspores. Thus, some protein matter enzyme precursors

Fig. 9. PMC at the beginning of the diakinesis ; time of supply : 2 h. If we compare this with fig. 8 (30 mn), we find increased activity of the periplasmodium. Fig. 10. PMC (pmc) at the beginning of diakinesis ; 2 h in ^{3}H-tryptophane then 2 h in a medium without radiotracer. The chromatin and especially the PMC (pmc) cytoplasm are clearly labelled (compare the present fig. with fig. 8 and 9). Fig. 11. Metaphase I ; 2 h of labelling, then 16 h without radiotracer. In addition to a distinct chromatic activity, the PMC show heavy cytoplasmic labelling indicated by the arrows. Fig. 12. Tetrad stage ; 2 h. Intensive activity of the periplasmodium ; very slight labelling of tetrads. Fig. 13. Tetrad stage ; 2 h in ^{3}H-tryptophane, then 16 h without radiotracer. The tetrads are clearly labelled at the expense of the labelling of the plasmodium. Fig. 14. Period 1 of microspores ; 2 h. Intensive activity of the periplasmodium ; the microspores (m) are only slightly labelled.

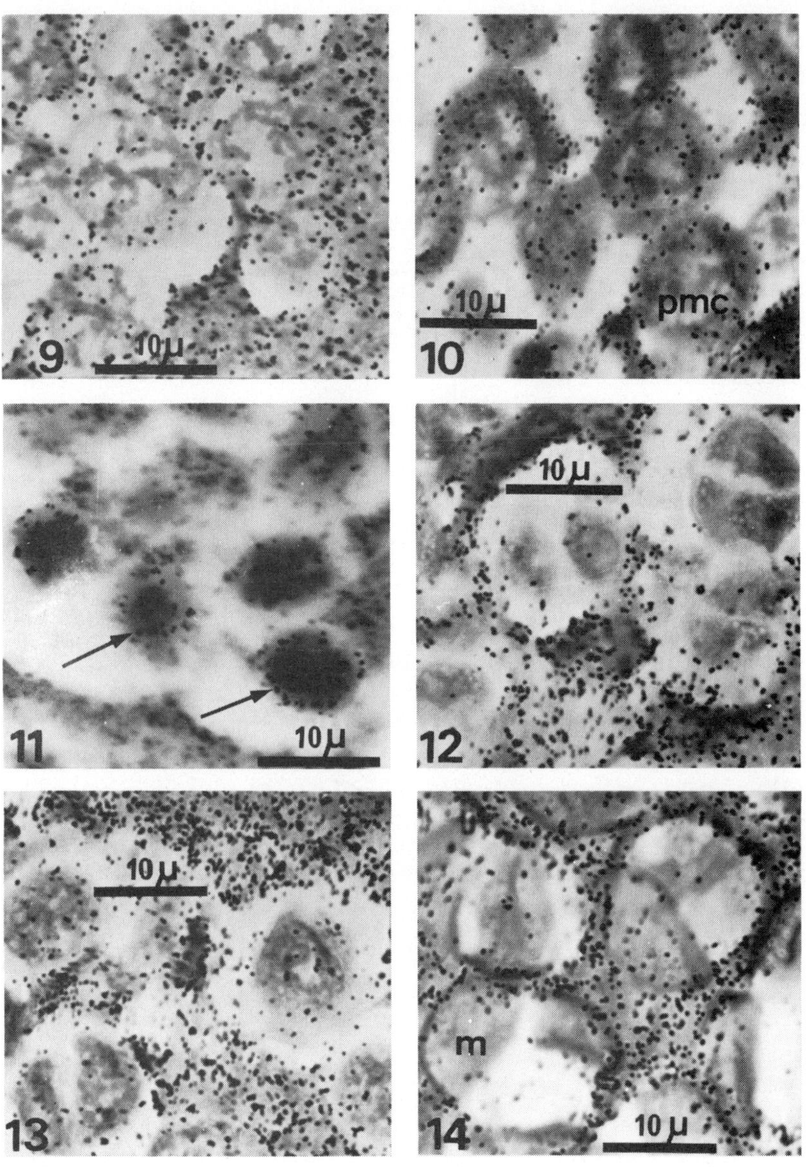
9
10 µ
10 µ
pmc
10
10 µ
11
10 µ
12
10 µ
13
10 µ
m
14

(anabolic, for instance) if not some enzymes themselves, which make up an important part of the non-histone proteins, could be transferred from the periplasmodium to the microspores according to a programmed plan in the tapetum.

References

1. Albertini, L., 1971, Rev. Cytol. et Biol. vég., 34,49.
2. Wang, T.Y., 1968, Exper. Cell Res., 53, 288.
3. Kamiyama, M. and Wang, T.Y., 1971, Biochim. Biophys. Acta, 228,563.
4. Kostraba, N.C. and Wang, T.Y., 1972, 262,169.
5. Tristram, G.R. and Smith, R.H., 1963, IN : The proteins, vol. I, ed. H. Neurath (Academic Press, N.Y.), p. 45
6. Bonner, J., 1965, in : Plant biochemistry, eds Bonner and Warner (Academic Press, New York), p. 38.
7. Vendrely, R. and Vendrely, C., 1966, Protoplasmatologia, V/3/c, 1.
8. Autran, J.C. and Bourdet, A., 1973, C.R. Acad. Sc., France, 277, 2553.
9. Horn, E.C., 1962, Proc. Nat. Acad. Sci., 48, 257.
10. Ts'o, P., Bonner, J. and Dintzis, H., 1958, Arch. Biochem. Biophysics, 76, 225.
11. Taleporos, P., 1959, J. Histochem. Cytochem., 7, 322.
12. Butler, J.A.V., Cohn, P. and Simson, P., 1960, Biochim. Biophys. Acta, 38, 386.
13. Cave, M.D., 1968, Chromosoma, 25, 392.
14. Yonesawa, Y. and Tanaka, R., 1973, Bot. Mag., Tokyo, 86, 63.
15. Albertini, L., 1970, Bull. Soc. Hist. Nat. Toulouse, 106, 352.
16. Ficq, A., 1961, Monographie n° 9, Institut Interuniversitaire des Sciences Nucléaires, Bruxelles.
17. Albertini, L., 1963, C.R. Acad. Sc., France, 256, 3490.
18. Barrnett, R.J. and Seligman, A.M., 1952, Science, 116, 323.
19. Rowley, J.R., 1959, Grana Palynol., 2, 3.
20. Mepham, R.H. and Lane, G.R., 1969, Protoplasma, 68, 175.

Fertilization in Higher Plants, ed. H.F. Linskens.

CYTOPHOTOMETRIC STUDY OF THE INFLUENCE OF COLD ON DNA SYNTHESIS IN THE STAMINAL TISSUES OF THE RHOEO DISCOLOR HANCE

A. Souvré and L. Albertini

Laboratoire de Biologie Végétale, Université P. Sabatier, Toulouse, France
Laboratoire de Cytologie, E.N.S.Agronomique, Toulouse, France

1. INTRODUCTION

We have already noted[1] that the authors who have studied the action of cold on DNA synthesis, on both animal and plant material, by cytologic methods and various measures, obtained quite conflicting results. Thus in the case of Trillium erectum roots, exposed to cold (3° C), Evans[2] measured a loss of 19% in the DNA content by two-wavelength photometry, whereas Woodard et al.[3], in similar conditions, but by microphotometry (plug-method) and microdensitometry, did not observe any quantitative variation of the DNA. According to Rodkiewicz[4], the nuclear DNA content in Hyacinthus roots is maximum at 4° C, whereas according to La Cour et al et al.[6], Heyes and Shaw[6], it falls from 15 to 20% in the roots of different species exposed to cold (0° C).

Evans[2], who, after treatment by cold, observed a decrease (20%) of the nuclear DNA content in species (Trillium erectum and T. sessile) with extensive heterochromatic zones and an increase of 22% in a species (Tradescantia edwarsiana) without clearly delimited heterochromatic zones, thinks that the loss takes place at the labile DNA associated with heterochromatin. That is not so according to La Cour et al.[5] who measured a decrease in DNA content throughout mitosis, without taking into account the species, the presence or the lack of heterochromatin.

According to Wake et al.[7] the loss (30%) of DNA content determined in the Trillium kamtschaticum could be caused by a modification of the DNA-protein complex which alters the heterochromatin staining.

An autoradiographic study (Souvré[8]) about the action of cold on our material i.e. the anthers of the Rhoeo discolor, showed that cold (2° C) considerably reduces ^{3}H-thymidine incorporation in the DNA (fig. 1 T; 2 F; 3 T; 4 F) and that of ^{3}H-uridine in the RNA of the meiocytes (PMC) and the tapetum. The aim of these experiments is to determine whether the activity variations of the nuclear structures, showing a decrease of synthesis in DNA and RNA, already noticed in the anthers exposed to cold, are in relation to a fall of DNA content, comparable to that measured by Evans[2], La Cour et al.[5], Heyes and Shaw[6] and Wake et al.[7].

2. MATERIALS AND METHODS

Sample plants in pots are taken from a clone of Rhoeo discolor cultivated in a greenhouse at 15-20° C. One part of this (control) is put into a glazed enclosure where the temperature is regulated at 20-21° for 4 days. The second part (cooled sample) is exposed in the same enclosure for an equal length of time, at a temperature varying from 0° C to 1° C. At the end of these treatments the inflorescences of two samples are fixed by a mixture of ethanol-acetic acid (AA : 4/1; 2 h) or in Hamant's[9] blue fixative (*). In order to reveal the synthesis variations in DNA, we thought it advisable to use two totally different fixatives to determine the incidence of the fixation on the results. Most of the authors who study the action of cold on the DNA have not taken this trouble, and use only one type of fixative, i.e. ethanol-acetic acid (Woodard et al.[3], Rodkiewicz[4], Evans[2]), freezing-drying (Li and Weiser[10]). In their reports, some of them do not even mention which type of fixing they have used (La Cour et al.[5], Heyes and Shaw[6], Wake et al.[7]). After fixation, the inflorescences are treated with usual cytologic methods; the sections (12 μ) undergo the reaction of Feulgen (HCl 1 N at 55° C : 20 mn; staining by using Schiff's reagent: 2 h) before photometry.

The values in arbitrary units of nuclear DNA content are calculated by a two-wavelength method (490 mμ, 514 mμ) after having measured the transmissions on a MPM Leitz cytophotometer. Moreover, the calculation of apparent areas of the nuclei is made after measuring the diameters with an ocular micrometer.

The action of cold on the nuclear DNA content, has been studied on three of the anther tissues: the PMC at synizesis, the tapetum at prophase I (value 4C) or at the post-mitotic G1 phase (value 2C) and the connective. Under normal conditions (Albertini[11]) the metablic activities of these tissues, at the indicated stages, are different: the PMC during synizesis, no longer synthetize DNA, and RNA synthesis decreases by 50% as early as the leptotene. On the contrary, the tapetum in its G1 phase during synizesis shows intensive metabolic activity (considerable synthesis of cytoplasmic RNA); as for the connective, the cytoplasm of the cells of which is slight, has an activity of minor importance.

3. RESULTS

The essential part of the results is recorded in the histograms of fig. 5 (PMC), fig. 6 (Tapetum), fig. 7 (Connective) and in a recapitulory, table 1.

In the case of the PMC, by using AA fixative, we measure a fall of 8,4% in

(*) fixation (24 h) followed by washing in running water (24 h)

Comparison of incorporation of ^{3}H-thymidine (20 μCi/ml ; 3 h) by the excised anthers of control (fig. 1T, 3T) and of plants treated by cold (fig. 2F, 4F; 3 days at 0°C to 1°C).
Fig. 1T, 2F : Premeiotic resting stage. Nuclear incorporation of pollen mother cells (PMC). At this stage, the tapetal nuclei are exempt from significant labelling. Observe reduced activity of PMC treated by cold.
Fig. 3T, 4F : Synizesis. Nuclear incorporation in the tapetum. At this stage, the PMC no longer synthetize the DNA. Observe reduced activity of cooled tapetum nuclei.

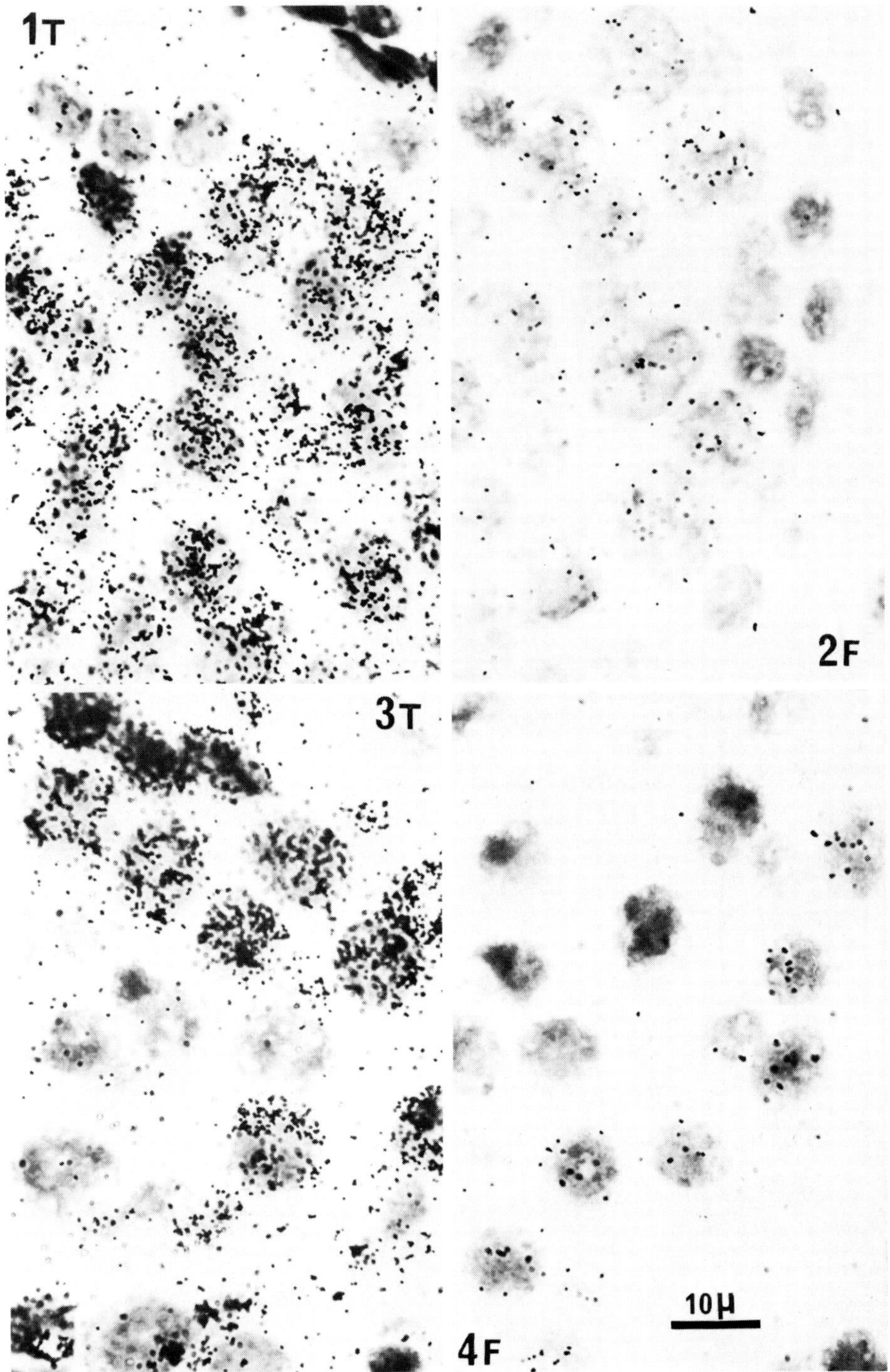
1T
2F
3T
4F
10μ

the DNA content in the cooled nuclei, parallel to an approximately 10% shrinking of the apparent surface (control: 149 μ^2 ; cooled: 134 μ^2). On the contrary, with Hamant's fixative [9] we determine no decrease of the DNA content in the nuclei treated by cold and the apparent surface is 5% lower than that of the control (control: 122 μ^2 ; cooled 116 μ^2).

In the case of tapetum, in order to compare the DNA content of the nuclei, we bring this content down to 2C value for the measures done in G2 or in prophase. The experiments aF6 (fig. 6), which correspond to nuclei (Albertini[11]) stopped by cold during endomitotic synthesis, are not taken into account. With AA fixative, we notice a 10,1% decrease of the DNA content of the tapetal nuclei treated by cold on the contrary with the Hamant[9] fixative, we have a 6,7% content increase with the same tapetal nuclei.

The histograms of fig. 7 show that the nuclear DNA content of the connective

Table 1

Study of the action of cold on nuclear DNA content of the *Rhœo discolor* staminal tissues (fixatives ethanol-acetic acid (AA) and Hamant[9]). The values are expressed in arbitrary unities for the control (T) and cooled (R) samples. (*) These averages are accompanied by their confidence interval for a 95% safety factor.

		Variation limits of the biggest class		Average of the totality of nuclei tested		Extreme values of averages (*) per pollen sac	
		A A	Hamant	A A	Hamant	A A	Hamant
PMC (4C)	T	400-420	360-420	427	405	410 ± 7	388 ± 14
						450 ± 12	424 ± 2
	R	360-460	380-420	391	407	363 ± 10	399 ± 11
						427 ± 9	417 ± 8
TAPETUM	T	190-230 (2C)	190-260 (2C)	207 (2C)	221 (2C)	366 ± 24	166 ± 19
						429 ± 12 (4C)	204 ± 8 (2C)
	R	140-220 (2C)	200-240 (2C)	186 (2C)	236 (2C)	389 ± 15	235 ± 12
						427 ± 12 (4C)	237 ± 12 (2C)
CONNECTIVE (2C)	T	180-220	200-240				
	R	180-240	200-220				

Fig. 5,6,7 : Action of cold on the synthesis of the nuclear DNA of Pollen Mother Cells (fig. 1) the Tapetum (fig. 2) and the Connective (fig. 3) in the *Rhœo discolor*.
The frequency distribution of the measures in nuclear DNA content (Feulgen) are represented by histograms. In abscissa : DNA content per nucleus in arbitrary units ; the limits of the classes are indicated. In ordinate : frequency ; number of nuclei in each class.
A, a, α : ethanol-acetic acid fixative ; B, b, β : Hamant[9] fixative. T : control ; F : treated by cold (4 days at 0°C to 1°C).

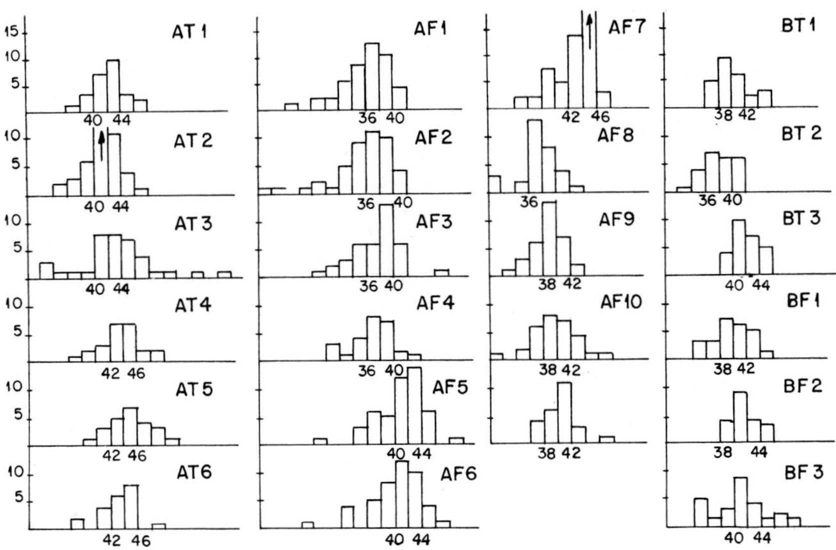

Fig. 5 : Pollen Mother Cells (PMC)

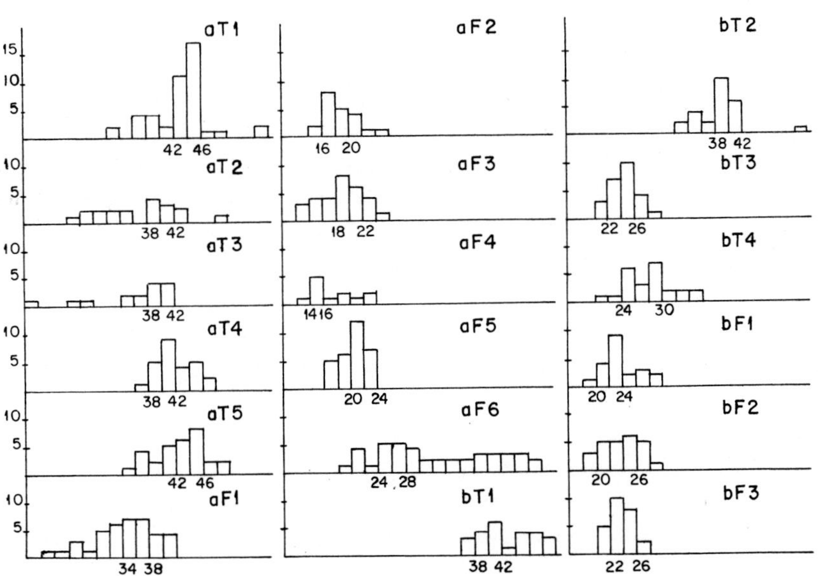

Fig. 6 : Tapetum

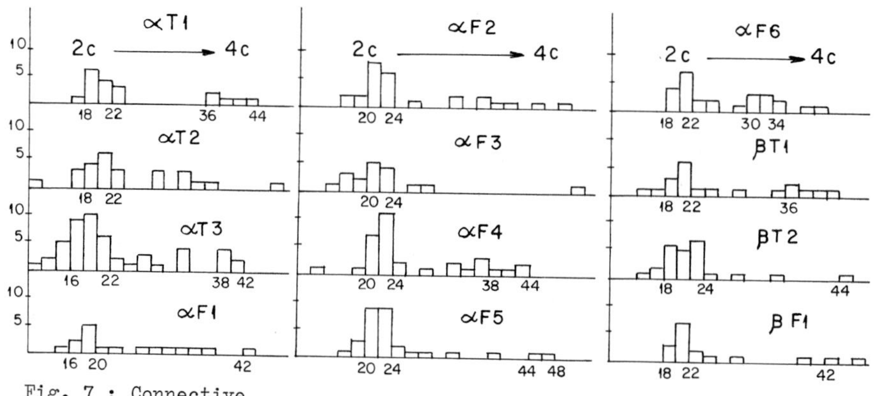

Fig. 7 : Connective

nuclei at 2C level is not modified by the treatment by cold, and the same thing seems to apply to the nuclei of content 4C.

4. DISCUSSION

We must stress the importance of the technical work involved by this photometric study on the influence of cold on the nuclear DNA content of PMC, the tapetum and the connective. Indeed, our study, for the whole of these three tissues, led us to analyse 53 groups of measures (53 histograms), each group including the determination of the optic density of 12 to 50 nuclei (mostly 30-35 nuclei). Moreover, let us point out that these multiple measures are made with 3 types of tissues at different metabolic stages, and this with two methods of fixation. The essential technical conditions seem, therefore, sufficiently fulfilled to allow the determination of the quantitative variations of nuclear DNA synthesis after action of the average length of steady cold.

Cold does not seem to bring about a loss of DNA in the PMC or the connective nuclei. The decrease of 8% that can be noticed in the PMC, using only AA fixation, and according to a Student's average comparison test, is not very significant and very close to the variability coefficient of the experimentation. Indeed, if we take the measures for the whole of the anthers of the same plant (AF 1, 2, 3, 4, 8; AF 5, 6, 7; AF 9, 10, 11), the fall of DNA content is respectively -10%, 0%, -5%.

In the case of the tapetum, the greater variability of the results obtained after the action of cold (nuclear DNA content of the treated plants: -10%, AA fixative; +6,7%, Hamant[9] fixative) is inherent at the variable physiological state of the nuclei which can start to synthetize some RNA at a more or less early stage during synizesis (Albertini[11]). Let us once more stress the incidence of histological fixation in the results we have obtained. The fall in DNA content

(-8% for the PMC, -10% for the tapetum) that we observe with AA fixative, is certainly caused by fixation, for we do not rediscover these negative variations with the Hamant[9] fixative. We notice that the decrease in DNA content, measured after AA fixation, is, in every case inferior to those measured by Evans[2] on Trillium erectum and T. sessile roots, by La Cour et al.[5] on radicular meristems of various species, or by Wake et al.[7] on the Trillium kamtschaticum ovule.

If our previous autoradiograph studies[8,12] prove that cold considerably reduces DNA (and RNA) synthesis we do not think that such a treatment can significantly reduce the DNA content of PMC, tapetum or connective nuclei in the Rhoeo discolor, and on that point our results agree with those of Woodard et al.[3]. But if, as Pelc[13] thinks, cold has an effect on metabolic DNA, the limits set by the variability of measures do not perhaps allow us to find and quantitatively estimate duch a change.

References

1. Souvré, A., 1971, Thèse Doct. Spécialité, Toulouse.
2. Evans, W.L., 1956, Cytologia, 21, 417.
3. Woodard, J., Gorovski, M. and Swift, H., 1956, Science, 151, 215.
4. Rodkiewicz, B., 1960, Exp. Cell Res., 20, 92.
5. La Cour, L.F., Deeley, E.W. and Chayen, J., 1956, Nature, 177, 272.
6. Heyes, J.K. and Shaw, G.W., 1958, Nature, 181, 1337.
7. Wake, K., Ochiai, H. and Tanifuji, S., 1968, Jap. J. Genet., 43, 1, 15.
8. Souvré, A., 1974, C.R. Acad. Sci. Paris, D, 278, n° 26.
9. Hamant, C., 1954, Recherches cytologiques sur la reproduction de quelques espèces du genre Mnium, Gomès imp. Toulouse.
10. Li, P.H. and Weiser, C.J., 1969, Plant Cell Physiol., 10, 1, 21.
11. Albertini, L., 1971, Rev. Cytol. et Biol. Végét., 34, 49.
12. Souvré, A., 1971, Ann. Univ. et A.R.E.R.S., 9, 214.
13. Pelc, S.R., 1972, Int. Rev. Cytol., 32, 327.

Fertilization in Higher Plants, ed. H.F. Linskens.

EVOLUTION OF THE PLASTIDIAL SYSTEM DURING THE MICROSPOROGENESIS IN IMPATIENS BALSAMINA L.

Franceline DUPUIS
Faculté des sciences, Laboratoire de Biologie végétale,
33, rue Saint Leu, 80039 AMIENS.

The study of the plastidial system in microspores has already been done in numerous works. MARUYAMA[1] (1968) has studied plastids and mitochondria during pollen development in *Tradescantia paludosa*. ECHLING and GODWIN[2] (1968) in *Helleborus foetidus*, HOEFERT[3] (1969) in *Beta vulgaris* and MEPHAM[4] (1970) in *Tradescantia bracteata* have pointed out changes at the level of the plastidial system, according to the stages considered, but also different structures of the plastids and a variable organization of their reserves in accordance with the considered species. This is why, we have thought interesting to follow the evolution of these organelles during microsporogenesis in *Impatiens balsamina L.* Our first observations begin in the young cells of the sporogenous tissue and continue to the two-celled pollen grain during maturation. During this period we notice the continuous presence of plastidial elements but under variable aspects, with phases of alteration clearly linked to the age of the considered cells. Consequently, we intend to expose here chronologically the result of our observations.

Anthers of *Impatiens balsamina L.* are removed from floral buds, whose sizes vary from 6 to 10 mm. They are fixed for 3 hours in a 3% glutaraldehyde solution in phosphate buffer, pH 7,3 or in cacodylate buffer, pH 7,6. They are then post-fixed for 1 hour in 1% osmium tetroxyde in the Palade buffer. Embedded in araldite, objects are sectioned in ultrathin slices which are stained with uranyl acetate and lead citrate according to VENABLE and COGGESHALL[5] (1965) technique. Certain preparations are subjected to the Thiery test[6] (1967) in order to reveal an eventual presence of polysaccharides.

Before their isolation in a callosic matrix, the mother-cells of pollen grains have a cytoplasm rich in various organelles. The plastids are numerous, very long in form, dispersed in the whole cell. They show a dense stroma, short crests and almost always, only one grain of starch. It is rare to meet several of them in the cells of the young sporogenous tissue, but their number increases as it develops. Very quickly, the starchy synthesis intensifies, in such a way that the original plastid is distorted and takes the aspect of a "tadpole" (fig. 2), with an enormous head, inflated by the distension of the starchy vesicle and with a reduced tail which contains a dense matrix where lamellate formations appear.

When meiosis begins in the nucleus, a modification of the localization of all the cytoplasmic organelles starts. It continues during meiosis to end at a zonal, concentric disposition, different from the phenomenon of segregation described by GENEVES[7] (1971) in Ribes rubrum and which persists until the four haploïd nuclei are organized. Tetraspores issued from the partition of the mother-cell receive equally each a part of the organelles. So, the starchy plastids are distributed in every cell. They contain one, two or three grains of starch surrounded by one or two rows of circular lamellae squashed in the periphery of the plastid. In the reduced and dense stroma sometimes appear zones as dark in the electrons as the inclusions of phytoferritine, but we are not able to disclose the characteristic cristallin arrangement of that substance (fig. 1).

The starchy reserves continue during meiosis but also in the course of the setted of the membranes which will separate the four daughter-cells, a phenomenon which follows the formation of the haploïd nucleus. In the meantime, while the thick matrix of callose uniting the tetraspores has not completely disappeared and while we assist at the setting of probacula of the future wall of the microspore, we do not find more starch in the plastids. Its hydrolysis is probably a very fast process, because we had only once the opportunity to observe in the same cell one starchyplastid and proplastids. On the other hand, at the same time, the zone of building of the microsporal wall shows important polysaccharidic concentrations (fig. 5), that should correspond to a transfer of the polysaccharides from the starchyplastids to the wall and to their using for the synthesis of the latter.

When the microspores are isolated, the starch has disappeared from the plastids. Then, we observe proplastids of a large size and with a rounded or feebly stretched-out form, having a very clear stroma, only a limited number of very flexuous lamellae, quite often circular and distended in places. Moreover, groupings of tubular formations, or their cutting, appear frequently in the stroma (fig. 5). As all membranes, they react positively to silver impregnation, even without preliminary hydrolysis by periodic acid. These tubular formations cannot be compared to the prolamellae corpus described by FARINEAU[8] (1970) in the etioplastids of maize leaves. Some dark places are seen in the stroma of that pro-

---

Fig. 1 - During the meïotic stage we find plastids with a dense stroma where zones so electron-dense that the inclusions of phytoferritine appear (arrow).
(G X 36000) - s, starch.

Fig. 2 - Cytoplasmof a microspore during the accumulation of callosic matrix. Arrows show the communication between plastid and vacuole.
(G X 24000) - s, starch; v, vacuole.

Fig. 3 - Lens of starch disposed between the intraplastidial lamellae in a plastid of the vegetative cell. (G X 60000) - s, starch.

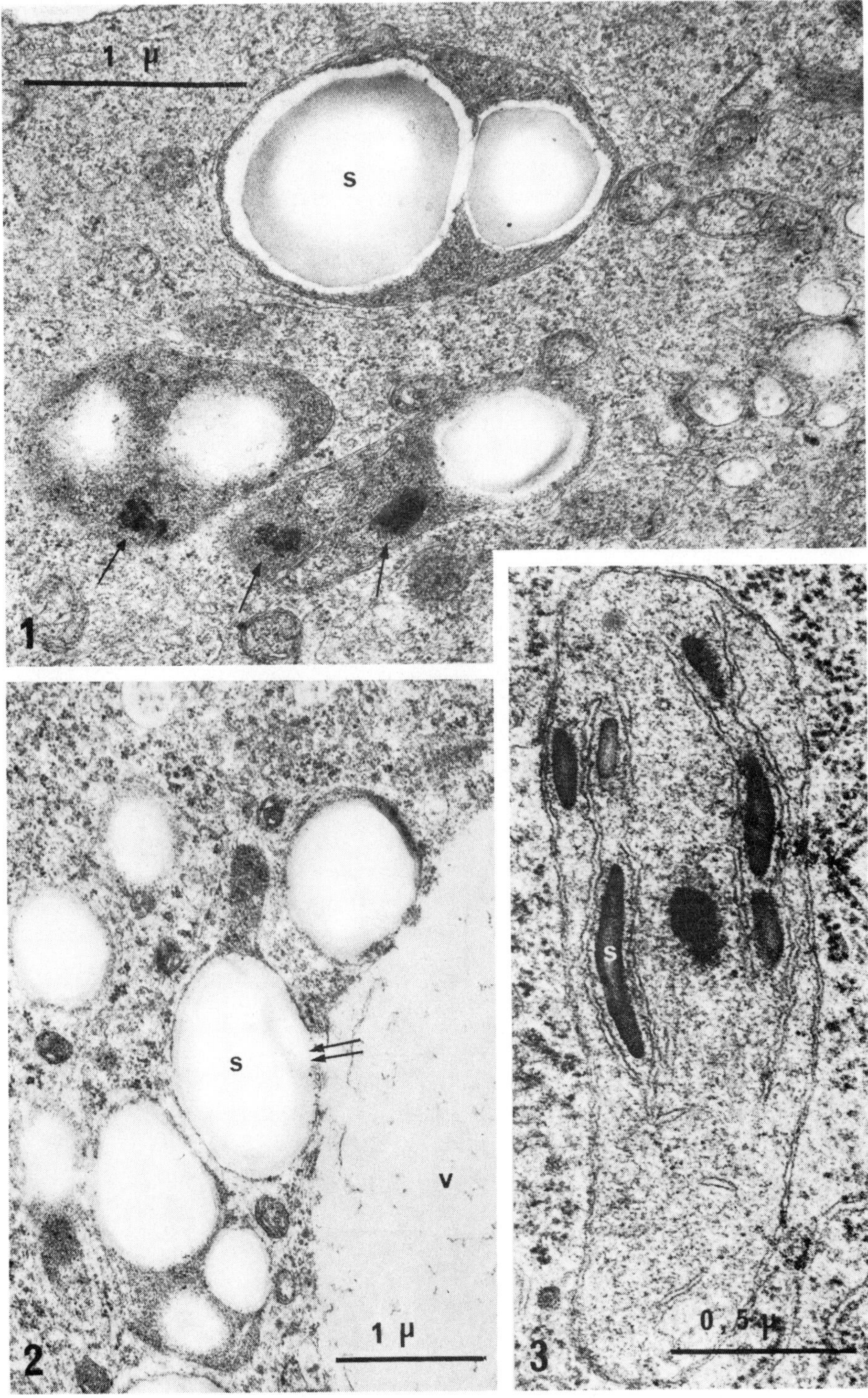
1 μ
s
1
s
v
1 μ
2
s
0,5 μ
3

plastids. They have neither sharp boundaries nor well defined shapes and remain particularly unreactive to the Thiery test (fig. 4 and 5). This might perhaps agree with the persistancy of starch traces in these plastids after its hydrolysis. We observe a third type of inclusion from the preceding ones in these organelles: they are drops rarely isolated, but reassociated in a group and with a variable sizé. They act like lipids after the Thiery reaction.

The plastidial system is thus in an indifferentiated state, not only during the period where the pollen grain is one-celled, but also during the first pollinic mitosis. Besides, the distribution of organelles between the two cells is very unequal. The vegetative cell inherits the majority of them (DUPUIS 1972)[9] and it is in the latter that we had observed a new modification of the plastidial apparatus. Its elements remain equal in number, they are little provided for in lamellae and crests, their stroma is almost as clear as the cytoplasm of the cell, but new accumulations have appeared between the lamellae: they are lenses of starch disposed in the direction defined by the intraplastidial lamellae (fig. 3). These plastids are very comparable with these of Bryum observed by KOFLER et al[10] (1970). Later, the plastidial stroma becomes even darker, and the size of the starch pile increases. This phenomenon is the beginning of the general accumulation of reserves in the cytoplasm. When the sepals of flower buds half-open and allow the colored petals to come into view, the pollen grains at the point of dissemination, are completely blocked by cytoplasmic reserves. We hardly find the usual organelles: mitochondria, endoplasmic reticulum, ribosomes, Golgi bodies are masqued by newly synthetised products. The plastids are not numerous, dispersed between formations scarely reactive to the Thiery test and are composed of polysaccharidic accumulations in the cytoplasm which is becoming dehydrated. Moreover, some lipidic drops complete these reserves.

If during our study, we had noticed the presence of starchplastids at a precise moment, we had also, parallel to the morphologically changes in the plastidial system, observed that very early in the mother-cells, the contingent of plastidial elements seemed to be formed, for during the evolution of the microspores, and afterwards, during the maturation of pollen grains, we had not observed an increase of the plastids.

Fig. 4 and 5 - Preparations subjected to the Thiery test. - dp, dark place; l, lipid; m, mitochondria; tf, tubular formation; w, wall. (G X 60000).

Fig. 4 - Preparation without hydrolysis by the periodic acid. In a microspore isolated we can see large size proplastid where dark places and lipidic drops are observed.

Fig. 5 - In a microspore at the same stage that in fig. 4, we find proplastid which stroma is clear, with very flexuous lamellae, dark places and cutting of tubular formations.

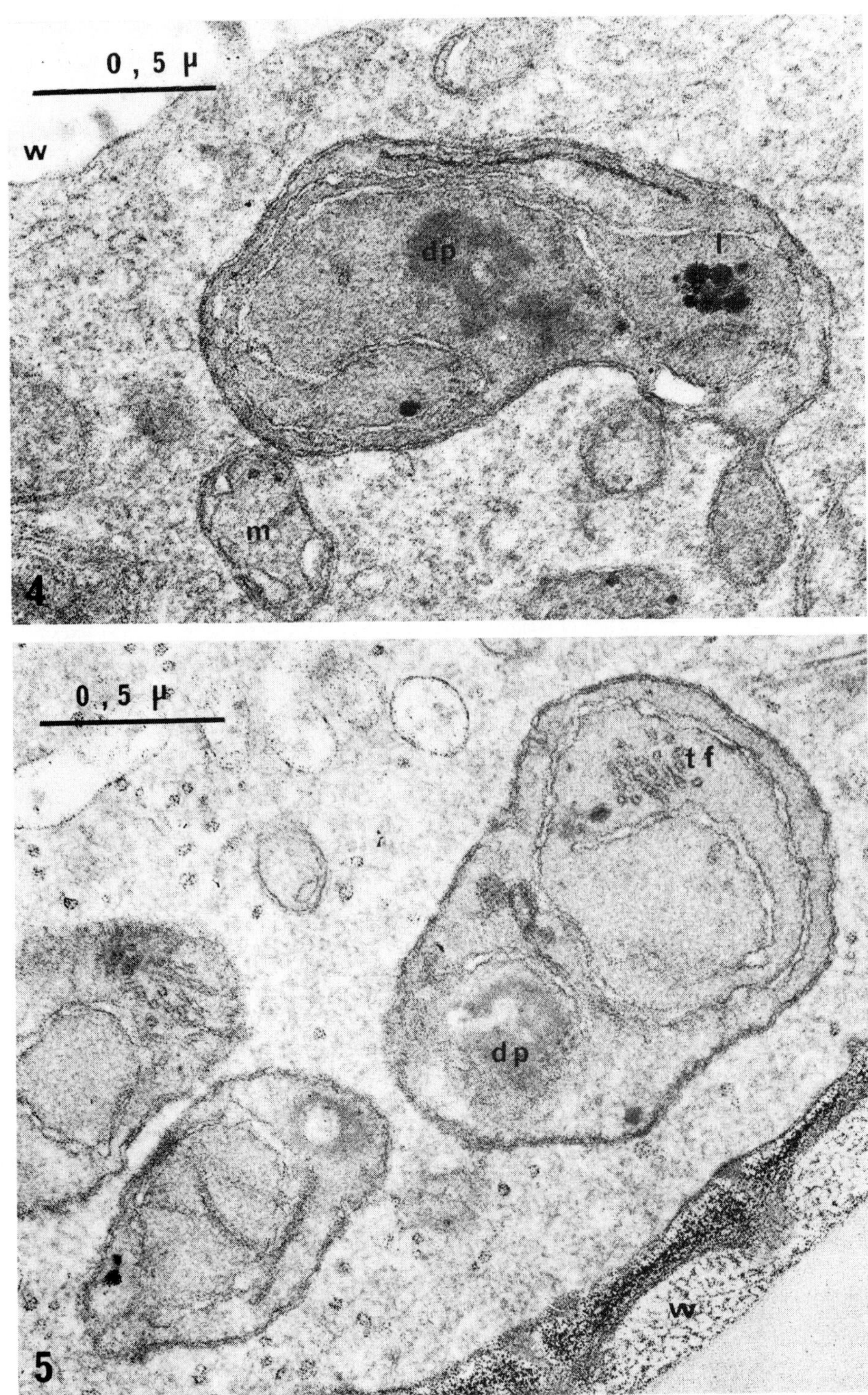
0 , 5 μ
w
dp
l
m
4
0 , 5 μ
tf
dp
w
5

There is no starch genesis in the one-celled microspores which are surrounded with the exine and that state goes on after the first pollinic mitosis; but on the other hand, the periods which come before and after correspond to the continuance of the starchplastids in the cell.

Comparing the evolution of the plastidial system in Impatiens balsamina L. to that observed by HOEFERT in Beta or MARUYAMA in Tradescantia, we notice a large diversity for for the periods where starch is present. HOFFERT and MEPHAM who only began their study at the tetrad stage have particular results for each example: in Beta the polysaccharidic reserves are always present, whereas in Tradescantia they only appear after the first pollinic mitosis and otherwise decrease at the end of the maturation of pollen. But, MARUYAMA who followed the moving forward of the plastidial elements from the mother-cells of pollen, remarked on the presence of starch essentially during meiosis, in the young tetraspores, in the "old" microspores and in the vegetative cell of the maturing grain pollen. There too, as in Tradescantia, the starch decreases in the pollen of flowers which are bloomed.

If it seems evident that the second wave of starch genesis participates in the general accumlation of reserves in the pollen grain before its dissemination, then its germination, we can wonder to what physiological process the presence of starch in premeiotic cells corresponds. We have not collected here all the work relevant to the evolution of the plastidial system during the microsporogenesis, but we notice, nevertheless, that in the few chosen examples, the beginning of the tetrad state shows polysaccharidic reserves which disappear in the microspore except in Beta, perhaps due to the late development of its exine. In Impatiens balsamina L., all trace of starch disappears from the beginning of the exine building. So, the first starch genesis falls in with the organization and accumulation of callosic matrix and we can imagine that there might exist a direct relationship between the presence of starchyplastids and the callosic synthesis, around sporogenous cells. The polysaccharides accumulated in plastids can be discharged into the vacuoles where they will be degraded allowing their products from hydrolysis to participate in the elaboration of callose (fig. 2).

On the other hand, the disappearing of starch in the plastids in microspores seems to correspond to the beginning of exine organization, the place where we find again numerous polysaccharidic traces. As the tetrad is still set in a thick matrix of callose, these polysaccharides come from microspores and may to some extent, come from the hydrolysis of starch previously stored up in the plastids.

References

1. MARUYAMA K. (1968).- Electron microscopic observations of plastids and mitochondria during pollen development in Tradescantia paludosa. Cytologia, 33, 482-497.

2. ECHLING P. and GODWIN H. (1968).- The ultrastructure and the ontogeny of pollen in Helleborus foetidus L. J. Cell Sci., 3, 175-186.

3. HOEFERT L. H. (1969).- Ultrastructure of Beta pollen. I. Cytoplasmic constituents. Amer. J. Bot., 56 (4), 363-368.

4. MEPHAM R. H. et LANE G.R. (1970).- Observation on the fine structure of developing microspores of Tradescantia bracteata. Protoplasma, 70, 1-20.

5. VENABLE J. H. and COGGESHALL R. (1965).- A simplified lead citrate stain for use in electron microscopy. J. Cell Biol., 25, 407-408.

6. THIERY J. P. (1967).- Mise en évidence des polysaccharides sur coupe fine en microscopie électronique. J. Microscopie, 6, 987-1018.

7. GENEVES L. (1971).- Phénomènes ultrastructuraux au cours de la méîose staminale chez Ribes rubrum L. Bull. Soc. bot. Fr., 118, 481-524.

8. FARINEAU L. (1970).- Etude comparée de l'action exercée par la lumière blanche et par diverses lumières monochromatiques sur l'évolution ultrastructurale et la biosynthèse pigmentaire des étioplastes de feuilles de maïs ; Soc. bot. Fr., Mémoires, 27-42.

9. DUPUIS F. (1972).- Formation de la paroi de séparation entre la cellule génératrice et la cellule végétative dans le pollen d'Impatiens balsamina L.Bull. Soc. bot. Fr., 119, 41-50.

10. KOFLER L., NURIT F. et VIAL A.M. (1970).- Germination des spores de mousse et évolution de leurs plastes en présence de DCMU. Soc. bot. Fr., Mémoires, 285-310.

Fertilization in Higher Plants, ed. H.F. Linskens.
© 1974, North-Holland Publishing Company – Amsterdam, the Netherlands.

THE ISOLATION AND ULTRASTRUCTURE OF POLLEN PROTOPLASTS

Y.P.S. Bajaj[1] and M.R. Davey

Department of Botany, University of Nottingham,
Nottingham, England

1. Introduction

Protoplasts have been isolated from almost every part of the plant, and have been used for a variety of purposes[1,2]. Isolated pollen protoplasts may be useful for studying pollen ontogeny, since their behaviour in culture may indicate the nature of wall materials being secreted and deposited by the protoplast independent of the surrounding somatic tissues. In addition, these protoplasts might be induced to produce haploid tissues/plants; and for somatic hybridization, fusion of two haploid pollen protoplasts would be analogous to natural fertilization. Pollen grains of angiosperms are coated with sporopollenin[3] which is remarkably durable and chemically inert[4], and is one of the most resistant materials in the organic world[5]. It is a polymer of carotenoids and carotenoid esters[6], and can be dissolved only by treatment with fused potassium hydroxide, strong oxidising solutions and certain organic bases[7]. Partial degradation of the exine has been reported by the action of stigmatic substances[4] and also by certain micro-organisms[8]. However, as yet no enzyme is known which can digest the exine, The present investigation is an attempt to denude mature pollen by a combination of enzymatic and mechanical means.

2. Materials and Methods

Pollen grains were obtained from _Nicotiana tabacum_ cv. White Burley, _Petunia hybrida_ cv. Satelite and _Triticum aestivum_ cv. Kolibri. They were squeezed from young anthers dissected from flower buds, or collected by shaking mature anthers excised from open flowers. The pollen was sterilized with 1-2% sodium hypochlorite solution (lo min), centrifuged into a pellet (3oog for 5 min.), and washed twice with sterile distilled water. Pollen was then incubated in various combinations and concentrations of Cellulase-P 5ooo, Helicase, Rhozyme

---

[1] Present address: Institut für Pflanzenphysiologie und Zellbiologie, Freie Universität Berlin, D-1 Berlin 33 (Dahlem).

HP 15o and Macerozyme prepared in 1o-2o% w/v sucrose (pH 5.8) for 24-48 h at 23°C. One ml of enzyme mixture was used per anther. Agitation during incubation by gentle shaking, by stirring with a glass rod, by slowly sucking the pollen into a Pasteur pipette, or by slight pressure under a cover slip,facilitated protoplast release. The method for the preparation of material for electron microscopy has earlier been described[9].

3. Results and Discussion

In earlier communications [1o,11,12] the enzymatic isolation of protoplasts from pollen tetrads and pollen mother cells was reported. These protoplasts are readily released from their massive callose walls when treated with o.75% w/v Helicase in 1o% sucrose solution. This callose is an unbranched β-1,3 glucan[13], and is simple compared to the complex and durable wall materials of mature pollen grains[14].

In the present investigation, Cellulase, Helicase, Rhozyme and Macerozyme when used alone were ineffective in liberating protoplasts from maturing pollen grains. Some protoplasts were released using Cellulase (2% w/v) with Helicase (1% w/v). The best results were, however, obtained with a mixture of Cellulase (2%), Helicase (1%), Rhozyme (1%) and Macerozyme (1%) with potassium dextran sulphate (o.1%) in 15% sucrose. In *Petunia*, up to 4o% of the pollen grains were observed to give rise to protoplasts. Protoplasts were liberated from their walls in the following ways:

(a) Weakening of the germ pore - The pollen walls (Fig.15) appeared to be more amenable to the action of enzymes following treatment with chlorine water during sterilization. Since the intine is largely pecto-cellulosic in composition[15], it was degraded through the germ pores by the enzyme mixture. Fig. 1-3 and 16-18 show stages in protoplast release via a germ pore.

Fig. 1,2. A bi- and a trinucleate pollen of *Petunia* and *Triticum* respectively, showing release of protoplasts through their weakened germ pores. Fig. 3. A trinucleate protoplast of *Triticum*;note the densely stained small generative and a large vegetative nucleus. Fig.4. A freshly isolated pollen protoplast. Fig.5. Same, after 2 wks in culture. Fig.6. 8-wk-old culture showing division of what appears to be a multinucleate protoplast. Fig. 7,8. Giant protoplasts (formed as a result of fusion of a number of protoplasts) showing budding.

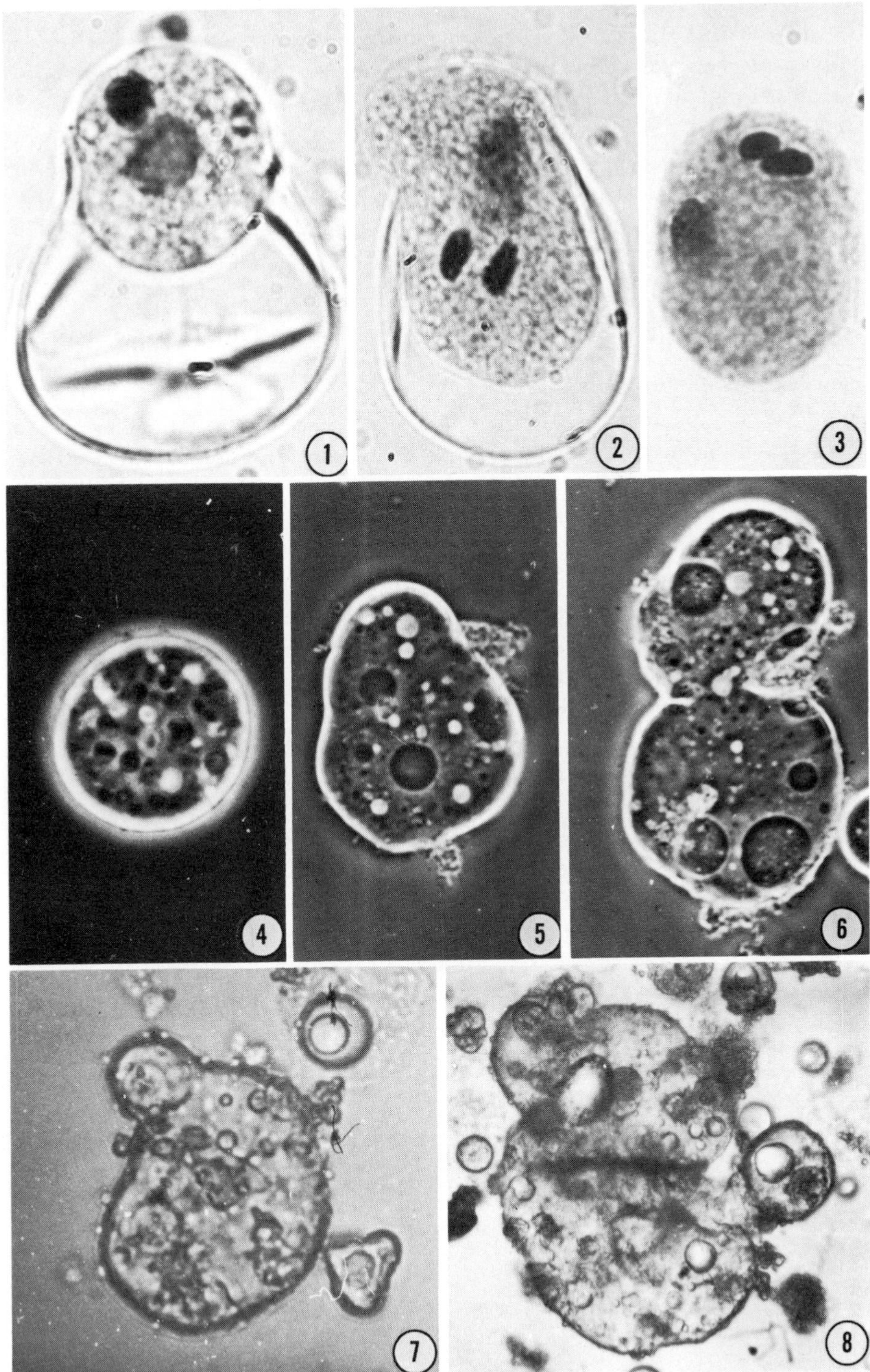
1
2
3
4
5
6
7
8

(b) Partial dissolution and mechanical rupture of the exine - The enzyme mixture partially dissolved the exine (Fig.19), causing it to swell (Fig.9) and to become soft and transparent. It then began to disintegrate in the form of globules which dispersed (Fig.11,12). The isolation time depended on the stage of pollen development and the extent to which walls had developed. Although pollen grains with a thin exine liberated protoplasts relatively easily, grains with a thick exine were more amenable to subsequent mechanical manipulations. The latter caused rupture and sloughing of the exine (Fig.19). Freshly isolated protoplasts were spherical (Fig.4,1o) with dense cytoplasm containing stored materials. They were vacuolate (Fig.2o) in contrast to pollen tetrad or pollen mother cell protoplasts which are highly cytoplasmic. Gentle shaking of the pollen during enzyme incubation appeared to increase the viability of released protoplasts as judged by fluorescene diacetate staining[16]. In a few instances three sub-protoplasts (Fig.13,14) were released from a mature pollen grain. There appeared to be two generative and a vegetative protoplast. Some pollen grains germinated when 2o% sucrose was used as plasmolyticum, and sub-protoplasts, similar to those of tobacco pollen[17], were released from the tip of germinating pollen tubes.

When centrifuged and left undisturbed in the enzyme mixture, the protoplasts tended to fuse with one another to form multinucleate 'tuber-like' giant protoplasts (Fig.8). In cultures, occasionally the protoplasts showed elongation (Fig.5), division (Fig.6) or budding (Fig.7).

In summary, of all the methods used, best results were obtained with the chlorine water-treated Petunia pollen in an enzyme mixture (cellulase 2%, macerozyme 1%, helicase 1%, rhozyme 1%, potassium dextran sulphate o.1% in 15% sucrose) incubated for 24-48 h at 25 C. High concentrations of enzymes over long incubation periods are not conducive for the successful culture of released protoplasts. Attempts are therefore being made to refine the techniques described.

Fig. 9,1o. Petunia pollen after 24 and 48 h in an enzyme mixture, note the thinning and dissolution of walls. Fig. 11,12. Partial dissolution of exine showing dispersal of wall material in the form of globules. Fig. 13,14. Liberation of three subprotoplasts from a pollen. There appear to be two generative and a vegetative protoplast.

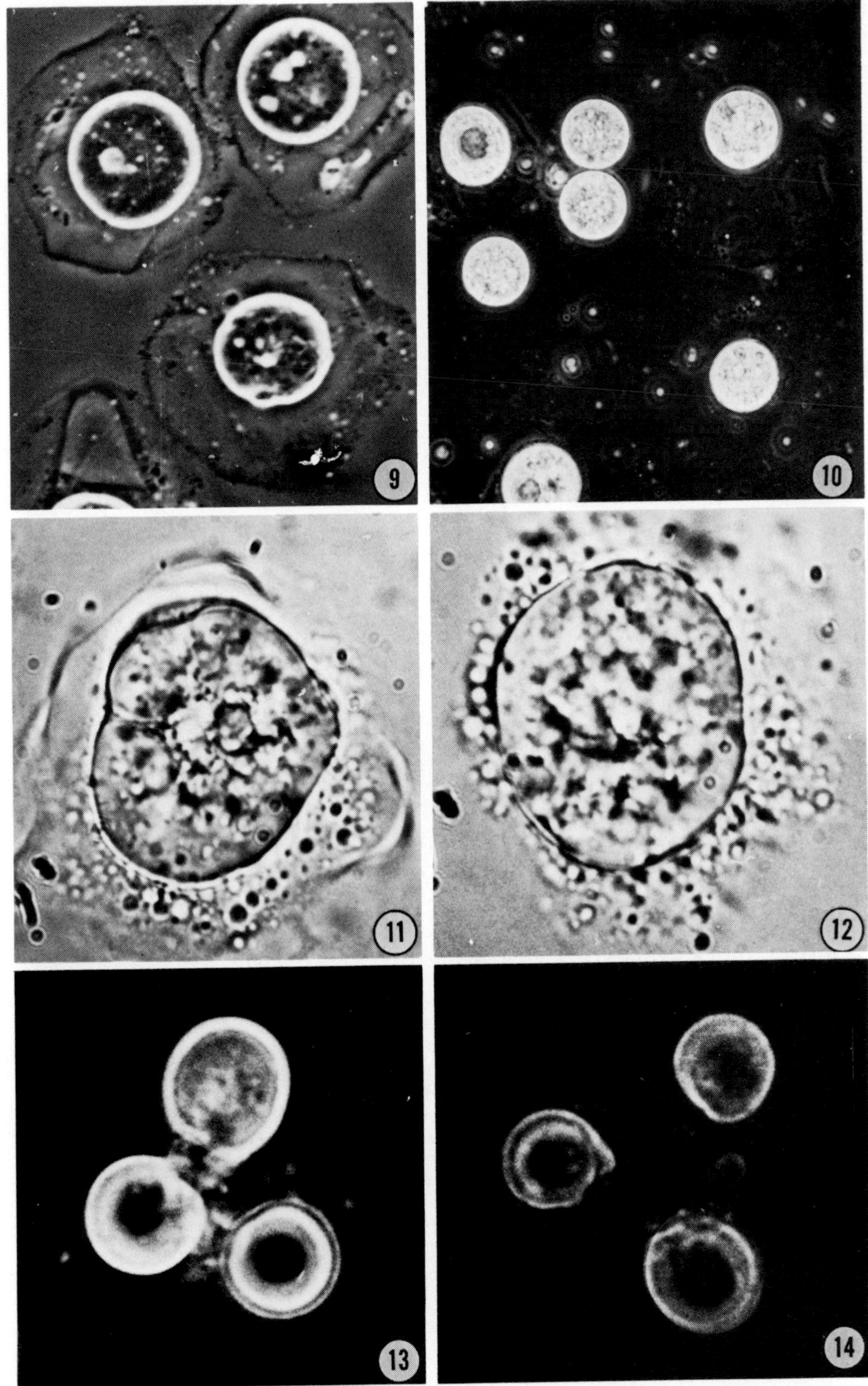

9
10
11
12
13
14

4. Acknowledgements

Grateful acknowledgement is made to Professor E.C. Cocking for providing the facilities for this work which was supported by a grant from the Agricultural Research Council, and The Lord Rank Research Centre, High Wycombe, U.K. Appreciation is also expressed to Mr. B.V. Case for assistance with photography.

References

1. Cocking, E.C., 1972, Ann. Rev. Plant Physiol.23, 29.
2. Bajaj, Y.P.S., 1974, Euphytica 23 (3).
3. Zetsche, F., 1932, In: Handbuch der Pflanzenanalyse, ed. G. Klein, Springer-Verlag, Berlin, p. 2o5.
4. Gherardini, G.L. and Healey, P.L., 1969, Nature 224, 218.
5. Faegri, K. and Iversen, J., 1964, Textbook of pollen analysis. Munksgaard, Copenhagen.
6. Shaw, G., 1971, In: Sporopollenin, eds. J. Brooks, P.R. Grant, M. Muir, P. van Gijzel and G. Shaw. Acad. Press, N.Y. p. 3o5.
7. Southworth, D., 1974, Amer.J.Bot., 61, 36.
8. Elsik, W.C., 1971, In: Sporopollenin, eds. J. Brooks, P.R. Grant, M. Muir, P. van Gijzel and G. Shaw. Acad. Press, N.Y. p. 48o.
9. Davey, M.R. and Short, K.C., 1972, Protoplasma 75, 199.
1o. Bhojwani, S.S. and Cocking, E.C., 1972, Nature New Biol.239, 29
11. Bajaj, Y.P.S. and Cocking, E.C., 1972, In: Proc. 3rd Internatl. Symp. Yeast Protoplasts, Salamanca (Spain), p.79.
12. Bajaj, Y.P.S., 1974, Plant Sci.Letters 3, 93.
13. Clowes, F.L. and Juniper, B.E., 1968, In: Plant Cells, Blackwell, Oxford.

Fig. 15. Electron micrograph of a plasmolysed *Triticum* pollen grain. The thick exine wall surrounds the protoplast. X 1,5oo. Fig.16. A *Triticum* pollen grain after 24h treatment with enzyme showing breaking of the exine (annulus) at the germ pore; the protoplast is beginning to extrude. X 2,5oo. Fig. 17,18. Further stages in protoplast release through the weakened germ pore. X 6,ooo and X 4,5oo. Fig.19. An enzyme-treated *Petunia* pollen grain. The protoplast has withdrawn from the partially dissolved exine; note the broken germ pore. X 4,ooo. Fig. 2o. A *Petunia* protoplast released from the confines of the pollen wall. The protoplast is vacuolate and the cytoplasm densely staining. V = vacuole. X 5,ooo.

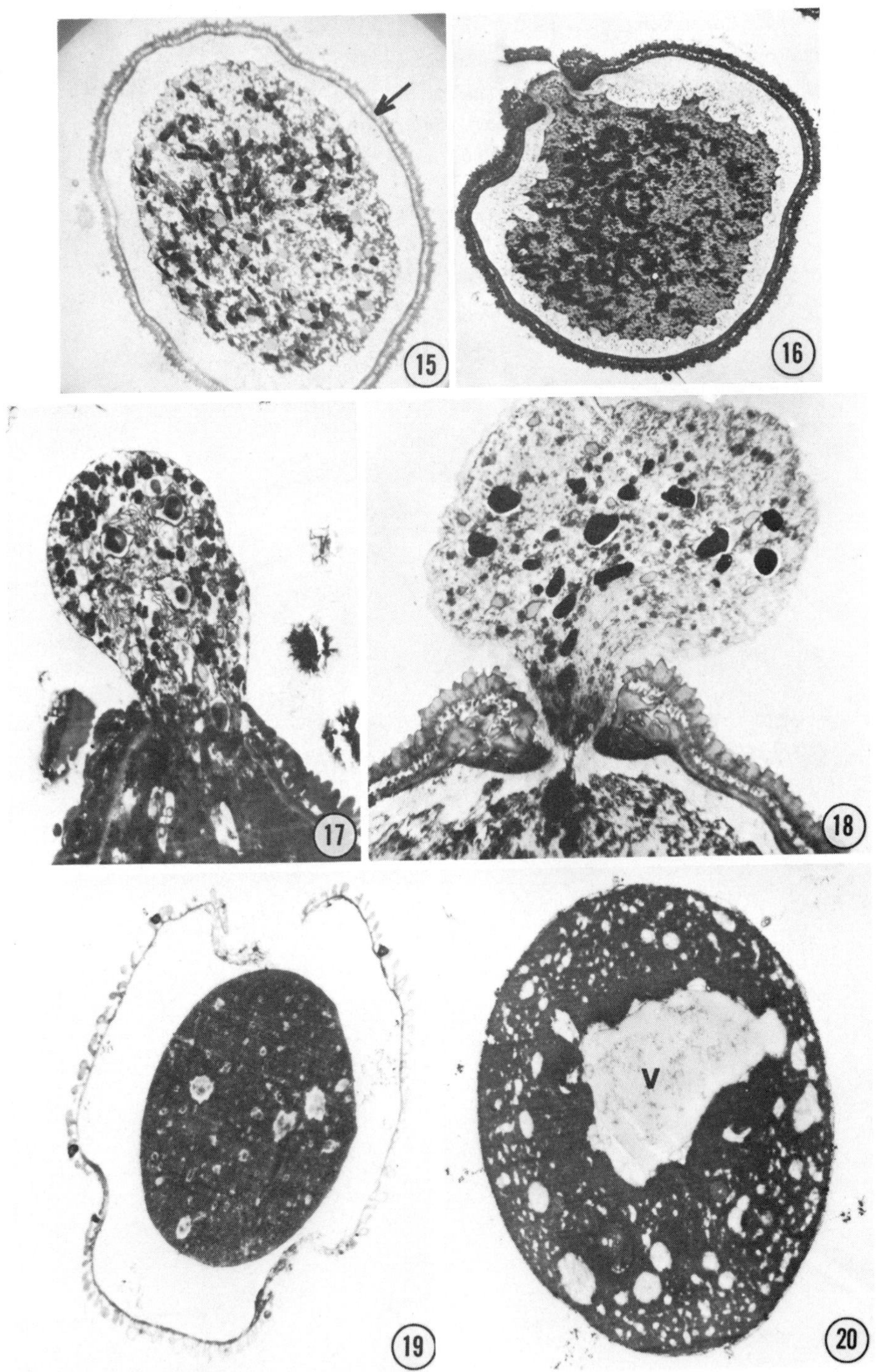
15
16
17
18
V
19
20

14. Heslop-Harrison, J., 1971, In: Pollen: development and physiology, ed. J. Heslop-Harrison, Butterworth, London, p. 277.
15. Sitte, P., 1953, Mikroskopie 8, 29o.
16. Widholm, J.M., Stain Technol., 47, 189.
17. Power, J.B., 1973, In: Plant tissue and cell culture, ed. H.E. Street, Blackwell, Oxford, p. 118.

Fertilization in Higher Plants, ed. H.F. Linskens.

THE ULTRASTRUCTURE OF IMPATIENS POLLEN

J. L. van Went

Department of Botany
Agricultural University, Wageningen
The Netherlands

1. Introduction

The numerous light microscopical studies of Angiosperm pollen have revealed a general and relatively uniform concept of pollen development and structure[1]. However, various electron microscopical studies have shown that the ultrastructure of mature pollen can be highly specific[2-12].
In this paper the characteristic ultrastructure of *Impatiens* pollen, which differs significantly from that of other species, is presented and discussed.

2. Material and Methods

Mature pollen grains of *Impatiens walleriana Hook. f.* were collected by dissecting the whole ovaries and attached loculi shortly before opening of the anthers. After drying for 24 hours at room temperature the released pollen grains were fixed for 2 hours in a solution of 5% glutaraldehyde in 0.1 M phosphate buffer, pH 7.2, to which 1.5 M saccharose had been added. The pollen grains were then washed for 45 minutes in 0.1 M phosphate buffer, pH 7.2, containing 1.5 M saccharose and postfixed for 2 hours in 2% OsO_4 in 0.1 M.phosphate buffer, pH 7.2, also containing 1.5 M saccharose. The entire procedure was carried out at room temperature. The material was dehydrated in ethanol and embedded in Epon. The sections were stained with Reynold's lead citrate.

3. Results

The *Impatiens* pollen are oval in shape, approximately 45 µm long and 25 µm wide. Usually there are four slit-like germination pores. The pollen wall consists of a pilate exine and an intine which is thickened near the pores (Fig. 1). Between the pilae of the exine a strongly stained Pollenkitt is present.

<u>The cytoplasm of the vegetative cell</u>

The most conspicuous feature is the presence of a tremendous number of spherical vesicles, approximately 0.25 µm in diameter, which are randomly distributed. The vesicles are surrounded by a unit-membrane and have an electron-translucent content with some fine fibrillar material. After staining of the sections with lead citrate and prolonged electron radiation in the electron microscope, both the content of the vesicles and the intine become granular in appearance in a similar way.

Mitochondria, dictyosomes and plastids are, like the vesicles, randomly distributed, but considerably less numerous. By counting in an 500 μm^2 cytoplasmic area the average ratio of vesicles, mitochondria, plastids and dictyosomes in sections was established at 150 : 5 : 1 : 1. The mitochondria are spherical in shape and approximately 0.45 µm in diameter. They contain numerous cristae, often oriented parallel to each other and some small plastoglobuli (Fig. 2). The plastids consist of a spherical part containing a single starch grain, and a tail-like part filled with electron-dense stroma (Fig. 5). The average diameter of the starch grains is 0.90 µm. Frequently the plastid surface is lined with rough endoplasmic reticulum (RER). The dictyosomes consist of 4-5 straight cisternae of which the endings are slightly swollen and surrounded by several small vesicles (Fig. 2).

A number of spherical lipoid bodies of varying size lie randomly distributed in the cytoplasm. Usually each lipoid body is almost completely surrounded by a RER cisterna, of which the membrane facing the lipoid body is always covered by ribosomes (Fig. 3). These ribosomes are arranged in a very regular pattern.

The endoplasmic reticulum (ER) is abundant. Most of it is smooth (SER) and lies scattered among the vesicles (Fig. 2 and 4). This SER appears to be highly vesiculated or tubular, since only short cisternae and vesicles of varying diameter are visible. The content of the SER varies from very light to electron-dense. Both SER and RER cisternae form a distinct layer directly beneath the plasma membrane covering the entire surface area (Fig. 3).
The relatively small number of RER cisternae are preferentially located near the surfaces of the vegetative nucleus (Fig. 4), the generative cell, the lipoid bodies and the plastids. Free ribosomes are rare, whereas polysomes are apparantly absent.

Fig. 1. Longitudinal section through *Impatiens* pollen showing the homogeneously structured vegetative cytoplasm, the vegetative nucleus (VN) and the thickened intine near the pore regions (arrows).

Fig. 2. Enlarged portion of the vegetative cytoplasm showing dictyosomes (D), mitochondria (M), vesicles (V) and smooth endoplasmic reticulum (arrows).

Fig. 3. Enlarged portion of the vegetative cytoplasm showing the intine (I), lipoid bodies (L), and starch (S). The arrow points at a tangential view of the ribosomes close to a lipoid body in a characteristic regular arrangement.

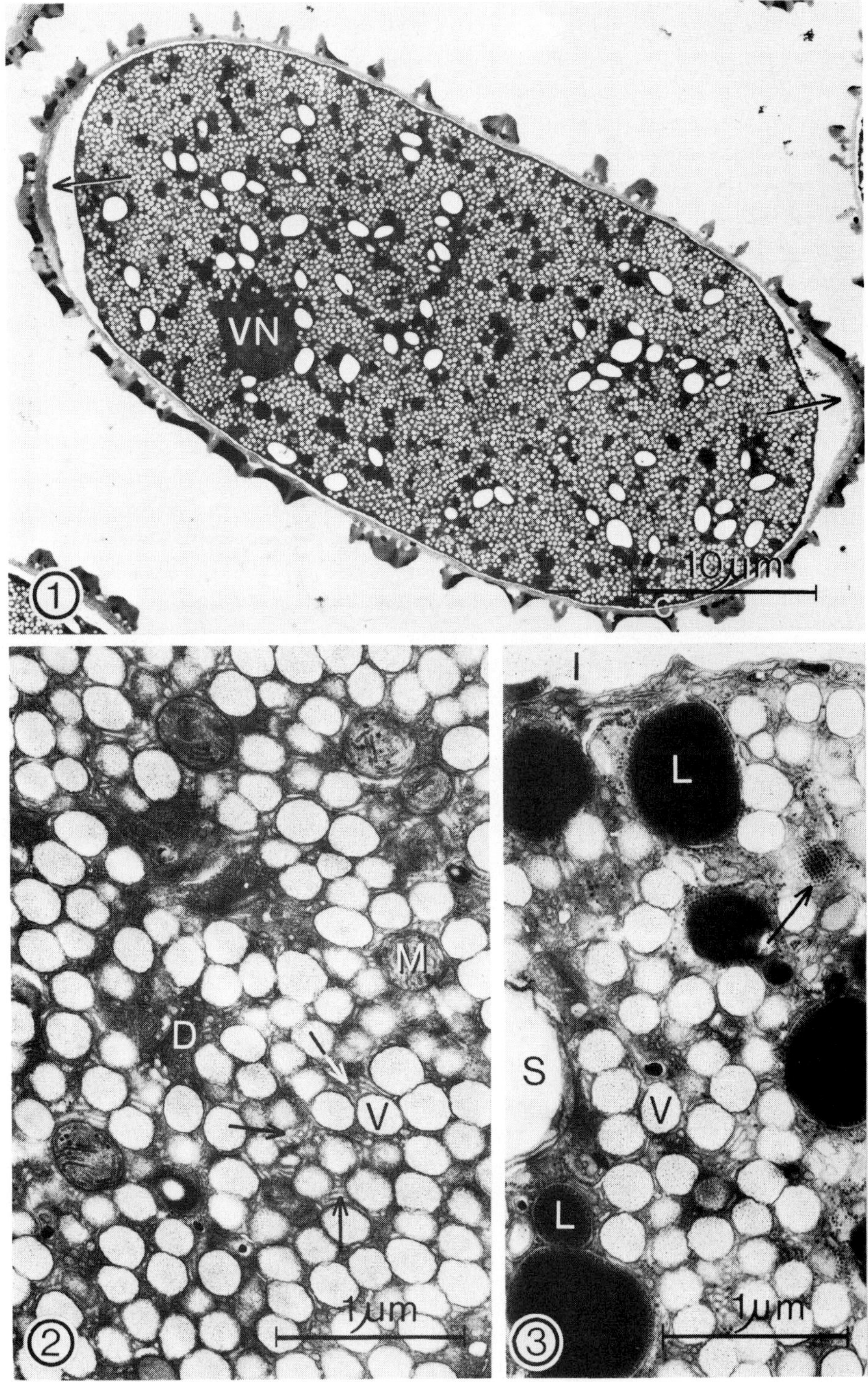

VN
10 µm
1
M
D
V
1 µm
2
I
L
S
V
L
1 µm
3

The vegetative nucleus

The round-shaped vegetative nucleus shows, in cross section, various invaginations (Fig. 4). Its nuclear envelope has many pores, only few attached ribosomes and is strongly wrinkled. Occasionally parts of the membranes of the nuclear envelope as well as membranes of near RER cisternae are very close to each other (Fig. 4). The vegetative nucleus is always in close contact with the generative cell. Many protrusions of the latter, marked by the electron-translucent space between the surrounding plasma membranes, can be observed in the invaginations of the vegetative nucleus (Fig. 4). The ultrastructure of the nuclear content varies. Sometimes it appears homogeneously electron-dense without further detail. In other cases it shows chromosome-like structures consisting of very fine granular material, together with numerous randomly distributed and strongly-stained dots. All vegetative nuclei observed lacked a definite nucleolus.

The generative cell

The generative cell is elongate in shape and has a strongly folded surface (Fig. 6). It is a definite cell since it is at least surrounded by two plasma membranes. The space in between the two plasma membranes is electron-translucent. The cytoplasm contains numerous free ribosomes, but polysomes could not be observed. Some RER is present, most of it arranged parallel to and near the plasma membrane. There are spherical-shaped mitochondria, which are smaller and have less cristae than those of the vegetative cell. There are few dictyosomes present, but plastids could not be observed.

The ultrastructure of the generative nucleus varies. In most cases there is a complete nuclear envelope of which the two composing membranes lie very close to each other. The nuclear content consists of chromosome-like structures, lined and accompanied with some strongly-stained dotlike material (Fig. 6). As in the vegetative nucleus a definite nucleolus appears to be lacking.

Fig. 4. Enlarged portion of the vegetative nucleus and adjacent cytoplasm. Near the nuclear envelope (NE) parallel arranged rough endoplasmic reticulum (RER) is present. In the invaginations of the vegetative nucleus portions of the generative cell (GC) can be seen.

Fig. 5. Enlarged portion of the vegetative cytoplasm showing starch containing plastids.

Fig. 6. The generative cell surrounded by a cell wall (CW) and containing numerous ribosomes. The generative nucleus (GN) contains chromosome-like structures (CHR).

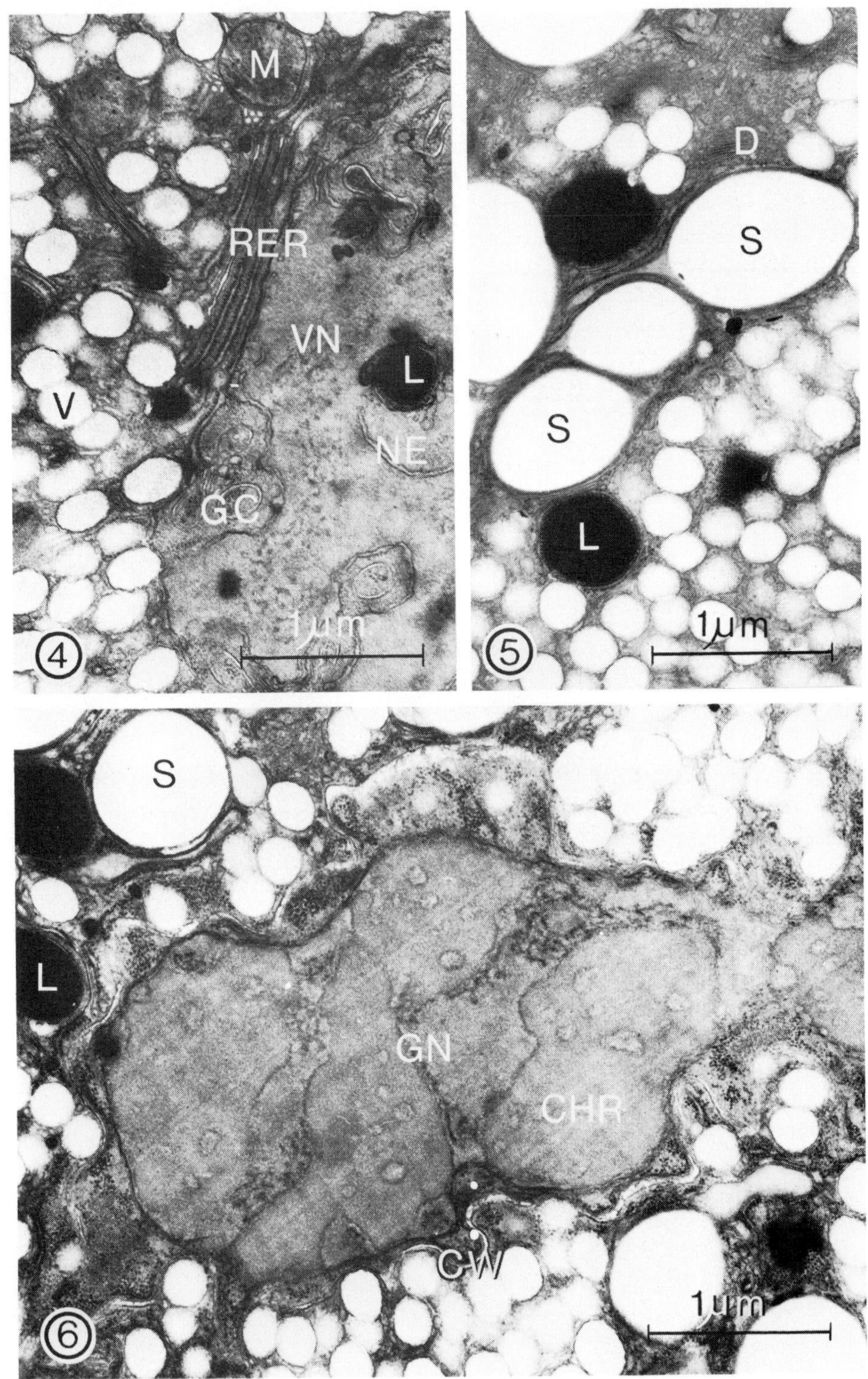
M
RER
VN
L
V
NE
GC
1 µm
4
D
S
S
L
1 µm
5
S
L
GN
CHR
CW
1 µm
6

4. Discussion

Only in a few aspects the ultrastructure of *Impatiens* pollen is comparable with that described for other pollen[2-12]. The presence of spherical mitochondria, abundant ER, an invaginated vegetative nucleus and poorly differentiated plastids are common characteristics of mature pollen. However, most of its ultrastructural features appear to be unique for *Impatiens* -pollen. This holds especially for the relatively small amount of RER, the small number of ribosomes, the special relation between RER cisternae and lipoid bodies, the presence of an extremely large number of vesicles and the ultrastructure of the content of the vegetative nucleus.

For most pollen species studied, the existence of a large protein--synthesizing machinery in the mature pollen grain, necessary for subsequent pollen tube growth, could be concluded from the presence of abundant ribosomes or extensive RER[2-6-7-10]. However, the ultrastructural features (small number of ribosomes and small amount of RER) of mature *Impatiens* pollen indicate that its protein-synthesizing machinery is relatively small. Moreover, the location of most RER cisternae close to the lipoid bodies suggest a relationship between them. Although the regular arrangement of the ribosomes indicates a steady-state, the RER might have been involved in production of the lipoid bodies during maturation of the pollen grain, or it may become involved in the breakdown of the bodies during pollen germination and pollen tube growth.

The chromosome-like state in which the DNA of the vegetative nucleus is present, together with the absence of a nucleolus strongly suggest that the rate of RNA synthesis in the mature pollen, needed for ribosome formation and subsequent protein synthesis is rather low. Since the pollen grains of *Impatiens* germinate extremely rapidly and the subsequent growth of the pollen tube is fast, it is very likely, that also during these stages of development no large production of RNA will occur. Absence of ribosomal RNA production during pollen tube growth was shown for *Lilium* by Steffensen[12] and concluded for cotton by Jensen[7].

Finally, in mature *Impatiens* pollen there is no indication that proteins are stored as could be observed in cotton by Jensen[7].

In my opinion the present data indicate that in *Impatiens* no large quantities or mass production of proteins are needed for both pollen germination and pollen tube growth.

To prevent the pollen from swelling, germinating and producing tubes during fixation, 1.5 M saccharose had to be added to the fixation and washing media. This clearly shows the high osmotic value of the pollen content and the importance of its ability to take up water quickly. In this respect the abundant 0.25 µm vesicles may be involved. They may represent a highly specialized vacuolar system with an extremely large membrane-surface/volume ration. By subsequent uptake of water and gradual fusion of the vesicles the volume of the entire vacuolar system increases enormously, leading to both the expansion and continuously filling up of the increasing pollen tube volume. In this way they might account for the concluded type of germination and pollen tube growth without synthesis of a large amount of protein and cytoplasm.

The relatively small number of dictyosomes in the mature pollen is puzzling, because large amounts of tube wall material has te be available suddenly. Either a rapid production of dictyosomes must take place or the tube wall material must already be present in the mature pollen in one way or another. An indication for the latter possibility forms the similar reaction of the intine, c.q. tube wall and the content of the 0.25 µm vesicles after prolonged electron radiation in the electron microscope. Tube wall material in the vesicles in a precursor form also many account for the proposed high osmolarity.
Vesicles similar to those of *Impatiens* have been reported to be present in the pore regions of *Lychnis* pollen. According to Crang and Miles[2] they contain fibrous material that resembles the structural component of the intine indicating a structural relationship.

The function of the abundant SER is not clear. Their random distribution among the vesicles suggest a relationship. One possibility is that they are involved in the synthesis of lipoids needed for the production of vesicle membrane material. Another noteworthy possibility is that their ultimate function in the mature pollen grain is the comparting of the cytoplasm, since in pollen tubes distinct accumulations of SER are found (unpublished results).

The data on the generative cell are in agreement to those reported by other investigators[4-7-8-9-11]. However, the presence of a true wall around the generative cell could not be established. Difficulties in identifying plastids in the generative cell have been reported previously[7-8-9-11] and Jensen[7] even supposed that during its development the generative cell loses its plastids. Apparently the generative cell of *Impatiens* lacks plastids as no plastids or plastid-like organelles could be identified. However, according to Richter-Landmann[13] plastids are present in the generative cell of *Impatiens glandulifera*. Additional studies are needed to clarify these contradicting meanings concerning the presence or absence of plastids.

The ultrastructural data of the generative nucleus are in agreement with the light-microscopical observations of Wulff[14], who described the nucleus to be in a prometaphase stage.

To summarize the previous discussion, in our opinion the ultrastructural data indicate that the mature pollen grains of *Impatiens* form a highly efficient transport system, completely equipped and provided with all materials needed for the transport of generative, c.q. sperm cells to the female gametophyte. The proposed way of action is primarily based on the uptake of water by vesicles containing precursors of tube wall material. The fusion of vesicles would account for the increase of the pollen tube volume, whereas the formation of the pollen tube wall is based on the fusion of vesicles with the plasma membrane.

However, to prove the foregoing hypothesis more detailed information is needed on the histochemistry of mature pollen and on the ultrastructure and histochemistry of developing microscope and pollen tube.

References

1. MAHESWARI, P., 1950, An Introduction to the Embryology of Angiosperms. (McGraw-Hill, New York).
2. CRANG, R. E. and MILES, G. B., 1969, Amer. J. Bot. 56, 398.
3. DIERS, L., 1963, Z. Naturforschg. 18b, 562.
4. DIERS, L., 1963, Z. Naturforschg. 18b, 1092.
5. ECHLIN, P., 1972, J. Cell Sci. 11, 111.
6. HOEFERT, L. L., 1969, Amer. J. Bot. 56, 363.
7. JENSEN, W. A. et al., 1968, Planta 81, 206.
8. LARSON, D. A., 1965, Amer. J. Bot. 52, 139.
9. SANGER, J. M. and JACKSON, W. T., 1971, J. Cell Sci. 8, 303.
10. SANGER, J. M. and JACKSON, W. T., 1971, J. Cell Sci. 8, 317.
11. SASSEN, M. M. A., 1964, Acta Bot. Neerl. 13, 175.
12. STEFFENSEN, D.M., 1966, Exp. Cell Res. 44, 1.
13. RICHTER-LANDMANN, W., 1959, Planta 53, 162.
14. WULFF, H. D., 1934, Ber. Dtsch. Bot. Ges. 52, 43.

Fertilization in Higher Plants, ed. H.F. Linskens.

DISTRIBUTION OF ORGANELLES AND STARCH GRAINS DURING MEGASPOROGENESIS IN EPILOBIUM

B. Rodkiewicz and J. Bednara

Department of Biology, M. Curie-Skłodowska University
20-032 Lublin, Akademicka, Poland

1. Introduction

Polarization of the megasporocyte and megaspore tetrad in Angiosperms is an obvious phenomenon which eventually results in the formation of an active megaspore from a row of four. This privileged cell lies at the micropylar end of a tetrad in plants with Oenothera type of embryo sac development /fig. 1-5/ and at the chalazal end in Polygonum type; the remaining megaspores undergo degeneration. The visible symptoms of polarization can be easily shown by investigating callose distribution in the cell wall. During the I meiotic prophase,callose occurs in almost the entire megasporocyte wall leaving a space at the micropylar apex in species with Oenothera type of embryo sac development and at the chalazal apex in species with Polygonum type. In further stages of megasporogenesis, callose is laid out in cross walls of diads and tetrads, but the original space of wall without callose remains principally unaltered /1, 2/.

Polarized organelle distribution was described in the megasporocyte of Ginkgo biloba /3/. In Paphiopedilum spicerianum with bisporic embryo sac development organelles and starch grains are gathered at the chalazal end of the megasporocyte. Later they occupy only the two-nucleate embryo sac mother cell /4/. In Oenothera lamarckiana, plastids are grouped at two poles of megasporocyte and in further development are present only in two opposite apical megaspores /5/.

2. Material and methods

Ovules of Epilobium palustre /Onagraceae/ were fixed in ethyl alcohol and acetic acid /3:1/. After hydrolysis in 1N HCl callose was identified in squash preparations by aniline-blue fluorescence method /1/. The periodic acid Schiff /PAS/ reaction /6/ was carried out on in toto ovules. After the procedure, ovules were rinsed in water with detergent and a squash preparation made. Ovules for electron microscopy were fixed in 2% $KMnO_4$, embedded in Epon and sections were stained with lead citrate /7/.

3. Results

Callose occurs in the wall of the elongated megasporocyte of Epilobium palustre at the I meiotic prophase. In the early callose phase the whole cell wall shows vivid fluorescence /fig. 6/; later fluorescence disappears at the micropylar apex or becomes extremely weak /fig. 7/. Some other changes in fluorescence intensity are also visible; at first stronger fluorescence is displayed in the micropylar half of the megasporocyte wall, subsequently in the chalazal region. In diads /fig. 8/ and tetrads /fig. 9/ strongly fluorescent cell plates and cross walls are built. Hence each inactive megaspore is enclosed in fluorescing cell wall,whereas there is no fluorescence at the micropylar apex of active megaspore. The side walls of active megaspore loose fluorescing material before those of the three other megaspores /fig. 10/.

The megasporocyte cell wall contains also some PAS-positive material although the PAS reaction is rather weak. Strong PAS reaction is given by the diad and tetrad cell plates and by cross and side walls.

Epilobium palustre megasporocytes /and megasporocytes in some species of Fuchsia, Oenothera and Clarkia/ contain grains of PAS-positive material. Dense groups of these grains are localized exclusively at both ends of the elongated megasporocyte /fig. 1 and 2/. It appears that in most of the 120 megasporocytes which have been seen, the micropylar group is denser and consists of more

---

Fig. 1-5. Megasporocytes and tetrads of Epilobium palustre after PAS reaction.

Fig. 6-10. Callose fluorescence in cell wall of megasporocytes, diad and tetrads of Epilobium palustre.

Fig. 11. Micropylar pole of a megasporocyte at the early I meiotic prophase; four plastids, part of the nucleus, ER cisterns and mitochondria are visible.

Fig. 12. Micropylar pole of a megasporocyte at the end of I meiotic prophase with numerous plastids.

Fig. 13. Micropylar pole of the active megaspore in a tetrad.

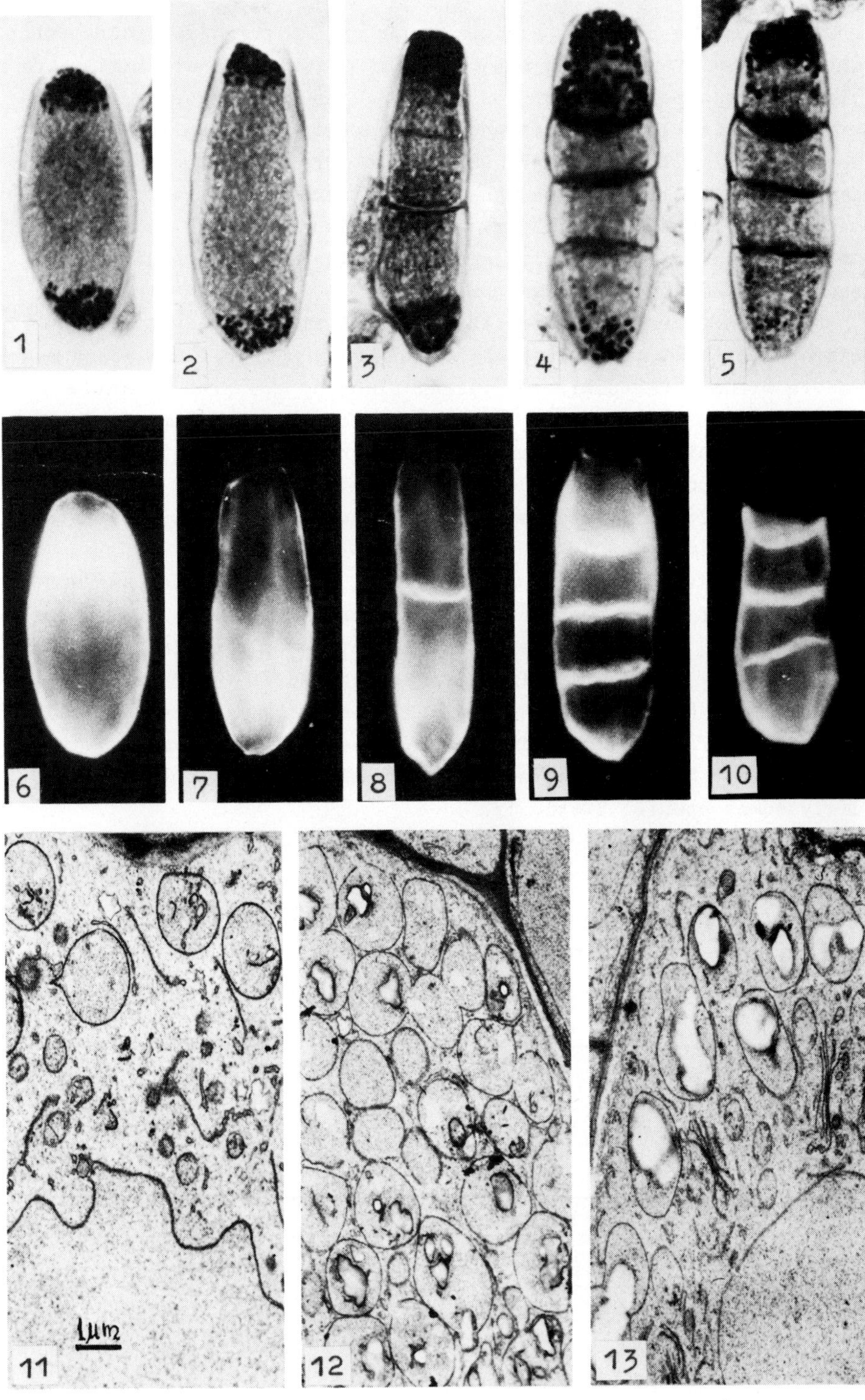
1
2
3
4
5
6
7
8
9
10
1µm
11
12
13

grains than the chalazal group. Groups of PAS-positive grains, once set up, remain unmoved in the course of meiosis and eventually are enclosed in two polar megaspores /fig. 3/. In both megaspores, the grains originally are dispersed in the region between nucleus and apical cell wall. The number and size of grains in the chalazal megaspore gradually decrease when in the micropylar megaspore new ones are synthetized /fig. 4/. This process ends with filling up of micropylar megaspore with grains and their complete disappearance from the chalazal megaspore.

Electron microscopy shows that distribution of plastids coincides with the distribution of PAS-positive grains. In a young megasporocyte without PAS-positive grains, plastids are predominantly scattered at the two poles /fig. 11/. The cell contains single cisterns and vesicles of ER, mitochondria and few and small dictyosomes. Both poles of an older megasporocyte are packed with plastids /fig. 12/; dictyosomes are more numerous and mostly situated in perinuclear zone.

A young tetrad with its chalazal cell still undivided was sectioned and complete preparations from three different levels were obtained. The tetrad consisted of: 1/ active micropylar megaspore /fig. 13/, 2/ its sister, inactive megaspore /fig. 14/ and 3 + 4/ two-nucleate cell where the cross wall was not yet formed after the second meiotic division /fig. 15/. In the pictures of this tetrad the area of the cells was measured and plastids, mitochondria and dictyosomes counted /table 1/.

Table 1

Average number of organelles in 100 μm^2 of megaspore sections from a megaspore tetrad

Megaspore	Active	Inactive	Two-nucleate
Total area in μm^2	760	535	1036
Plastids	3,5	-	1
Mitochondria	13	13,8	13
Dictyosomes	2,6	5,4	3,6

Fig. 14. Inactive megaspore in a tetrad in Epilobium.

Fig. 15. Two-nucleate chalazal cell after the II meiotic division.

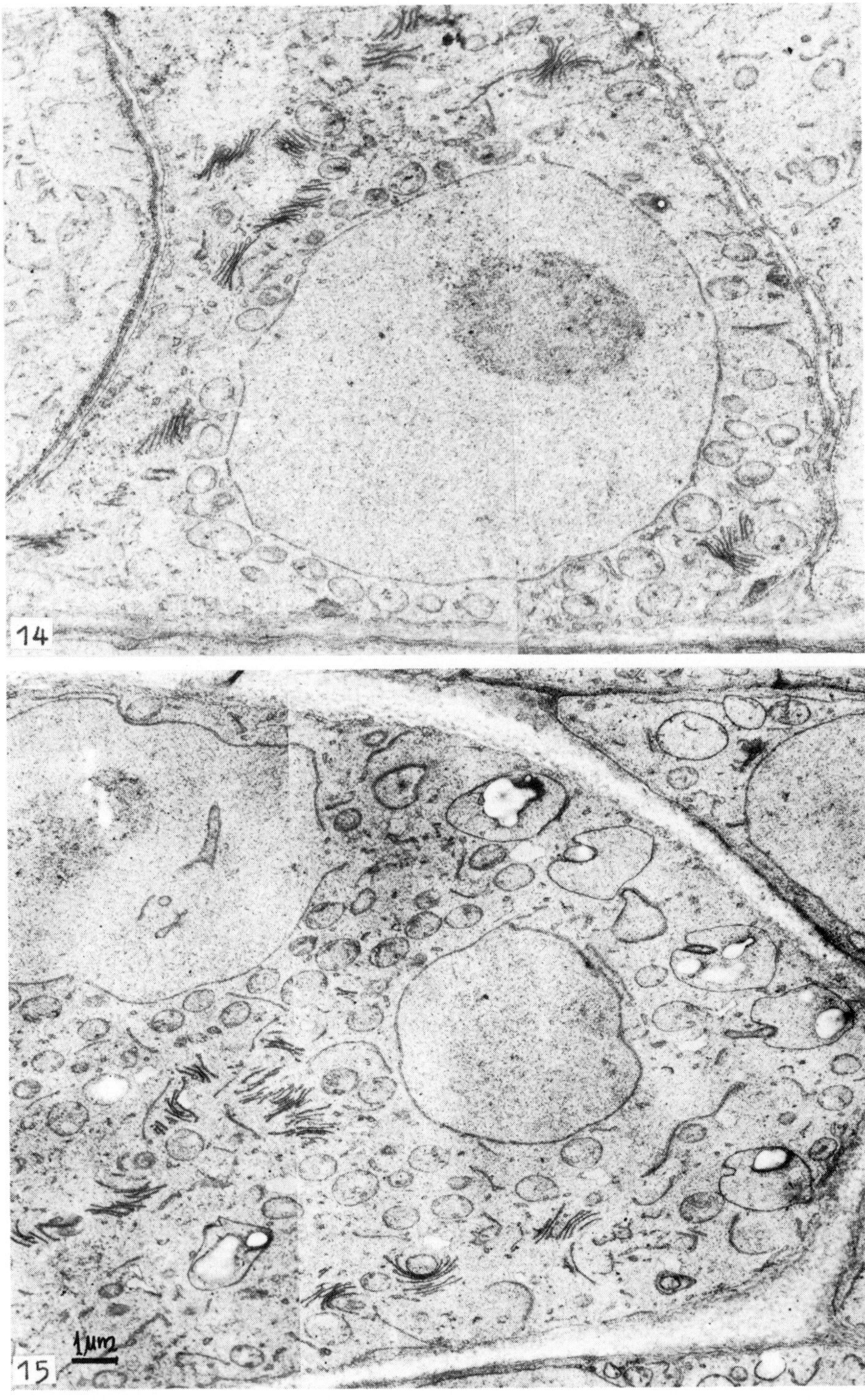
14
1µm
15

In the active megaspore, plastids are concentrated in the space between the nucleus and micropylar apex, similarly they are only present in the chalazal part of the two-nucleated cell. Plastids are conspicuously lacking in the middle megaspore /fig. 14/. Dictyosomes are well developed with cisterns bordered by vesicles. It seems that the populations of the dictyosomes is denser in the middle megaspore and inside parts of both apical cells. Mitochondria are more or less evenly distributed in the cytoplasm of all tetrad cells /see table 1/.

4. Discussion

Some processes occuring in megasporogenesis in Epilobium palustre may be interpreted as being in direct relation to the differentiation of active megaspore. At the early meiosis, the megasporocyte cell wall is undergoing chemical change and new material i.e. callose is laid down in the wall. The distribution of callose is uneven. The micropylar apex of meiotic megasporocyte is free of callose and this region persists during the whole megasporogenesis; consequently in a megasporocyte and in active megaspore there is the region of better permeability than that of the remaining cell wall.

During development, plastids are grouped exclusively at both poles of megasporocyte, already enclosed in the wall with callose. These plastids are synthetizing starch grains, which appear to be more numerous at the micropylar apex. Plastids are not dislocated when the megasporocyte divides into four megaspores, and the two middle megaspores are without plastids. These two megaspores must be excluded as potential embryo sac mother cells. Both polar megaspores, however, contain plastids and seem to be fully equipped for further development, in fact in some Onagraceae each one could play an active role. But it may be assumed that the distribution of plastids and dictyosomes which seems to be unequal, and the insulation of the chalazal megaspore by the cell wall with callose handicap chalazal megaspore in its development into an embryo sac.

Megaspore tetrad appears to function as a physiological unit. Three inactive megaspores are equipped with a denser population of dictyosomes than the micropylar megaspore. Starch grains localized in the chalazal megaspore disappear while in the micropylar megaspore existing starch grains grow and new ones are formed.

Intensive metabolism of three inactive megaspores is denoted by abundance of functioning dictyosomes. Increase in dictyosome number comes about in the late I meiotic prophase and possibly then and in diad stage they are mainly localized in the central and chalazal parts of cell.

Megaspores are separated by thick cross walls consisting of callose and a large amount of PAS-positive material, but as has been shown in older tetrads of Epilobium palustre /8/, callose partially disappears from the cross walls which then have large patches without callose. Such cross walls are somewhat similar to the sieve plates and may be easily transgressed by solutes coming from three inactive megaspores into the active one.

Acknowledgements. The authors wish to thank Miss Emilia Paleń and Prof. Franciszek Kadej for their assistance in electron microscopic work.

References

1. Rodkiewicz, B., 1970, Planta /Berl./ 93, 39.
2. Kuran, H., 1972, Acta Soc. Bot. Polon. 41, 519.
3. Stewart, K.D. and Gifford, Jr., E.M., 1967, Amer. J. Bot. 54, 375.
4. Corti, E.F. and Cecchi, A.E., 1970, Caryologia 23, 715.
5. Jalouzot, M.F., 1971, Ann. Univ. ARERS /Reims/ 9, 36.
6. Jensen, W.A., 1962, Botanical Histochemistry /Freeman, San Francisco/.
7. Reynolds, E.S., 1963, J. Cell Biol. 17, 208.
8. Rodkiewicz, B., 1973, Caryologia 25 /Suppl./, 59.

Fertilization in Higher Plants, ed. H.F. Linskens.

MEGAGAMETOGENESIS AND FORMATION OF NEOCYTOPLASM IN PINUS SYLVESTRIS L.

M. T. M. Willemse

Department of Botany
Agricultural University, Wageningen
The Netherlands

1. Introduction

From morphological studies of megagametogenesis, fecondation, formation of the neocytoplasm and proembryogenesis in species of *Pinus*, *Larix*, *Cryptomeria*, (Camefort[1-2-3]), *Biota*, *Juniperus*, *Pseudotsuga*, *Chamaecyparis* (Chesnoy[4-5-6-7]) and *Sciadophyta* (Gianordoli[8]), it appears that there are similarities and variations. Referring to these descriptions, in this study mainly some special characteristics during megagametogenesis and formation of the neocytoplasm in *Pinus sylvestris* are presented.

2. Materials and Methods

During May and June megasporangia of *Pinus sylvestris*, originating from one tree, were collected. Prothallia in different stages of development were fixed for 1 hour in 1% OsO_4 at 0° C in phosphate buffer pH 7,2 or 1 hour in 1% $KMnO_4$ at 0° C in veronal buffer pH 7,2. The specimens were embedded in Epon 812 and examined with the Philips EM 300 electron microscope at 60 KV.

3. Results

3.1 The follicle cell

The young follicle cell has many vacuoles and contains, mainly around a large nucleus, a small number of plastids and some mitochondria without cristae. The outer nuclear membrane of the follicle cells and of the other prothallial cells shows some blebs (fig. 1, 2). In the cytoplasm of the follicle cell around the central cell vacuoles are absent. It contains now a great number of vesicles, some strands of rough endoplasmic reticulum (RER), dictyosomes and ribosomes. A small number of mitochondria are present. Plastids dividing simultaneously lie close to each other in the shape of bowed bar-bells (fig. 3). The follicle cell of the mature egg cell has a large nucleus without a blebbing outer membrane and contains some nucleoli. At this stage many plastids and small mitochondria with short cristae are present, and also dictyosomes, small vesicles, RER and ribosomes (fig. 4).

Cell wall formation around the central cell starts near the neck cells and is produced mainly by the central- and egg cell and only for a small part from the follicle cell. In the wall there are plasmodesmata, but also large pores through which elements of the cytoplasm of the follicle cell may pass into the developing egg cell (fig. 5, 6).

3.2 The central cell

In the young central cell the nucleus with some nucleoli shows also blebs of its outer membrane. The cytoplasm around the nucleus has whimsical-shaped plastids, some with a starch granule. The plastids start to enlarge and will become the "large inclusions". Mitochondria are very difficult to observe. Small vesicles fuse to form the membrane of the vacuoles. Between these growing vacuoles some dictyosomes and ribosomes are observed.

Before division, the blebs in the outer nuclear membrane have disappeared; many great vacuoles are formed and all the plastids are expanding.

3.3 The egg cell and the neocytoplasm

The young egg cell has a lobed nucleus containing strands of fibrillar structures. The vacuoles disappear, plastids still enlarge and the mitochondria remain difficult to recognize. The formation of the "small inclusions" starts (fig. 7).

During maturation, the nucleus is more rounded and the number of nucleoli increases. Around the nucleus a zone of short strands of ER is present and thereupon a zone of the small inclusions mixed with indistinct electron transparent spots (fig. 8). Near the nucleus some of the short strands of ER run parallel and make a bend around very electron transparent spots and enclose them (fig. 9, 10). These spots are also observed in mitochondria of follicle cells and in the mature egg cell (fig. 4, 11). At this stage clusters of mitochondria can be observed near to the nucleus. Later on they are distributed over the whole

---

The line on the figures represent a length of 1 µm. Unless mentioned otherwise $KMnO_4$ fixation is used.

Fig. 1. In vivo isolated prothallial cell nucleus (N) with blebs (arrows); fase contrast protograph.
Fig. 2. Young follicle cell. Nucleus with bleb (arrow). OsO_4 fixation.
Fig. 3. Follicle cell with simultaneous dividing plastids (P) OsO_4 fixation.
Fig. 4. Follicle cell around a mature egg cell. M: mitochondria.
Fig. 5. Cell wall with pores around the mature egg cell; fase contrast photograph.
Fig. 6. Passage of the part of a follicle cell nucleus (N) through the cell wall pore into the mature egg cell.

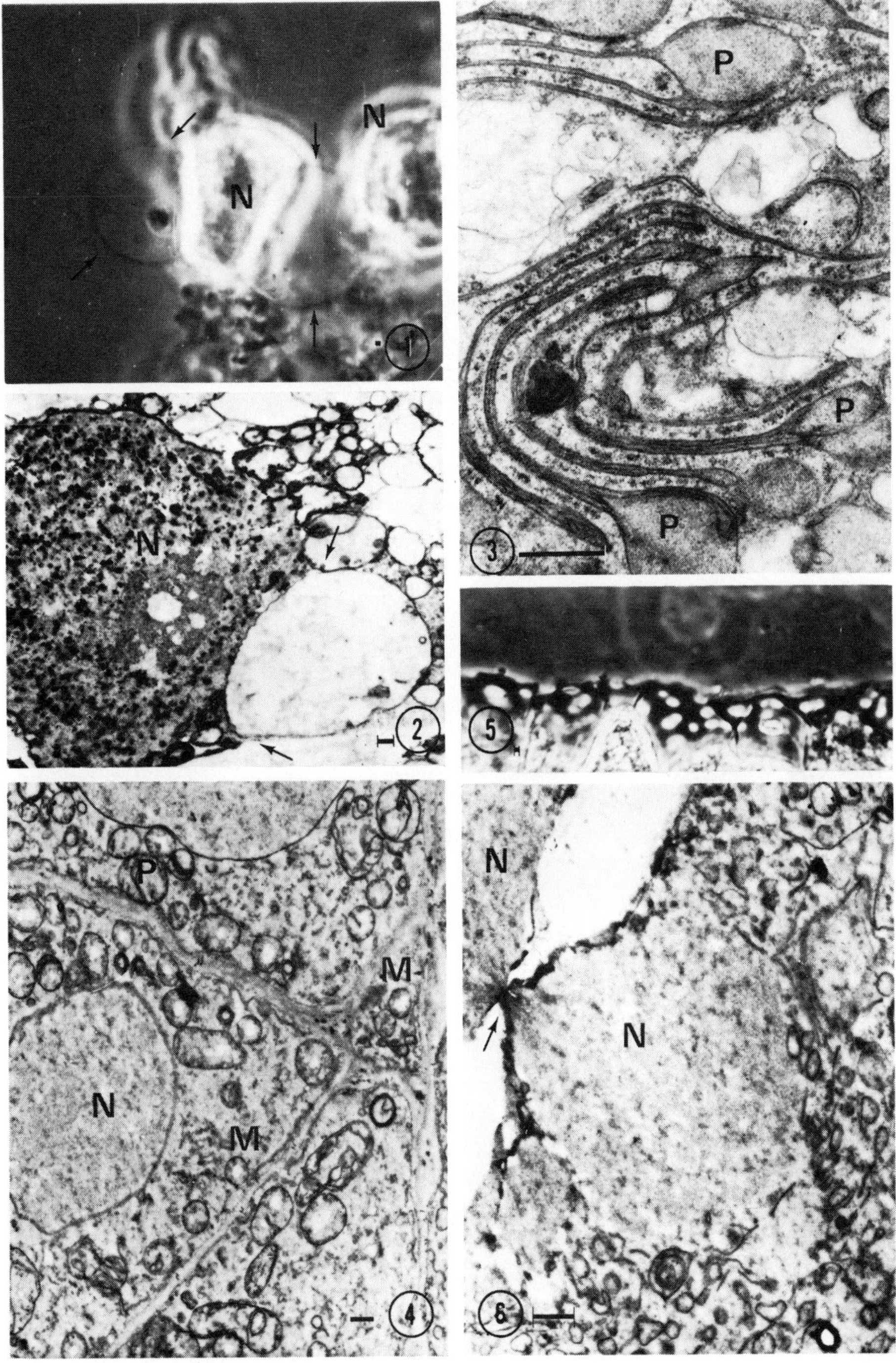
N
N
1
N
P
P
P
3
N
2
5
P
M
N
M
4
N
N
6

cytoplasm of the egg cell. Just before fecondation the number of nucleoli is diminished. Around the nucleus long strands of ER, small mitochondria and small inclusions are present, while some lipid droplets appear (fig. 11). Sometimes long rolled strands of ER are situated on the margin of the egg cell; dictyosomes are very rare.

After fecondation,the male plastids, in the beginning,situated around the male nucleus, are dispersed in the cytoplasm. During the formation of the neocytoplasm, mitochondria of the sperm cells are not observed.

After the first mitosis the cytoplasm around the nuclei gets more organelles. A narrow zone with strands of ER and some small mitochondria appears. This zone enlarges and lipid droplets and plastids are included (fig. 12).

4. Discussion and conclusion

In general few differences in megagametogenesis and formation of the neocytoplasm of *Pinus sylvestris* can be noted when compared with the studies of other Gymnosperms. Some observations in *Pinus sylvestris* are in agreement with the descriptions for *Pinus nigra* (Camefort[1-8-9-10-11]): the formation of the great inclusions originating from the plastids; the formation of the vacuolar membrane by fusion of vesicles; the formation of the small inclusions and the simultaneous division of plastids in the follicle cells. The bleb formation of the outer nuclear membrane is also reported in *Ginkgo* (Dexheimer[12]).

The plastids in the neocytoplasm originate probably from the male cytoplasm. All female plastids enlarge and form large inclusions. The plastids in the sperm cells, around the sperm nucleus in the female cytoplasm and in the neocytoplasm have the same structure. In $KMnO_4$-fixation the plastid membrane is very electron dense (see fig. 12).

The appearance of lipid droplets just before fecondation and the augmentation in the neocytoplasm is in accordance with observations in *Pseudotsuga*[13].

The presence of mitochondria in the early stages of development of the central cell is indistinct. Only during the maturation of the egg cell small

---

Fig. 7. Young egg cell with lobed nucleus containing fibrillar structures (arrows) and a small inclusion (I).

Fig. 8. Maturing egg cell with around the nucleus ER and an indistinct electron transparent dot (arrow).

Fig. 9. Maturing egg cell, around the nucleus (N) mitochondria (M) are formed.

Fig. 10. Detail possible formation of mitochondria, note the very electron transparent spots (arrows).

Fig. 11. Mature egg cell before fecondation, around the nucleus (N) mitochondria (M), ER, small inclusions (I) and lipid droplets (L).

Fig. 12. Neocytoplasm after the first mitosis around the nucleus (N) plastids (P), ER, mitochondria (M) and lipid droplets (L).

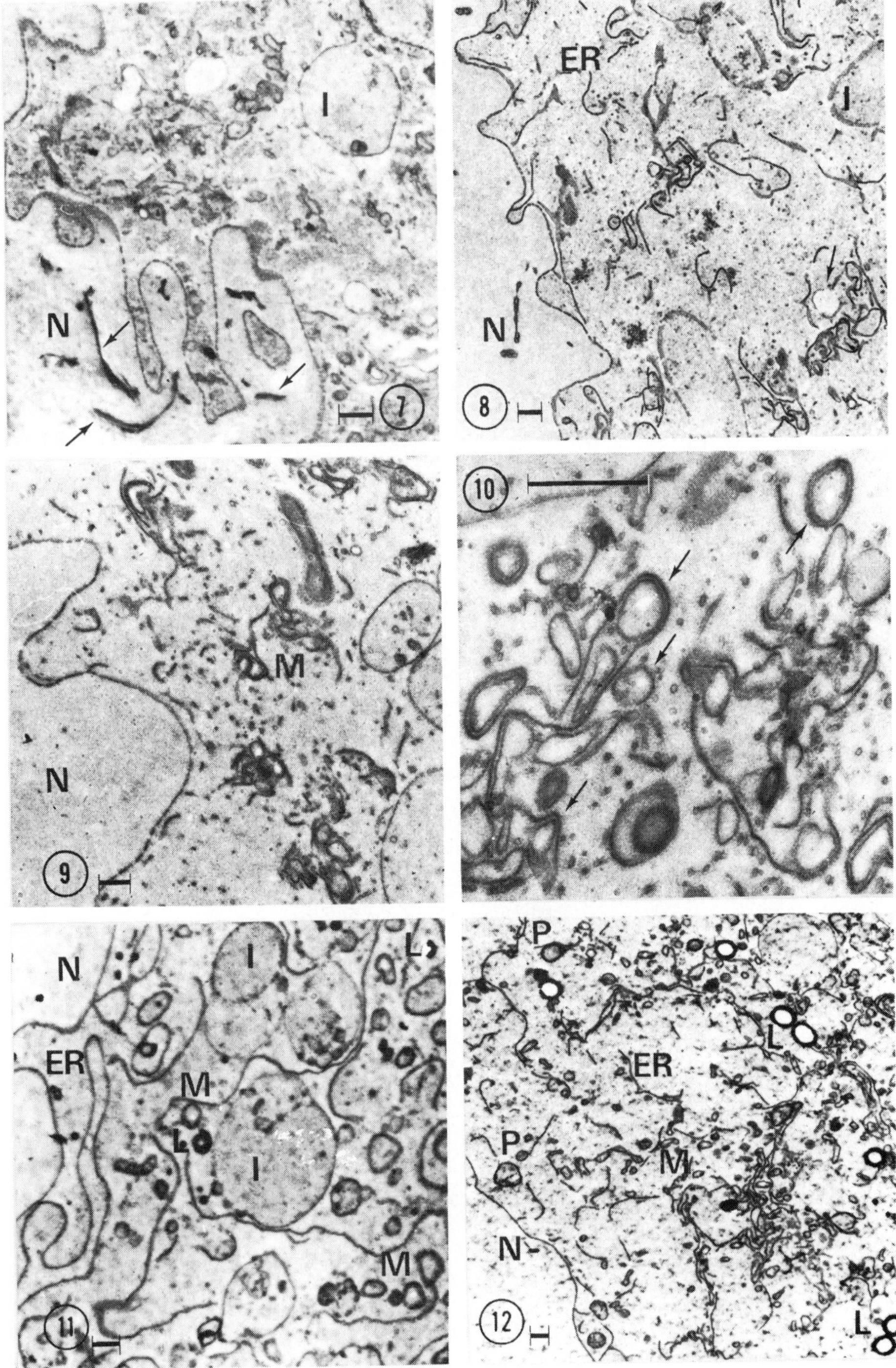
I
N
7
ER
I
N
8
M
N
9
10
N
I
L
ER
M
L
I
M
11
P
L
ER
P
M
N
12
L

mitochondria become visible in clusters around the nucleus and later throughout the whole cytoplasm. The mitochondria fixed in $KMnO_4$ are marked by an electron transparent spot, probably a reaction of nucleic acids. By these feature the small mitochondria are easy to recognize in the egg cell, neocytoplasm and follicle cell. Because of their quick appearance and great number it may be suggested, that as in *Pseudotsuga*[13] a quick division or migration to the nucleus of female mitochondria occurs. But because of their indistinct presence in early stages and the presence of mitochondria-like structures around the nucleus (fig. 10, 9) it may be possible that in relation to the ER, formation of mitochondria takes place. During this stage the egg cell of *Pseudotsuga*[6, 13] and *Larix*[2, 14] shows a zone with many mitochondria, microtubules and D.N.A. around the nucleus. In *Pinus sylvestris* probably for a short duration formation of mitochondria takes place by folding and fusion of strands of ER which seem to include cytoplasmatic elements and nucleic acids. Another possibility that cell organelles may migrate from the follicle cell to the egg cell, can not be excluded. The dimension of the mitochondria in the neocytoplasm give an indication that they mainly originate from the egg cell, the mitochondria of the intact sperm cell are larger and are not observed in the egg cell. Further study will explain the origin of mitochondria in the egg cell and the neocytoplasm in *Pinus sylvestris*.

Acknowledgements: the author is much indepted to Mr. J. S. de Block for the correction and to Miss T. Kuijt, Mr. W. Scheepmaker and T. Zaal for their assistance.

References

1. Camefort, H., 1967, Ann. Univ. A.R.E.R.S. 5, 75.
2. Camefort, H., 1969, Rev. Cytol. et Biol. vég. 32, 253.
3. Camefort, H., 1970, Ann. Univ. A.R.E.R.S. 9, 16.
4. Chesnoy, L., 1967, C. R. Acad. Sci. Paris, 264, 1016.
5. Chesnoy, L., 1969, Rev. Cytol. et Biol. vég. 32, 273.
6. Chesnoy, L. et Thomas, M. J., 1969, C. R. Acad. Sci. Paris, 268, 55.
7. Chesnoy, L., 1973, Caryologia 25, suppl. 223.
8. Giranordoli, M., 1969, Rev. Cytol. et Biol. vég., 32, 183.
9. Camefort, H., 1962, Ann. Sci. Nat. Bot. 12e serie, 265.
10. Camefort, H., 1965. Traveaux dediés à Lucien Plantefol, 407. Masson & Cie, Paris.
11. Camefort, H., 1966, C. R. Acad. Sci. Paris, 263, 959.
12. Dexheimer, J., 1973, C. R. Acad. Sci. Paris, 276, 2789.
13. Thomas, M. J. et Chesnoy, L., 1969, Rev. Cytol. et Biol. vég. 32, 165.
14. Camefort, H., 1967, C. R. Acad. Sci. Paris, 265, 1293.

THE PROGAMIC PHASE

Fertilization in Higher Plants, ed. H.F. Linskens.

THE HISTOLOGY AND PHYSIOLOGY OF POLLEN GERMINATION AND POLLEN TUBE GROWTH ON THE STIGMA AND IN THE STYLE

Indra K. Vasil*
Department of Botany, University of Florida,
Gainesville, Fla. U.S.A.

1. INTRODUCTION

The rapidly increasing world population, coupled with declining food reserves, will inevitably bring man face to face with widespread hunger and death, with catastrophic social, economic an political repercussions. Most countries are now making serious attempts to check the rate of population growth. In addition, biologists are attempting to use revolutionary new techniques, like somatic hybridization[1,2], genetic transformations[3,4,5], etc., to produce new and improved varieties of plants. However, conventional methods of plant hybridization are still the principal means for the genetic improvement of plant species used by man. In order to facilitate inter-specific and inter-generic hybridization, it is essential to understand the control of pollen germination and pollen tube growth in vivo, so that such knowledge can then be applied to solving the complex problems of incompatibility, and other barriers to hybridization. During recent years much new information about the structure and physiology of the stigma and the style, and their relationship to the germination of pollen grains and the growth o' pollen tubes in vivo, has become available. Important aspects of such work are reviewed in the following pages.

2. THE STIGMA

Stigmas have been classified into two principal types based on the presence or absence of stigmatic exudate at the time of pollination. WET STIGMAS, like those of _Aegle marmelos_, _Nicandra physaloides_[6], and _Petunia hybrida_[7] are covered by a sticky secretion at the time of pollination. DRY STIGMAS, as in cotton[8], do not produce any secretory exudate[9].

---

* This review was prepared while the author was the recipient of a Faculty Development Award (Sabbatical) of the University of Florida. During this period he was also supported by a Climat Laboratory Senior Research Fellowship, at the Plant Physiology Division, Department of Scientific and Industrial Research, Palmerston North, New Zealand.

The wet stigma of Petunia shows several randomly distributed 2-celled papillae on its surface[7]. In a developing stigma, the epidermis is covered by a continuous, thin cuticle, and the sub-epidermal cells are densely cytoplasmic without any intercellular spaces. In a mature stigma, the cells of the sub-epidermal zone elongate to form a secretory zone with large schizogenous cavities filled with a lipoidal secretion. This secretory zone is delimited from the basal part of the stigma by a storage zone which comprises 1-3 layers of small, compact, parenchymatous cells. The cells of the stigma contain numerous amyloplasts and a large population of lipid globules. The latter gradually coalesce and migrate to the peripheral part of the cytoplasm, and eventually find their way out of the cell. In the epidermal cells and the papillae, the lipoidal exudate accumulates between the cell wall and the cuticle. In the secretory zone, the exudate fills the large, inter-cellular schizogenous cavities. At the time of anthesis, the epidermis becomes disorganized, the cuticle is discarded in the form of small flakes, and the accumulated exudate escapes and spreads over the entire surface of the stigma. A very thin layer of water is trapped below the unevenly spread oily layer on the stigma, and plays an important role in the germination of pollen.

The dry stigma of cotton (Gossypium hirsutum) are covered with long, unicellular hairs[8]. At the time of pollination, the stigmatic hairs show a distinct and continuous cuticle which is closely appressed to the thin wall. Immediately below the stigmatic hairs are several layers of a thin-walled parenchymatous tissue with large inter-cellular spaces. Farther in, the size of the inter-cellular spaces gradually decreases until no such spaces are present, and the cell walls thicken with a heavy pectic content. A clear transition is thus seen from a thin-walled tissue filled with large air spaces to a closely packed tissue with thick, amorphous cell walls. This latter tissue provides a connecting link from the stigma to the transmitting tissue.

3. THE STIGMATIC EXUDATE

The exudate appearing on the wet stigmas is a highly viscous, refractive and adhesive substance. It is ideally suited for its role in trapping pollen grains, and generally appears in the form of tiny droplets due to its high surface tension. Traditionally, the stigmatic exudate has been considered to be a sugary solution. The stigma has thus been compared to the floral or extra-floral nectaries[9]. However, recent histochemical and chemical analyses in a variety of genera and species show that free sugars are at best only minor constituents of the stigmatic exudate, which consists of a complex mixture of lipids and phenolic compounds[6,10-13].

The lipid compounds of the stigmatic exudate protect the stigma from desiccation as well as wetting, prevent the pollen grains from getting washed off the stigma, and regulate the availability of water to the pollen grains. In Petunia the stigmatic exudate has no nutritive role and hence is not suitable for the germination of pollen[10].

The phenolic compounds found in the stigmatic exudate occur as esters or glycosides and probably serve as sources of nutrition for the pollen, and may selectively stimulate or inhibit pollen germination[12]. Phenolic also conserve the sugars of the stigma by protecting the stigma from insects and other pests. Enzymes diffusing out of the pollen grains on to the stigma[14,15] probably release free sugars from the phenolic glycosides which then provide proper osmotic conditions for the germination of pollen and initial nutrition for the growth of the pollen tubes.

Reducing sugars are known to be present in the stigmatic exudate of *Aegle marmelos*[6]. Glucose, fructose, and sucrose have been identified in the pollination drop of *Pinus*[16], *Taxus*[17], and the stigmatic exudate of *Antirrhinum*, *Cammelia*, *Gladiolus*, *Hibiscus*, *Lilium*[18], and *Petunia*[10]. In *Ephedra* only sucrose was detected[17]. Xylose and other similar substances appear in the stigmatic extracts a day or two after pollination, probably as a result of the degradation of cell wall materials. The pollination drop of gymnosperms and the stigmatic exudate of angiosperms do have some common functions, but they are very unlike each other in methods of production and chemical composition.

Pistils of *Lilium longiflorum* secrete large quantities of an exudate which accumulates on the surface of the stigma in the form of droplets[19,20]. The stylar canal is also filled with this secretion which is an aqueous solution (99 per cent water) with about 95 per cent of the solutes in the form of a high molecular, protein-containing polysaccharide composed of galactose, arabinose, rhamnose, glucuronic acid, and galacturonic acid, and a monosaccharide composition similar to plant gum exudates[21,22]. The high water and polysaccharide content of the exudate present on the stigma and in the stylar canal of *Lilium* is in sharp contrast to the largely non-aqueous and lipoidal stigmatic exudate found in most other plants. It is not surprising, therefore, that the stigmatic exudate of *Lilium* has been found to be a good medium for the germination of *Lilium* pollen[23]. Polysaccharidic gum exudates play an important role in the sealing of wounds[24], and the large amount of acidic polysaccharides found in the exudate of *Lilium* may be involved in protecting the fragile pollen tubes during their growth, in addition to providing a source of carbohydrate residues for pollen tube wall biosynthesis[22].

The stigmatic papillae of *Lilium* lack the characteristic secretory zone seen in canal cells[25], and the stigmatic exudate is known to appear before pollination and before the release of the secretion product from the canal cells into the stylar canal. The "stigmatic exudate" of *Lilium*, therefore, may actually be a secretion product of the canal cells which is transported to the stigmatic surface through the inter-cellular spaces of the stylar tissue rather than through the stylar canal[26]. This explains the marked difference in the function, the chemical composition and the nutritive role of the stigmatic exudate of Lilium as compared to the exudate of other plants described earlier.

4. THE STYLE

Hanf[27] described two principal types of styles. In the OPEN STYLES a stylar canal is present which is lined with a well-developed glandular epidermis, the latter functioning as the transmitting tissue. Open styles are characteristic of monocotyledons. The SOLID or CLOSED STYLES have a compact core of transmitting tissue, and are common in dicotyledons, especially the Gamopetalae.

During their passage through the style, pollen tubes are restricted to a specilized tissue which serves to connect the stigma to the interior of the ovary. Esau[9] and Konar and Linskens[7] have termed it the stigmatoid tissue due to the apparent cytological and physiological similarity of this tissue with the cells of the stigma, and because of its "continuity" with the stigmatic tissue. The term transmitting tissue has been used by many other authors[6,27-31]. The structure as well as the function of the cells comprising the transmitting tissue in closed styles is quite different from the stigmatic cells[8]. Even in open styles the glandular cells lining the stylar canal have a much more elaborate structure and function as compared to the cells of the stigmatic surfaces[25]. I, therefore, favor the use of the term transmitting tissue.

A cross section of the closed style of cotton shows an epidermis with stomata, a cortex of thin-walled parenchyma cells with several vascular bundles, and strands of transmitting tissue[8]. The cells of the transmitting tissue have thin transverse walls but their lateral walls are 7-10 µm thick and consist of several distinct and concentric layers. The innermost part of the wall, wall layer 1, is composed of pectic substances and hemicellulose, and is about 2 µm thick. Surrounding this is the 0.5 µm thick wall layer 2, which is darker, thinner, and similar in composition to wall layer 1 but with a large hemicellulose content. Wall layer 3 is loosely textured, 4-6 µm thick, and shows concentric rings of a fibrous material. This layer is poor in hemicellulose, but is rich in pectic substances and also contains small amounts of non-cellulosic polysaccharides and cellulose. Wall layer 4 is represented by the middle lamella region, which is distinctive in appearance, 0.5-1 µm thick, and is primarily pectic in nature. Small amounts of protein are also present in wall layers 3 and 4, while wall layer 3 contains masses of small vesicles, similar to those seen in the wall of the stigmatic cells of cotton. The cells of the transmitting tissue contain many mitochondria and active, vesicle-forming dictyosomes. The plastids are large with numerous amyloplasts. Polysomes and abundant rough ER are seen, along with 1 or 2 lipid bodies which may be several microns in diameter. Transmitting tissue cells have a spherical or slightly ellipsoidal vacuole which is 7-9 µm in diameter; frequently these may also contain a much larger, 20-40 µm in diameter, vacuole which contains a druse presumably composed of calcium salts. Nuclei of the transmitting cells are large and frequently lobed indicating their highly active metabolic state.

Open styles of *Aegle marmelos*, *Fritillaria roylei*, *Lilium tigrinum*[6] and *L. longiflorum*[25,26] have variable numbers of stylar canals, depending on the number of carpels. The epidermal cells of the stylar canals divide actively and become papillate in acropetal succession, and in *L. tigrinum* contain 1-5 nuclei which often fuse to form large polyploid masses[6]. The stylar canals thus become lined by highly glandular and secretory cells which show a characteristically domed and thick outer tangential wall facing the stylar cavity. These cells are better described as the canal cells[25] rather than as stigmatoid cells. The thickened outer tangential wall of the canal cells of *L. longiflorum* is smooth on the outside but is highly convoluted towards the interior of the cell. This domed region is presumably the secretion zone, and its 8-14 µm thick wall shows three regions. An outer, 1 µm thick, fibrillar layer corresponding to the true cell wall (layer 1); an inner, 7-13 µm thick, granular-fibrillar layer with irregular projections into the cytoplasm and many osmiophilic islands which may be continuations of the cytoplasm in the secretion zone and are reminiscent of similar continuities of the pollen cytoplasm into the intine (layer 2); and an irregular interface between layer 2 and the cytoplasm containing aggregates of tubules and vesicles recognized as paramural bodies[26,32]. Layer 1 contains protein, pectin and cellulose. The outer part of layer 2 is primarily fibrillar in nature with sparse granular contents and contains pectin which is probably complexed with protein. The inner part of layer 2 consists of randomly dispersed microfibrils, which may be cellulosic in nature, with a high concentration of granular components.

The canal cells have a large nucleus (25-30 µm), and often become multinucleate. The cytoplasm of canal cells is rich in mitochondria, dictyosomes, free ribosomes or polysomes, smooth and rough ER, and occasional amyloplasts. Very often the mitochondria and the dictyosomes are localized between the nucleus and the secretion zone in the wall, while there is a large vacuole between the nucleus and the basal part of the cell. Conspicuous dictyosome activity, characteristic of secretory cells in general, is lacking in the canal cells of *Lilium*. The secretion product - or its precursor material or the organelle from which it is released - can not be identified in the canal cells until it is excreted through the secretion zone in the wall and is contained by a layer of cuticle covering the domed region until anthesis. It is possible that a major portion of the secretion product is transported to the canal cells from the neighboring parenchyma cells through the numerous plasmodesmatal connections, and then it is further elaborated in, and passes through, the highly developed wall area in the secretion zone of the canal cells. It is also likely that at least a part of the secretion product is elaborated within the canal cell. The structure of the thickened portion of the canal cell wall is quite like that of the transfer cells[33], which provide a greatly increased surface area for the transfer of material between neighboring cells.

According to Vasil'ev[34], the Golgi apparatus of the canal cells of *Lilium regale* and *L. davidii* secretes a non-cellulosic and amorphous, polysaccharide-containing mucilage during the bud stage. This secretion is easily transported to the stylar canal because of the absence of a cuticle on the outer walls of the canal cells; in *L. longiflorum* the secretion products of the canal cells are retained with the help of a thin and continuous layer of cuticle until after pollination[26]. Vasil'ev[34] also compared the canal cells of *Lilium* with sex hormone-producing cells of animals and the glandular cells of terpenoid-secreting plants, and suggested that the canals cells secrete terpenoids and isoprenoids which may serve as sexual attractants (as chemotropic factors) and as sex hormones.

5. POLLEN TUBE GROWTH IN VIVO

The stigma provides appropriate conditions for the retention and germination of pollen grains. Receptivity of the stigma is generally limited to a short period before and after anthesis. A rapid increase in the permeability of the stigmatic papillae of grasses takes place immediately after the pollen attaches to the papilla and germination takes place.

It has been shown recently that extra-cellular enzymic proteins localized in the pollen grain wall are related to the germination of pollen grains on the stigma, penetration of the stigma by the pollen tube, and the early growth of the pollen tube[30,35]. Other fractions are involved in recognition responses which control inter- and intra-specific incompatibility[36,37]. The proteins are of sporophytic or ganetophytic origin, and are present at different sites in the pollen grain wall. Sporophytic proteins, which probably serve as recognition substances for pollen germination on the stigma, originate in the tapetum and are stored in the cavities of the exine. Gametophytic proteins are injected into the intine from the microspore cytoplasm during the growth of the cell wall, and are probably involved in the germination and early nutrition of the pollen grain, and in gametophytically controlled incompatibility systems. Sporophytic proteins leach out from the cavities of the exine within seconds after pollen lands on the stigma or is placed in an appropriate medium. Gametophytic proteins held in the intine are slower to move out and are detected after several minutes. It has thus become possible to facilitate the germination of incompatible pollen by extracting pollen wall proteins from compatible pollen and supplying these during interspecific crosses. Mattsson et al.[38] have recently described the presence of an external protein coating, the pellicle, which lies over the cutinised wall of the stigmatic papillae. The pellicle appears to be functionally important in the capture and hydration of pollen grains, and may also be the site of the recognition reactions involved in incompatibility responses.

In the Cruciferae, the stigmatic papillae are completely covered by a cuticular layer and no exudate is produced. Pollen grains break down the cuticle of the stigma enzymatically and come in direct contact with the stigmatic papillae[39,40]. Pollen grains are then able to absorb water from the turgid cells of the stigmatic surface and germinate readily. The walls of the stigmatic papillae of *Brassica nigra* consist of an outer layer of cuticle, a thin intermediate pectic layer, and an inner layer of pectin and cellulose. After cross-pollination the pollen tubes penetrate the cuticle and the intermediate pectic layer and actually grow in between the cellulose lamellae of the innermost pectin-cellulose layer by dissolving only the pectic constituents of the wall[41]. In *B. oleracea* the stigmatic papillae have been shown by scanning electron microscopy to be covered by an additional waxy layer, and it is only after piercing the waxy layer that the pollen grains come in contact with the cuticle[42]. In *Diplotaxis tenuifolia* also, another member of the Cruciferae, the pollen tubes enter the stigmatic papillae by dissolving the cuticle and grow inside the pectic-cellulose layer of the wall[43]. Further growth of pollen tubes takes place in the middle lamellae of the stigmatic tissue and in the intercellular spaces of the transmitting tissue, both of which are pectic in nature. In *Pinus silvestris* the growth of the pollen tube in the nucellus brings about the degeneration of adoining nucellar cells, principally by affecting the pectin and hemicellulose content of the cell walls[44,45]. Enzymes for the breakdown of cutin and pectin have been demonstrated in pollen grains[46,47].

In cotton the pollen grains land on the surface of stigmatic hairs, and produce a pollen tube within an hour which grows down the surface of the hair and then between the cells of the stigma at the bases of the hairs and beyond[8,48]. The cytoplasm of the stigmatic hair degenerates, no exudate is secreted, and the cuticle remains unbroken and closely appressed to the cell wall. The pollen tube never penetrates the cuticle or enters the cells of the stigma, but continues its further growth through the intercellular spaces of the thin-walled cells of the transmitting tissue. After reaching the thick-walled cells of the main strands of transmitting tissue, it actually grows through wall layer 3 and not through the middle lamella as reported for solid styles in much of the literature. (Pollen tubes of *Petunia* grow within the compac matrix of the middle lamellae of the transmitting tissue by enzymatically creating a pipe-like path in front[49]). No depletion of starch or lipids takes place in the cells of the transmitting tissue in relation to pollen tube growth, and there is no change in the ER, and in ribosome population of aggregation. There is increased dictyosome activity and the cell become thicker. Callose is deposited in the pit fields on the transmitting tissue cells after the passage of the pollen tubes. The passage of the pollen tube probably changes the permeability of the cells and callose is formed as a wound response and as a reaction against cell leakage. Once the pollen germinates and the pollen tube has penetrated the stigmatic tissue, the path of the pollen tube through the rest of the stigma and the style appears to be determined by the nature and structure of the cell walls, and the morphology and distribution of the transmitting tissue in the stigma and the style[8].

The pollen tube in the stigma is filled with cytoplasm containing numerous mitochondria and dictyosomes. The number of dictyosomes cisternae is reduced from 5-7 in the pollen grain to 3-4 in the tube. Large vesicles associated with the dictyosomes seem to be incorporated in the pollen tube wall. There is abundant ER, and polysomes are present in free form or attached to the ER. Pockets of tubular elements and small vesicles are found adjacent to the pollen tube wall. The wall of the pollen tube in the stigma and style has a complex structure showing two distinct regions: the outer part of the wall is strongly PAS positive in nature, while the inner portion is thicker, more homogeneous, much less reactive in the PAS test, and is rich in callose[48]. The dense cytoplasm of the pollen tube in the style contains vesicles of various sizes, ER, ribosomes (these might be derived from ribosomes previously attached to the ER as no new ribosomes are formed during the growth of the pollen tube), and a few poorly developed plastids with swollen outer membranes. The outer membrane of the short, and often rod-like mitochondria is dark with a dense matrix. Dictyosomes are quite numerous, with 4-5 cisternae, and produce vesicles up to 0.5 µm in diameter containing a diffuse filamentous material. The vesicles appear to fuse with the plasma membrane of the pollen tube and their contents from the inner part of the tube wall. A very large population of small, spherical vesicles, 0.15-0.17 µm in diameter, is scattered throughout the pollen tube cytoplasm.

The ER in the pollen grains and during early growth of the pollen tube has extended cisternae, and apperently serves as a storage site for proteins[8,48]. As the pollen tube grows down the style, the ER shows the more common variety of narrow cisternae, indicating that the protein present in the ER is gradually being utilized during pollen tube growth. The ultrastructure of the distal region of the pollen tube and the wide variety of cell organelles found in it, are indicative of active carbohydrate and protein metabolism which are necessary to sustain the rapid growth (2 mm/hr in cotton) of the pollen tube. The part of the pollen tube immediately behind the distal tip region shows less dense cytoplasm and more dispersed organelles. Occasionally the ER is greatly expanded to form localized sacs which are 5-10 µm long, and can be easily seen with the light microscope. The sacs stain densely with aniline blue black indicating proteinaceous contents. The more mature parts of the pollen tube contain only a thin layer of cytoplasm closely appressed to the wall, and large vacuole which occupy the rest of the space. Plugs of wall material, mostly callose, serve to separate the older parts of the pollen tube from the growing distal region. The plugs originate as rings on the inside of the wall and grow like the closing of an iris diaphragm.

Structural changes are known to take place in the transmitting tissue of solid styles during and after the growth of pollen tubes through it. However, no detectable fine structural differences are seen between canal cells of open styles from pollinated or unpollinated pistils of Lilium longiflorum[26]. The pollen tubes growing through the stylar canal are entwined to each other and form a thick thread-like structure. Such a mass of pollen tubes grown in close proximity to, or on the surface of, canal cells through an exudate which fills the stylar canal. The exudate is not released into the canal until after anthesis and pollination due to the presence of a continuous layer of cuticle which covers the secretion zone to the canal cells. Pollination and germination of pollen causes release of hydrolytic enzymes from pollen grains[14]. Cutinases released from the pollen grains[38,40] could dissolve the cuticle covering the secretion zone of the canal cells and thus cause the release of the exudate into the stylar canal. In Fritillaria the pollen tubes grow ectotropically along the surface of the canal cells which stain darker during the passage of the pollen tubes. The tips of the canal cells facing the stylar canal thicken within two days after pollination and stain negatively for cellulose and lignin[6].

6. NUTRITION OF THE POLLEN TUBE IN VIVO

The surface of the stigma and the stigmatic exudate primarily provide favorable conditions for the germination of the pollen grain, as in Petunia, and are not directly involved in the nutrition of the germinating grains (the stigmatic exudate of Lilium, on the other hand, serves as a favorable medium for pollen germination). This is evident from the earlier discussion of the role and composition of the stigmatic exudate. However, the nutritive role of the transmitting tissue for the growth of the pollen tubes through the style was recognized as early as 1824 by Amici (see Vasil and Johri[6]). Pollen tubes of Lilium and Petunia are said to draw nourishment - sugars and amino acids - from the stylar tissues tissues[19,50-53]. Pollen tubes of Oenothera organensis utilize stylar carbohydrates particularly sugars, during their growth[54]. Growth of pollen tubes through the style causes an increased in-flow of carbohydrates into the pistils, and pollen tubes use sugars from the stylar tissues[55].

In Aegle marmelos cells of the parenchymatous tissue surrounding the stylar canals show an optimal concentration of starch just before pollination[6]. Subsequently, as the starch is digested, the canal cells and the basal portions of the stigmatic papillae show the presence of reducing sugars which also disappear within three days after pollination. Disappearance of storage starch from stylar tissues has also been observed in Fritillaria roylei, Lilium tigrinum, Catasbaea spinosa, Pavonia zeylanica, and Zephyranthes ajax[6].

There are significant differences in the fine structure of the tips of Lilium pollen tubes growing in compatible and incompatible pistils[56-58]. Tubes growing in incompatible pistils have a compartmented cap similar to that seen in vitro; tips of tubes growing in compatible pistils show deep embayments but no compartments. On the basis of such evidence, it has been postulated that compatible tubes undergo a transition from autotrophic nutrition, characterized by the compartmented cap of Golgi-derived vesicles, to heterotrophic nutrition in which the secretion product of the secretory cells of the stylar canal enters the tip of the tube through the deep embayments. Pollen tubes growing in compatible pistils are unable to make this transition and are unable to continue their growth due to the exhaustion of endogenous food reserves.

Metabolic products of myoinositol, a specific precursor of pectic substances in plant cell walls, are utilized in the synthesis of stigmatic and stylar canal exudate, and the cell wall material of canal cells in _Lilium longiflorum_[59]. The pollen tube wall is composed primarily of polysaccharides. Since the pollen grain has only limited food reserves, and a relatively large amount of new pollen wall material is synthesized during growth in vivo, it is reasonable to assume that at least a part of the substrate needed for the synthesis of pollen tube wall materials is derived from the polysaccharides present in the tissue of the pistil. Electron microscopic and other studies indicate that the pectic wall material of the transmitting tissue in solid styles is hydrolysed, and it is assumed that the hydrolysis products are then metabolized by the growing pollen tubes for tube wall formation[41,43,50,53,60]. Actual use of the polysaccharides present in the canal cell walls and the sigmatic and stylar exudate for pollen tube wall biosynthesis has been demonstrated by Kroh et al.[61], and Kroh, Labarca and Loewus[62]. Further, Labarca and Loewus[22] have shown that the polysaccharide component of the stigmatic exudate of _Lilium longiflorum_ is incorporated into the cytoplasm of the growing pollen tubes and later a specific fraction of the incorporated exudate is extensively metabolized before being utilized for pollen tube wall biosynthesis.

7. METABOLISM OF POLLEN TUBES IN VIVO

Pollination and the growth of pollen tubes initiates dvelopment of the female gametophyte of _Gingko biloba_ and ovules of _Pinus radiata_[63,64], stimulates the differentiation of ovules in orchids, prevents abscission of the flower, and begins the growth of the ovary resulting in fruit development. Fertlization is necessary only for seed formation but not for fruit growth. Pollen from unrelated species, nonviable pollen, or even pollen extracts can prevent abscission of the flower and cause swelling of the ovary and formation of near-normal but seedless, parthenocarpio fruits. Pollen grains contain auxin (indoleacetic acid) and gibberellins, the two plant growth substances which are known to be involved in the post-pollination enlargement of the ovary and the development of the fruit[64-68].

The initial and relatively small amounts of indoleacetic acid, or other auxin-like substances, and gibberellins supplied by the germinating pollen to the pistil serve to initiate some minimal growth and metabolic processes, as a result of which enzymes liberate additional amounts of auxin from the tissues of the style and the ovary[63,68-70]. Such a system seems to work at least in the case of Nicotiana tabacum where formation of indoleacetic acid from the tryptophan present in pollinated pistils has been indicated[71-75]. One of the several possible routes for the biosynthesis of indoleacetic acid is by oxidative decarboxylation, or possibly by a Cannizzaro-type reaction, from indolepyruvic acid, which in turn is formed from tryptophan by transamination[68]. The auxin released as a result of pollination initiative growth also in the fertilized ovule, which later produces appreciable amounts of auxin and gibberellins in the endosperm, and auxin and cytokinins in the developing embryo. Thus the initial supply of auxin and gibberellin from germinating pollen not only begins the development of the fruit, but is also responsible for the release and production of additional amounts of plant growth substances in the tissues of the pistil for the development of a normal fruit.

The actual oxygen tension in the stigma and at various levels of the style and ovary can be measured before, during, and after pollen tube growth with the help of a Clark microelectrode[76]. In most of the earlier studies of the metabolism of pollinated and unpollinated pistils the respiration of entire styles and stigmas was measured[52,77-81]. Such experiments included large amounts of vegetative tissues not directly related to pollen tube metabolism, and therefore could not be expected to give an accurate measurement of oxygen tension changes in the tissues supporting pollen tube growth. The use of the microelectrode enables accurate measurement of oxygen tension in the stylar canal in the region of pollen tube growth. In the unpollinated pistils of Hippeastrum hybridum very high oxygen tension exists from the stigma down through most of the style, and an abrupt and sharp drop in oxygen tension is seen in the lower-most 5 mm of the style and in the ovary. During pollen tube growth a marked drop in oxygen tension is seen in the region of the style containing the tips of pollen tubes; this region of low oxygen tension moves down the style progressively with the growth of the pollen tubes. After the passage of the pollen tubes the original high level of oxygen tension is restored, though not completely. It appears that the pollen tubes grows aerobically through the stigmatic and stylar tissues and it is only in the lower-most region of the style and in the ovary, characterized by a very low level of oxygen tension, that the tubes become anaerobic. The growth of the pollen tube from the stigma to the ovules is not bases on an oxygen tension gradient.

No net synthesis of RNA or DNA takes place in the stigma and the stylar after pollination[82]. The slight increase in the amount of DNA (0.2-0.3 µg/style) seen in pollinated styles is roughly the amount of DNA contributed by the pollen grains to the pistil tissues during pollination. An interesting difference in the activity of ribonuclease is seen between open and closed styles with a transmitting tissue is about 20 times more than in open styles. Most of the enzyme activity is localized in the transmitting tissue and is not affected by pollination. The enzyme prevents any net synthesis of RNA and thus helps us to maintain a constant level of RNA in the style during pollen tube growth.

REFERENCES

1. Carlson, P.S., H.H. Smith, and R.D. Dearing, 1972, Proc. Nat. Acad. Sci., U.S.A. 69, 2292.
2. Vasil, V., and I.K. Vasil, 1974, In Vitro 9.
3. Ledoux, L. (ed.), 1971, Informative Molecules in Biological Systems (North-Holland, Amsterdam).
4. Hess, D., 1972, Naturwiss. 59, 348.
5. Doy, C.H., P.M. Gresshoff, and B. Rolfe, 1973, in: The Biochemistry of Gene Expression in Higher Organisms, ed. J.K. Pollak and J. Wilson Lee (D. Reidel Publ. Co., Boston).
6. Vasil, I.K., and M.M. Johri, 1964, Phytomorphology 14, 352.
7. Konar, R.N., and H.F. Linskens, 1966, Planta, Berl. 71, 356.
8. Jensen, W.A., and D.B. Fisher, 1969, Planta, Berl. 84, 97.
9. Esau, K., 1965. Plant Anatomy. 2nd ed. John Wiley, New York.
10. Konar, R.N., and H.F. Linskesns, 1966, Planta, Berl. 71, 372.
11. Martin, F.W., 1969, Amer. J. Bot. 56, 1023.
12. Martin, F.W., 1970, Ann. Bot. 34, 835.
13. Martin F.W., and L. Telek, 1971, Amer. J. Bot. 58, 317.
14. Stanley, R.G., and H.F. Linskens, 1965, Physiol. Plant. 18,47.
15. Mäkinen, Y., and J.L. Brewbaker, 1967, Physiol. Plant. 20, 477.
16. McWilliam, J.R., 1958, Bot. Gaz. 120, 109.
17. Ziegler, H., 1959, Planta, Berl. 52, 587.
18. Iwanami, Y., 1959, J. Yokohama Munic. Unive. 116C, 1.
19. Yamada, Y., 1965, Jap. J. Bot. 19, 69.
20. Labarca, C., and F. Loewus, 1972, Plant Physiol. 50, 7.
21. Aspinall, G.O., 1969, Adv. Carbohyd. Chem. Biochem. 24, 333.
22. Labarca, C., M. Kroh, and F. Loewus, 1970, Plant Physiol. 46, 150.
23. Rosen, W.G., 1961, Amer. J. Bot. 48, 889.
24. Smith, F., and R. Montgomery, 1959, Amer. Chem. Soc. Monograph No. 141 (Reinhold, New York).
25. Rosen, W.G., and H.R. Thomas, 1970, Amer. J. Bot. 57, 1108.

26. Dashek, W.V., H.R. Thomas, and W.G. Rosen, 1971, Amer. J. Bot. 59, 909.

27. Hanf, M., 1935, Beit. bot. Zbl. 54A, 99.

28. Arber, A., 1937, Biol. Rev. Camb. 12, 157.

29. Eames, A.J., 1961, Morphology of the Angiosperms (McGraw-Hill, New York).

30. Vasil, I.K., 1973, Naturwiss. 60, 247.

31. Kapil, R.N., and I.K. Vasil, 1963, in: Recent Advances in the Embryology of Angiosperms, ed. P. Maheshwari (Intern. Soc. Plant Morphol., Delhi).

32. Marchant, R., and A.W. Robards, 1968, Ann. Bot. 32, 457.

33. Pate, J.S., and B.E.S. Gunning, 1972, Rev. Plant Physiol. 23, 1973.

34. Vasil'ev, A.E., 1970, Soviet Plant Physiol. (Fiziologiya Rastenii) 17, 1240.

35. Heslop-Harrison, J., Y. Heslop-Harrison, R.B. Knox, and B. Howlett, 1973, Ann. Bot. 37, 403.

36. Heslop-Harrison, J., R.B. Knox, and Y. Heslop-Harrison, 1974, Theoret. App. Genet. 44, 133.

37. Dickinson, H.G., and D. Lewis, 1973, Proc. Royal Soc. B183, 21.

38. Mattsson, O., R.B. Knox, J. Heslop-Harrison, and Y. Heslop-Harrison, 1974, Nature 247, 298.

39. Christ, B., 1959, Z. Bot. 47, 38.

40. Heinen, W., and H.F. Linskens, 1961, Nature, Lond. 191, 1416.

41. Kroh, M., 1964, in: Pollen Physiology and Fertilization, ed. H.F. Linskens (North-Holland, Amsterdam).

42. Roggen, H.P.J.R., 1972, Euphytica 21, 1.

43. Kroh, M., and A.J. Munting, 1967, Acta Bot. Neerl. 16, 182.

44. Willemse, M.Th.M., 1968, Acta Bot. Neerl. 17, 330.

45. Willemse, M.Th.M., and H.F. Linskens, 1969, Rev. Cytol. Biol. Vég. 32, 121.

46. Paton, J.B. 1921, Amer. J. Bot. 8, 471.

47. Linskens, H.F., und W. Heinen, 1962, Z. Bot. 50, 338.

48. Jensen, W.A., and D.B. Fisher, 1970, Protoplasma 69, 215.

49. van der Pluijm, J., und H.F. Linskens, 1966, Der Züchter 36, 220.

50. Schoch-Bodmer, H., und P. Huber, 1947, Vjschr. Naturforsch. Ges. Zurich 92, 43.

51. Bhattacharjya, A.S., and H.F. Linskens, 1955, Sci. Cult. 20, 370.

52. Linskens, H.F., 1955, Z. Bot. 43, 1.

53. Linskens, H.F., und K. Esser, 1959, Proc. Kon. Ned. Akad. Wetenschap, 62C, 150.

54. Kumar, S., and A. Hecht, 1970, Biol. Plant., Praha 12, 41.

55. Tupý, J., 1961, Biol. Plant., Praha 3, 1.

56. Rosen, W.G., and S.R. Gawlik, 1966, Protoplasma 61, 181.

57. Rosen, W.G., and S.R. Gawlik, 1966, in: Electron Microscopy - Proc. VI Intern. Congr. Electron Microsc., Kyoto (Maruzen, Tokyo).

58. Rosen, W.G., 1968, Ann. Rev. Plant Physiol., 19, 435.

59. Kroh, M., H. Miki-Hirosige, W. Rosen, and F. Loewus, 1970, Plant Physiol. 45, 86.

60. Steffen, K. 1963, in: Recent Advances in the Embryology of Angiosperms, ed. P. Maheshwari (Intern. Soc. Plant Morph., Delhi).

61. Kroh, M., H. Miki-Hirosige, W. Rosen, and F. Loewus, 1970, Plant Physiol. 45, 92.

62. Kroh, M., C. Labarca, and F. Loewus, 1971, in: Pollen: Development and Physiology, ed. J. Heslop-Harrison (Butterworths, London).

63. Sweet, G.B., and P.N. Lewis, 1969, Planta, Berl. 89, 380.

64. Nitsch, J.P. 1971, in: Plant Physiology - A Treatise, ed. F.C. Steward, Vol. 6A (Academic Press, New York).

65. Johri, B.M., and I.K. Vasil, 1961, Bot. Rev. 27, 325.

66. Barendse, G.W.M., A.S. Rodrigues-Pereira, P.A. Berkers, F.M. Driessen, A. van Eyden-Emons, abd H.F. Linskens, 1970, Acta Bot. Neerl. 19, 175.

67. Mitchell, J.W., N. Mandava, J.F. Worley, J.R. Plimmer, and M.V. Smith, 1970, Nature, Lond. 225, 1065.

68. Thimann, K.V., 1972, in: Plant Physiology - A Treatise, ed. F.C. Steward, Vol. 6B (Academic Press, New York).

69. Wright, S.T.C., 1961, Nature, Lond. 190, 699.

70. Sastry, K.K.S., and R.M. Muir, 1963, Science 140, 494.

71. Muir, R.M., 1942, Amer. J. Bot. 29, 716.

72. Muir, R.M. 1951, in: Plant Growth Substances, ed. F. Skoog (Univ. Wisconsin Press, Madison).

74. Lund, H.A., 1956, Plant Physiol., 31, 334.

75. Lund, H.A., 1956, Amer. J. Bot. 43, 562.

76. Linskens, H.F., and J. Schrauwen, 1966, Planta, Berl. 71, 98.

77. White, J., 1907, Ann. Bot. 21, 587.

78. Maige, P., 1909, Rev. gen. Bot. 21, 32.

79. Hsiang, T.T., 1951, Plant Physiol. 26, 708.

80. Stanley, R.G., 1964, Sci. Prog. 52, 122.

81. Tupý, J., 1962, Biol. Plant, Praha 4, 69.

82. Godfrey, C.A., and H.F. Linskens, 1968, Planta, Berl. 80, 185.

83. Schrauwen, J., and H.F. Linskens, 1972, Planta, Berl. 102, 277.

Fertilization in Higher Plants, ed. H.F. Linskens.

SOME ASPECTS OF STIGMATIC SECRETION IN FORSYTHIA

C. DUMAS

Biologie Végétale, Université Claude Bernard, Villeurbanne (F)

1. Introduction

This work is devoted to the study of the genus Forsythia. The reason for choosing this plant is that it is a heterostylic species from the family of Oleaceae. Forsythia or ("Mimosa of Paris") is a hybrid, growing in natural conditions and resulting from cross-breeding between two species: F.suspensa Vahl var.fortunei Rehd (short styles) x F. viridissima Lindl (long styles). The stigma of these flowers corresponds to the terminal portion, capped by the upper part of the style, which is covered by a large number of papillate hairs. The width of the bilobed receptive surface (fig.2) of the pistil varies sligthly from the short-styled to the long-styled plant. The same phenomenon exists for the stigmatic papillae. On the other hand, there is a great difference between the length of styles for the two forms. In this dimorphous species, the thrum has short style with stamens overhanging the stigma. In the pin, the style is long and the stamens are situated below the stigma (fig.1). The cultivars, which produce many flowers, were obtained from the Botanical Garden of Lyon. Each shrub corresponds to a true natural clone.

An exploratory investigation into the fine structure of stigma material and its lipidic chemical analysis in Forsythia, is the subject of this research. Investigations were carried out using two plants: F. intermedia Zabel, short- and long-styled.

2. The glandular region of the stigma

Some few studies do exist on the stigma of the plant and its role in the production and release of the exudate[1,2,3].

a/ Histological and histochemical results

Some authors[4,5] have shown the apparent presence of two well distinct zones in the stigma. Similarly, in Forsythia, one can distinguish a superficial region or stigmatic zone covered by the papillae and another deeper region or stigmatoid zone, a continuation of the stylar tissues. The distinction between these two zones is sharper after the application of certain histochemical tests[6] (fig.5). By microscopic studies, one can observe exudate droplets (fig.3) on and between the stigmatic papillae. These droplets are coloured characteristically by different stains used for the detection of lipids. A relatively universal reagent on lipids is the sulfate of Nile blue. These different stains can be removed by immersing the stigma in a mixture of solvents Furthermore, by chelation with aluminium salts in ethanolic solution, we can obtain a bright yellow secondary photoluminescence (seen under the microscope) or fluorescence superimposable at the glandular zone,after the exposure of the primary fluorescence (fig.6,7). Primary denotes luminescence by substances or cell structures themselves. This group incluses some pigments and lipids. This proves the existence of flavonoidic aglycons, probably free, in the superficial zone. The same results were obtained in certain glands[7] or by chemical analysis of some stigmatic exudates in other species[2,8].

HO, O, OH, OH, O ⇄ ($AlCl_3$ / aqu.HCl) HO, O, O—Al-Cl, O

Scheme illustrating the type of complex that $AlCl_3$ could found form with certain flavone in presence or absence of acid.

Moewus[9] has already reported the presence of such compounds in *Forsythia* but his conclusions were very controversial[10].

b/ A survey of ultrastructural aspect

The ultrastructural studies of the stigmatic zone in *Forsythia* show that during the secretory process, different stages can be identified leading to release of the stigmatic exudate[3]. The post-meristematic stage is characterized by the appearance of membranous profiles, resembling the smooth endoplasmic reticulum (ER) filled with electron dense products which leads by the vesiculisation process to the formation of electron opaque vesicles[11]. These vesicles then migrate

---

Fig.1. Heterostyli in *Forsythia intermedia* Zabel. Fig.2. The stigma has a bilobed receptive surface. Fig.3. Stigmatic papillae observed with scanning microscope show exudate droplets (arrows)(C.Dumas and M.Lecocq). Fig.4. These papillae accumulate numerous osmiophilic grains (arrows). Fig.5.These droplets are coloured characteristically (red) with the sulfate of Nile blue (arrow).
The glandular zone (g.z.) is distinct from the stigmatoid zone (s.z.) after the application of histochemical test[6] (Nile blue), in Fig.7, or with a bright photoluminescence, under 360nm (U.V.), obtained with $AlCl_3$ - ethanol mixture, in Fig.6.
s:stigma, st:style, ov:ovary, pa:stigmatic papillae, N:nucleus, V:vacuole, Ex: Exudate, gr:osmiophilic grains.

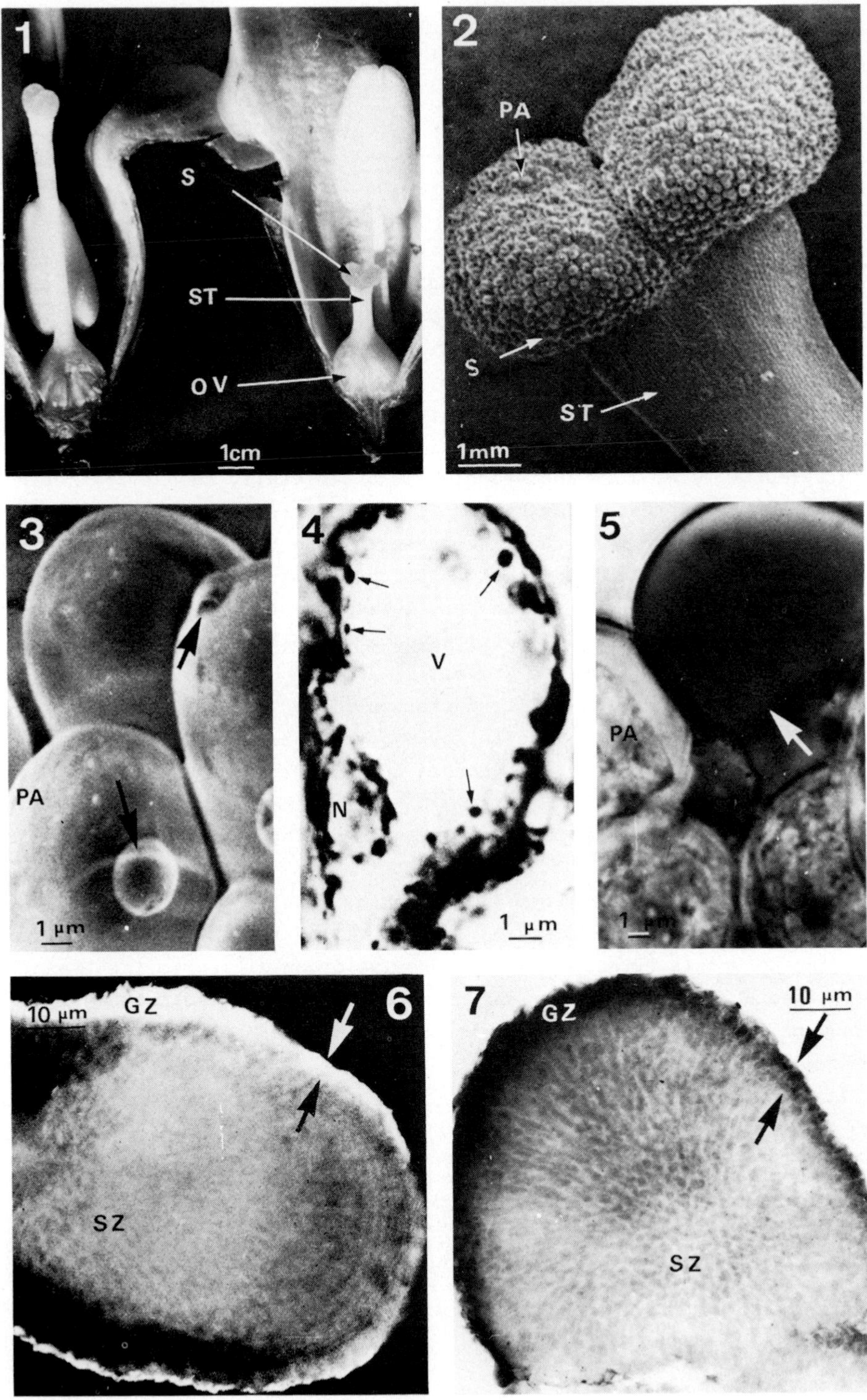
1
S
ST
OV
1cm
2
PA
S
ST
1mm
3
PA
1 µm
4
V
N
1 µm
5
PA
6
10 µm
GZ
SZ
7
GZ
10 µm
SZ

through the cytoplasm and the cell wall and are then accumulated under the cuticle, which eventually bursts freeing the secretory droplets. This is a typical granulocrine secretion[12] similar to that described by Kroh[13].

One of the particularities of the secretory activity in Forsythia is accumulation of electron dense grains.This accumulation is not limited by a membrane and is more or less associated with the tonoplast; it develops an argentaffin reaction after thiosemicarbazide-silver proteinate treatment (fig.9) losing its contents after a controlled oxidization by H_2O_2 (fig.8) or by periodic acid (fig.10). It is likely that these substances contain lipo-polyphenolic compounds[14] (fig. 11), but the absence of specific cytochemical tests (with T.E.M.) for lipids and polyphenols prevent us from concluding this certainty.

In the stigmatic cells, a close relationship between ER (or Golgi, ER,Lysosome: G.E.R.L.) and vacuole has occasionally been noted[16] similar to that described by Fineran[16] in frozen-etched root tips. It has been suggested that the ER ensheathing the vacuole forms a "collecting center"; the functional relationship between the two organelles is possibly that of a transport system for substances to and / or from the vacuole. Such observations have not been made in the stigmatoid zone of the stigma and style.

In Forsythia, the stigmatic secretion formed chiefly by neutral lipids[6] seems to involve the following structures: smooth endoplasmic reticulum (or G.E.R.L.), vacuole and plasmalemma.

3. Neutral lipids analysis of the stigmas of the"thrum" and"pin"forms

Although the stigma plays a determining role in the physiological reproduction of the Angiosperms, it has failed to draw the attention of the botanists as more than a secretive organ linked to the "sexual sphere". Without doubt, this is due to the very small quantity of exudate liberated at the anthesis. A small number of results available were published[17,2].

Fig.8. After H_2O_2/thiosemicarbazide/silver proteinate-treatment the content of peri-vacuolar grains have disappeared.
Fig.9. It develops an argentaffin reaction after thiosemicarbazide/ silver proteinate treatment, stronger than proteinate alone (Fig.11).
Fig.10. This peri-vacuolar accumulation has its contents which is extracted after a controlled oxidization by periodic acid. (treatment by : periodic acid/thiosemicarbazide/silver proteinate described elsewhere[12]).
V:vacuole, gr:grain, N:nucleus, p:plastid, CW:cell wall, Ex:exudate

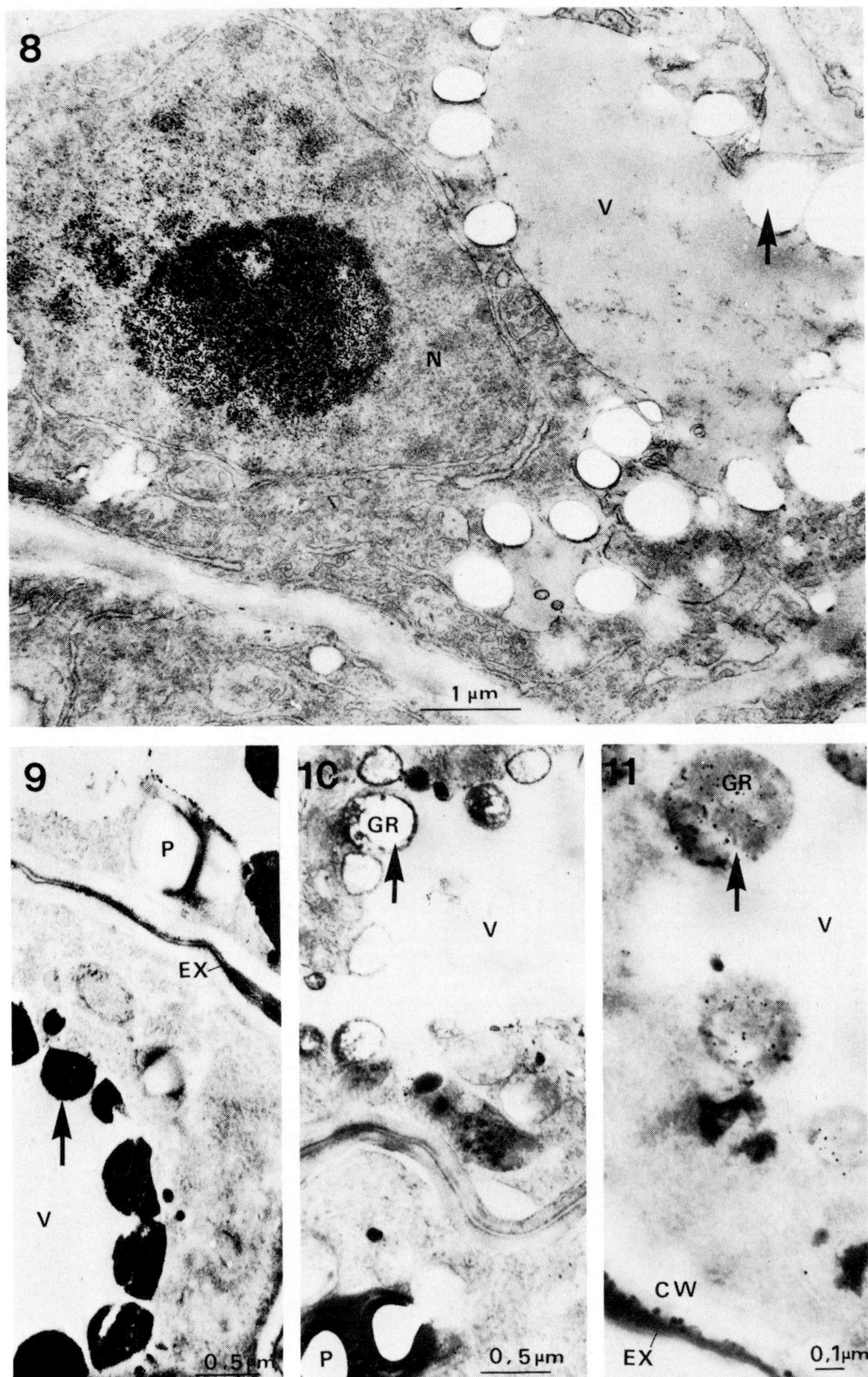
8
V
N
1 µm
9
P
EX
V
0,5 µm
10
GR
V
P
0,5 µm
11
GR
V
CW
EX
0,1µm

A very large number of flowers (many hundred thousands) are required for the lipid analysis of stigmas in F.intermedia. The experimental process used will be described elsewhere. After thin layer chromatographic analysis on the silica gel plates with the help of a solvant system adapted[18], we can observe that the neutral lipids are chiefly found in a glyceridic mixture (mono-di-triglycerides). There are neither free fatty acids nor sterols. On the other hand, hydrocarbons with perhaps terpens or similar compounds are present at the solvent front. The methylic esters fatty acids obtained are analysed in gas chromatography by the technique of double chromatography on polar and non polar column (SE 30 and D.E.G.S.)[18]. These can be characterized by the length of their carbon atom chains which are between C:7 and C:22, with the maximum for the unsatured form being C:18 (unpublished results).

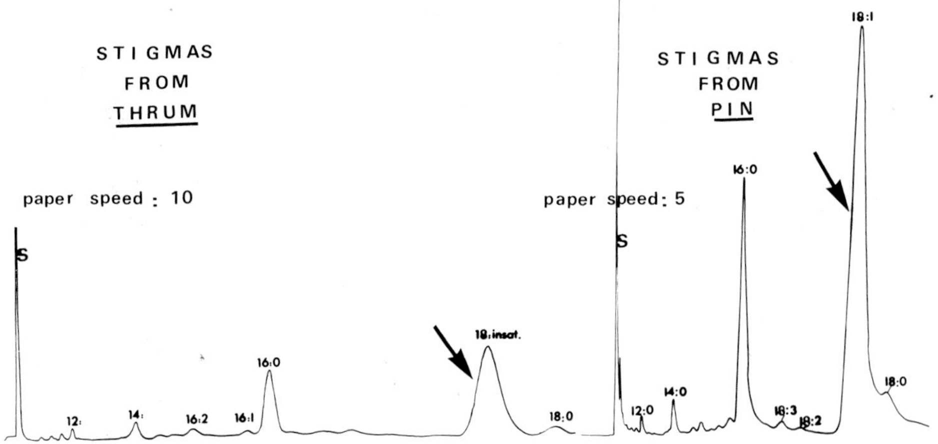

Gas chromatograms of methyl esters of fatty acids (total fatty acids) of stigmas (F.intermedia Zab.) The column was 10% SE 30 with 128 like attenuation and 5 or 10 paper speed.

There is no apparent difference between the neutral lipids and the fatty acids analysed from the stigmas of the"thrum" and the"pin"forms It should be noted that this technique does not exactly reflect the analysis of stigmatic exudate, nevertheless, due to the absence of neutral lipids in the stigmatoid tissue, we can conclude that most of the analysed neutral lipids are present in the glandular layer.

4. Role of the stigmatic lipids and phenols

The function of stigmatic fluid, essential contact with the environment, in the pollen germination process has not been clearly elucidated[19], except in _Lilium_[20,21]. Neutral lipids produced by the stigma of _Forsythia_ are insignificant, both in quality of lipids observed and in the nature of fatty acids identified. Different authors[17] [2,6], have reported the constant presence of lipids in the stigmatic exudate. Some hypothesis were formulated on their intervention: in hydratation of the pollen grain, formation of a water gradient in the exudate[17], on stimulation or inhibition on pollen germination[22,23]. These prevent dessication of stigmatic surface and trap pollen grains [17]. Lipids are oxidized (autoxidation); but under natural conditions, the lipids are found at the stigmatic surface. This proves the existence of antioxidant compounds. The phenols demonstrated here, can play this role. The actual substances involved in inhibition and their modes of action are unknown. Some authors[25] suggest that phenolic compounds are the active inhibitors.

Although not a single sex hormone has been found in the pistil, it is out of questions to think that they do not exist. The stigmatic fluid "probably conveys the chemical message"[25]. Some lipidic substances, possessing hormonal character have been isolated from pollen[26] Other lipids substances stimulating the pollen germination have been found[27]. The relationships between lipids and auxins (IAA) are still not well known. However, certain authors have reported a certain contain of auxin in the stigma[28]. Now, simple phenolics may stimulate or inhibit the pollen germination; this could not be demonstrated here.

The pollen tube probably derived a portion of its nourishment from pistil and/or eventually structural material from its secretion[19]. Besides, the stigmatic exudate might provide as a carrier for exogenous substance[30] and its lipids can be involved in the transport of metabolites like free flavonoids aglycons and enzymes; in this latter case they act as co-factors.

In pistils with"solid styles", the stigmas will produce mainly oils. These results are different in hollow style species[20] and in _Coniferae_[1] Then, the supposition that the secretion of stigmatic surface of flowering plants has been considered to be a sugary solution is"a myth of modern botany"[25]. Our observations show that the glandular stigmatic zone functions as an oil gland or a polyphenol-and-oil gland[12].The respective role of these sorts of compounds remains to be elucidated.

Acknoledgements: I thank Dr.Grantham for reviewing this English manuscript and Dr.Pham Liem Quang for his invaluable assistance in the gas chromatography.

References

1. Linskens, H.F., 1971, in: Fertilization Mechanisms in higher plants vol.2, eds. C.Metz and A.Monroy (Academic Press, N.Y.) p.197

2. Martin, F.W. and Brewbaker, J.L., 1970, in: Pollen, ed.J.Heslop-Harrison (Butterworths, London) p.262

3. Dumas, C., 1973, Z.Pflanzenphysiol., 69, 35

4. Vasil, I.K. and Johri, M.M., 1964, Phytomorphology, 14, 352

5. Konar, R.N. and Linskens, H.F., 1966, Planta, 71, 356

6. Dumas, C., 1974, Acta histochemica, 48, 115

7. Charrière, Y.,and Tissut, M., 1972, C.R.Acad.Sci, Paris, 274, 2659

8. Martin, F.W., 1970, New Phytol., 69, 425

9. Moewus, F., 1950, Forschgn.u.Fortschr., 26, 101

10. Visser, T., 1956, Proc.Kon.ned.Akad.Wet., 59, 685

11. Dumas, C., 1973, Z.Pflanzenphysiol., 70, 119

12. Dumas, C., Perrin, A., Rougier, M. and Zandonella, P., 1974, in: Plant Cell Differentiation in International Symposium (Lisboa,in press)

13. Kroh, M.,1967, Planta, 77, 250

14. Dumas, C., 1973, C.R.Acad.Sci, Paris, 277, 1479

15. Dumas, C., 1974, Le Botaniste, 56, 59

16. Fineran, B.A., 1973, J.Ultr.Res., 43, 75

17. Konar, R.N. and Linskens, H.F., 1966, Planta, 71, 372

18. Christie, W.W., 1973, Lipid analysis (Pergamon Press, N.Y.)

19. Rosen, W.G., 1974, Lin.Soc.Sympos. on the male gamete (in press)

20. Kroh, M.,Miki-hirosige, H., Rosen, W.G. and Loewus F., 1970, Plant Physiol., 45, 92

21. Labarca, C. and Loewus, F., 1973, Plant Physiol., 52, 97

22. Linskens, H.F. and Kroh, M., 1970, in:Current Topics in developmental biology, vol.5, (Academic Press inc., N.Y.) p.89

23. Kroh, M., 1967, Rev.Palaeobot.Palynol.,3, 197

24. Keularts, J.L.W. and Linskens, H.F., 1968, Acta bot.neerl., 17,267

25. Martin, F.W., and Ruberté, R., 1972, Phyton.Argent., 30, 119

26. Mitchell, J.W., Mandava, N., Worley, J.F.and Drowne, M.E., 1971, J.Agric.Food Chem., 19, 391

27. Koshimizu, K.,Kobayashi, A.,Mitsui, T., Matsubara, S. and Tsukamoto, Y., 1972,Bull.Inst.Chem.Res., Kyoto, 50, 142

28. Lund, H.A., 1956, Amer.J.Bot., 43, 562

29. Galston, A.W. and Hillman, W.S., 1961, in: Encyclopedia of Plant Physiology, vol.14, ed. W.Ruhland (Springer-Verlag, N.Y.)

30. Acher, P.D., and Drewlow, L.W., 1970, J.Amer.Soc.Hort.Sci., 95,706

Fertilization in Higher Plants, ed. H.F. Linskens.

ELUTABLE SUBSTANCES OF POLLEN GRAIN WALLS

E. G. Kirby and J. E. Smith
Forest Physiology-Genetics Laboratory
School of Forest Resources and Conservation
University of Florida
Gainesville 32611

Introdūction

The majority of angiosperms shed their pollen in the binucleate condition. However, Brewbaker[1] has shown that in 30% of 2,000 species studied, division of the generative cell takes place prior to shedding. Such pollen grains are shed in the trinucleate condition. It was initially proposed by Schürhoff[2] and later confirmed by subsequent studies[3,4,5] that trinucleate pollen was the derived condition and, thus, phylogenetically advanced.

In addition to cytological differences between binucleate and trinucleate pollen, certain physiological differences have also been reported. Brewbaker and Majumder[6] list four distinct characteristics that are strongly correlated with the number of pollen nuclei. Binucleate pollen is not usually difficult to germinate _in vitro_, whereas trinucleate pollen germinates with considerable difficulty. Binucleate pollen can normally be stored for considerable periods of time under proper storage conditions; trinucleate pollen cannot be stored for an appreciable length of time. Intraspecific incompatibility is generally observed in the style or ovary for species having binucleate pollen, whereas species having trinucleate pollen usually display incompatibility reactions in the stigma. Binucleate species are usually characterized by gametophytic incompatibility systems; trinucleate systems are characterized by sporophytic incompatibility systems.

There are notable exceptions, however, to the listed physiological differences. Some trinucleate pollens germinate readily _in vitro_ (e.g. _Brassica_ spp.), or germinate well in incompatible crosses; i.e. inhibition takes place in the style (e.g. _Beta_ spp.). In addition, grasses, which have trinucleate pollen, have a well defined gametophytic incompatibility system.

Explanations for the above phenomena are generally based on metabolic requirements for mitosis of the generative cell, which occurs prior to shedding in trinucleate pollen. This mitotic activity apparently deprives the pollen protoplast of substrates essential for: germination _in vitro_; extended storage; and growth of pollen tubes into the style in incompatible matings. Required substrates may be made available to pollen only by genetically compatible stigmas following the action of enzymes or recognition substances released from the pollen walls.[7]

The present work was undertaken to clarify and establish the chemical and physiological characteristics of binucleate and trinucleate pollen in an attempt to further illucidate the biological function of pollen surface compounds.

Materials and Methods

Pollen from 42 species representing 25 families of angiosperms was collected during the 1973-1974 growing season or purchased from the C. G. Blatt and Co., Independence, Missouri, USA (See Table 1). Pollen was stored at -5°C with silica gel as dessicant.

Table 1

Binucleate and trinucleate species included in analyses

Binucleate Pollen Species:	Trinucleate Pollen Species:
Betulaceae	Amaranthaceae
Alnus sp.	*Amaranthus* sp.
Betula papyrifera	*Acnida tamariscina*
Euphorbiaceae	Cactaceae
Ricinus communis	*Opuntia* sp.
Fagaceae	Caprifoliaceae
Quercus virginiana	*Sambucus* sp.
Fagus sp.	Chenopodiaceae
Juglandaceae	*Kochia* sp.
Juglans nigra	*Beta vulgaris*
Carya glabra	*Chenopodium album*
Leguminosae	Compositae
Acacia sp.	*Chrysanthemum* sp.
Magnoliaceae	*Artemisia dracnuculus*
Magnolia grandiflora	*Taraxicum* sp.
Moraceae	*Helianthus* sp.
Cannabis sativa	*Baccharis* sp.
Morus rubra	*Chrysothamnus* sp.
Myricaceae	*Ambrosia elatior*
Myrica sp.	Graminae
Myrtaceae	*Festuca* sp.
Eucalyptus sp.	*Zea mays*
Oleaceae	Plantaginaceae
Fraxinus sp.	*Plantago lanceolata*
Olea sp.	Polygonaceae
Palmae	*Rumex* sp.
Caryota sp.	Typhaceae
Rosaceae	*Typha* sp.
Rosa sp.	Ulmaceae
Pyrus communis	*Ulmus americana*
Salicaceae	*Celtis occidentalis*
Populus sp.	
Simarubaceae	
Ailanthus sp.	
Urticaceae	
Urtica sp.	

Samples of 50 mg were extracted for 1 hr at 4°C on a shaker using Coca's solution minus phenol (5.0 g NaCl, 2.75 g $NaHCO_3$ in 1000 ml distilled water).

Aliquots of the extracts were analyzed for proteins by the Lowry procedure[8] and for carbohydrates by α-naphthol-sulfuric acid. In this procedure aliquots of eluents containing not more than 100 μg carbohydrate were added to 5.0 ml α-naphthol reagent (2.0 g α-naphthol in 500 ml conc. H_2SO_4), mixed well and heated in boiling water for 10 min. After cooling optical density readings were taken at 555 nm on a Beckman DB spectrophotometer. The amount of total eluable substances was determined on a dry weight basis.

Results

All determinations or proteins, carbohydrates and total elutable compounds have been calculated as micrograms per one million (10^6) pollen grains. This represents an effort to minimize any differences related to pollen size.

Table 2

Quantitative determinations of surface compounds of angiosperm pollens. Determinations were made on 42 pollen species representing 25 families. Values reported are mean values

Nucleate Condition	Binucleate	Trinucleate
	μg/10^6 pollen grains	
Carbohydrates (α-naphthol)	9.40 ± 1.83**	5.75 ± 1.83
Proteins (Lowry)	4.98 ± 0.57**	3.85 ± 0.57
Total elutable compounds (dry weight basis)	370.97 ± 20.48**	330.15 ± 20.48

Significance:
** = 0.01

These quantitative differences are reported in Table 2. The results show clearly significant differences between binucleate and trinucleate conditions regarding total elutable wall compounds, as well as elutable carbohydrates and proteins. This is evident in the greater quantities of surface compounds in binucleate pollens.

Discussion

Tsinger and Petrovskaya-Baranova[9] concluded from the presence of proteins and other compounds that pollen grain walls are "...living, physiologically active structures playing a very responsible role in the processes of interchange between pollen grain and its substrate." Studies of Mäkinen and Brewbaker[10] and Stanley and Search[11] indicated that proteins and enzymes contained within pollen walls can be eluted within 5 sec, which indicates a rapid interchange.

Cytochemical studies[12,13] have shown that enzymes are associated with the intine layer of the pollen wall. More recently, attention has focused on gametophytic and sporophytic fractions of pollen wall compounds. The difference between these two fractions is the site of their synthesis. Heslop-Harrison et al.[14,15] reported that protein fractions as well as allergenic and antigenic fractions may be associated with exine and intine sites. Their observations indicate that intine-held compounds are gametophytically synthesized, while compounds located in the exine are sporophytically synthesized. Furthermore, it has been proposed that control of gametophytic intraspecific incompatibility systems is mediated through intine-held recognition substances, while exine-held compounds control sporophytic incompatibility systems.[14]

The results of this preliminary study indicate that cytologically distinct groups of angiosperm pollen (binucleate and trinucleate) that have been reported to differ in several physiological aspects, including type of incompatibility control, also differ quantitatively in the surface compounds that have been both gametophytically and sporophytically contributed. If indeed control of incompatibility is regulated through "recognition substances" carried on pollen grain surfaces, then qualitative studies characterizing distinct gametophytic and sporophytic fractions of surface compounds of binucleate and trinucleate pollen species could ellucidate possible control mechanisms involved in intraspecific incompatibility.

Acknowledgments

This work was supported by a grant from the Division of Sponsored Research of the University of Florida, under the biomedical program.

References

1. Brewbaker, J.L., 1967, Amer. J. Bot. 54, 1069.
2. Schürhoff, P.N., 1926, Die Zytologie der Blutenpflanzen (Enke Pbl. Co., Stuttgart).
3. Schnarf, K., 1939, Tabul. Biol. 17, 72.
4. Brewbaker, J.L., 1959, Indian. J. Genet. Plant Breed. 19, 121.
5. Rudenko, R.E., 1959, Biol. Zhurn. 44, 1467.
6. Brewbaker, J.L. and Majumder, S.K., 1961, in: Recent advances in botany, vol. 2 (University of Toronto Press), p. 1503.
7. Know, R.B., Willing, R. and Ashford, A.E., 1972, Nature 237, 381.
8. Lowry, O.H., Rosenbraugh, N.J., Farr, A.L. and Randall, R.J., 1951, J. Biol. Chem. 193, 265.
9. Tsinger, N.V. and Petrovskaya-Baranova, T.P., 1961, Dokl. Akad. Nauk. SSSR 138, 466.
10. Mäkinen, Y. and Brewbaker, J.L., 1967, Physiol. Plant. 20, 477.
11. Stanley, R.G. and Search, R.W., 1971, in: Pollen: development and physiology, ed. J. Heslop-Harrison (Butterworths, London), p. 174.
12. Knox, R.B. and Heslop-Harrison, J, 1969, Nature 223, 92.
13. Knox, R.B. and Heslop-Harrison, J., 1970. J. Cell Sci. 6, 1.
14. Heslop-Harrison, J., Heslop-Harrison, Y., Knox, R.B. and Howlett, B., 1973, Ann. Bot. 37, 403.
15. Howlett, B., Knox, R.B. and Heslop-Harrison, J., 1973, J. Cell Sci. 13, 603.

Fertilization in Higher Plants, ed. H.F. Linskens.

BORON IN POLLEN AND POLLEN CELL FRACTIONS

J. K. Peter and R. G. Stanley*
School of Forest Resources and Conservation
University of Florida, Gainesville, Florida 32611

1. Introduction

Since Agulhon[1] in 1910 first reported the requirement of boron in higher plants, much research has been directed to the symptoms of boron deficiency and toxicity and subsequently to the elucidation of its physiological role(s).

Although boron seems to be universally present in nature[2] this element does not appear to be essential for animals and fungi. It was observed[3] that Aspergillus niger and Penicillium glaucum, organisms which do not require boron or calcium are also incapable of synthesizing true pectic compounds. The hypothesis emerged that boron was required for plants capable of photosynthesis. It was shown[4] that the diatom Cylindrotheca fusiformis requires boron both for autotrophic growth and heterotrophic culture in the dark, ruling out the possibility that boron is required in photosythesis exclusively.

One of the early but most persistent theories concerning the physiological role of boron was its involvement in sugar uptake and translocation. Although at length defended,[5] much evidence has accumulated that boron was only secondarily involved.[6,7]

Boron also influences the flavonoid-lignin metabolism. Boron deficiency causes accumulation of phenolics, probably resulting from decreased ability to synthesize lignin.[8,9] Interesting in this respect is the observation[10] that boron seems to play a role in partitioning metabolism between the glycolytic and pentose shunt pathways; borate inhibits (in vitro) 6-phosphogluconate dehydrogenase. Absence of borate results in increased metabolism via the pentose shunt, supposedly resulting in increased production of 3-deoxy-D-arabinoheptulonic acid, a precursor of phenolic acids. This is just one example of the many enzyme systems which have been shown to be influenced by boron.

Timashov[11] reported that boron deficiency in mitochondria, isolated from sunflower roots, resulted in uncoupling of oxidative phosphorylation. The resulting depletion of the cell's energy must have immediate and far-reaching effects on the entire metabolism of the cell.

More recent research indicated that RNA metabolism is immediately affected when boron levels are manipulated.[12,13] The addition of certain nitrogen bases could

---

*Deceased April 15, 1974.

alleviate boron deficiency symptoms and application of base analogs induced deficiency symptoms in the presence of boron.[14]

Finally, research on pea roots[15] showed that absence of boron leads to decreased amounts of histones in the chromatin.

It appears that an integrated picture of the physiological role(s) of boron in plants is still unavailable.

This study deals with pollen; a convenient material for boron studies since it is monocellular, non-photosynthetic and does not form lignin.

2. Materials and Methods

Pollen Germination: Pear pollen was germinated for three hours at 30°C in a calcium phosphate buffer (pH = 6.0), containing 0.4 M raffinose and 3 or 80 ppm boron in the form of boric acid.

Boron Determination: A satisfactory ashing procedure was determined experimentally. Twenty-five mg $Ca(OH)_2$ was added to the pollen samples. The samples were ashed in covered porcelain crucibles, at 475°C for exactly 8 hours. Although ashing was incomplete, well reproducible results were obtained and the boron recovery was excellent. With each experiment a standard curve was determined (see Fig. 1, a typical example of a standard curve). The ashed samples were taken up in 2 ml 0.06 N HCl, and 0.5 ml was pipetted into polyethylene containers. Subsequently, a boron-curcumin complex was formed in anhydrous medium.[16] After formation of the curcumin complex and addition of buffer, a three-hour period was required to allow precipitation of calcium. The precipitate was removed by filtering through Whatman No. 1 using vacuum. Absorbance was determined at 545 nm.

Isolation of Cell Fractions: Cell fractions were obtained, using a method adapted from Van Der Woude.[17] For each experiment 1 g of pear pollen, distributed over 10 erlenmeyers, was germinated in 10 ml medium per flash, Germination was checked microscopically (range of 30-50%) and the pollen was centrifuged and washed twice in 0.1 M sodium phosphate buffer (pH = 7.2), containing 0.5 M sucrose and 0.001 M EDTA. The pollen was homogenized for 45 seconds in a teflon pestle tissue grinder and disruption of the pollen tubes was examined. The sample was centrifuged at 500 x g for 10 minutes, resuspended in the aforementioned buffer and centrifuged. The obtained pellet is referred to as the cell wall fraction. The washing and the supernatant were combined and centrifuged at 30,000 x g for 45 minutes. The subsequent pellet--referred to as mitochondrial fraction--was resuspended and centrifuged. The supernatants were combined and centrifuged at 98,000 x g for 45 minutes. The final pellet, highly enriched in vesicles, was examined for purity using electron microscopy.

3. Results and Discussion

The method used for boron determinations in organic material was very satisfactory, a linear standard curve was obtained (Fig. 1) for quantities between 0.1 and 1.24 µg boron (as B) and results were reporducible.

It is known that most pollens require boron for germination in vitro. It appears that pollens which require relatively high levels of boron in the nutrient medium also show high endogenous levels. The boron levels in various pollens were determined (Fig. 2). Angiosperm pollens contained generally more boron than

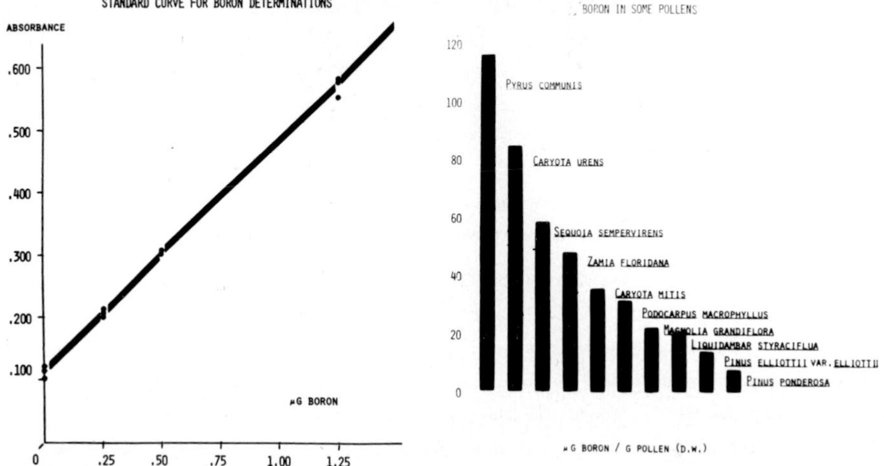

gymnsoperms. This may be related to the time required for germination. Pear pollen, with an optimum concentration of 80 ppm boron in the medium, germinates in approximately 2 hours. Pine pollen, for example P. elliottii var. elliottii, requires 40 to 70 hours for germination in pure water. Pine pollen, however, may obtain boron from the female tissue since this contains higher levels (Table 1). It was shown in our laboratory that addition of 3 ppm boron increases in vitro germination by approximately 5%.

Determination of Boron in Female Tissue of Pinus elliottii var. elliottii

Dry Weight (%)	Boron (µg/g DW)
69.8	34.4
72.6	36.3
71.1	31.3

*Female cones were between 4-6 weeks old, and 13 mm long.

The endogenous boron levels in pear pollen varied considerably (Table 2), however, the percentage germination was not affected. The fact that boron levels varied so much may be a reflection of some fertilization scheme in the pear orchard, but this could not be verified since the pollen is a mixed sample obtained from commercial orchards. Unfortunately, an adequate amount of female tissue of pear flowers could not be obtained in time, for determination of endogenous boron levels.

Variation of Boron Concentrations and % Germination in Pollen of Pyrus communis.

Year	μg B/g Pollen	% Germination
1968	47	50-59
1970	89	55-60
1972	108	50-55
1973	116	40-45

Note: Germination was determined within one year of harvest of pollen.

Since boron has been implicated in various physiological functions it seemed proper to determine boron levels in various cell fractions (Table 3). It is difficult to distinguish between adsorbed and absorbed boron; and, in addition, leakage cannot be prevented. However, it is known that boron is accumulated and a certain amount is "bound" in the cell. The data obtained show that boron is not accumulated to any extent in any specific fraction. Although the value of the data (expressed as g boron/gram dry weight) may be debatable, the concentration of boron in the different fractions was of the same order of magnitude and possibly reflected a constant amount per unti dry weight of membrane material.

Boron in Cell Fractions of Pear (Pyrus communis) Pollen*

Fraction	Total Boron μg B (aver)
Medium after germination and centrifugation	81.0
Supern. of washings in P-buffer + EDTA	7.5
Supern. after centrif. of all fractions	5.4
Cell wall fraction (500 x g)	3.5
Mitochondria fraction (30,000 x g)	1.4
Vescicle fraction (98,000 x g)	0.27
TOTAL	99.1

*Obtained from 1.0 gram pollen (F.W.) The medium contained 30 μg boron total and the pollen contained 110 μg total.

Table 4 shows the total boron budget of all pellets and supernants. The total recovery was 99.1 μg, which is 71% of the combined amount in the germination medium and the ungerminated pollen. The fact that the pollen was germinated in 10 vessels, each containing 3 μg boron, may account for the small losses due to adsorption to the vessel walls.

Boron in Cell Fractons of Pear (Pyrus communis) Pollen (after centrif. of medium and washing with Phosphate-EDTA buffer).

	Boron in Medium (μg/ml)	Dry Weight (g)	μg B/g(DW) (average of triplicate)
Vescicles	3	0.0501	9.36
	3	0.0666	8.00
	80	0.0684	3.68
Mitochondria	3	0.2640	4.27
	3	0.1213	8.68
	80	0.1049	7.83
Cell Wall	3	0.6154	7.87
	3	0.6808	7.20
	80	0.6483	7.85
Supernatant	3	------	2.72
	3	------	2.34
	80	------	3.18
		Boron (μg)	Dry Weight (g)
Total	3	24.22	0.9295
	3	26.60	0.8687
	80	22.54	0.8216

Future research may be directed to identification and characterization of the compound(s) to which boron is bound in the various cell fractions.

4. Acknowledgements

Thanks are due to Joel E. Smith who isolated the various cell fractions, and Carolyn Napoli who examined the purity of these fractions using electron microscopy.

5. References

1. Agulhon, H., 1910, Ph.D. Thesis, Univ. of Paris.
2. Ploquin, J., 1967, Extrait du bulletin de la Société de Scientifique d'Hygiene Alimentaire. 55(1)(2):70.
3. Winfield, M.E., 1945b, Australian J. Exptl. Biol. Med. Sci. 23:267.
4. Lewin, J.C., 1966, J. Exp. Bot. 17(52):473.
5. Gauch, J.G. and Dugger, W.M., Jr., 1954, Bulletin A-80 (Technical) College Park, Md.
6. Skok, J., 1958, In: Trace elements. C.A. Lamb, et al., eds. Academic Press, New York.
7. Weiser, D.J., Blaney, L.T. and Li, P., 1964, Physiol. Plant. 17:589.
8. McIlrath, W.J. and Skok, J., 1964, Bot. Gaz. 125(4):268.
9. Troitskaya, E.A., Dranik, L.I. and Shkol'nik, Ya.M., 1971, Fizoilogiya Rastenii 18(2):393.
10. Sung, Lee and Aronoff, S., 1967, Science 158:798.
11. Timashov, N.D., 1967, Fiziologiya Rastenii 15(4)597.
12. Shkol'nik, M. Ya and Maevskaya, A.N., 1961, Fiziologiya Rastenii 2(3):270.
13. Crosswell, C. F. and Nelson, Helen, 1973, Am. Bot. 37(151):427.
14. Johnson, D.L. and Albert, L.S., 1967, Plant Physiol. 42(9):130.
15. Khuzhanazarov, S.H.M., Sherstnev, E.A. and Borshchenko, G.A., V.U. Komarov Inst., Acad. Sci. U.S.S.R. Leningrad. Publ. Naukava Dumka, Kiev.
16. Upström, L.R., 1968, Anal. Chim. Acta 43:475.
17. Van Der Woude, W.J., Morré, D.J. and Bracker, C.E., 1971, J. Cell Sci. 8:331.
18. Bobko, E.V. and Priadilshchikova, T.D., 1945, Comptes Rendus (Doklady) de l'Academie des Sciences de l'URSS Vol. XLVII(5):358.

Fertilization in Higher Plants, ed. H.F. Linskens.

PROTEIN SYNTHESIS DURING GERMINATION AND POLLEN TUBE GROWTH IN TRADESCANTIA

Joseph P. Mascarenhas, Barry Terenna, Anthony F. Mascarenhas* and Linda Rueckert

Dept. of Biological Sciences, State University of N.Y., Albany, N.Y. 12222, USA

*Permanent address: Biochemistry Div., National Chemical Lab., Poona, India

Protein synthesis is initiated during the early stages of Tradescantia pollen germination prior to tube outgrowth[1]. Similar results have been found with Petunia pollen[2]. Inhibition of protein synthesis with inhibitors such as cycloheximide results in either a reduction in the germination of pollen grains and/or an inhibition of tube growth[3,4,5], and generative cell division[6,7].

RNA synthesis occurs during pollen germination and tube growth (see ref. 3 for review). The RNA synthesized is probably messenger RNA (mRNA) since no ribosomal or transfer RNAs are synthesized in Tradescantia pollen tubes[8,9]. When RNA synthesis is blocked with actinomycin D (AmD), germination and early tube growth are not inhibited in Tradescantia and several other plant species[10,11].

These results indicate that in Tradescantia and possibly other plants as well, most of the proteins required for germination are already present in the mature pollen grain. In addition, the mature pollen grain contains pre-existing mRNAs whose translation into protein is required for later tube growth and the division of the generative cell.

The purpose of this report was to study the changes in the rate of RNA and protein synthesis and the number and types of proteins synthesized at different times during germination and tube growth. In addition, we wished to determine the number and size of proteins synthesized on pre-existing mRNA when RNA synthesis was blocked by actinomycin D.

Materials and Methods

Pollen of Tradescantia paludosa was collected and stored as previously described[1]. The pollen was grown in shaking cultures in growth medium containing 50 μg/ml of chloramphenicol to inhibit bacterial growth. This concentration of chloramphenicol does not affect pollen tube growth or generative cell division adversely. The growth medium consisted of equal volumes of Walker's medium[12] and our normal pollen medium[10]. Sterile glassware and solutions were used.

To study RNA synthesis 5 mg of pollen was grown in 2.5 ml growth medium. At various times after the addition of pollen to the medium 10 μc/ml of adenosine-(8-^{3}H), (Schwarz/Mann, Orangeburg, N.Y.), was added and the pollen grown for 1 hr longer. To terminate the experiment pollen was transferred with an excess of ice cold growth medium to a centrifuge tube and the pollen pelleted at low speed. To the pellet 1.5 ml of a 1% sodium dodecyl sulfate (SDS) solution in 10 mM NaCl,

10 mM Tris-HCl (pH 7.5) was added. It was mixed on a Vortex shaker at 25° for about 5 min, transferred to ice and trichloroacetic acid (TCA) added to a concentration of 5%. After 15 min the suspension was filtered through Whatman GF/C glass fiber filters and washed with cold 5% TCA. The filters were dried and counted in a toluene based scintillation fluid (Liquifluor, New England Nuclear) in a Packard 3375 Liquid Scintillation Spectrometer.

To study the rate of protein synthesis 12 mg of pollen was grown in 2 ml of growth medium (except Walker's medium minus casamino acids was used), containing 4 μc of ^{14}C-labeled reconstituted protein hydrolyzate (Schwarz/Mann) in each of several flasks. At various times after start of the experiment a sample was taken for growth measurements and the pollen pelleted as described for RNA synthesis. The pollen was homogenized in a Dounce homogenizer with 0.5 ml of sample buffer[13] (0.5 M Tris-HCl, pH 6.8, 1.0 ml; mercaptoethanol, 0.1 ml; glycerol, 1.0 ml; and H_2O, 7.9 ml). The homogenate was centrifuged for 10 min at 2000 g. To the supernatant, 20 μl of a 25% SDS solution was added and the mixture immediately heated at 95°C for 2 min. To a 25 μl aliquot of this solution and to the pollen residue, 2 ml of a 10% TCA solution was added and the tubes heated at 95°C for 10 min. After cooling in ice the proteins from the soluble fraction were filtered through Millipore HA 0.45μ nitrocellulose filters and the pollen residue through Whatman GF/C glass fiber filters. After washing with 5% TCA the filters were dried and counted as described earlier.

For an analysis of the proteins synthesized during germination and tube growth, a procedure identical to that described for protein synthesis was used. 25 μl of each soluble fraction was analyzed by electrophoresis in a thin slab of polyacrylamide prepared in an apparatus similar to that of Studier[14] and using the discontinuous SDS buffer system of Laemmli[13]. This procedure separates proteins on the basis of their molecular weights. The separating gel contained 15% acrylamide and the stacking gel 5% acrylamide. Both acrylamide and bisacrylamide were recrystallized[15]. After electrophoresis for about 2 1/2 hr at 110 volts, the gel was stained overnight in a solution of 0.1% Coomassie blue in 25% TCA. It was destained in 7% acetic acid in 20% ethanol and dried on a piece of filter paper as described by Maizel[16]. Autoradiographs of the gels were made with Kodak No-Screen Medical X-ray film. To determine molecular weights the following protein standards were used: bovine serum albumin (68,000 daltons), ovalbumin (43,000) and chymotrypsinogen (25,000).

Results

The changes in the rates of RNA synthesis during pollen tube growth are shown in Fig. 1. In this experiment pollen tubes were pulse labeled for 1 hr at different times during their growth with ^{3}H-adenosine and the TCA insoluble radioactivity determined. The rate of RNA synthesis is highest during the first hour of growth and decreases continuously thereafter.

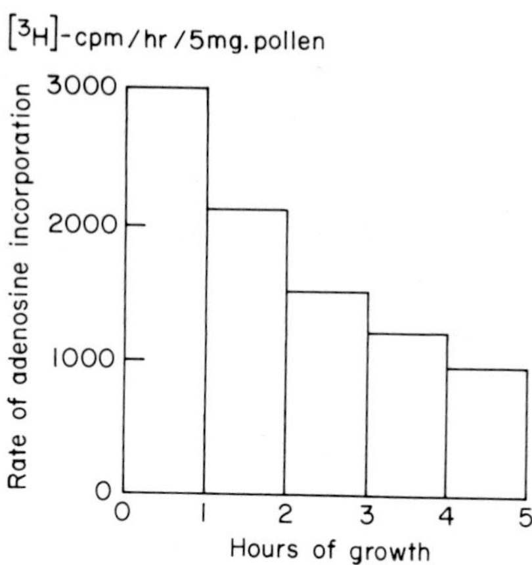

Fig. 1. Rate of RNA synthesis during different periods of pollen germination and tube growth.

To determine the rates of protein synthesis pollen samples were grown continuously for increasing intervals of time with a mixture of ^{14}C-amino acids and the incorporation of radioactivity into hot TCA precipitable material determined. The data in Fig. 2 show that the rate of protein synthesis is high during the first two hours. Thereafter there does not seem to be any net incorporation of radioactivity into proteins. Similar results have been obtained with pulse labeling experiments (unpublished results). The soluble labeled proteins seem to diminish slightly with time whereas the insoluble proteins associated with the cell wall fraction seem to remain constant after 3 hr. The growth measurements indicate that the drop in the rate of protein synthesis after two hours is not caused by a reduction in the rate of pollen tube growth. It is not possible to measure pollen tubes beyond a length of 1.5 mm as they get tangled in masses.

The electrophoretic analysis of proteins from pollen tubes labeled continuously for periods of 1 to 6 hr is shown in Fig. 3. The Coomassie blue stained band pattern appears almost identical for all periods of labeling except for one band indicated by an arrow that seems to disappear after one or two hours of growth. The autoradiograms of 1 and 2 hr labeled pollen tube proteins show 4 protein bands that are heavily labeled. In addition there are at least 16 other less radioactive bands. No new labeled protein bands appear during later periods of growth although at least two proteins with molecular weights less than 36,000 daltons (arrows) seem to disappear after 2 to 3 hr of pollen tube growth.

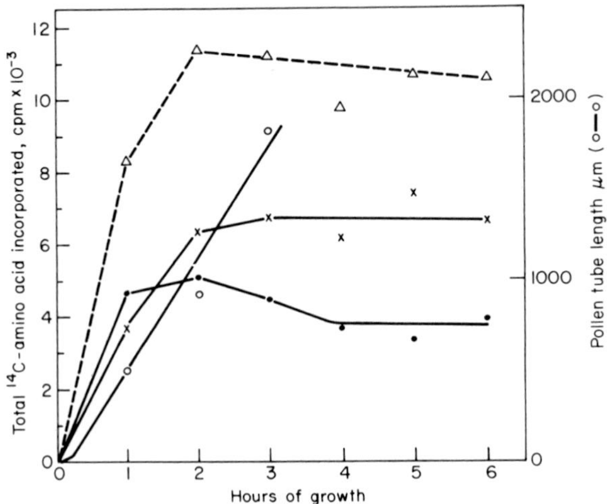

Fig. 2. Incorporation of ^{14}C-amino acids into the soluble, insoluble and total proteins of pollen tubes grown for different periods of time.(•——•), soluble proteins; (x——x), insoluble proteins; (Δ--Δ), total proteins (soluble + insoluble).

In order to determine which of the labeled proteins were translated on pre-existing mRNAs, pollen was grown for one hour in growth medium with and without 30 μg/ml of AmD. The proteins were isolated and analyzed by SDS-polyacrylamide gel electrophoresis. The data in Fig. 4 show very clearly that whether the synthesis of RNA is blocked or not, exactly the same pattern of synthesis of proteins is obtained. In another experiment pollen tubes were grown with 30 μg/ml of AmD for 1 hr, ^{14}C-labeled amino acids were then added and after a further hour the proteins were analyzed by SDS-gel electrophoresis and autoradiograms prepared. Although the proteins from AmD treated tubes were about 20% less radioactive than the control, the pattern of radioactive protein bands was qualitatively very similar in the two treatments.

Fig. 3. SDS acrylamide gel electrophoresis of pollen tube proteins. A = Coomassie blue stained gels; B = autoradiograms. The numbers 1 to 6 indicate the hours of growth of pollen with the ^{14}C-amino acid. Numbers on right are approximate molecular weights determined by electrophoresis of protein standards.

Fig. 4. SDS-polyacrylamide gel electrophoresis of proteins from pollen grown with ^{14}C-amino acids without (1,2) and with (3,4) actinomycin D. 1 and 3 = Coomassie blue stained gels; 2 and 4 = autoradiograms of 1 and 3 respectively. The numbers at the left are molecular weights.

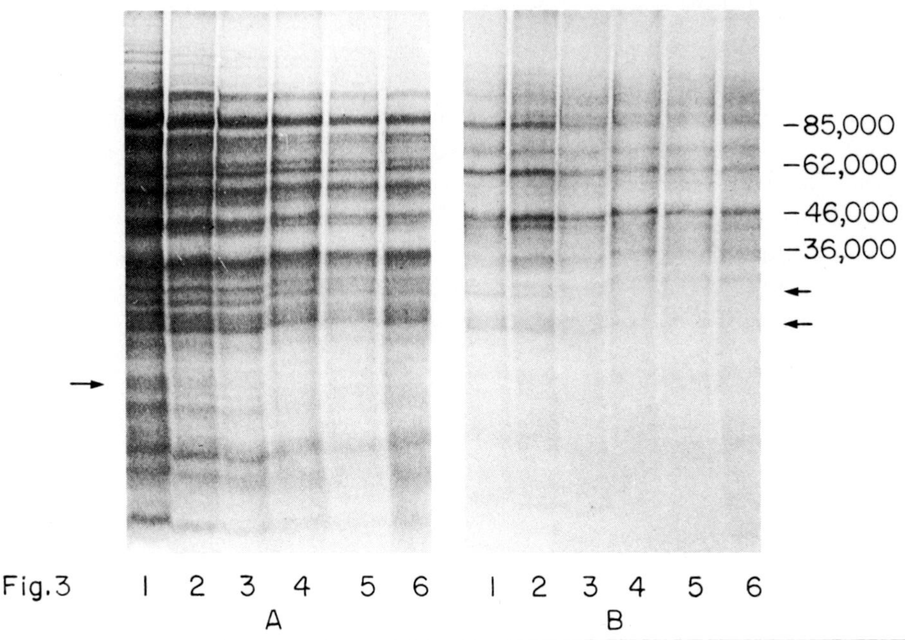
-85,000
-62,000
-46,000
-36,000
1 2 3 4 5 6
A
1 2 3 4 5 6
B

Fig. 3

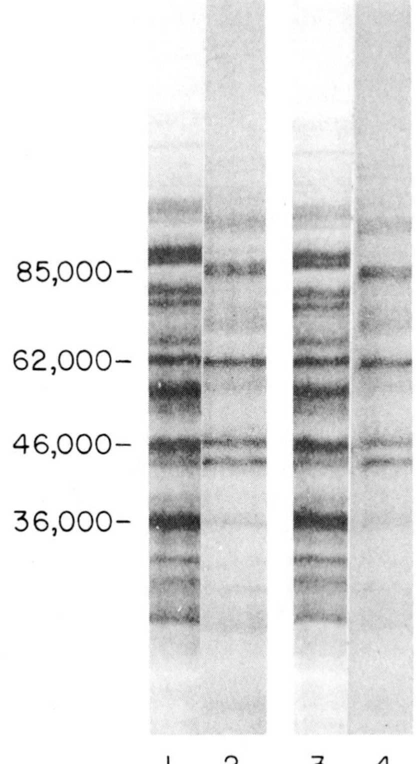
85,000-
62,000-
46,000-
36,000-
1 2 3 4

Fig. 4

Discussion

The rate of synthesis of both RNA and proteins is high during the first hour of pollen tube growth. Thereafter both rates rapidly decline with time. It appears that the RNA species and the proteins required for pollen tube growth and generative cell division are synthesized early after germination. This is in agreement with protein and RNA synthesis inhibitor studies with Tradescantia[4] which show that if AmD (20 μg/ml) is added to the growth medium two hours after start of pollen germination, it has no effect on generative cell division, indicating that the RNA species required for division are synthesized during the first two hours of pollen tube growth. Generative cell division is first seen at about 5 hr with most divisions being completed by 8 to 9 hr.

When cycloheximide (100 μg/ml) was added at the time of pollen germination, tube growth was rapidly inhibited and progress of the generative cell towards division was prevented. If applied 3 or 4 hr after start of germination, it did not prevent division and the formation of the two sperm cells[14]. Thus the proteins synthesized during the first two to three hours of pollen tube growth are required for pollen tube growth and completion of generative cell division. In Petunia there is a similar change in the rate of protein synthesis after the first hour of adding pollen to a growth medium[2]. In Impatiens balsamina cycloheximide inhibited the division of the generative cell but had no effect on pollen germination and tube growth[7]. Our own unpublished inhibitor studies with pollen of Antirrhinum majus and Amaryllis belladonna would seem to indicate that there are differences between different pollens in the dependence of germination, tube growth and generative cell division on the synthesis of new RNA and proteins.

In Tradescantia a fairly large number of proteins are synthesized during the early stages of pollen tube growth. There appear to be no qualitative differences, however, between the labeled protein bands in SDS-acrylamide gels obtained from pollen tubes grown with and without AmD. This indicates that the proteins made on newly synthesized RNA are not any different from the proteins translated from the pre-existing mRNAs in the mature pollen grain.

References

1. Mascarenhas, J.P. and Bell, E. 1966. Biochim. Biophys. Acta 179, 199.
2. Linskens, H.F., Schrauen, J.A.M., and Konings, R.N.H. 1970. Planta 90, 153.
3. Mascarenhas, J.P. 1971. In: Pollen Development and Physiology, ed. J. Heslop-Harrison (Butterworths, Lond.), p. 201.
4. LaFleur, G.J., Mascarenhas, J.P. and Whipple, A. (Manuscript in preparation).
5. Franke, W.W., Herth, W., VanDerWoude, W.J. and Morre, D.J. 1972. Planta 105, 317.
6. Niitsu, T., Hanaoka, A. and Uchiyama, K. 1972. Cytologia 37, 143.

7. Shivanna, K.R., Jaiswal, V.S. and Mohan Ram, H.Y. 1974. Planta 117, 173.
8. Mascarenhas, J.P. and Bell, E. 1970. Develop. Biol. 21, 475.
9. Mascarenhas, J.P. and Goralnick, R.D. 1971. Biochim. Biophys. Acta 240, 56.
10. Mascarenhas, J.P. 1966. Amer. J. Bot. 53, 563.
11. Dexheimer, J. 1968. Compt. Rend. Acad. Sci., D. 267, 2126.
12. Walker, G.R. 1957. Proc. Genet. Soc. Canada 2, 18.
13. Laemmli, V.K. 1970. Nature 227, 680.
14. Studier, F.W. 1973. J. Mol. Biol. 79, 237.
15. Loening, V.E. 1967. Biochem. J. 102, 251.

Acknowledgements: Work supported by National Science Foundation Grant BO-33805 and Public Health Service Grant GM-02014.

Fertilization in Higher Plants, ed. H.F. Linskens.

THE RELEASE OF RNA FROM POLLEN TUBES

J. Tupý, Eva Hrabětová and Věra Balatková

Department of Genetics, Institute of Experimental Botany, Czechoslovak Academy of Sciences Praha

1. Introduction

The mutual interactions between pollen tubes and pistil controlling the progamic phase of fertilization may result from the biochemical activity of substances moving from the tubes. So far, attention has been paid to the diffusion of proteins. In artificial pollen tube culture, various proteins are present in the medium[1] and their diffusion from germinating pollen already starts before tube protrusion occurs[2]. The released protein includes a number of enzymes, whose effect on pistil substrates may be essential for normal pollen tube growth[3]. Besides protein, an abundant diffusion of amino acids from artificially cultivated pollen is reported[4]. In this paper the results described provide evidence that RNA and also ribosomes are released from pollen tubes into the cultivation medium.

2. Material and methods

Pollen free of microbial contamination was collected from the surface sterilized anthers[5] of Nicotiana tabacum and stored at -20°. In all experiments the cultivation of pollen was carried out under aseptic conditions in autoclaved 0.3 M sucrose-0.001% boric acid in 100 ml Erlenmayer flasks. The suspension of 25 mg pollen in 10 ml of the solution was gently shaken during the whole cultivation period on a horizontally moving water bath at 25°. For the rapid estimation of pollen tube growth, a simple method was developed based on the weighing of the mass of pollen tubes recovered by sucking out the medium through a glass sintered funnel under constant conditions. This method will be described in detail elsewhere.

To isolate RNA for chromatography on kieselguhr coated with methylated albumin (MAK), the medium was mixed with two volumes of ethanol and kept at -20° at least overnight. The precipitate was dissolved in 10 mM Tris-HCl (pH 7.6), 150 mM NaCl, 1% SDS (sodium dodecyl sulphate) at ambient temperature. After about 10 min, the solution was made to a final concentration of 0.5 M NaCl (using 5 M NaCl), cooled and deproteinized with cold chloroform. The RNA was precipitated from the aqueous phase with 2 volumes of ethanol. For the preparation of cytoplasmic and "nuclear" RNA, the pollen tubes were homogenized at about 0° in extraction solution (Tris-HCl, pH 7.6, 10 mM; sucrose, 0.3 M; $MgCl_2$, 5 mM; mercaptoethanol, 5 mM) and centrifuged at low speed (1,000 g, 10 min). The pellet was washed 3 times with the same cold solution and the pooled extracts were mixed with 2 volumes of ethanol. The RNA from the alcoholic precipitate and from the nuclear and wall pellet was isolated in the same manner as from the alcoholic precipitate from the cultivation medium, with the exception that for the isolation of "nuclear" RNA the concentration of SDS was 2%.

For the isolation of ribosomes, the cultivation medium was mixed with concentrated buffer (Tris-HCl, pH 7.6, 0.1 M; magnesium acetate, 0.12 M; KCl, 0.6 M; mercaptoethanol, 0.14 M) in the proportion of 9:1. The mixture was cooled and centrifuged for 20 min at 30,000 g at 2°. The ribosomes from the supernatant were then pelleted by centrifugation at 105,000 g for 150 min at 2°. The sedimentation constant of ribosomes was determined by centrifugation on a sucrose gradient using S70 ribosomes from E.coli strain MRE 600 as reference standard.

3. Results and discussion

The first indications of the presence of RNA in the cultivation medium were obtained from UV-absorption spectra (fig. 1). The material with an absorption maximum at 260 nm is released from germinating pollen much later than the protein, being practically absent after 2 hours of cultivation. This material is precipitable with ethanol and the absorption spectra of the extracts from the precipitate obtained with hot perchloric acid indicate the presence of RNA. The chromatography on a MAK column showed that the released RNA includes low-molecular-weight RNA (tRNA + 5S) as well as the two high-molecular-weight components of rRNA (fig. 2).

A further experiment describes the changes in the amount of the released (extracellular) RNA, of the cytoplasmic RNA remaining in pollen tubes and of the "nuclear" RNA during 16 hours of pollen cultivation. The great increase of the mass of germinating pollen during the first 2 hours' interval is due to pollen grain imbibition in addition to tube elongation. In further intervals it corre-

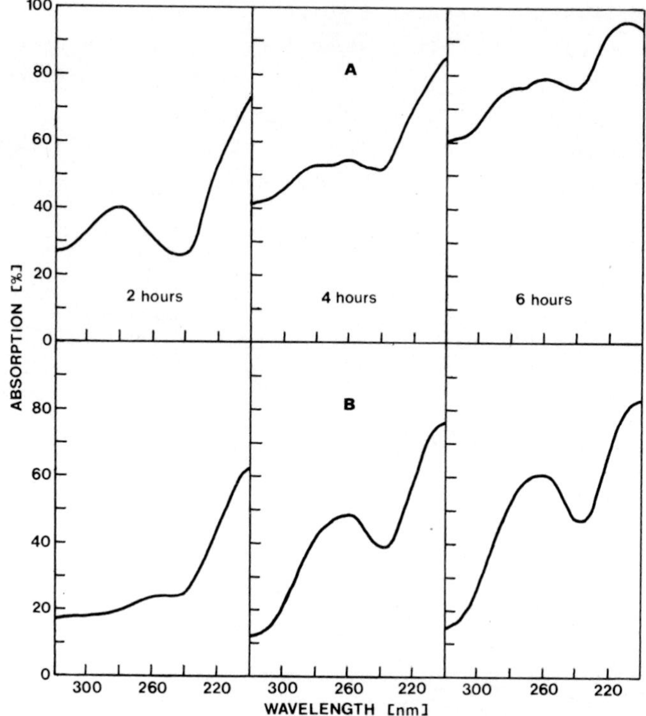

Fig. 1. Ultraviolet spectra of the material released from pollen tubes after 2, 4 and 6 hours of pollen cultivation. A: cultivation medium diluted 10 times. B: perchloric acid extracts from alcohol precipitates of the medium (2 ml of the medium was mixed with two volumes of 0.56 N $HClO_4$ in alcohol and kept overnight at -20°; the precipitate was extracted twice with 2.5 ml of 1 N $HClO_4$ at 70° for 30 min and the pooled extracts were diluted to 25 ml).

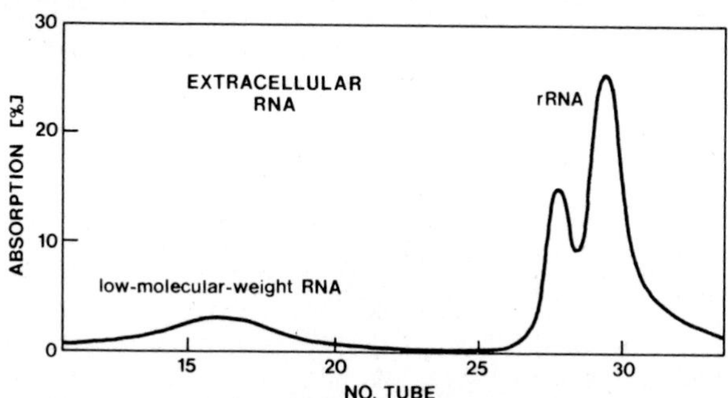

Fig. 2. MAK column elution profile of RNA present in the medium at 6 hours of pollen cultivation; linear gradient from 75 ml each of 0.3 M and 1.1 M NaCl.

sponds to pollen tube growth. A weight increase of 10 mg was related to an increase of about 35 μ in tube length. The course of growth over the 16 hour period (fig. 3) shows a significant depression at 6 hours followed by a temporary enhancement of tube elongation which ceases after 12 hours of cultivation. A similar growth pattern was observed in several other experiments.

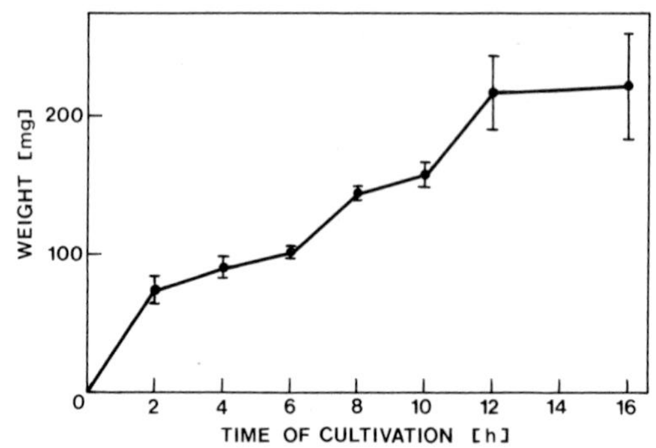

Fig. 3. Weight increase of the mass of pollen culture in sucrose-boric acid solution. Mean values from 3 replications with their 0.5 per cent confidence intervals.

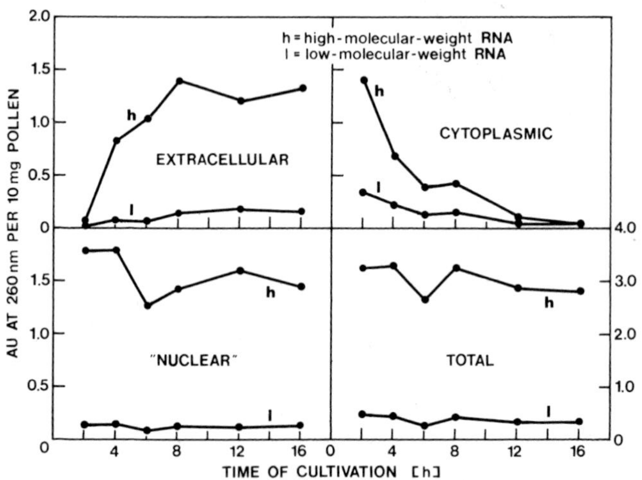

Fig. 4. Changes in proportions of RNA in pollen tube culture. Values were obtained from A 260 nm measurements of pooled fractions of low-molecular-weight (tRNA + 5S) RNA and high-molecular-weight (ribosomal) RNA separated on a MAK column as seen in fig. 2.

The amount of RNA in the medium rises rapidly between 2 and 8 hours after which it remains almost constant (fig. 4). There is a corresponding decrease in pollen tube cytoplasmic RNA which is very low at 12 hours and practically absent after 16 hours of cultivation. This loss of RNA may be the reason for the observed cessation of the growth. On the other hand, the level of "nuclear" RNA shows no great change and at the end of the experiment, it is only slightly decreased. Even smaller changes are seen as regards the total RNA in pollen tube culture. It is of interest that a decrease in all classes of RNA most apparent in the case of high-molecular-weight "nuclear" RNA coincides with the depression of growth observed between 4 and 6 hours. The reason for this depression is unknown, but as it mainly concerns the "nuclear" RNA it can be related to pollen tube mitosis. On the whole, the course of changes in high-molecular-weight RNA and low-molecular-weight RNA shows a similar pattern.

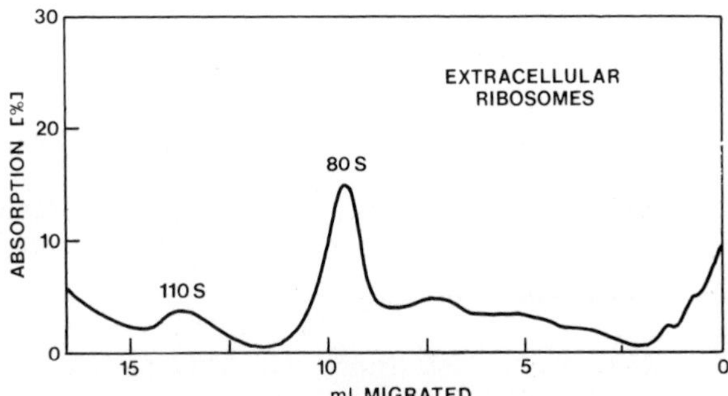

Fig. 5. Sucrose gradient sedimentation analysis of ribosomes isolated from the cultivation medium after 4 hours of pollen germination. The ribosomal pellet was resuspended in buffer containing: Tris-HCl, pH 7.6, 10 mM; KCl, 60 mM; magnesium acetate, 12 mM; mercaptoethanol, 7 mM. The suspension was layered over a linear gradient of 5 to 20% (w/w) sucrose (16 ml) in the same buffer and centrifuged for 5 hours at 25,000 rpm in Beckman SW-27.1 rotor at 2°.

In further work evidence was obtained that the rRNA is released as ribonucleoprotein. An important amount of extracellular ribosomes with sedimentation coefficients of 80S and 110S, corresponding to the content of rRNA determined by MAK chromatography, was found after only 4 hours of pollen germination (fig. 5). The continuation of the growth of the pollen tubes and the great difference in the diminution of endogenous cytoplasmic and "nuclear" RNA exclude the possibility that the ribosomes enter the medium through the bursting of the tubes. This was confirmed by the microscopical examination which showed that there were no burst tubes present in the culture. The growing tips of pollen tubes contain an abundance of vesicles rich in RNA[6]. These vesicles are reported to coalesce frequently with the outer cap of the tip contributing their contents to the cap compartments. In the process in which the relatively thin non-compartmented wall of the subapical region is formed from the cap, this contents may be released from pollen tubes.

Whether the released ribosomes retain their protein-synthesizing activity remains to be determined. The release of tRNA reported here and the rapid movement of amino acids from pollen tubes[4] together with the occurrence of a new protein component in the medium of pollen tube culture[1] suggest this possibility. The importance of extracellular RNA in enzyme synthesis would open a new approach to the investigation of the regulation of pollen tube growth in the pistil.

References

1. Tupý, J., 1963, in: Genetics To-day 1 (Pergamon Press, Oxford) p. 212.
2. Stanley, R.G. and Linskens, H.F., 1965, Physiol. Plant. 18, 47.
3. Mäkinen, Y. and Brewbaker, J.L., 1967, Physiol. Plant. 20, 477.
4. Linskens, H.F. and Schrauwen, J., 1969, Acta Bot. Neerl. 18, 605.
5. Petrů, E., Hrabětová, E. and Tupý, J., 1964, Biol. Plant. 6, 68.
6. Rosen, W.G. and Gawlik, S.R., 1966, Protoplasma 61, 181.

Fertilization in Higher Plants, ed. H.F. Linskens.

ENZYMATIC ACTIVITY OF POLLEN OF OENOTHERA MISSOURIENSIS BEFORE AND DURING GERMINATION IN VITRO

B. Bris
Université des Sciences de Lille
Laboratoire de
Cytogénétique et d'Ecologie
Villeneuve D'Ascq

INTRODUCTION

Oenothera missouriensis is an autosterile plant whose incompatibility is determined gametophytically. On the incompatible stigma the pollen germinates, but the growth of the pollen tube is blocked in the upper layers of the style.

Biosynthesis at the level of the pollen tube during growth involves intense metabolic activity. Several enzyme systems have been studied, among which those that are involved either in the development of pollen tube material or those involved in bioenergetic processes.

A first step has been devoted to the study of the material *in vitro*. A technique for germination on culture medium has been designed in order to show enzyme activity during growth of the pollen tube.

The material used belongs to three distinct genetic clones. They are:

	Plant	Pollen
clone S1	S1S1	entirely S1
clone Bb	S1S2	S1 + S2
clone Bg	S3S4	S3 + S4

The analyses were carried out on fresh material, pollen stored at -20°C and pollen germinated on nutrient medium.

The following enzymes have been studied: glycan hydrolases and acid and alkaline phosphatases.

RESULTS

a) Glycan hydrolases:

Specific activity of non-germinated pollen

1. Enzyme extract before lyophilization

	S1	Bb	Bg
α-Gal	46	29.7	38
β-Gal	180	408.2	200
α-Man	25	25.1	22
N-actyl-Glc	430	228	310
N-actyl-Gal	180	114	170

S1 (277.5/ml)   Bb (437/ml)   Bg (370/ml)

2. After lyophilization and storage at -20°C

	S1	Bb	Bg
α-Gal	46	28	31
β-Gal	200	406	234
α-Man	20	18	32
N-actyl-Glc	430	70	248
N-actyl-Gal	184	42	142

Evolution of enzyme activity as a function of germination time
(determined on genotype S1 only)

	30 min	1 h	2 h	3 h	4 h
α-Man	40	46	130	111	125
α-Gal	62	84	104	148	147
β-Gal	195	219	227	270	320
N-acetyl-Glc	439	463	472	506	554
N-acetyl-Gal	186	244	254	280	305

b) Phosphatase activities: study on genotype S1 only

Specific activity for non-germinated pollen

Pollen extract: 24.8

Lyophilized and frozen pollen extract: 18

Evolution of enzyme activity during pollen tube growth

Time	0	30 min	1 h	2 h	3 h	4 h
Specific activity	25	29	23	19	17	15

CONCLUSION

The results obtained with mixed populations of pollen (Plants S1S2 or S3S4) do not permit us to know whether there exists a relation between the amount of enzymes studied and the action of each allele, or possibly their mutual action.

For pollen carrying only a single defined allele (plant S1S1), pollen tube growth is accompanied by a steady increase in enzyme activity related to the activation of the metabolism in progress; nevertheless, the activity of the acid phosphatases decreases. These results are in accord with changes observed in <u>Petunia hybrida</u> (Linskens, 1969).

The problem posed for the future is to know whether the kinetics of the enzyme activity are modified during the incompatibility reaction.

The technical details of the experiments are given elsewhere.

REFERENCE

Linskens, H.F., Havez, R., Linder, R., Salden, M., Randoux, A., Laniez, D., Coustaut, D., 1969, C. rend. Acad. Sci. (Paris), Sér.D., 209, 1855-1857

Fertilization in Higher Plants, ed. H.F. Linskens.

BRANCHING OF POLLEN TUBES IN SPINACH

H. J. Wilms

Department of Botany
Agricultural University, Wageningen
The Netherlands

1. Introduction

The mature male gametophyte of Angiosperms is still generally thought of as a monosiphonous structure of the pollen grain and pollen tube containing two sperms, preceded by a tube nucleus. The pollen tube is commonly pictured as an unbranched structure, which grows unerringly from the stigma through the style to the ovule. However, branching of the pollen tube has sometimes been observed (for literature see Johnston[1] and Steffen[2]). In spinach Ramanna and Mutsaerts[3] also have observed an unusual behaviour in the growth of pollen tubes. They report that in the style 10-12% of the pollen tubes produce branches; near the micropyle of the ovule the tubes grow like fungus mycelium and produce haustoria-like structures.

In this article pollen tube branching in spinach has been investigated at light-microscopical level.

2. Materials and Methods

The cultivars Heraut (2n=12) and Prévital (2n=12) of spinach, *Spinacia oleracea L.*, were grown in the greenhouse. The female plants were isolated from the males just at the time of flowering, when sex determination is easy. The female plants were hand-pollinated and collected for fixation at ½ hour intervals from 2 to 9 hours, 1 hour intervals from 9 to 50 hours and 24 hours intervals from 72 to 144 hours after pollination.
Pollen tube growth was estimated by U.V.-fluorescence microscopy[4-5]. Fixation was performed in formalin-acetic acid-alcohol 96% (1 : 1 : 18) for at least 24 hours. The female flowers were washed in water and transferred to 5 N sodium hydroxide solution for 5 hours. After rinsing with water and separating the perianth from the ovaries, the pistils were stained with 2% water blue in 20% K_3PO_4. The stained pistils were observed through a microscope with ultraviolet illumination of a wavelength of about 356 mμ. Under these conditions the

callose, highly present in pollen tubes, exhibited a bright yellow-green fluorescence, contrasting markedly with the dark background. The pollen tubes were outlined by the callose and callose plugs.

3. Results

The rate of pollen tube growth decreases as the tubes elongate and approach the micropyle. Generally the tubes reach the micropyle after 6-7 hours. No or less branching is observed till this time. If branching occurs, it is at the beginning of the tube growth near the stigma papillae. At about 9 hours after pollination ingrowth in the nucellus tissue takes place. From 10-12 hours after pollination branching starts in the micropyle, between and around the inner and outer integuments (fig. 1). The growing process leading to fertilization is normal till the first tube reaches the embryosac (10-12 hours after pollination). Whereas many tubes enter the micropyle of an ovule, only a few penetrate into the nucellus to the embryosac (fig. 2). From the time fertilization takes place no further ingrowth of new tubes into the nucellus is observed. Branching of the present tubes in the nucellus can be seen. Some tubes in the micropyle end their growth, others start to branch. The branching proceeds either in a rather uniform way (fig. 3), or with one main tube and a number of short-branches (fig. 4).

In the stigmata and styles no differences in wall structure of the tubes is observed. However, in and around the micropyle of ovaries, fixed after 120 and 144 hours after pollination, the fluorescence of the branching tubes is different. The endgrowth of pollen tubes with protrusions and branches shows a general weak fluorescence of the total wall and a strong fluorescence of some parts of the wall (fig. 5).

4. Discussion

The female flower of spinach is monocarpous and only one ovule must be fertilized. So one fertile male gametophyte can result in an effective double

---

Fig. 1. The pistil of spinach 24 hours after pollination.
Ingrowth in the nucellus (nuc) has taken place and one or two tubes have reached the embryosac (es). In the micropyle, between the inner and outer integument (oi) as between the inner integument (ii) and the nucellus branching can be osverved.

Fig. 2. Ovule 24 hours after pollination. A mass of pollentubes have grown in the micropyle. Only a few have penetrated the nucellus tissue. One tube probably caused ferlilization because of the present plug (pl) at the entrance of the embryosac. Notice in the nucellus a short branching tube (arrow).

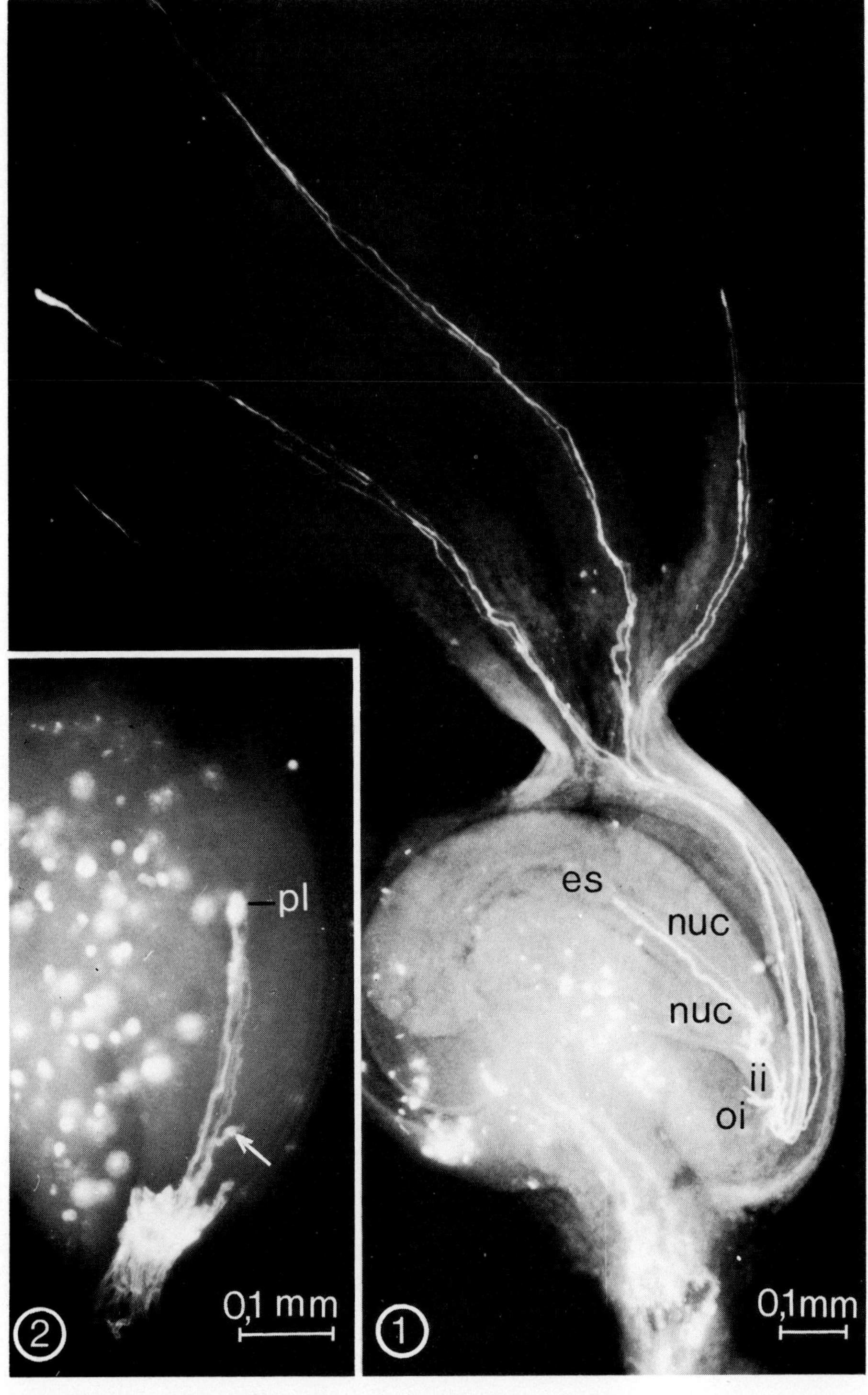
pl
0,1 mm
2
es
nuc
nuc
ii
oi
0,1mm
1

fertilization. Nevertheless a large number of pollen grains germinate and grow to the female gametophyte. Branching of the pollen tubes has been observed occasionally in the beginning of germination on the papillae, but mainly in and around the micropyle and sometimes in the nucellus tissue.

Till a tube reaches the embryosac,penetration of tubes into the nucellus has been possible. After that the nucellus does not allow any further penetration. The tubes in the nucellus that failed to fertilize, seem to be inhibited and some show short branching (arrow, fig. 2). Branching of any importance starts in all cases, when at least one pollen tube has reached the embryosac and probably fertilization has taken place. In similar experiments seed set has been as high as in normal crosses[3].

Branching in and around the micropyle occurs frequently and is complicated.

It has been suggested that the pollen tube may sometimes serve as a haustorial organ, not for its own benefit but for that of the embryosac or embryo[6-7-3]. Ramanna and Mutsaerts[3] also report that branching and penetration of protrusions into integuments, nucellus and other tissue occur, but these statements seem to be incorrect. In the nucellus some short branches appear, but neither in the integuments, nor in any other tissue penetration of tubes has been observed. They all grow between the nucellus surrounding tissues where they ramify and form protrusions. The hypothesis that haustorial-like structures are responsible for the nourishment of the growing embryo is wrong, because no haustorial-like structures are detected in or between the tissues.

Our results indicate that the branching phenomenon in spinach:

1) cannot be ascribed to the male gametophyte only, since branching occurs mainly from the time of fertilization. Initiation of branching in some growing tubes is latent and has to be induced. This induction can be caused by changes in factors, which the male gametophytes do not produce.

2) can be the result of the female tissue after an effective fertilization.

The female tissue produces a "hormone" which diffuses and causes an disturbed growth hormone metabolism. The vegetative nuclei of the tubes, responsible for growth direction, do not direct the growth anymore. However, the synthesis of pollen tube walls is not ended, so protrusions and branches appear.

In literature some examples of hormonal influence on the behaviour of the pollen tubes have been reported. A hormone, which caused a slight increase in

---

Fig. 3. Ovule 24 hours after pollination with branching pollen tubes. This branching proceeds in a rather uniform way.

Fig. 4. Short branching pollen tube in the micropyle 24 hours after pollination.

Fig. 5. Protrusions of the pollen tube 144 hours after pollination. General weak fluorescence of the total tube wall, but strong fluorescence of some wall parts (arrow).

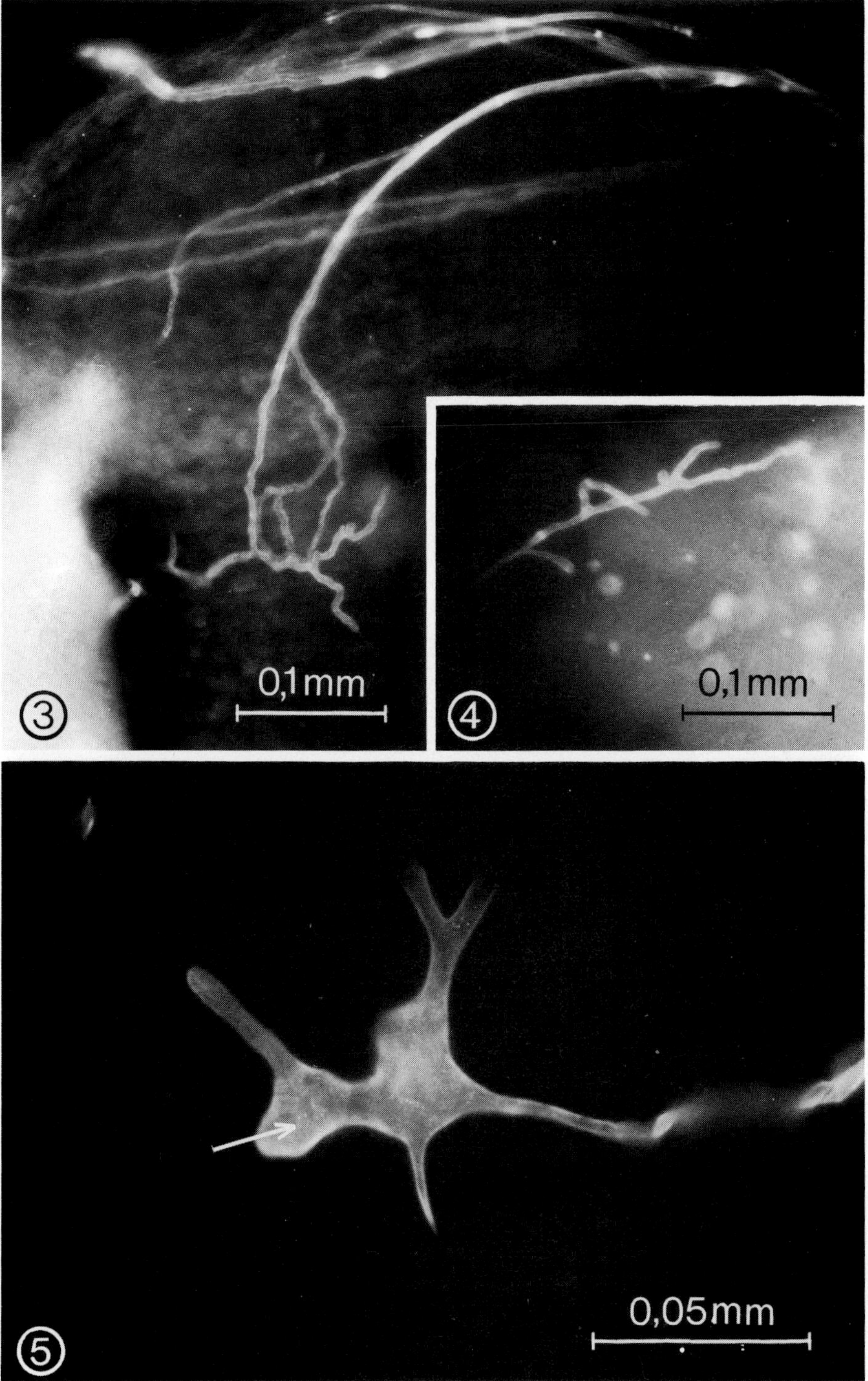
0,1 mm
③
0,1 mm
④
0,05 mm
⑤

branching of pine pollen tubes *in vitro*, has been indoleacetic acid (IAA)[8]. The ball formation in and around the micropyle in spinach after the time of fertilization is nearly similar to the incompatible pollen tube growth in the ovule of *Tulipa*[9]. In interspecific *Datura* crosses embryo inhibition by ovular tumors was caused by IAA[10].

If these statements are correct branching of pollen tubes in spinach can be seen as a postfertilization process. Investigations on the influence of growth hormones on the branching phenomenon may support this theory.

5. References

1. JOHNSTON, G. W., 1959. Phytomorph. 9, 130.
2. STEFFEN, K., 1963. In: Recent advances in the embryology of Angiosperms. P. Maheswari, Ed., 15.
3. RAMANNA, M. S. and MUTSAERTS, M. C. A., 1971. Euphytica 20, 145.
4. LINSKENS, H. F. and ESSER, K., 1957. Naturwiss. 44, 16.
5. MARTIN, F. W., 1959. Stain Technol. 34, 125.
6. LONGO, B., 1903. Ann. di Bot. 1, 71.
7. COOPER, D. C., 1949. Amer. J. Bot. 36, 348.
8. SZIKLAI, O. and HO, R. H., 1970. IUFRO, Finland.
9. KHO, Y. O. and BAËR, J., 1970. Zeiss Inform. 18, 54.
10. BLAKESLEE and collaborators, 1969. In: Fertilization 2, 241.

Fertilization in Higher Plants, ed. H.F. Linskens.

RADIATION INDUCED STIMULATION OF ELONGATION OF PINE POLLEN TUBES.

L.Zelles

Institut für Strahlenbotanik der Gesellschaft für Strahlen- und Umweltforschung. Hannover,FRG.

1. INTRODUCTION

The pollen grain is one of the best experimental objects to examine the effects of ultraviolet and ionising radiations. The inhibition of germination and the tube elongation by high doses have been frequently studied[2,3,6,7]. Effects causes by low doses of x-rays and uv-light, termed as radiation-induced stimulation[2,9], supplied longterm conflicting evidence. The great number of recent papers dealing with these phenomenon justify the interest for this effect.

Pollen grains of Pseudotsuga[5] and Pinus[4] irradiated with moderate and low doses of x- and γ-rays develop significantly longer tubes than the unirradiated control. Similar effects are observed with moderate doses of uv-light[9]. The mechanism or mechanisms by which low radiation doses give rise to increased tube elongation is not known. An understanding of the mechanism or mechanisms would permit the interpretation of the irregularities as well as help to elucidate the effect of irradiation in living cells.

2. PHENOTYPE OF STIMULATION

To study the way in which stimulated tube elongation occurs by irradiation, 1 mg of pollen grains (stored under vacuum in ampules at -18° C) is placed on a watch-glass in 1 ml of a 0,03% sterilized sucrose solution. The grains, being lighter than water due to their wings, float as a monolayer at the surface. By these means one of the two nuclei is facing the source of energy. The dehydrated pollen grains have taken up to 3 minutes before irradiation. The x-rays were supplied from an x-ray-tube (30 KV and 10 mA) with a Beryllium window, the uv-light (270-300 nm) is emitted by a mercury arc lamp with a reflection filter. Afterwards the cultures were illuminated continuously with 1000 Lx with a florescence lamp[9] for 3 days. For the evaluation of the experiment, 3 drops of each sample were distributed on a slide. 50 tubes were measured in each drop and classified into groups of increasing size. Each group represents a range of 40 μ.

The tube length is of normal distribution. Most of the unirradiated grains (62%) showed a tube length of 80-160 μ, 18% had shorter tubes and 20% longer tubes (see table 1). X-Ray treatment modifies this pattern of distribution. Most of the pollen irradiated with low doses are stimulated, whereas high dose irradiation inhibits the tube elongation. The mean value of the tube length increases after irradiation with low doses and decrease with high doses.

Table 1

Distribution of the length of pollen tubes after irradiation with different doses of x-rays.

radiation doses (R)	percent of pollen tubes						
	group						
	1	2	3	4	5	6	7
	µm						
	1-40	40-80	80-120	120-160	160-200	200-240	240-280
0	8±3	10±5	32±10	30±2	10±3	10±4	0
100	7±2	12±6	20±5	20±3	34±10	7±5	0
300	2±2	2±2	11±7	15±10	20±5	30±7	20±8
20000	12±15	50±9	32±2	6±3	0	0	0
40000	41±17	59±33	0	0	0	0	0

To characterise the differences between two treatments, the mean value of each group (i.e. 1 group 20 µ, 2 group 60 µ a.s.o.) is multiplied by the number of tubes belonging to this group, giving the summed length (SL).

3. PARAMETER INFLUENCING THE STIMULATION

The SL-value of pollen treated with 15 µg actinomycin-D is only 50% of the value of untretated pollen. The processes controlling tube elongation can be separated into a actinomycin-D sensitive and insensitive components. Which of the two components can be stimulated with low doses of x-rays and uv-light? Pollen irradiated by stimulating x-ray doses as well as uv-intensities, do not develop longer tubes in the germination solution containing 15 µg actinomycin-D than do the unirradiated pollen (table 2).

Table 2

Stimulation and actinomycin-D treatment

irradiated with	percent of control (SL)	
	treated with 15 µg actinomycin-D	not treated with actinomycin-D
0	46±3	100±2
x-rays 300 R	45±4	111±5
uv-light $2,4 \times 10^5$ erg/cm^2	49±4	117±4

The tube elongation of Pinus pollen is light-indifferent. After irradiation with stimulating (300 R) and with inhibiting (3000 R) doses of x-rays, the SL-value and the number of grains with tubes longer than 200 µ (actinomycin-D sensitive) are independent of the illumination conditions.

Pollen irradiated with $2{,}4\times10^{5}$ erg/cm^{2} uv-light and germinated in the light develop longer tubes. Germination in the darkness decreases the SL-value and the number of actinomycin-D sensitive pollen. Even pollen irradiated with inhibiting doses ($3{,}6\times10^{6}$ erg/cm^{2}) develop shorter tubes germinating in the dark than in the light. The mechanism of uv-stimulation which is probably of a repair kind, differs from that of x-ray stimulation.

Table 3

Tube length (SL) and number of pollen grains with tubes longer than 200 µ (Numb.) in relation to illumination during germination.

irradiation		percent of control			
		germination in light		germination in darkness	
		SL	Numb.	SL	Numb.
0		100 ± 3	100 ± 3	100 ± 4	100 ± 4
x-rays	300 R	116 ± 2	133 ± 10	112 ± 4	123 ± 10
	3000 R	82 ± 10	70 ± 12	88 ± 10	71 ± 13
uv-light	$2{,}4\times10^{5}$ $\frac{erg}{cm^{2}}$	112 ± 4	160 ± 18	79 ± 2	45 ± 15
	$3{,}6\times10^{6}$ "	70 ± 3	50 ± 20	55 ± 4	16 ± 6

Do the pollen need light during the whole germination time to display stimulation? Samples of control and stimulated pollen were transferred from dark to light at different stages of germination (figure 1). For stimulation, pollen tubes require visible light in the second part of tube elongation. The stimulated pollen

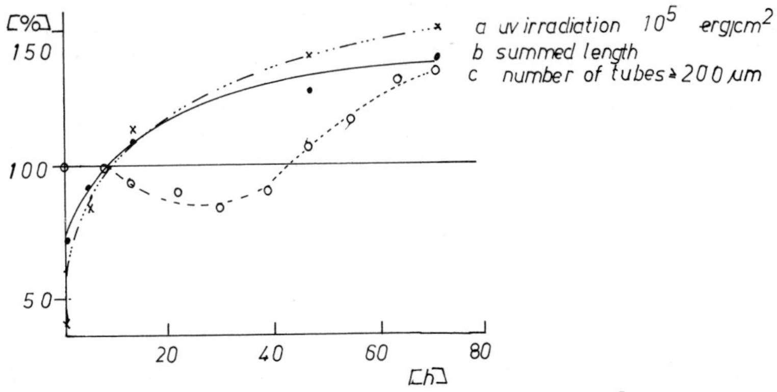

Fig. 1. Ratio between uv-light stimulated ($2{,}4\times10^{5}$ erg/cm^{2}) and unirradiated pollen; a) in different phases of tube development (SL-value), b) in correlation to the length of illumination (SL-value), c) in connection with the length of illumination (number of pollen with tubes longer than 200 µ).

grains also develop their tubes faster in the second part of tube development than do the unirradiated control (figure 1).

Radiation may be applied to test the physiological systems. Irradiation may be given at a high rate, with the exposure lasting only a short time, or it may be given at low rates. If the result is due to the cumulative action, we might expect to find that the effect of given doses is dependent on the dose-rate and uv-intensity, respectively. The natural explanation is that the organism is capable of recovery from the effect of radiation, providid the dose is applied sufficiently slowly[1].

Pollen were irradiated with the same dose, but with different dose-rates (fig. 2). With a low dose-rate (0.5 R/s) only small amounts of energy (50R) induced tube elongation. The tubes of grains irradiated with a dose-rate 10 times higher (5 R/s), are significantly longer in the ranges between 200-600 R. Stimulated tube length with the broadest dose range (100-1800 R) can be reached with moderately intensive (50 R/s) x-ray irradiation. A higher dose-rate (100 R/s) does not stimulate the tube elongation.

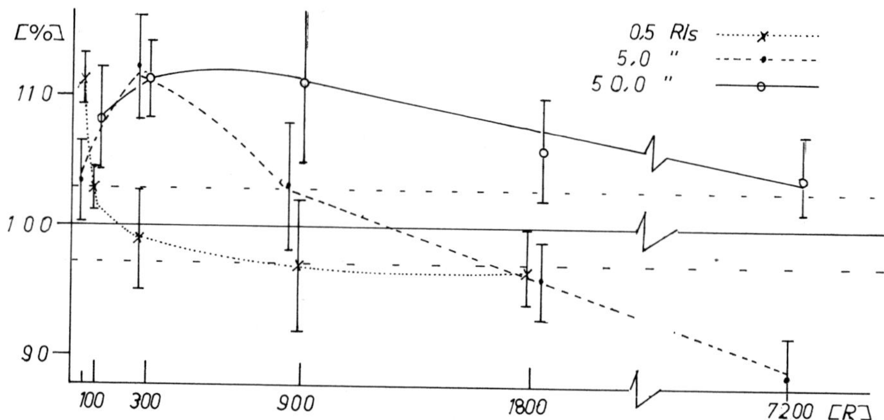

Fig. 2. X-ray-stimulation in dependence of the delivered dose-rates.

The same effect has been found with uv-irradiation. Unattenuated uv-light (100% in figure 3) induces stimulation only at an energy level of 10^5 erg/cm^2. Pollen irradiated with higher uv-doses display an effect of inhibition. The uv-light has been attenuated by filtering so that 33% more time is needed to deliver the same dose. Pollen irradiated in this way do not elongate tubes significantly longer nor significantly shorter than the control. The intensity was diminished down to 3% of the unfiltered uv-light (we now need 30 times more time for the transmission of the same dose). The tubes are significantly longer than the unirradiated control.

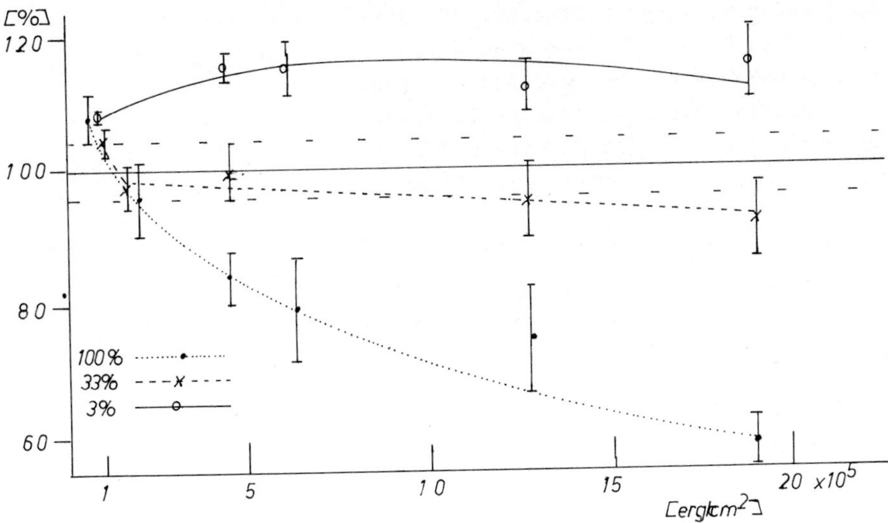

Fig.3. Uv-light stimulation in dependence of intensity.

4. DISCUSSION

The actinomycin-D sensitivity suggests that one of the nuclei must be involved with the stimulation effect. The activity of the generative nucleus with the stimulation effect. The activity of the generative nucleus is limited to the second part of tube elongation observed by Young and Stanley[8]. The irradiation causing tube elongation is also bound to this section of tube elongation.

The experiments with actinomycin-D show that the stimulation effect is connected with the newly synthetized RNA. The stimulation effect is surely not due to a primary product of irradiation. It suggests more a repair character supported by dose-rate and light-dependence. It can be assumed that some kind of repair products (not for DNA) can cause growth-stimulation. Its reproducibility is, to a great extent, due to a correct choice of dose-rates.

5. REFERENCES

1. Bacq, Z.M and Alexander, P., 1961, Fundamentals of Radiobiology (Pergamon Press, Oxford, London, New-york, Paris).
2. Brewbaker, J.L. and Emery, G.C., 1962, Rad.Bot., 1, 101.
3. Brewbaker, J.L., Espiritu, L. and Majumder, S.K., 1965, Rad.Bot., 5, 493.

4. Fendrik,J. and Zelles,L.,1971,Stimulation Newsletter,3,20.
5. Livingstone,G.K. and Stettler,R.F.,1971Rad.Bot.,13,65.
6. Pfahler,P.L.,1971,Rad.Bot.,11,233.
7. Pfahler,P.L.,1973,Rad.Bot.,13,13.
8. Young,L.T.C. and Stanley,R.G., 1963, The Nucleus,1,63.
9. Zelles,L. and Ernst,D., 1973,Biophysik,9,132.

Fertilization in Higher Plants, ed. H.F. Linskens.

TRANSMITTING TISSUE AND POLLEN TUBE GROWTH

M. Kroh and J.P.F.G. Helsper
Department of Botany
University of Nijmegen

1. Introduction

In styles with a transmitting tissue, pollen tubes grow within the intercellular substance of this tissue to the ovary[1-5]. In Petunia this material appears to be a mixture of mainly acidic carbohydrates[6]. From electron microscopical studies of pollinated styles it is assumed that the pollen tubes break down enzymatically the intercellular material and utilize it for growth[2,3]. First evidence for a possible flow of material from the style into the pollen tubes was achieved by Linskens and Esser[7] by means of labeling experiments. The present paper deals with preliminary studies on the utilization of carbohydrate material from intercellular substance of the transmitting tissue of Petunia for the synthesis of pollen tube wall.

2. Materials and Methods

Flowers from Petunia hybrida plants, grown under greenhouse conditions were used. Styles were labeled with 25 μC/style of myo-inositol-2-^{3}H (^{3}H-MI) or D-glucose-1-^{14}C (^{14}C-Glu) as described before[8]. Myo-inositol readily converts to uronosyl-, and pentosyl-units of pectic substances and pistil secretion products[9]. Label from ^{3}H-MI and ^{3}H- or ^{14}C-Glu is also readily incorporated into carbohydrate material of the intercellular substance of the transmitting tissue of Petunia styles. It can be extracted with water as electronmicroscopical and biochemical studies have shown[6,8]. The methods used for extraction of the transmitting tissue and fractionation of the water extracts on a column of Sephadex G-15 was the same as described earlier[6] with the exception that the dissected transmitting tissue was extracted with cold (3-5°C) in place of warm (39°C) water. Following fractionation of the water extract on Sephadex G-15 the bulk of label and carbohydrates is present in one peak (G-15-III) of low molecular weight material[6]. Pollen stored at -10°C were germinated "in vitro" in a medium of 10% sucrose and 0.01% boric acid (Suc-B) or in Dickinson's pentaerythritol-medium (D-P)[10]. Three series were germinated in 20 ml of Suc-B according to Schrauwen and Linskens[11]. To this medium was added unfractionated labeled water extract (~180.000 cpm) from transmitting tissue dissected from styles labeled with ^{3}H-MI. II. In 25 ml erlenmeyer flasks were added 7.5 mg of pollen, 1.0 ml Suc-B-medium and labeled fraction G-15-III (~7.200 cpm/flask) from the water extract of transmitting tissue from styles labeled with ^{3}H-MI. III. In 25 ml erlenmeyer flasks were added 15 mg of pollen, 2.0 ml Suc-B or D-P-medium and- ^{14}C-labeled material (~50.000 cpm) eluted from the origin and the region of pre-galactose of thin layer chromatograms of fraction G-15-III obtained from the transmitting tissue of styles labeled with ^{14}C-glucose. Earlier experiments had indicated that in styles labeled with ^{3}H- and ^{14}C-glucose, 50-60%, in styles labeled with ^{3}H-MI, 60-80% of the label from fraction G-15-III stayed at the origin and between origin and the region corresponding to galactose after thin layer chromatography[6]. To determine the distribution of tritium and ^{14}C-label in pollen tubes after germination "in vitro", samples incubated for 8 hours (I), 7 hours (II) and 6 hours (III) were ground in 0.1 M phosphate buffer (pH 7.2) (I and II), respectively in 80% ethanol (ETOH) (III). By washing the tube wall material in buffer, respectively ETOH and buffer it was separated into a buffer resp. buffer/ETOH -soluble and -insoluble fraction. The latter, corresponding to wall material, was further treated with pectinase to yield a pectinase-soluble fraction and a pectinase-insoluble residue. Monosaccharide fragments of the water-extract of the intercellular material, of fraction G-15-III, and of the pectinase-soluble fractions of pollen tube walls were separated on ion exchange and paper- or thin layer chromatography and the areas corresponding to location of known sugars as well as the origin and the area between origin and galactose, resp. galacturonic acid eluted as described before[6]. Labeled material of eluted areas was counted in a Packard liquid scintillation spectrometer.

3. Results and Discussion

The intercellular material of the transmitting tissue of styles can be looked at as substrate for pollen tubes growing "in vivo". Because the carbohydrate material of the intercellular substance is easily labeled and extracted by water, it was possible to check whether pollen germinating "in vitro" in the presence of labeled carbohydrate that originates from water-extract of the transmitting tissue is able to take up some of this label and incorporate it into tube wall carbohydrates. Pollen was germinated in the presence of I. tritiated water-extract, II. tritiated fraction G-15-III that contains the bulk of label and carbohydrate of the water-extract, and III. ^{14}C-labeled carbohydrate material eluted from the origin of chromatographed fraction G-15-III. The origin of the different sources of label is given in Figure 1; their carbo-

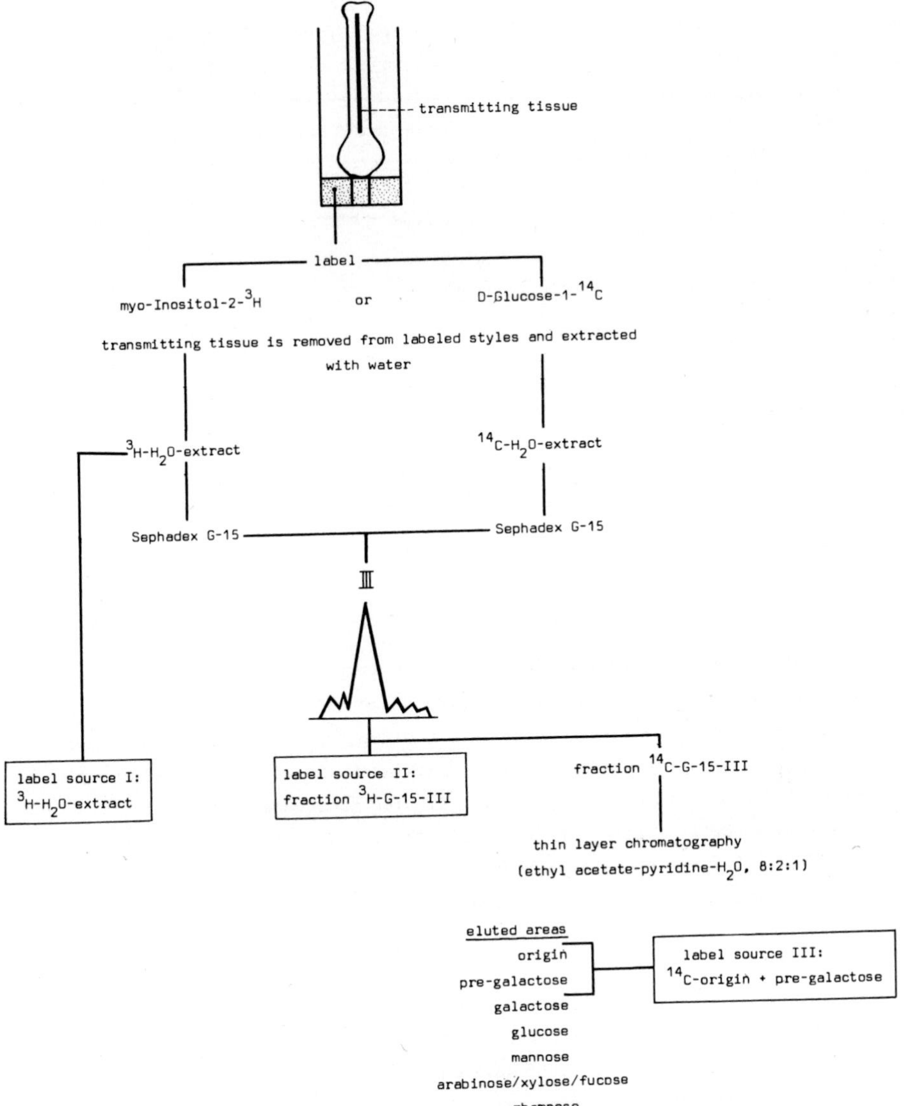

Fig. 1. Origin of the three label sources ^{3}H-H_2O-extract (I), ^{3}H-G-15-III (II), and ^{14}C-origin + pre-galactose (III) used for labeling pollen germinating "in vitro"

hydrate composition, so far as it is known from preceding studies, is listed in Table 1. Fraction G-15-III contains 60% to 80% of the total radioactivity

label source	carbohydrate compounds
^{3}H-H_2O-extract	material of molecular weight ≥ 1500 oligosaccharides + monosaccharides (= G-15-III)
fraction ^{3}H-G-15-III	oligosaccharides of uronic acid nature (= origin + pre-galactose-material) monosaccharides (hexoses, pentoses, uronic acids)
^{14}C-origin + pre-galactose-material	olisaccharides of uronic acid nature with glucuronic acid predominating over galacturonic acid

Table 1. Carbohydrate compounds present in the different label sources

and total carbohydrate present in the water-extract[6]. As revealed by chromatography 60% of this radioactivity is present in oligosaccharides of uronic acid nature that are found at the origin and the region of pre-galactose of the chromatograms[6]. The monosaccharides of fraction G-15-III are possibly in part products of autohydrolysis of the intercellular substance during the extraction procedure, in part originating from cells destroyed during the excision procedure of the transmitting tissue. Table 2 shows the uptake of label from the different sources and its distribution into different fractions of pollen. With all label sources the uptake of label by germinating pollen appears to be low. However, it is striking that more label is taken up from fraction G-15-III and from the oligosaccharide material eluted from the origin and the region of pre-galactose than from the water-extract. If the germination percentages and pollen tube lengths in these media would have equalled that in the medium with labeled water-extract, the percentage of uptake would increase from 3 to 9% for the medium with labeled fraction G-15-III. For the medium containing the label from origin + pre-galactose the percentage would increase from 5% to 22%, respectively 27%. Pollen germinated in Dickinson's pentaerythritol-medium lacks any metabolizable source of carbohydrate. In this medium a possible competing influence of additional carbohydrates on the uptake of label is eliminated. The percentage of label bound to tube wall material is higher with pollen that has been labeled with ^{14}C-origin + pre-galactose-material than with ^{3}H-water-extract

exp. series	Source of label added to medium	germination			average tube length in pollen grain diameter	uptake	buffer^{+}/ ETOH-buffer^{++} soluble	buffer^{+}/ ETOH-buffer^{++} insoluble (=wall material)	wall bound radioactivity	
		medium	time hours	%		radioactivity			pectinase soluble	pectinase insoluble
						%	%	%	%	%
I	^{3}H-H_2O-extract	Suc-B	8	72	6	2	46^{+}	54^{+}	73	26
II	fraction ^{3}H-G-15-III	Suc-B	7	47	3	3	46^{+}	54^{+}	70	30
III	^{14}C-origin + pre-galactose-material	Suc-B	6	32	3	5	38^{++}	62^{++}	80	20
		D-P	6	26	3	5	35^{++}	65^{++}	71	29

Table 2. Uptake and distribution of label from different sources into fractions of pollen incubated 6 to 8 hours in a sucrose-boric acid (Su-B)-, resp. Dickinson's pentaerythritol (D-P)-medium.

or ^{3}H-G-15-III. Although the possible influence of the different washing procedures on the percentages found may not be ruled out completely, the differences in the percentage of uptake and incorporation into tube wall material may be caused by the different label sources present in the germination media. Possibly, only the carbohydrate material from origin + pre-galactose corresponds in its composition to intercellular material "in situ", and therefore may be preferentially utilized by germinating pollen. In a medium that contains this carbohydrate material as the only label source, the pollen could utilize this material without being interfered by other labeled carbohydrates. This would then explain the increased uptake and incorporation of label by pollen germinated in the medium with labeled origin + pre-galactose. The experiments, however, have to be repeated by more sophisticated methods before final conclusions can be drawn in this matter.

Pectinase treatment of the insoluble wall material obtained from pollen germinated in the three different media released 70% to 80% of the bound label (Table 2). This corresponds with values found for pectinase-treated tube wall material of Lilium-pollen that had grown through myo-inositol-U^{14}C labeled styles[12].

The distribution of label among eluted areas from chromatograms corresponding to location of known sugars was determined from the neutral and acidic material of the pectinase-hydrolyzates of tube wall material as well as of the label sources ^{3}H-water-extract and fraction ^{3}H-G-15-III (Table 3). At the label sources, the pectinase-hydrolyzates of tube wall material contained labeled material that stays at the origin and between the origin and the region of galactose, respectively galacturonic acid after chromatography. The amount of label, however, at these areas is reduced as compared to that of the water-extract and fraction G-15-III. The neutral fractions of these two label sources contain at these areas 67%, respectively 64% of the total neutral carbohydrates, while the corresponding values for the neutral fractions of tube wall material are 54% and 22%. The value for the wall material from the label source ^{14}C-origin + pre-galactose is 27%. That means, that the wall material from pollen germinated in the presence of fraction ^{3}H-G-15-III and ^{14}C-origin + pre-galactose contains about 50% less label in this region than the wall material of the water-extract.

As the neutral fractions, the acidic fractions of the wall material show a reduced amount of label present at the origin and the region between origin and pre-galacturonic acid if compared to that of the acidic fractions of the ^{3}H-water-extract and fraction G-15-III (50% vs. 62%; 51% vs. 77%). With pollen germinated in the presence of ^{14}C-origin + pre-galactose 31% of its acidic wall material could be eluted from this region.

position on chromatogram	H_2O-extract (^3H)	tube wall medium: Suc-B label: ^3H-H_2O-extract	G-15-III (^3H)	tube wall medium: Suc-B label: ^3H-G-15-III	tube wall medium: D-P label: ^{14}C-origin + pre-galactose from ^{14}C-G-15-III
neutral material⁺	%	%	%	%	%
origin + pre-galactose	67	53	64	22	27
galactose	8	6	6	10	11
glucose	3	2	5	4	11
mannose	4	3	5	18	6
arabinose/xylose/fucose	14	32	16	43	36
rhamnose	4	4	4	3	9
	100	100	100	100	100
acidic material⁺⁺	%	%	%	%	%
origin + pregalacturonic acid	62	50	77	51	31
galacturonic acid	19	23	6	26	58
glucuronic acid	19	27	17	23	11
	100	100	100	100	100

Table 3. Distribution of label among areas eluted from chromatograms of ^3H-H_2O-extract, ^3H-G-15-III, and of pectinase- hydrolyzates from tube walls of pollen germinated "in vitro" in the presence of ^3H-H_2O-extract, ^3H-G-15-III, and ^{14}C-labeled material eluted from the origin and the pre-galactose-region of chromatographed ^{14}C-G-15-III. Suc-B = Sucrose-Boric Acid, D-P = Dickinson's Pentaerythritol-Medium. +ethyl acetate-pyridine-water, 8:2:1, v/v; ++ethyl acetate-pyridine-acetatic acid-H_2O, 5:5:1:3, v/v, acetone-n-butanol-phosphate buffer (pH = 4,6), 4:2:3, v/v.

Whether the labeled wall-carbohydrates present at the origin and the area between origin and galactose, resp. galacturonic acid consist of acidic oligosaccharides as the carbohydrate material of the label sources eluted from identical places of the chromatograms or of other material, has to be found out. In the first case, a part of this material should have been incorporated into tube wall more or less unchanged.

The label distribution between areas corresponding to known neutral sugars shows for the wall fractions a distinct concentration of label at the area of arabinose/xylose/fucose. The amount of label in this region equals or is higher than the total amount of radioactivity distributed over the hexoses. Just the opposite is true with the label sources. In the ^{3}H-water-extract and fraction ^{3}H-G-15-III the hexoses are labeled more intensively than the pentoses.

Concerning the presence of sugar acids in the wall fractions, an increase in amount of label is observed in the region corresponding to galacturonic acid, if one compares wall material originating from ^{3}H-water-extract, ^{3}H-G-15-III, and ^{14}C- labeled material from origin + pre-galactose. The latter wall material contains about twice as much galacturonic acid as the wall material from the water-extract and fraction G-15-III (58% vs. 23% and 26%).

The studies have shown that pollen, germinating in Dickinson's pentaerythritol-medium in the presence of ^{14}C-labeled acidic oligosaccharide material originating from the intercellular substance, is able to incorporate some of the label into pentosyl- and uronosyl-units of wall pectin. From these results one may conclude that pollen germinating "in vivo" is also able to utilize carbohydrate material from the intercellular substance of the transmitting tissue for the synthesis of the wall material.

It is not yet known, whether germinating pollen resp. pollen tubes break down the acidic oligosaccharides to monosaccharides during the process of incorporation, or whether the material is taken up in part unchanged. If there is a degradation of oligosaccharides it is an open question, whether this takes place outside at the tube wall or within the cytoplasm of the tube. For Lilium, it has been found that a significant portion of polysaccharide material from the stylar exudate enters the tube without undergoing complete degradation. Only in the cytoplasm is it metabolized and utilized for tube wall synthesis[13]. Before the above questions can definitively answered for Petunia, more information about the composition of the intercellular substance is needed.

Acknowledgment

The authors are grateful to Mr. B. Knuiman for his skilful assistance and to Miss J.P.M. Tummers for correcting the English text.

References

1. Schoch-Bodmer, H. and Huber, P. 1947, Vj. Schr. Naturforsch. Ges. Zûrich 92, 43.
2. van der Pluijm, J. and Linskens, H.F. 1966, Der Züchter 36, 220.
3. Kroh, M. and Munting, A.J. 1967, Acta Bot. Neerl. 16, 182.
4. Jensen, W.A. and Fischer, D.P. 1969, Planta (Berl.) 84, 97.
5. Sassen, M.M.A. 1974, Acta Bot. Neerl. 16, 182.
6. Kroh, M. 1973, in: Biogenesis of plant cell wall polysaccharides, ed. F. Loewus (Academic Press, New York) p. 195.
7. Linskens, H.F. and Esser Kl. 1959, Proc. Kon. Ned. Akad. v. Wetensch. 62, 150.
8. Kroh, M. and van Bakel, C.H.J. 1973, Acta Bot. Neerl. 22, 106.
9. Loewus, F. 1969, Ann. N.Y. Acad. Sci. 165, 577.
10. Dickinson, D.B. 1967, Phyiol. Plantarum 20, 118.
11. Schrauwen, J.A.M. and Linskens, H.F. 1967, Acta Bot. Neerl. 16, 177.
12. Kroh, M. et al. 1969, Plant Physiol. 45, 92.
13. Labarca, C. and Loewus, F. 1972, Plant Physiol. 50, 7.

THE FUSION

Fertilization in Higher Plants, ed. H.F. Linskens.

EXPERIMENTAL STUDIES ON POLLEN AND FERTILIZATION

B.M. Johri and K.R. Shivanna

Department of Botany, University of Delhi, Delhi 110007, India

ABSTRACT

At the Department of Botany, University of Delhi, one of the main lines of investigations has been on pollen and fertilization - both descriptive and experimental. Experimental studies on pollen have been conducted on development, germination, storage, and viability. Recent studies on the effect of cycloheximide, an inhibitor of protein synthesis, on cultured pollen grains of *Impatiens balsamina* and *Trigonella foenum-graecum* have indicated that, in some systems, the proteins required for pollen germination and tube growth are already by the time pollen is shed, and those required for gamete formation are synthesized during pollen tube growth. Whereas, in other systems, proteins responsible for all these processes are synthesized only after pollen grains are put in culture medium.

Studies on fertilization have been carried out both in vivo and in vitro using different techniques with the main aim of overcoming sexual-incompability. The technique of intra-ovarian pollination has been standardized, and applied to many members of Papaveraceae. The technique of test-tube fertilization, which involves the culturing of pollen grains and ovules together on a nutrient medium and achieving double fertilization and seed development in test-tube, has been devised and applied in many systems. Extensive studies have been carried out in *Petunia axillaris*, using a modified technique of test-tube fertilization - "placental pollination", and through this technique it has been possible to overcome self-incompatibility.

INTRODUCTION

Since its inception, the Department of Botany, University of Delhi, has taken a leading role in studies on fertilization and seed development in higher plants. Initially, this school devoted its attention largely to the descriptive studies using conventional techniques, and valuable data were obtaines on sporogenesis, embryogenesis, pollination, fertilization, and seed development in a large number of taxa. In the 1950s the scope was extended to experimental aspects also. Until the 1960s experimental studies were confined to pollen physiology, and were carried out with the main aim of understanding the process of meiosis by using the technique of aseptic culture of anthers. By culturing anthers at leptotene-zygotene stage on a medium containing 4 nucleotides of RNA, 2-celled pollen grains were obtained in Allium and Rhoeo. Optimal conditions for pollen storage, pollen germination, and pollen tube growth were also studied in numerous taxa.

During the 1960s experimental studies were further extended to fertlization, and seed development. Investigations both on pollen and fertilization are being continued. In this article some of our recent studies on pollen and fertilization are briefly reviewed. For earlier investigations, the reader is referred to Maheshwari (1950, 1964), Johri and Vasil (1961), Maheswari and Kanta (1964), and Maheshwari and Rangaswamy (1965).

STUDIES ON POLLEN

During the last 2-3 years we have investigated the effect of various chemicals on pollen physiology, both in vitro and in vivo. Effects of 2 non-ionic surfactants, which are commonly used in many biological studies, have been investigated on pollen germination and pollen tube growth in Trigonella foenum-graecum (Shivanna, 1972). Tween 80 (polyoxy-ethylene sorbitan monooleate) had no effect on these processes, whereas Triton X-114 (alkyl phenoxypolyethoxy ethanol) drastically reduced both pollen germination and pollen tube growth at 100 ppm, and totally inhibited pollen germination at 200 ppm (Fig. 1). Morphactin, which has turned out to be the most

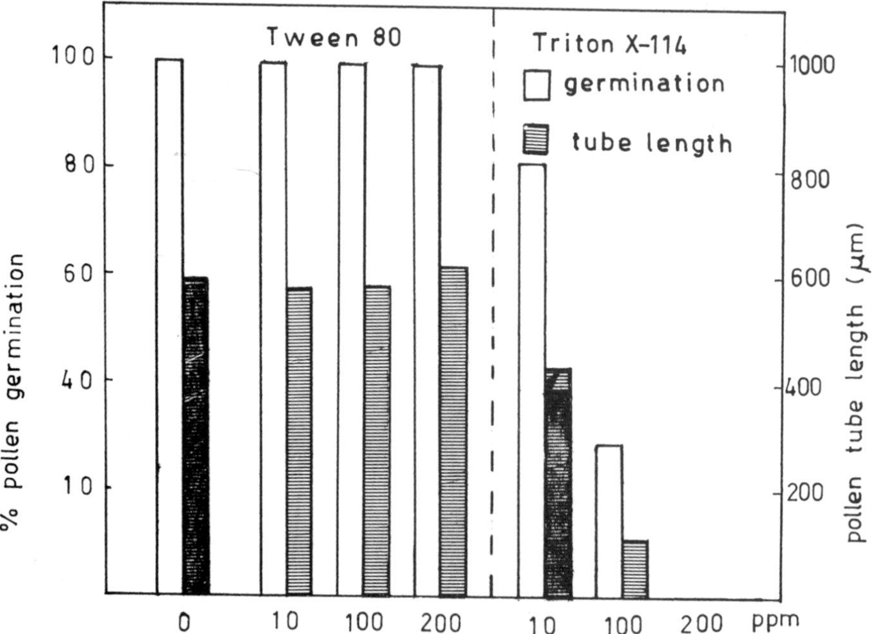

Fig. 1. Effect of Tween 80 and Triton X-114 on pollen germination, and pollen tube growth in Trigonella foenum-graecum. Culture period: 3 hr (from the data given in Shivanna, 1972).

potent chemical in altering the morphogenetic processes in higher plants, has also been tested on the pollen system in Nicotiana rustica (Shivanna, 1973), and Trigonella foenum-graecum (Shivanna unpublished. In cultures pollen grains of both these systems to morphactin chloroflurenol (CFl) inhibited both pollen germination and pollen tube growth (Fig. 2). Post-pollination-effects of this morphactin

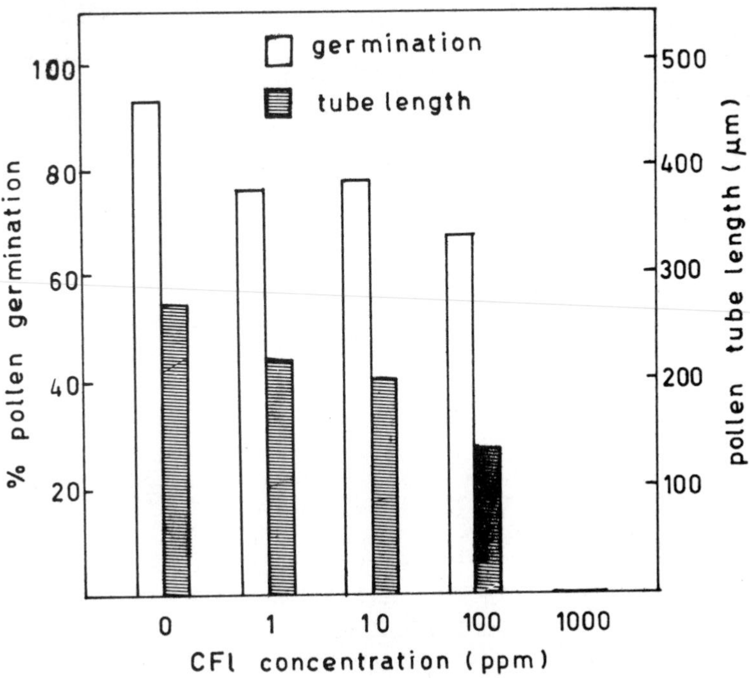

Fig. 2. Effect of chloroflurenol (CFl) on pollen germination, and pollen tube growth in Nicotiana rustica. Culture period: 3 hrs (from the data given in Shivanna, 1973).

were also investigated in details, in vivo, in Nicotiana rustica (Shivanna, 1974). Unlike in cultured pollen grains, morphactin did not affect pollen germination, pollen tube growth, and fertilization even up to 1000 ppm when the plants were sprayed with this chemical. However, it induced abscission of many of the developing fruits, and drastically reduced seed-set at concentrations higher than 1 ppm (Fig. 3).

Inhibitors of protein synthesis such as cycloheximide, puromycin, and chloramphenicol have been demonstrated to reduce pollen germination and pollen tube growth in a few system and, hence, it is suggested that proteins synthesized in the initial stages of pollen germination are required for pollen germination and initial tube growth (Mascarenhas, 1971). We have investigated the effect

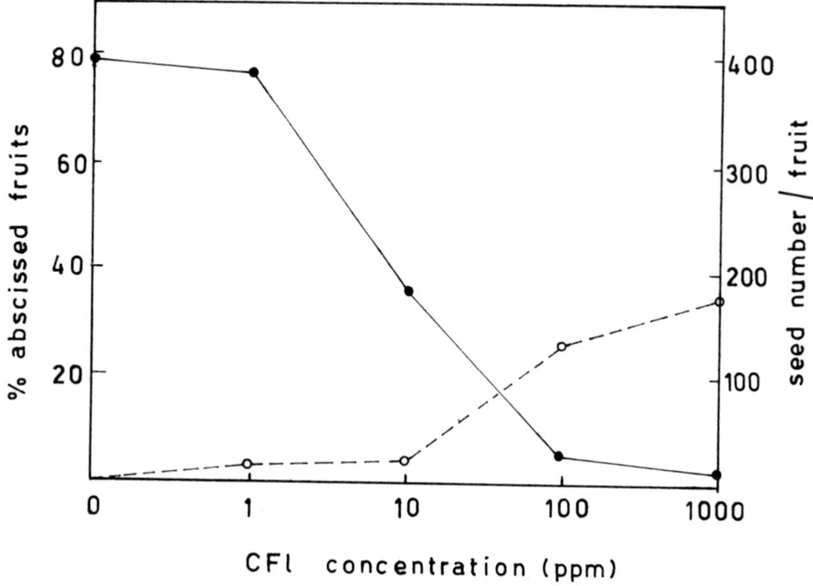

Fig. 3. Effect of CFl on fruit abscission, and seed-set in *Nicotiana rustica* (from the data given in Shivanna, 1974).

of cycloheximide (CH) on pollen germination, pollen tube growth, and gamete formation in cultured pollen grains in two systems - *Impatiens balsamina* (Shivanna et al., 1974a), and *Trigonella foenum-graecum* (Shivanna et al., 1974b). In *Impatiens*, CH did not affect pollen germination and pollen tube growth but, invariably, inhibited gamete formation by arresting the division of the generative cell at metaphase (Fig. 4), at all the concentrations tried, This inhibition was reversible up to 6 hr by replacement of the CH-medium with CH-free medium (Fig. 5). In *Trigonella foenum-graecum*, on the other hand, CH inhibited all these processes, i.e. pollen germination, pollen tube growth, and gamete formation, Although no direct evidences on the mechanism of action of CH in inhibiting gamete formation are available, other studies on the effect of CH on mitosis (Arora et al., 1970; Niitsu et al., 1972) suggest that this inhibition is mediated through inhibition of the synthesis of proteins of the kinetochore substance which takes part in the formation of kinetochore fibres. Inhibition of the formation of kinetochore fibres

Fig. 4. Propionocarmine squash preparations of pollen tubes of *Impatiens* grown for 3 hr on control medium (A), and on cycloheximide (CH) medium (B). Gametes have formed in A, and in B the division of generative cell is arrested at metaphase and 7 chromosomes are clear (after Shivanna et al., 1974).
Fig. 5. Recovery of generative cell division in *Impatiens* after different periods of CH treatment (after Shivanna et al., 1974).

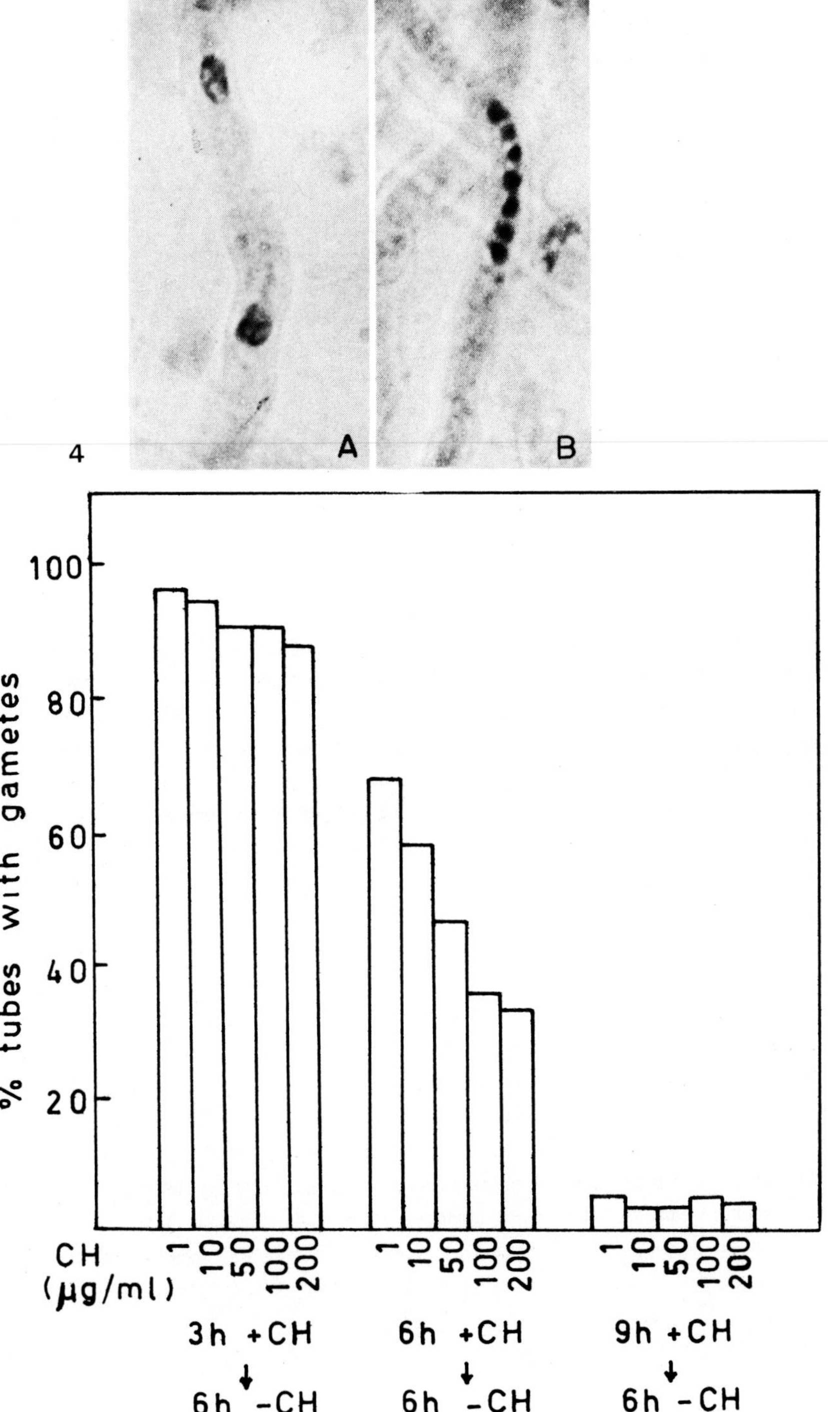
4
A
B
% tubes with gametes
100
80
60
40
20
CH
(μg/ml)
1
10
50
100
200
3h +CH
6h -CH
6h +CH
6h -CH
9h +CH
6h -CH

5

prevents the separation of sister chromatids and, thus, results in the failure of gametic formation.

No information is available on the nature of protein synthesis in generative cell, although ribosomes have been observed in the generative cell of many species (see Mascarenhas, 1971). It appears that, at least, a fraction of protein synthesized in the generative cell during pollen tube growth is concerned with the formation of kinetochore fibres. The results with *Impatiens* and *Trigonella*, in this laboratory, and those of Mascarenhas (1971) with *Tradescantia*, on protein synthesis inhibitors, indicate that different species show variation in the time of synthesis of proteins required for pollen germination, tube growth, and gamete formation. In *Impatiens* the proteins required for the former two processes seem to be already synthesized by the time pollen is shed, and those required for gamete formation are synthesized during pollen tube growth. In *Trigonella* and *Tradescantia*, on the other hand, proteins required for all these processes are synthesized only after the pollen grains are put in the culture medium+ It would be worthwhile to screen more systems on these lines, particularly those having 3-celled pollen grains.

STUDIES ON FERTILIZATION

Studies on fertilization have been carried out both in vivo and in vitro, using different techniques, with the chief objective of overcoming sexual-incompatibility. The technique of intra-ovarian pollination was standardized and successfully applied in many members of Papaveraceae (Kanta and Maheswari, 1963a). In *Petunia axillaris* self-incompatability could be successfully overcome by bud-pollination (Shivanna and Rangaswamy 1969). For this, buds 3 days before anthesis proved to be most suitable. Smearing the stigma of the bud with stigmatic exudate, from a mature pistil, improved seed-set nearly 10-fold both in self- and cross-pollinated buds. Delayed pollination (up to 7 days), as well as pollination with stored pollen (up to 4 wk), were not effective in overcoming self-incompatibility although compatible pollination produced viable seeds in both the treatments.

Under in vitro condition, fertilization has been studied using pistil culture as well as ovule culture. Unpollinated pistils of *Petunia* (Shivanna, 1965), *Nicotina* (Rao, 1965), and *Antirrhinum* (Usha, 1965), which were pollinated in test tubes on a rather simple nutrient medium, have been successfully reared to mature fruits containing viable seeds. Pollen germination, pollen tube growth, fertilization and further growth of the seed and fruit were comparable to those in vivo. Retention of sepals in the cultured pistils significantly improves seed-set. In addition to its utility in fundamental studies on fertilization, and fruit and seed development, pistil cultures may also be useful in overcoming prefertilization barriers, especially precocious abscission of the flower.

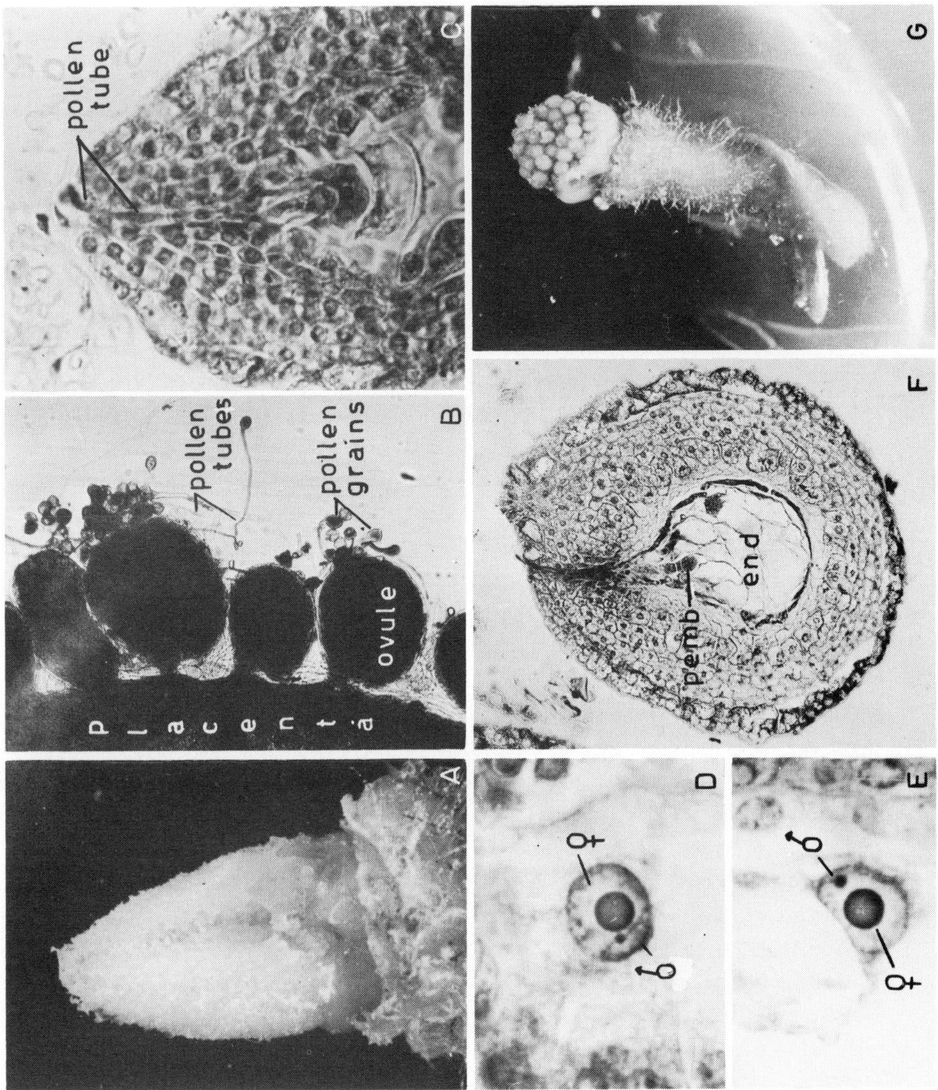

Fig. 6. Placental pollination in Petunia axillaris. A explant consisting of ovule mass borne on placentae, together with a short length of pedicel, made ready for culture. Self-pollen grains are deposited on the ovule mass. B. Free-hand transection of a part of ovule mass, 24 hr after culture, to show pollen germination and profuse of tubes. C. L.s. ovule 24 hr after placental self-pollination to show entry of pollen tube into embryo sac. D,E. L.s. micropylar part of ovule 2 days after placental self-pollination; showing syngamy (D) and triple fusion (E). F. L.s. young seed, 7 days after self-pollination. Note the pro-embryo (pemb) and endosperm (end). G. Placental culture, 3 wk after self-pollination, to show mature seeds (after Rangaswamy and Shivanna, 1971a).

The most effective technique devised and standardized in this laboratory to overcome pre-fertilization barriers has been the technique of test-tube fertilization. The technique involves culturing of unfertilized ovules and pollen grains together on a suitable nutrient medium, and achieving double fertilization and seed development in vitro. Through this technique test-tube seeds have been obtained in many members of Papaveraceae, and a few others (Kanta et al., 1962; Kanta and Maheshwari, 1963b; Rangaswamy and Shivanna, 1969). Extensive studies have been carried out in a self-incompatible taxon Petunia axillaris (Shivanna, 1969). As the original technique of test-tube fertilization was not successful in this system, a modified technique termed "placental pollination" (Rangaswamy and Shivanna, 1967, 1971a) was devised. In placental pollination, instead of isolated ovules or groups of ovules, the entire ovule mass of an ovary, together with a short length of pedicel, was cultured undisturbed and the pollen grains were deposited directly on the ovules and placentae (Fif. 6A). This prevented injury to the ovules, and caused least disturbance to the original arrangement of ovules. Subsequent to placental pollination, pollen grains germinated readily. (Fig. 6B), pollen tubes entered the ovules (Fig. 6C), and double fertilization (Fig. 6D,E) and subsequent development of embryo and endosperm (Fig. 6F) proceeded normally. Mature seeds were obtained in 3 wk after culture (Fig. 6G). Unlike stigmatic pollination in which self-pollination does not work, in placental pollination there was no difference in the details of fertilization and seed development, irrespective of whether the placentae were self- or cross-pollinated.Thus, through placental pollination it was possible to overcome successfully self-incompatibility repeatedly for many generations.

Also, a technique was devised, with Petunia (placental pollination), to treat the ovules of the two placentae of the same ovary differently (Rangaswamy and Shivanna, 1971a; Shivanna, 1971). A slit was made between the placenta, and a piece of sterilized cellophane was inserted in the slit (Fig. 7A). This effectively prevented pollen tubes from one placenta traversing to the other, thus allowing both self- and cross-pollinations to be performed with ovules of the same ovary (Fig. 7B). In addition to reducing sample variation between the treatments to a minimum, this technique facilitates a direct deposition of pollen grains of the desired kind in definitive loci on the ovule mass.

A method for carrying out pollinations at two sites, the stigma and placenta, in the same pistil, was devised (Rangaswamy and Shivanna, 1971b). To perform 2-site pollination to ovary wall covering one of the placentae was carefully removed retaining the stigma and style (Fig. 7C.D), and pollination was carried out on the exposed placenta (Fig. 7E,F). By using technique the influence of stigmatic pollination on placental pollination, and vice versa, particularly concerning self-incompatibility, has been investigated. These studies have demonstrated that selfincompatible reaction is confined to the style, and it has no effect on the

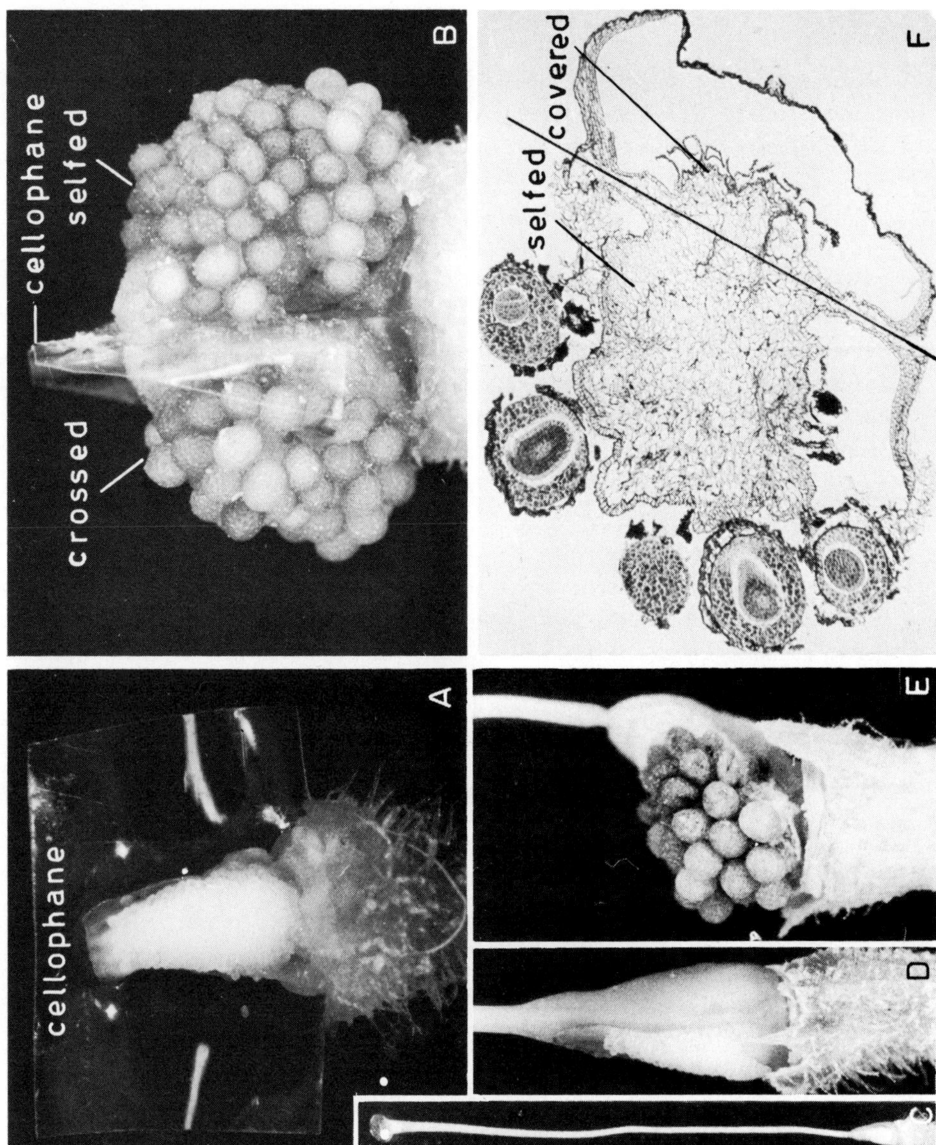

Fig. 7. Differential pollination (A,B), and 2-site pollinations (C,D) in Petunia axillaris. A. Explant after insertion of cellophane between two placentae as seen in face view of one of the placentae. B. Placental culture, 3 wk differential pollination (side view). Seed have developed equally well on selfed as well as on crossed placentae. C. Pistil made ready for 2-site pollinations by exposing the ovules on one of the placentae. D. Magnified view of exposed placenta (left), and covered placenta (right) in profile. E. 3-wk-old culture in which both stigma and exposed placenta were self-pollinated. Note the seeds on exposed placenta. F. F. Transection through the placentae of culture shown in E. Normal seeds have formed on exposed placenta only; all the ovules on the covered placenta have degenerated (after Rangaswamy and Shivanna, 1971a,b).

receptivity of ovules either to compatible or incompatible pollen. Stigmatic self-pollination is incompatible, no matter what treatment is given to the placenta, and placental self-pollination is compatible whether or not stigmatic self-pollination is carried out.

Because of the efficacy of test-tube fertilization in overcoming prefertilization barriers, it has attracted the attention of many other investigators. Zenkteler (1967, 1970) has made significant progress in applying this technique successfully to achieve interspecific and even inter-generic hybridization. Balatková and Tupý (1968) have demonstrated the utility of this technique in achieving fertilization and seed development by applying pollen tubes on the ovule mass (after obtaining pollen germination and pollen tube grwoth on the nutrient medium). The technique of pollination with pollen tubes, in addition to eliminating the problem of pollen germination, if any, on the ovule mass, will facilitate the treatment of only pollen tubes without affecting the ovules. Recently, the technique test-tube fertilization has also been applied to overcome self-incompatibility in *Petunia hybrida* (Niimi, 1970; Wagner and Hess, 1973). Wagner and Hess (1973) have utilized the technique of 2-site pollinations to study the competition between the pollen grains deposited on the stigma, and those deposited on the ovules, in effecting fertilization.

Thus, these techniques of in vitro pollination and fertilization offer great promise not only in overcoming barriers to fertilization, but also in other basic studies concerning fertilization and seed development.

REFERENCES

1. Arora, P.P., Shah, V.C., Rao, S.R.V. and Dass, C.M.S., 1970. Effect of cycloheximide on cell division and macromolecular synthesis in root tip cells of *Vicia faba* L. Indian J. exptl. Biol. 8: 121-125.

2. Balatková, V. and Tupý, J., 1968. Test-tube fertilization in *Nicotiana tabacum* by means of artificial pollen tube culture. Biol. Pl. 10: 266-270.

3. Johri, B.M. and Vasil, I.K., 1961. Physiology of pollen. Bot. Rev. 27: 325-381.

4. Kanta, Kusum and Maheshwari, P. 1963a. Intraovarian pollination in some Papaveraceae. Phytomorphology 13: 215-229.

5. Johri, B.M. and Vasil, I.K., 1963b. Test-tube fertilization in some angiosperms. Phtomorphology 13: 230-237.

6. Johri, B.M., Rangaswamy, N.S. and Maheshwari, P. 1962. Test-tube fertilization in a flowering plant. Nature (Lond.) 194: 1214-1217.

7. Maheshwari, P., 1950. An Introduction to the Embryology of Angiosperms. McGraw Publ. Co., New York.

8. Maheshwari, P. (ed.) 1964. Recent Advances in the Embryology of Angiosperms. International Society of Plant Morphologists, Delhi.

9. Maheshwari, P. and Kanta, Kusum, 1964. Control of fertilization: 187-197. In Linskens, H.F. (ed.) Pollen Physiology and Fertilization. North-Holland Publishing Co., Amsterdam.

10. Maheshwari, P. and Rangaswamy, N.S. 1965. Embryology in relation to genetics: 219-321. In Preston, R.D. (ed.) Advances in Botanical Research. Vol. 2. Academic Press, London.

11. Mascarenhas, J.P., 1971. RNA and protein synthesis during pollen development and the growth: 201-222. In Heslop-Harrison, J. (ed.) Pollen Development and Physiology. Butterworths, London.

12. Niimi, Y., 1970. In vitro fertilization in the self-incompatible plant Petunia hybrida. J. Japanese Soc. hortl Sci. 39: 346-352.

13. Niitsu, T., Hanaoka, A. and Uchiyama, K., 1972. Reinvestigations on the spindle body and related problems. II. Effects of cycloheximide upon the development of kinetochore fibres in the pollen mitosis of Ornithogalum virens in vivo. Cytologia 37: 143-154.

14. Rangaswamy, N.S. and Shivanna, K.R., 1967. Induction of gamete compatibility and seed formation in axenic cultures of a diploid self-incompatible species of Petunia. Nature (Lond.) 216: 937-939.

15. Rangaswamy, N.S. and Shivanna,K.R., 1969. Test-tube fertilization in D Dicranostigma franchetianum (Prain) Fedde. Curr. Sci. 38: 257-259.

16. Rangaswamy, N.S. and Shivanna, K.R., 1971a. Overcoming self-incompatibility in Petunia axillaris (Lam.) B.S.P. II. Placental pollination in vitro. J. Indian bot. Soc. 50A: 286-296.

17. Rangaswamy, N.S. and Shivanna, K.R., 1971b. Overcoming self-incompatibility in Petunia axillaris (Lam.) B.S.P. III. Two-site pollinations in vitro. Phytomorphology 21: 284-289.

18. Rao, P.S., 1965. The in vitro fertilization and seed formation in Nicotiana rustica L. Phyton (Argentina) 22: 165-167.

19. Shivanna, K.R., 1965. In vitro fertilization and seed formation in Petunia violaceae Lindl. Phytomorphology 15: 183-185.

20. Shivanna, K.R., 1969. Elimination of Self-Incompatibility in Petunia axillaris (Lam.) B.S.P. Ph.D. Thesis, Univ. Delhi.

21. Shivanna, K.R., 1971. Overcoming self-incompatibility in Petunia. Differential treatment in vitro of whole placentae. Experientia 27: 864-865.

22. Shivanna, K.R., 1972. Effect of non-ionic surfactants on pollen germination and pollen tube growth. Sci. 41: 609-610.

23. Shivanna, K.R., 1973. Effect of morphactin on pollen germination and pollen tube growth in tobacco (Nicotiana rustica L.). Indian J. exptl. Biol. 11: 257-258.

24. Shivanna, K.R. 1974. Effect of morphactin on fruit and seed development in Nicotiana rustica Linn. Z. Pfl. Physiol. 51: 30-36.

25. Shivanna, K.R. and Rangaswamy, N.S., 1969. Overcoming self-incompatibility in Petunia axillaris (Lam.) B.S.P. I. Delayed pollination, pollination with stored pollen and bud pollination. Phytomorphology 19: 372-380.

26. Shivanna, K.R., Jaiswal, V.S. and Mohan Ram, H.Y., 1974a. Inhibition of gamete formation by cycloheximide in pollen tubes of Impatiens balsamina. Planta (Berl.) 117: 173-177.

27. Shivanna, K.R., Taiswal, V.S. and Mohan Ram, H.Y., 1974b. Effect of cycloheximide on cultured pollen grains of Trigonella foenum-graecum. Plant Science Letters (In Press).

28. Usha, S.V., 1965. In vitro pollination in Antirrhinum majus L. Curr. Sci. 34: 511-513.

29. Wagner, G. and Hess, D., 1973. In vitro-Befruchtungen bei Petunia hybrida. Z. Pfl. Physiol. 69: 262-269.

30. Zenkteler, M., 1967. Test-tube fertilization on ovule in Melandrium album Mill. with pollen grains of several species of Caryophyllaceae family. Experientia. 23: 775.

31. Zenkteler, M., 1970. Test-tube fertilization on ovules in Melandrium album Mill. with pollen grains of Datura stramonium L. Experientia 26: 661-662.

Fertilization in Higher Plants, ed. H.F. Linskens.

CONTRIBUTION TO THE STUDY OF FERTILIZATION IN THE LIVING EMBRYO SAC

O. Erdelská

Institute of Botany
Slovak Academy of Sciences, Bratislava

1. Introduction

Three groups of plants are suitable as a material to investigate the processes taking place in living, intact embryo sacs of angiosperms.

The first group includes such species whose ovules are transparent, such as the Monotropa hypopitys which was Strasburger´s[10] classical object of research and Monotropa uniflora, research object of Shibata[9]. The Cypripedium insigne, Calanthe veitchii and Dendrobium nobile were successfully used by Poddubnaja-Arnoldi[7,8] to investigate megasporogenesis, megagametogenesis, fertilization and embryogenesis. Heitz[6] recommends the Brodiaea uniflora species. Alexandrov[1] worked with ovules of some cereals. The Jasione montana species was used by ourselves[2,3] for the cytologic and microcinematographic study of the first development stages of the endosperm and the embryo.

The second group may include species with embryo sacs that can be fully or partly isolated from the ovule. This group may be represented e.g. by the Galanthus nivalis /Fig.1/.

A special group represente species the embryo sac of which grows out of the micropyle into the placenta or style, prior to fertilization. A suitable object of this group is e.g. Torenia fournieri /Fig.2/. Subramanyam[11] and Haustein[5] present a survey of some other species with the embryo sac growing out of the ovule.

Though the majority of vital observations of embryo sacs was carried out shortly before or shortly after fertilization, the investigation of the fertilization process proper meets methodical difficulties. In our previous work[4] we succeded in recording microcinematographically the process of the fusion of nucleoli of male and female origin in the prophase of the first division of primary endosperm nucleus of Jasione montana. The same phase of fertilization is followed in the case of Galanthus nivalis in this paper.

2. Materials and methods

The flowers of Galanthus nivalis were castrated approximately 24 hours before anthesis and after 24 hours they were pollinated with pollen grains from other flowers. Work was carried out with cut off plants immersed with they stems in water, or with isolated pistils with their ovary base dipped into an agar medium / 1% agar with 5% sucrose/ in a small covered vessels. The maximum of the pollen tubes grew into the ovules approximately 24 - 36 hours after pollination at a temperature of 25 C. The ovules were released from the placenta into a drop of silicone fluid / Silicone fluid MS 200, Midland Silicones Ltd./on a microscope slide and the embryo sacs were excised under a microscope with the aid of entomological pins. Exstirpation uncovered only the micropylar and the central regions of the embryo sac. The base of the embryo sac retained its coherence with the rest of the ovule tissues. The embryo sacs survived much better if they were left covered with one layer of the integument. The enzymatic isolation of embryo sacs that was also tested, did not yield satisfactory results.

During the microcinematographical process the objects were covered with a teflone membrane / YSI 5352, Yellow Spring Instruments Co., INC./. For microcinematography a Pentaflex - 16 camera / VEB, GDR/ with time lapse equipment and the Zeiss /NfpK/ microscope with a normal optics was used. The shot frequency on a Fomapan - 17 DIN / Meopta / inverse film was 4 - 8 frames per minute.

3. Results

The last phase of sperm cell fusion with the secondary nucleus under double fertilization comes off in the proximity of the antipodals. The vacuolar activity of the nucleolus of female origin is relatively high in this period.The nucleolus releases the content of nucleolar " vacuoles " into the nucleus content very intensively.

Fig. 1. Partly isolated embryo sac of Galanthus nivalis.
Fig. 2. Micropylar region of the ovule of Torenia fournieri.
Fig. 3a - f. Process of nucleoli fusion in the primary endosperm nucleus of Galanthus nivalis.

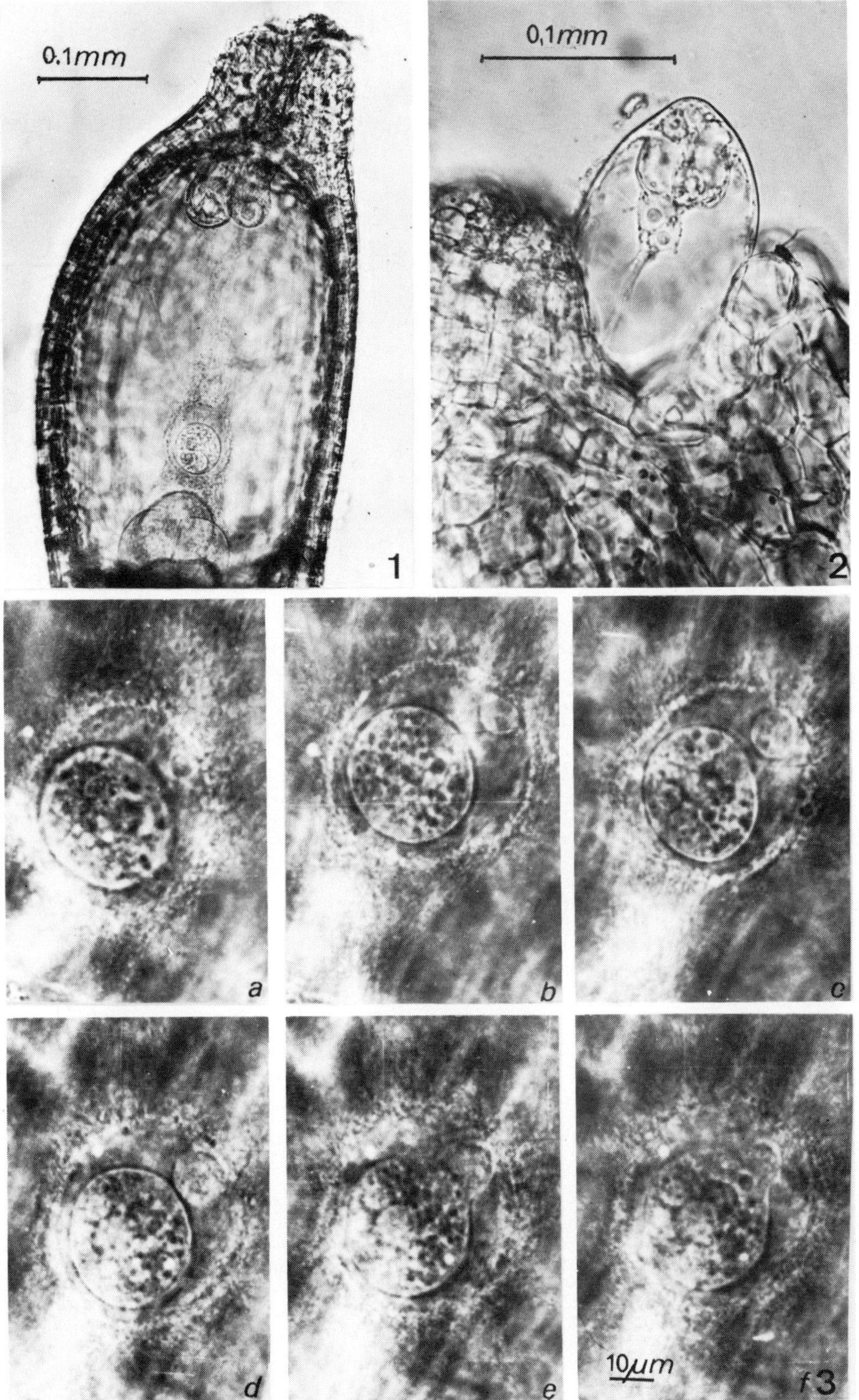
0.1mm
1
0,1mm
2
a
b
c
d
e
10μm
f 3

Cytoplasmic organels and reserve material accumulate in the environment of the nucleus so that we did not contrive to observe the penetration of the sperm cell into the secondary nucleus. We have registered microcinematographically only the growth and the differenciation of the male nucleolus/ Fig.3 a - d /. This process takes about 120 - 150 minutes. Following this period the male nucleolus attains the size approximately corresponding to one fifth of the size of nucleolus of the secondary nucleus. No vacuolar activity of the male nucleolus has been observed. Its content remains rather optically homogeneous in course of the entire growth.

In consequence of the sperm cell penetration the nucleolus of female origin shifts over the reverse side of the nucleus and flattens visibly / Fig. 3 a - d /. On acquiring its final size the male nucleolus approaches the female one and fuses with it. The fusion process itself takes about 10 - 15 minutes. In the course of the fusion the vacuolar activity of the nucleolus slightly declines and revives only after the completion of the fusion. The nucleoli get fused several hours before the prophase of the first mitosis in the primary endosperm nucleus. Under our experimental conditions, we observed in some cases the disappearence of the nucleolus in a late prophase only approximately 10 hours after the fusion of nucleoli of male and female origin.

4. Discussion

Though the majority of the vital observations of embryo sacs of angiosperms were made shortly before or shortly after fertilization, the fertilization process proper is very hard to trace. The problem lies in the low transparency of the micropylar region of the embryo sac at the time of fertilization and in the limited probability of getting the embryo sac isolated immediately after the penetration of the pollen tube. It would be ideal to follow up continuously in vitro the entire process of penetration of the pollen tube into the ovule and of fertilization. So far however, we did not succeed in setting up a medium warranting an oriented growth of the pollen tubes into the isolated embryo sacs and, at the same time , allowing the observation of the entire process.

Despite the fertilization was observed on the living material[7-10] we did not meet any photographic or cinematographic documentation of this process. The microcinematographic registration that would help to reveal e.g. the laws by which the sperm cells move in the embryo sac and ascertain the time parameters of individual partial processes and their interrelations in the living embryo sac is still to be realized.

5. Summary

With the aid of microcinematography the differentiation process of the nucleolus of male origin and its fusion with the nucleolus of the secondary nucleus as part of double fertilization in the living embryo sac of the Galanthus nivalis L. species was studied.

The paper also gives a survey of the species suitable for vital cytological investigation of the embryo sac.

References

1. Alexandrov, V.G., 1951, Dokl. Ak. nauk SSSR, 78, 1231.
2. Erdelská, O., 1969 a, Planta 84, 43.
3. Erdelská, O., 1969 b, Rev. Cytol. et Biol. Vég. 32, 397.
4. Erdelská, O., 1973, Film C 1075/ 1973, Inst. für den wiss. Film Göttingen, Germany.
5. Haustein, E., 1967, in Encyklopedia of plant Physiology, vol.18, ed. W. Ruhland / Springer/, p. 433.
6. Heitz, E., 1953, Ber. Schweiz. Bot. Ges. 63, 194.
7. Poddubnaja-Arnoldi, V.A., 1956, in Proceedings of the embryologists conference / Leningrad/, p. 63.
8. Poddubnaja-Arnoldi, V.A., 1960, Phytomorphology 10, 185.
9. Shibata, K., 1902, Flora 90, 61.
10. Strasburger, E., 1900, Bot. Ztg. 58, 293.
11. Subramanyam, K., 1960, J. Madras Univ., B., 30, 29.

Fertilization in Higher Plants, ed. H.F. Linskens.

FERTILIZATION IN ORCHIDACEAE

G.I. Savina

Laboratory of Embryology, Komarov
Botanical Institute, Leningrad,
U.S.S.R.

The family of orchids presents itself as an example of Angiospermae where the formation of the endosperm mostly does not take place. The embryological research of this family was started long ago, but the special attention of the scientists was drawn to this family after the publication of the work by S.G. Navashin[1] in which the term "double fertilization" was first mentioned. It later found wide application both in the Russian and foreign scientific literature.

Having discovered the fact of participation of both sperms in the process of fertilization in Liliaceae, S.G. Navashin suggested that it might be inherent in other representatives of Angiospermae. Besides, he was interested whether the fusion of the sperm with the central cell nucleus of the embryo sac takes place in cases when the endosperm is known not to be found. In order to further investigate these questions, he did research on the process of fertilization in Compositae and Ranunculaceae as well as in Orchidaceaea the latter being an exception to the rule because of the absence of the endosperm formation.

S.G. Navashin showed that the double fertilization is inherent in Ranunculaceae and Compositae. He observed an absolutely different behaviour of the sexual nuclei in orchids. On the example of three tropical species (Phajus blumei, Phajus sp., Arundia speciosa) he established that their polar nuclei do not fuse before fertilization but remain closely pressed to each other before and after it. In the process of fertilization the nucleus of the sperm joins them, although no fusion takes place. The nuclei remain to be isolated and, consequently, as S.G. Navashin noted, no endosperms are formed.

After research by S.G. Navashin the amount of the studied species has considerably increased and information on the embryology of the orchids was enriched due to the application of modern research methods. A considerable number of publications was dedicated to the orchids embryology both in the Soviet Union[2,3,4,5,6,7,8,9] and other countries. Among the latter are the general surveys[10,11,12].

As a result of the research at the light-optical level, a few conclusions on the specific embryology of this family has been made. They can be formulated as follows:

The orchids are characteristic by the reduction and variability of the number of nuclei and divisions during the development of the female generative sphere.

The macrosporogenesis here may finish with the formation of a tetrad of macrospores, a row of three cells (triad) or a dyad of two cells. The tetrads and triads are characteristic for the subfamily of Monandrae and triads occur in orchids twice as often as tetrads.[12] The formation of dyads is characteristic for the subfamily of Diandrae.

It should be noted that in a number of the family representatives a variable character of macrosporogenesis is observed within the same species or even the same individual[13,14].

In the orchids family the tendency has been revealed to the reduction in the number of the embryo sac nuclei from 8 to 4, this reduction being a result of various irregularities in the behaviour of the nuclei of the embryo sac chalazal part. These irregularities reduce the number of nuclei in the central cell and antipodal apparatus and therefore provide the decrease in the total number of the embryo sac nuclei. This can be accomplished in different ways: at the cost of reducing the number of nucleus divisions in the chalazal part of the embryo sac[5,8,9,13,15,16]; as a result of the fusion of spindles in the devided chalazal nuclei[6,13]; or due to the fusion of the embryo sac central cell nuclei[8,14,16].

The antipodal apparatus in orchids has a tendency not only to the reduction of its components but also to the change of organization from the cellular to the nuclear one. In many species the structure of the antipodal apparatus is clearly defined; it has either cellular or nuclear organization. In the eight-nuclei embryo sacs

---

Fig. 1-4. Fusion stages of Cypripedium calceolus sexual nuclei.
Fig. 5-10. Fusion stages of Listera ovata sexual nuclei.
Fig. 11. The already formed Listera ovata sperm.

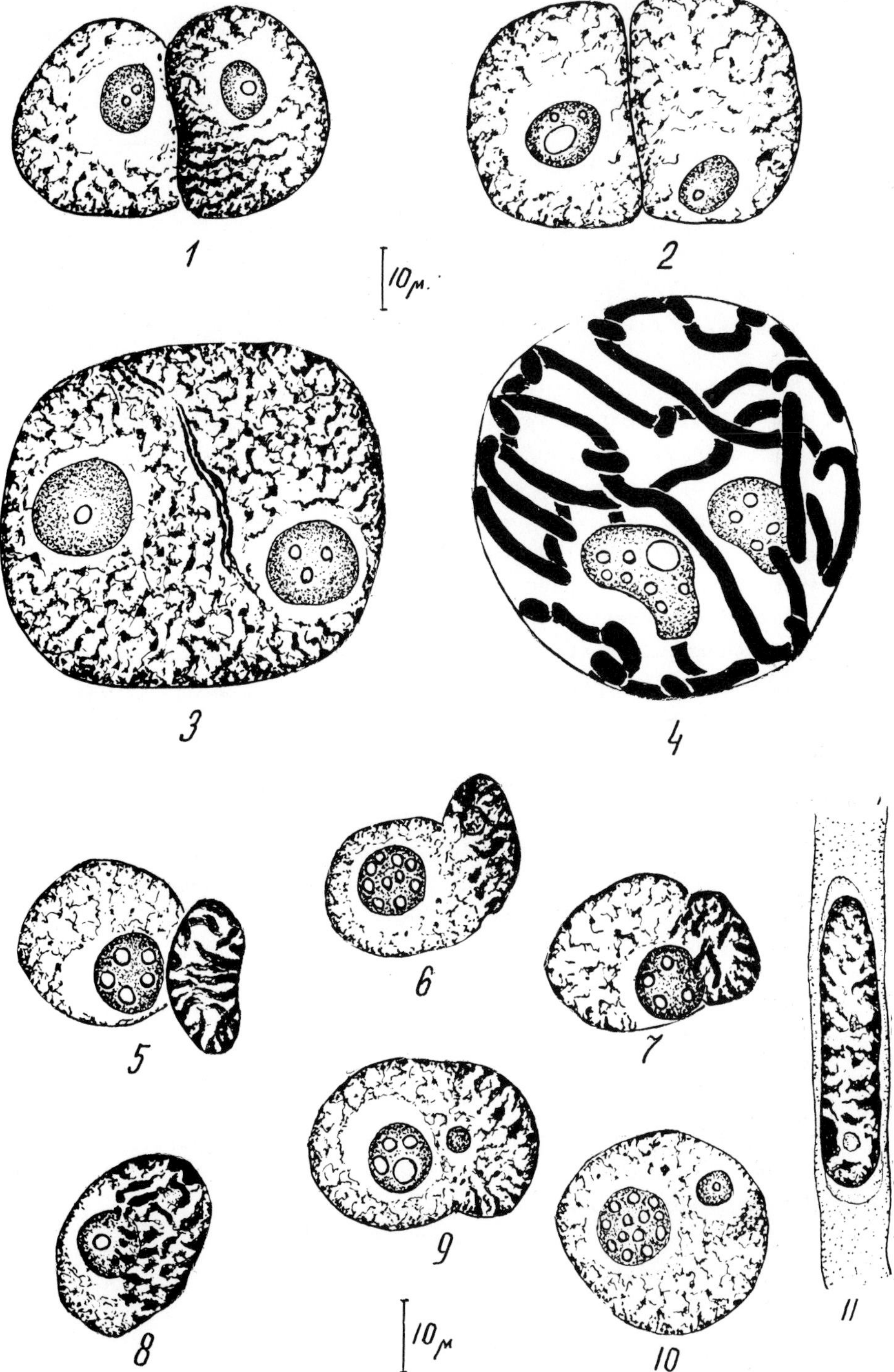
1
2
10μ
3
4
5
6
7
8
9
10
11
10μ

the antipodes are usually represented by three cells; in five and six-nuclei embryo sacs one or two free nuclei are usually present at the chalazal end. They can approach the polar nucleus,forming a polar-antipodal (polar-chalazal) complex[8,12,16]. In certain family representatives the antipodes of the same species and even of an individual may consist partly of cells and partly of nuclei [13,14]; the number of elements composing the antipodal apparatus may be unstable varying within the limits of the same species.

The spermogenesis in orchids is known to occur in the pollen tube. In the already formed sperm-cell a small quantity of fine-grained cytoplasm is concentrated around the nucleus. The male cell nucleus is more or less chromatized, gives an intensive Feulgen reaction and contains a small nucleolus (Fig. 11).

The fusion of the sexual nuclei is carried out in a different way in various family representatives. For example, in a number of species that we have studied, including Cypripedium calceolus, the sperm nucleus, having come into contact with the female sexual nucleus, changes its shape,getting rounded; its Feulgen reaction weakens and the size of the nucleolus is increased. As a result of these changes the sperm nucleus takes the resemblance of the female nucleus (Fig. 1,2). Then, after a while, the Feulgen reaction of the contacting nuclei as well as their chromatization get stronger which apparently testifies their transfer to mitosis. The gradual dissolving of a wall between them is simultaneously observed and, finally, the zygote nucleus enters the prophase with clearly expressed chromosomes (Fig. 3,4). This type of sexual nuclei fusion should be referred to the postmitotic type, according to the classification of Gerassimova-Navashina[17].

At the same time, another type of the sexual nuclei fusion can be observed within the limits of the orchids family. For instance, in the studied species of Listera ovata[18] a strongly chromatized sperm does not get rounded after its contact with the female nucleus as is observed in the species with the postmitotic type of the sexual nuclei fusion, but starts to fuse preserving at first its prolongated shape and intensive Feulgen reaction (Fig. 5-7). The sperm despiralization takes place eventually, the zygote nucleus obtains a homogenious structure and, after a certain period of rest enters the mitosis (Fig. 8-10). The fusion of the sexual nuclei is slow enough to thoroughly study the successive stages of the male and female sexual nuclei fusion. The above mentioned type of the sexual nuclei fusion can be classified as premitotic[17].

In a great number of Orchidaceae species the double fertilization, i.e. the fusion of the sperms with the female sexual nuclei proceeds normally. At the same time, in some species various deviations from the usual course of double fertilization are observed. The irregularities occur mainly in the second link of the fertilization, that is, when the sperm nucleus and the central cell nucelus fuse. These irregularities can be expressed differently: from the lateness of the fusion up to a complete absence of the fusion[1,2,3,8]. In some of the species the irregular fusion of the sperm nucleus and the central cell nucleus occur[12,19].

In the case when the double fertilization takes place, the fate of the primary endosperm nucleus is different in various species. Only in some of the studied orchids the primary endosperm nucleus is divided forming several nuclei (Table 1).

Table 1

Orchidaceae species in which the endosperm formation takes place.

Subfamily	Species	Number of nuclei	Author
Diandrae	Paphiopedilum insigne	2	Afzelius[13]
	Cypripedium spectabile	2-4	Pace[20]
	C. parviflorum	2-4	2 "
	C. gutattum	4	Prosina[6]
	C. insigne	6	Poddubnaya-Arnoldi[8]
	C. calceolus	2-4	Savina[15]
Monandrae	Vanilla planifolia	10	Swamy[21]
	Galeola septentrionalis	16	Kimura[22]
	Epipactis latifolia	2-6	Hagerup[23]
	E. atrorubens	4	Savina[24]
	Cephalanthera longifolia	few	Hagerup[25]
	C. damasonium	"	"
	Bletilla striata	4-8	Tohda[26]
	Lecanorchis japonica	4	Tohda[27]
	Pogonia japonica	2	Abe[28]
	Bromhaedia finalysoniana	2	Jeyanayaghy and Rao[29]
	Neottia nidus avis	4	Terekhin and Kamelina[30]

According to the literature data, in the majority of the family representatives the primary endosperm nucleus degenerates without division.

In the literature various terms for the onset of the primary endosperm nucleus degeneration are mentioned: immediately after the fertilization[31], by the time of the first division of the fertilized egg cell[32], during the formation of two or four-cell embryo[14]. Only in a few of the studied species a prolonged existence of the primary nucleus or endosperm nuclei in the active state as well as late degeneration have been observed[5,26,30,33].

What is the reason of the disturbances in the second link of the orchids fertilization? Why does the second sperm in certain cases not fuse with the polar nuclei or with the central cell nucleus?

Hagerup[34] suggests that the reason for the absence of the sperm fusion with the polar nuclei is that by the moment of fertilizing the female nucleus, they are dead.

Gerassimova-Navashina[35] and Poddubnaya-Arnoldi[8] believe that irregularities in the orchids double fertilization are connected with the reduction of their embryo sac. That was demonstrated by Poddubnaya-Arnoldi on the example of three orchid species with various degree of the embryo sac reduction. A species with the most reduced sac had the extremely irregular double fertilization and no endosperm formation took place.

The use of the hystochemical method[8,36,37,38] made it possible to trace the localization and dynamics of plastic, physiologically active substances and ferments in the orchid ovule. It demonstrated that the orchid embryo sac differs greatly from the embryo sac of other Angiospermae by its sharply decreased physiological activity It was established that a peculiar feature of orchids is the depression of oxidative process and the loss of some physiologically active substances.

In addition to that, there has been revealed the inverse relationship between the systematic position of the orchid, activity of ferments and metabolites concentration as well as a correlation between the reduction in activity of the chalazal physiological mechanisms and the formation of the suspended haustorium.

As a result of the comparative hystological research on the orchids the scientists came to a conclusion that the morphological peculiarity of the orchids corresponds to their physiological peculiarity. The embryo sac reduction of the orchids is apparently connected with the depression of the oxidative processes, inertness of nitrogen metabolism, lack of the physiologically active substances (heteroauxin,ascorbic acid).

The hystochemical method allowed also to reveal a tendency for morphophysiological reduction of,endosperm in a number of orchids of different systematic groups.

Thus, the application of the above method proved to be highly valuable for a deeper penetration into the nature of the embryonal processes in the Orchidaceae family representatives. Further development of such research will undoubtedly contribute to the progress in the field of orchids embryology.

Recently, the ultramicroscopic method began to be used in orchids embryology. The research on Epidendrum scutella[39,40,41] provided the data concerning the structure of a mature embryo sac and changes in it after fertilization. Information has been also obtained on the ultrastructure of the germinating male gametophyte.

It has been established that for a non-fertilized egg-cell and the central cell of this species the ribosomes are characteristic. After the fertilization they combine into polysomes. This, as the authors noted, shows that the above mentioned cells of the embryo sac pass from relative rest to the active state.

As in E. scutella, the endosperm does not develop beyond the initial stage, the authors assume that the factors determining the abortion of endosperm in orchids are connected with the fenomena of the nuclei fusion or division.

Such are the first data that have been obtained as a result of research on the orchids embryology at the ultramicroscopic level.

Electron microscopy has only recently begun to be used in the orchids embryology. Further application of this method as well as the research of embryonic processes on living material with the use of hystochemical method will undoubtedly contribute to the progress in the study of the generative sphere development, fertilization and endospermogenesis of this peculiar family of plants.

References

1. Navashin S.G., 1970 in: Ibr.Tr. 1951,225.
2. Baranov, P.A., 1917, Journal Russk. bot. obsch. 2, 20.
3. Baranov, P.A., 1924, Journal Russk. bot. obsch. 9,5.
4. Baranov, P.A., 1925, Bull. Sredne-Az. Gos. Univ. 10, 181.
5. Modilevskiy, Y.S., 1918, Zap. Kievsk. obsch. est. 26, I.
6. Prosina M.N., 1930, Planta 12, 532.
7. Poddubnaya-Arnoldi, V.A., 1952, Bull. Gl. bot. sada AnSSSR 14,3.
8. Poddubnaya-Arnoldi, V.A., 1958, Bot. journ. 43,178.

9. Poddubnaya-Arnoldi, V.A.,1964,Bull.Gl.bot.sada AN SSSR,54,51.
10. Swamy, B.G.L.,1949,Amer.Midl.Nat.41, 181.
11. Wirth, M. and Withner, C.L.,1959,in:The Orchids,sci.survey,N.Y. 155.
12. Abe, K., 1972, Sci. Rep. z Tôhoku Univ. IV, 36, 179.
13. Afzelius, K., 1916, Svensk. bot. Tidskr. 10, 183.
14. Abe, K., 1972, Sci. Tôhoku Univ. IV, 36, 135.
15. Savina, G.I., 1964, Bot. journ. 49, 1317.
16. Savina, G.I., 1972, Bot. journ. 57, 118.
17. Gerassimova-Navashina, E.N., 1957, Bot. journ. 42, 1654.
18. Savina, G.I.,1971,Mat.V Vsesoyuzn.sov.po embr.rast.SSSR, Kishinev, 160.
19. Savina, G.I., 1972, Bot. journ. 57, 382.
20. Pace, L., 1907, Bot. Gaz. 44, 353.
21. Swamy, B.G.L., 1947, Bot. Gaz. 108, 449.
22. Kimura,C., 1968, Sci. Rep. Tôhoku Univ. IV, 34, 67.
23. Hagerup, O., 1945, Kl. Danske Vidensk.Selsk.,Biol.Medl. 19, 1.
24. Savina, G.I.,1968,Mat.Vs.simp.po embr.rast.SSSR,Kiev, 97.
25. Hagerup, O., 1947, Kl. Datske Vidensk. Selsk.,Biol.Medl.20, 1.
26. Tohda, H., 1968, Sci.Rep. Tôhoku Univ. IV,33, 83.
27. Tohda, H., 1971, Sci.Rep. Tôhoku Univ. IV, 35, 245.
28. Abe,K., 1968, Sci. Rep. Tôhoku Univ. IV, 34, 59.
29. Jeyanayaghy,S.,and Rao,A.N.,1966,Bull.Torrey bot.Club 93, 97.
30. Teryokhin,E.S. and Kamelina, O.P.,1969,Bot.journ. 54, 1373.
31. Strasburger, E., 1900, Bot. Ztg. 58, 293.
32. Brown, W.H., 1909, Bot. Gaz. 48, 241.
33. Kusano, S., 1915, J. Col. Agr. Tokyo Imp. Univ. 6, 7.
34. Hagerup, O., 1944, Dansk. bot. Arkiv 11, 2.
35. Gerassimova-Navashina,E.N.,1954,Dokt.diss., SSSR, Leningrad.
36. Zinger,N.V. and Poddubnaya-Arnoldi,V.A.,1958,Dok.AN SSSR 118,607.
37. Zinger,N.V. and Poddubnaya-Arnoldi,V.A.,1959,Tr.Gl.bot.sada AN SSSR 6, 90.
38. Zinger,N.V. and Poddubnaya-Arnoldi,V.A.,1964,Bull.Gl.bot.sada AN SSSR 55, 81.
39. Cocucci, A.E.,and Jensen, W.A., 1969, Amer.J. Bot. 56(6),629.
40. Cocucci, A.E. and Jensen, W.A., 1971, Kurtziana 6, 25.
41. Cocucci, A.E. and Jensen, W.A., 1969, Kurtziana 5, 23.

Fertilization in Higher Plants, ed. H.F. Linskens.

FERTILIZATION PROCESS OF CEREALS

T.B. Batygina
Laboratory of Embryology
Komarov Botanical Institute of the USSR Academy of Sciences
Leningrad, USSR

Although quite a number of works have been dedicated to the fertilization process of cereals, some aspects of this problem have not been sufficiently elucidated for a long time. Most of the authors dealing with the problem paid little attention to the structure of sexual nuclei. They did not follow all the details of the fusion process of sexual gametes and did not take notice of the organization and the structure of the embryo sac and its elements. Besides, these explorers studied only some isolated moments of fertilization and hardly investigated correlatively the development of the zygote and endosperm.

All this gave rise to some contradictory interpretations of the same structures and phenomena taking place in the fertilization process of cereals.

Thus, Sax[1] in his study of the fertilization process in wheat (T.durum hordeiforme Host. var. Kubanka) paid great attention to the cytological aspect ofthis phenomenon. He believed that one of the sperms as well as the egg cell nucleus with which it fuses is in the stage of prophase and the other sperm at the moment of its fusion with the polar nuclei is in the stage of early metaphase.But as we shall see below, the case is somewhat different.

Later Morrison[2] contended that the sperms at the moment of their fusion with female nuclei are in the stage of dormancy. But judging by his illustrations it is not quite so.

Special attention should be paid to Vazart's[3,4] work in which the author gives consideration to the details of the reproductive nuclei fusion in wheat, rye, barley, maize,sorgo. Dwelling at length on the reproductive nuclei types Vazart does not attach importance to the succession of their development stages and shares Sax's[1] opinion that dissolution of the sperm coincides in time with the prophase which at this moment the egg cell nucleus enters.

In their works dedicated to some phases of fertilization in

cereals , Modilevski and others mention mostly the structure of sexual nuclei at the moment of their fusion. They write about the chromatic net which, they think, resembles the prophase in female nuclei and about possible spireme stage of sperms (of which Sax writes). However, they consider it difficult to determine the state of the sperms at the moment of their fusing with female nuclei.

To throw more light upon the problem a thorough investigation of the fertilization process has been carried out on some wheat species[6-14] by standard and by remote hybridization and also on maize[15-18], sorgo[19] and barley[20-22].

Fertilization being a complicated biological process inseparable from the development of sexual elements[24-25] it is necessary to dwell upon the sperm structure in cereals[8,9,10,26]. Analysis of the literature and of our evidence has proved that in most cereals studied (barley, rye oat, wheat, maize, sorgo) division of the generative cell results in sperm-cell formation[5,8,15,26,27,28]. According to our data, in the newly formed sperm-cells of wheat (table I, 1-8) due to their structure (blunt-pointed from one end and caspidate from the other), the cytoplasm is not uniformly spread around the nuclei (table I, f.7). In the process of pollen grain formation in wheat and obviously in all the cereals the sperms change their form (lengthen, stretch), the distribution of the cytoplasm around the nucleus becomes even and also its structure alters (table I, f.8).

Most of the investigators suppose that the sperms of the cereals lose their cytoplasm in the process of the pollen grain maturation. The explorers think that in mature pollen grains, pollen tubes and in the embryo sac these are not sperm-cells but naked sperm nuclei in the stage of telophase. However, it must be noted that mature pollen grains and pollen tubes of cereals are characterized by the presence of a great quantity of starch and perhaps it makes it difficult to discover whether or not the sperms have cytoplasm and to determine their structure. More than once we noted the presence of cytoplasm in the sperms of mature pollen grains of wheat (table I, f.8). On these grounds it may be supposed to be present. Application of new methods (electron microscopy and oth.)

Table I. Spermiogenesis in a pollen grain of wheat (1-8), growth of pollen tubes in the pistil tissues (9-12), sperms of various wheat species (13 - T. monococcum, 14 - T.dicoccum, 15 -T.aestivum).

Табл. I

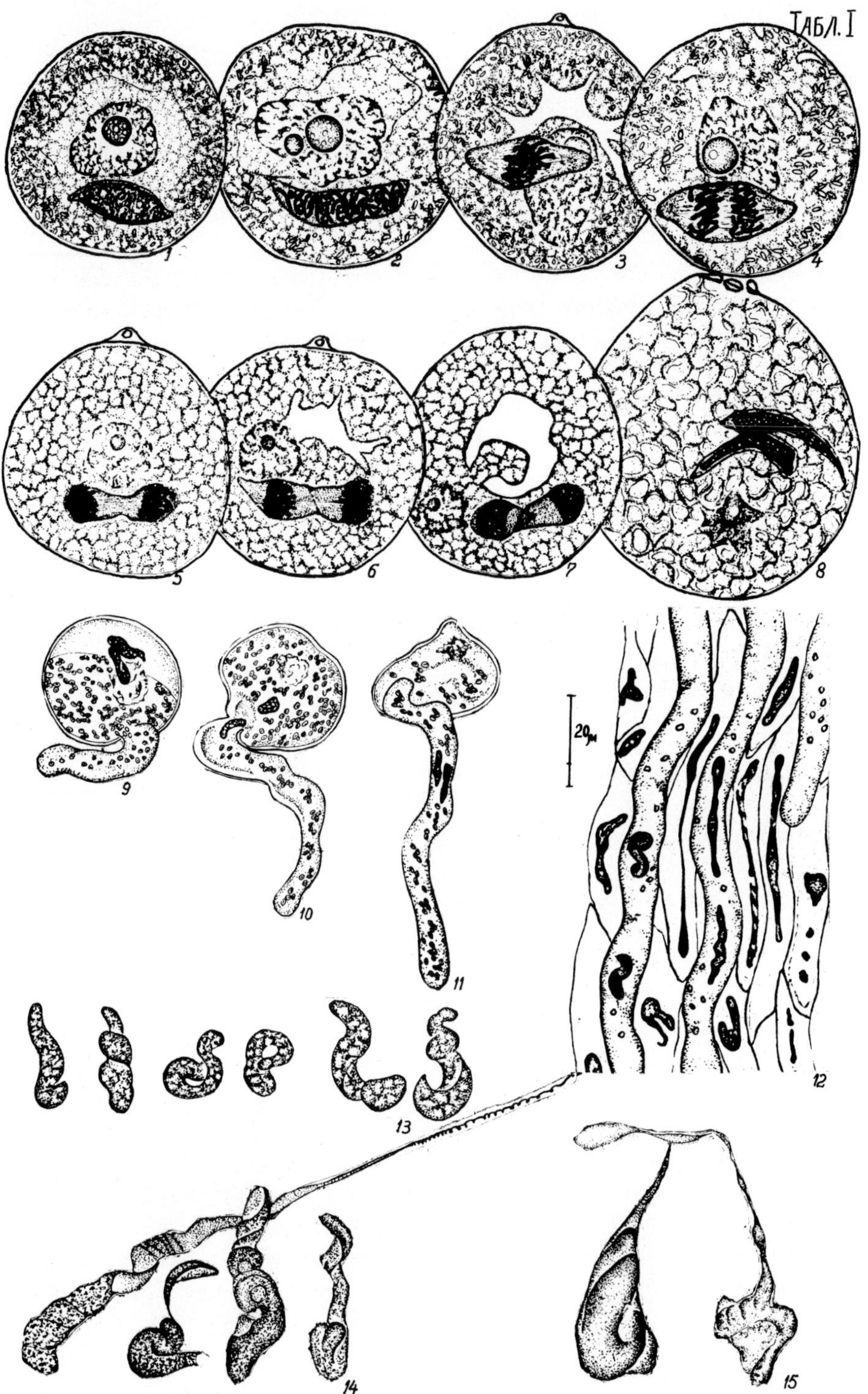

will make it possible to obtain more definite evidence, Besides, it should be pointed out that not in all the cereals sperms approach the dormant female nuclei in the state of telophase as it is noted by most of the explorers.[6,7,16,22] For example, Tatintseva[26] reports that in sorgo (Sorghum Caffrorum j.) at the end of spermiogenesis the sperms enter the interphasic state in which they approach the female nuclei.

Analysis of the literature dedicated to the fertilization process of cereals and our temporal study of syngamy, triple fusion and the development of the zygote and endosperm in various species of wheat have made it clear that in the main aspects it is very much the same. Therefore we have studied the fertilization process of cereals on the example of the polyploid row of wheat (T. monococcum L., n=7, T.dicoccum Schrank, n=14, T. aestivum L., n=21). Above all wheat appeared to be very convenient for investigation. The prolonged fertilization process of wheat makes it possible to follow all its stages, e.g. to observe the sperm in the synergida, in the egg cell cytoplasm, etc. Due to the prolongation of this period it is also possible to elucidate the correlation of syngamy and triple fusion proceeding in its various stages. And what is also convenient all the sexual elements of wheat are large enough.

P r o g a m i c   p h a s e. We began our study from germination of the pollen. In favourable conditions it starts germinating nearly as soon as it gets on the stigma , so 5-15 min. after heavy pollination a great number of pollen tubes may be seen in the stigma. Like pollen grains and sperms, the pollen tubes of the studied species have various size (table I, 9-15).

Wheat has a very short style and its stigma is nearly sessile. The pollen tubes pass through the lobes of the plumose stigma and grow in the conducting tissue of the style, moving apart the tightly closed cells which results in deformation of the latter .

By its position in the ovary the wheat ovule is apotropous and pollen tubes traverse rather a long way from the stigma to the micropyle[10,13]. From the style the pollen tubes get into the ovary, passing between its walls and the external integument; they then reach the internal integument that forms the micropyle. Not only one but several pollen tubes may enter both the ovary and the embryo sac. The cytoplasm of all the pollen tubes is filled with granular contents, there are also plastids and oils. The sperms in the pollen tubes of wheat slightly differ in shape from those in the pollen grains. With growth of the pollen tubes the sperms undergo some shape and structure changes. Within the limits of every pair they may also be different in their outward appearance. In the pollen tubes sperms may lie at diverse distances from each other. They may be various in shapes: vermiform, beltform or twisted in a loose or tight spiral; sometimes they despiralize, stretching in a long filament (table I, 13-15). The visible structure of sperms in the pollen tubes of different species of wheat is somewhat dissimilar. Thus, for instance, in the sperms of the low-chromosomic wheat T. monococcum (table I, 1,13) intervals between the chromonemas are distinctly seen and for this reason they seem to be more structuralized than the sperms of T. aestivum, that have close structure and seem to be homogenous (table I, 1, 15).

D o u b l e   f e r t i l i z a t i o n. Penetrating the embryo sac the pollen tube meets the synergidae and into them discharges its content which is seen in the form of streams transpiercing the synergida.

Destruction of either one or both synergidae in the process of fertilization is observed equally often in all the wheat species studied.

Degeneration of the synergida not affected by a pollen tube proceeds in a long period of time.

With degeneration of the synergidae their nuclei converse and often move to their apical part. In the pycnotic state the destroyed nuclei of synergidae have some likeness to the male gametes and because of this they are taken by some authors for additional sperms.

In the pollen tube content discharged into the synergida the beginning of sperm characteristic conversions may be seen: in the apical part of the synergida the sperms are mostly elongated and have a spiral shape; in the lower part they are twisted in tight spirals which sometimes are even difficult to be distincted and the sperms seem to be nearly orbicular. Thus, at the beginning of their stay in the embryo sac the sperms get twisted even more than in the pollen tube. Then, as it was found by Navashin[29] , the pollen tube content together with both sperms is delivered into the space between the egg cell and the central cell of the embryo sac. From there the sperms move in the opposite directions: one of them gets into the central cell and the other into the egg cell.

After having penetrated into the egg cell the sperm stays in its cytoplasm for 1 hour owing to which all the further stages of its transformation may be followed (table II). On the way to the egg cell nucleus which at the moment is in the state of dormancy the sperm begins getting friable; in this period its structure becomes most distinctly seen.

Near the egg cell nucleus and in contact with it the sperm has a peculiar shape: one of its ends is wide and the other narrow; the wide end is more friable, the narrow one is solid. In both ends of the sperm there are seen spiralized chromonemae. Despiralization of the sperm in the egg cell nucleus usually begins from the wide end that loses its outline. Some cases were observed when the wide end of the sperm had already been dissolved while the narrow one had not yet got into contact with the egg cell nucleus which proves that the sperm sinks into it gradually.

All the obtained data of the sperm structure in the pollen tube and pollen grain as well as in the embryo sac confirm once more the fact **that** wheat sperms approach female cells in the state of

---

Table II. Successive stages of form and structure changes in a wheat sperm from the moment of its penetration into the embryo sac up to its complete dissolution in the egg cell nucleus (premitotic type of fertilization) : а - T. dicoccum sperms from the synergidae; б - T. aestivum sperms from the slot; в -е T. aestivum, the sperms have entered the egg cell; ж - п - dissolution of the sperm in the egg cell nucleus; ж, з, н, п - T. monococcum; к, л, о - T. aestivum; м - T. dicoccum; р - the nucleus of a T. dicoccum zygote in the state of dormancy; с - the prophase of a T. monococcum zygote. By Felgen with lichtgrune colouring.

Table III. Successive stages of form and structure changes of a-sperm from the moment of approaching the central nuclei to its complete "dissolution" in the polar nuclei before the primary division of the endosperm. б - sperms on the border of two polar nuclei; в, г, е, ж - the sperm is fusing with one polar nucleus; д - the sperm fuses with both polar nuclei at the same time; з - the dormant nucleus of endosperm embryo cell; и, к - the endosperm prophase; л - the endosperm metaphase; д, з, и, к - T.aestivum; е, ж, п - T.monococcum.

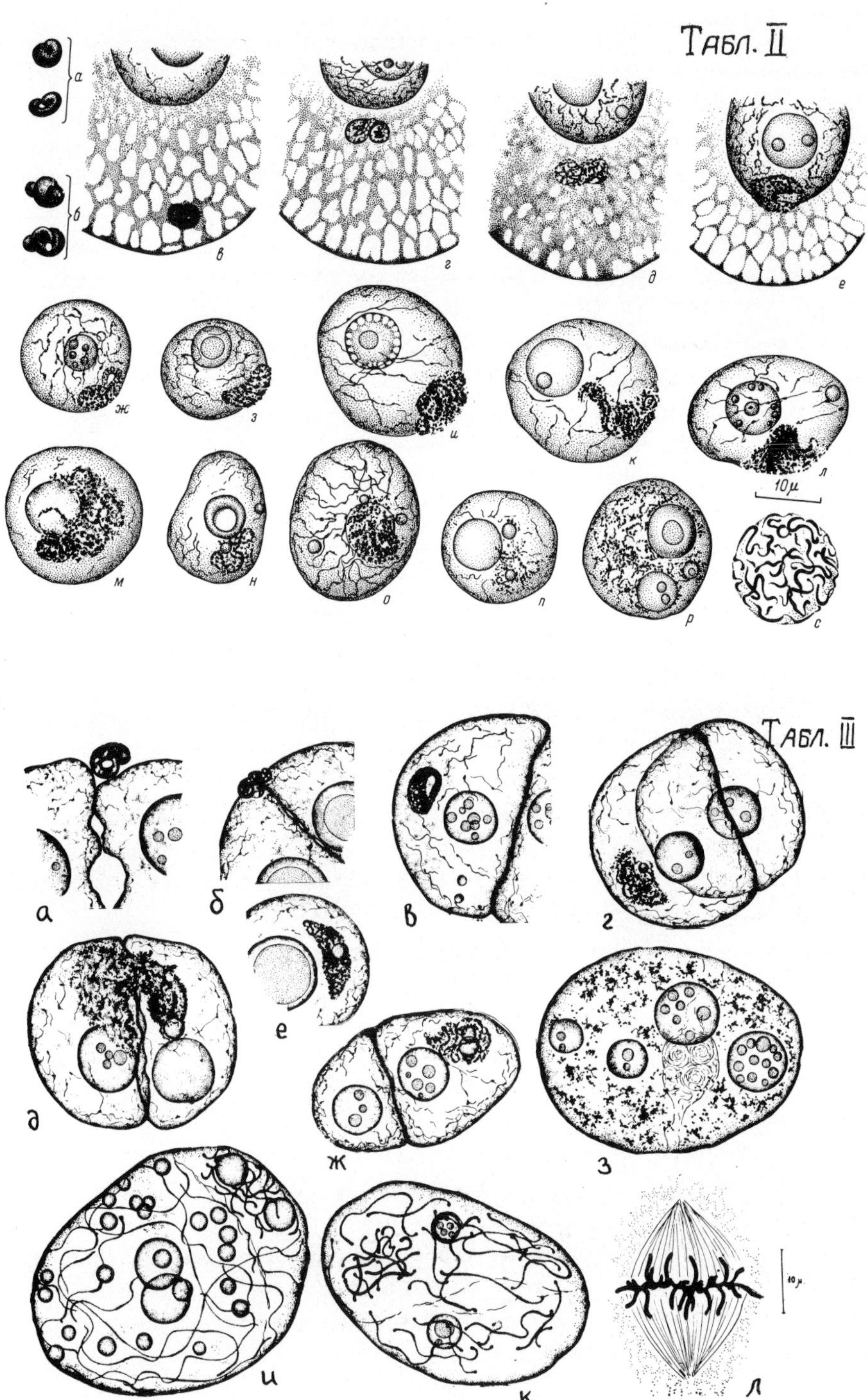
Табл. II
а
б
в
г
д
е
ж
з
и
к
л
10μ
м
н
о
п
р
с
Табл. III
а
б
в
г
д
е
ж
з
и
к
л
10μ

telophase because even with their considerable friability at the moment of contacting and sinking into the female nucleus the nucleolus yet cannot be found in the sperms[6-8]. It appeares at the moment of considerable despiralization, when the sperm chromonoma apparently loses its continuity. It goes from above that only under the influence of the dormant female cell the sperm at last accomplishes its development cycle and falls into the state of dormancy.

The size of a male nucleus obviously correlates with dissolution of the sperm in the female nuclei: in the course of this process the nucleolus notably increases in size. Sometimes the nucleolus becomes remarkable while the sperm still reserves its structure. A sperm of T.aestivum, T.dicoccum and T.monococcum discharge usually two nucleoli though in some cases there may be only one. We did not happen to observe the female nucleolus fusing with the male one but more than once we saw zygotes with one large nucleolus, which, obviously, is the proof of their having fused.

After fusion of the sperm with the egg cell nucleus has been accomplished the zygote falls into a long period of dormancy that lasts for 16-18 hours. In the zygote the male chromatin cannot be distinguished from the female one. During the period of dormancy the zygote is growing and developing intensively. At the same time structural transformations of the interphasic nucleus and cytoplasm are taking place , which are expressed in alternation of the vacuolization nature of the zygote and in disappearance of starch. It is evidently the result of such a long period of dormancy that to the division prophase the zygote comes as a whole unit 24 hours after pollination (table III).

The process of the sperm sinking into the nucleus of the cen tral cell is similar to the one in the egg cell but goes on faster (table III), whereas in the cytoplasm of the egg cell the sperm stays for more than half an hour, in the cytoplasm of the central cell it stays only for 15-30 min. Therefore it is very difficult to reveal alteration of the sperm in the cytoplasm of the central cell.

As it has been said, before fertilization the polar nuclei are drawn together but not fused. They usually fuse when the sperm gets into contact with the polar nucleus.

It happens more often that the sperm dissolves in one polar nucleus though cases are not rare when it dissolves simultaneously in both of them; it probably occurs if the sperm gets on the border of the nuclei (table III, a, б).

Despiralization of the sperm in the polar nucleus goes on in the same way as in the nucleus of the egg cell but at higher rates. As a rule, 2-3 hours after pollination the fusion of the sperm with the central cell nucleus is accomplished and the secondary nucleus is seen. On the spot of "dissolving" of the sperm 1-2 nucleoli are found. In the polar nuclei T.aestivum some time after their fusion there often appear a number of additional nucleoli (to 20) but in their size and coloration they greatly differ from those discharged by the sperm (table III, И). Analogous nucleoli are sometimes found in non-fertilized polar nuclei. The nature of these additional nucleoli is not clear so far.

The period of dormancy in the secondary nucleus is very short - about 0.5-1 hour. 3-8 hours after pollination the cell of the endosperm embryo enters the phase of primary division during which a separate group of prophatic filaments constituting the sperm nucleus (table III, И, К) is seen. The development of the sperm nucleus goes ahead of the beginning of the polar nuclei prophase which is also proved by different time of nucleoli disappearing. Perhaps this fact may be explained by a very short interval of dormancy which gives the male chromatin no time for uniform distribution in the female nucleus as may be observed in a wheat zygote.

A similar phenomenon, i.e.isolated prophase of the male nucleus in a polar one was noted also by Sax[1]. However, he noted the difference between male and female chromosomes also in the metaphase of the primary division of the endosperm. But we did not see such a difference in this phase (table III, Л). In barley[21,22] the sperm has no separate stage of prophase. The authors only note that the polar nucleus in which the sperm has been dissolved is chromatized to a higher degree than the non-fertilized one.

The process of female nuclei and sperms fusion in maize, barley, sorgo and rye is similar to the above described processes in wheat.

As appears from analysis of the sperm behavior in the egg cell and in the central cell they are very much alike and undergo similar conversions but each sperm at different rate. It evidently depends on the conditions in which the sperms are. Thus, in the egg cell the sperm dissolves in 4-5 hours while in the polar nuclei of the central cell this process is accomplished in 1.5-2 hours. The duration of the dormancy period is also different: in the zygote it goes on for about 18 hours and in the endosperm embryo only for 0.5-1 hour. Therefore it is rather difficult to discover the stage of dormancy in the endosperm embryo and only using a very fractional method of temporal fixations we succeeded founding its presence. It was probably for this reason that Sax[1] has not discover the stage of dormancy and has come to the wrong conclusion that in wheat the polar nuclei of the central cell enter the prophase without falling into the state of dormancy in the prophase stage where they start fusing with the sperm which is in the same state.

As each sperm of one pair passes separate development phases at different rates it may lead to the wrong conclusion that there is a great difference between them. The different rates of their passing through the development phases are apparently explained by the conditions of the sperms[7,9,10,16,21,22]. This applies to other cereals as well as to wheat.

So, as has been mentioned before,[10] in the process of development and "maturing" of the pollen grain, pollen tube growth and double fertilization the sperms of wheat,and obviously of all the cereals from the beginning of their formation to the despiralization and dissolution in the female nuclei,undergo considerable morphological and structural changes. Regular changeability of their shape and structure in the process of their development and motion in the pollen tube and embryo sac allows to assume the male gametes to be capable of independent motion parallel with the influence of the pollen tube plasmic currents. Morphological similarity of changes in the sperms of one cereal pair gives us grounds to suppose that their functional difference may depend on the structure of their nuclei (enantiomorphic) and also on the different structure of the female cell nuclei and their cytoplasm. This assumption agrees with Navashin's[30] idea of self-mobility and the sperm structure of the angiosperms.

As a result of thorough study of fertilization in some wheat species and of analysis of the data obtained by Sax[1], Morrison[2] and Vazart[3,4], Gerassimova-Navashina and we[6,7,9,10] have come to the conclusion that the premitotic type of fertilization, when sexual nuclei fusion is prior to mitosis, is inherent in wheat. The following works have confirmed the premitotic type of fertilization also in other cereal species such as maize,sorgo and barley[16-22].

Table IV. The apical part of embryo sac 30 min (1 - T.aestivum), 1 hour (2 - T.dicoccum), 1.5 hour (3 - T.aestivum), 2.5 hour (4 - T.aestivum) after pollination.

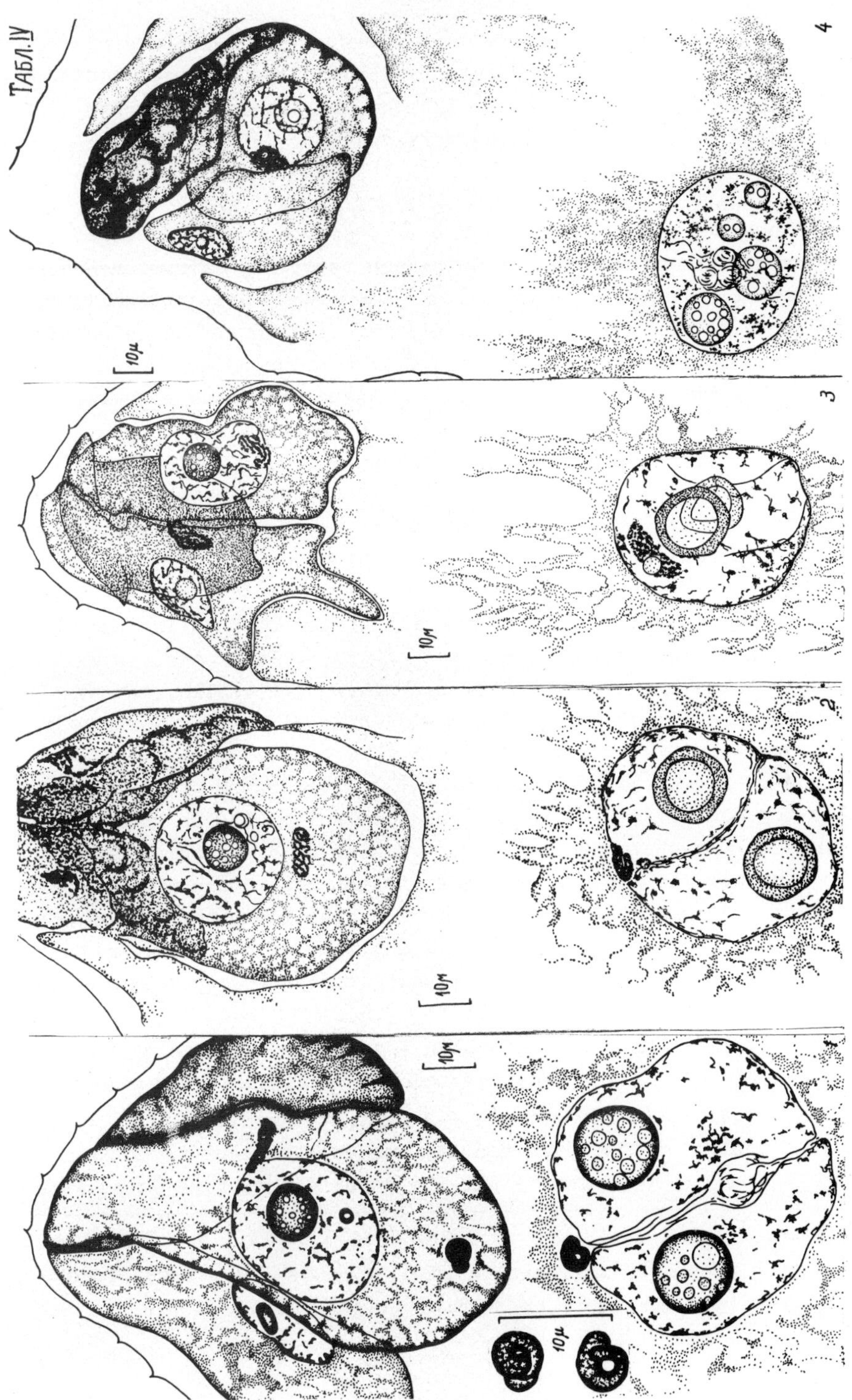
ТАБЛ.IУ
10μ
4
3
10м
2
10м
10м
10μ
1

It should be noted, however, that Tchebotar[18], when studying the fertilization process in maize, observed both pre- and postmitotic types of sperms and female cell fusion. Therefore the problem of the fusion type in maize requires more accurate definition.

C o r r e l a t i o n o f s y n g a m y a n d t r i p l e f u s i o n p r o c e s s e s. Quite a number of works deal with the problem of how much time passes between pollination and gamete fusion in cereals. However, all these data are contradictory and scrappy. Above that, scarcely any information on the rates of correlated development of syngamy and triple fusion may be found in these works. The most complete data of these processes correlation is is given in Pope's[32] work dedicated to the description of fertilization process in barley (Hordeum distichum Pal.). Though studies made on syngamy triple fusion, the zygote and endosperm development in various species of wheat allowed us to establish a definite correlation of these processes.

So, 15-20 min. after pollination the sperms usually are already in the synergide and 20-25 min. later they can be seen in the embryo sac between the central cell and the egg cell. This stage is rather difficult to be caught, for in 25-30 min. or even earlier, one of the sperms is lying near the polar nuclei and sometimes has already got in contact with them (table IV,1); 45 min. later it is in contact with the polar nuclei. All this time, the other sperm is in the egg cell cytoplasm moving to its nucleus (table IV,1,2). An hour after pollination the sperm usually begins fusing with the polar nuclei while the sperm in the egg cell has not yet got into contact with its nucleus (table IV, f.2) and only 1.5 hour later the fusion of the sperms with the egg cell nucleus may be seen starting. By this time in the polar nuclei the sperm has got nearly despiralized and has discharged a nucleolus (table IV, f.3).

2-3 hours after pollination, the sperm and polar nuclei fusion is accomplished and the secondary nucleus falls into the state of dormancy that lasts for about 0.5-1 hour (table IV, f.4). At this time, the fusion of the sperm and the egg cell nucleus is strongly pronounced . 30-20 min. after the polar nuclei have fused with

---

Table V. The apical part of embryo sac 3 hours (1 - T.aestivum), 5 hours (2 - T.monococcum), 6 hours (3 - T.monococcum), 7 hours (4 - T.monococcum) after pollination.

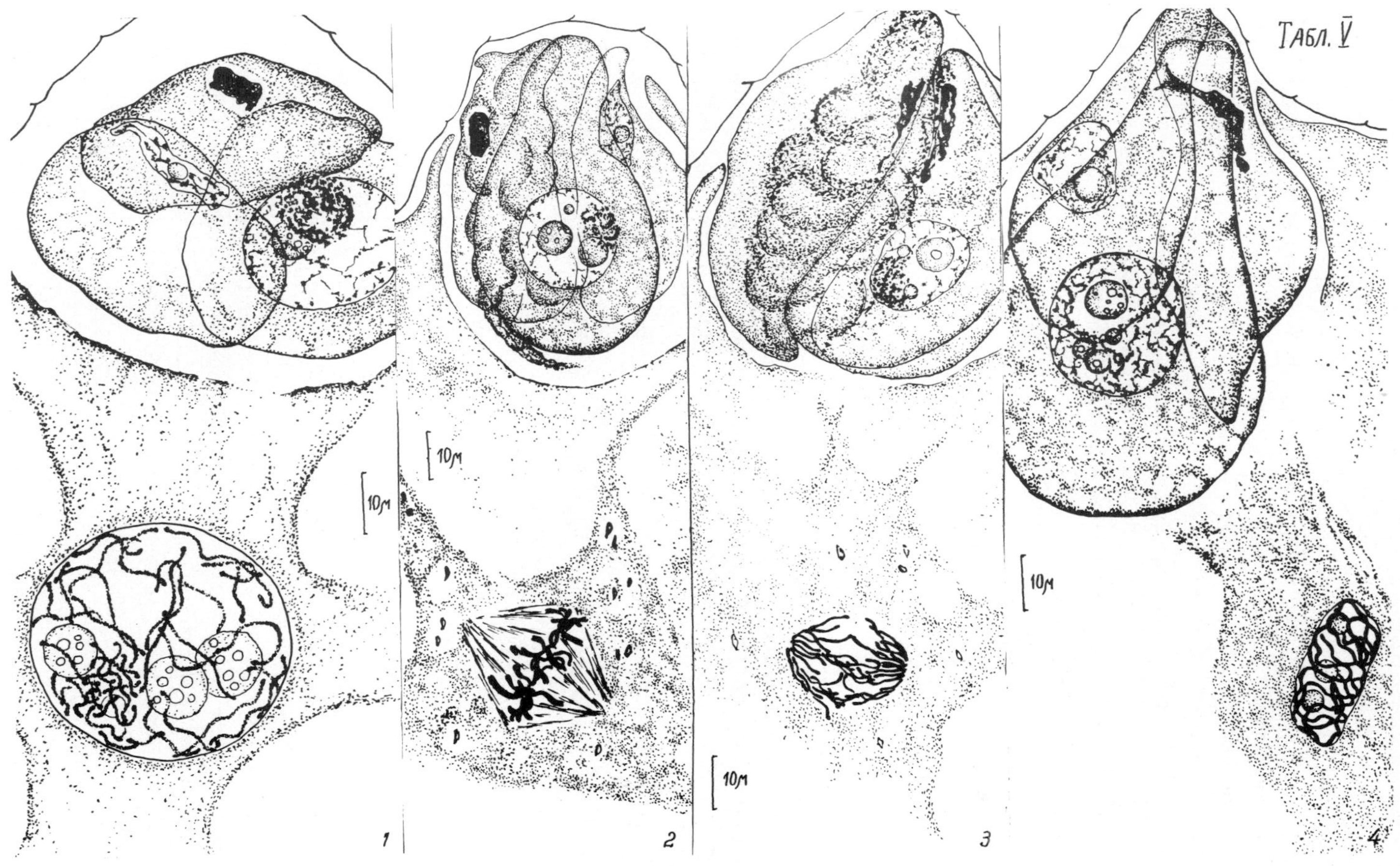
Табл. V
10м
10м
10м
10м
1
2
3
4

the sperm, i.e. 3-4 hours after pollination there comes a prophase, beginning as has already been said, first in the sperm and then in the secondary nucleus (table V,1). To this stage of the central cell development corresponds the phase of the sperm and the egg cell nucleus fusion. 5-6 hours after pollination, when metaphase or anaphase may be observed in the endosperm, the sperm in the egg cell is nearly completely despiralized (table V, f.2,3).The zygote falls into the dormancy only 6-7 hours after pollination (table V, 4). This stage lasts for about 16-17 hours. Thus, the zygote starts dividing 20-24 hours after pollination, when in the endosperm there are already 4-5 nuclei (table V, 2,3).

From this follows that despiralization of the sperm in the egg cell nucleus lasts for 4-5 hours while in the central cell polar nuclei this process goes on for 1.5-2 hours. The duration of dormancy period is also different: in the zygote it lasts for about 16-18 hours and in the cell of the endosperm embryo only for 0.5-1 hour.

Thus it is clear that both in all the wheat species studied and in other cereal species 5, 16, 17, 19-22 sperms fuse with the female nuclei of the embryo sac at different rates. However, it follows from the obtained data and from the analysis of the literature that in spite of their difference there exists quite a definite rate of each process proceeding and also their correlation, i.e. a certain state of an egg cell and of a zygote always corresponds with a certain state of polar nuclei and of endosperm. This correlation is found to be very little liable to the influence of external factors and practically does not depend on them. This has been confirmed by comparative study of the fertilization process under various conditions. However it should be noted that on the whole the rate of embryological processes depends upon the change of the environmental conditions.

1. Study of the fertilization process has revealed much likeness in various cereal species. All of them are characterized by the premitotic type of fertilization.

2. Comparative study of the fertilization process of various cereal species in dynamics has proved that in syngamy and triple fusion definite morphogenetic correlations (both temporal and structural) are found. The specific nature of the fertilization process in its different stages depends upon them. A breach of this corres-

pondence involves anomalies of the fertilization process.

3. From the moment of their coming into being to the moment of fusion with female nuclei cereal sperms undergo a number of morphological and structural transformations.

4. The sperms of one and the same cereal pair are similar and undergo the same transformations but not synchronically (the rate of the sperm and the egg cell nucleus fusion greatly differ from the rate of its fusion with the polar nuclei), which leads to the wrong idea of their being different.

5. On the grounds of gradual morphological similarity in the conversions of the sperms in a cereal pair their ability of independent motion may be assumed (without excluding the influence of plasmic currents) and their functional difference supposed to depend upon the sperm nuclei structure, the structire of the female cell nuclei (enantiomorphic) and on the quantity and the structure of female cell cytoplasm.

References

1. Sax K., 1918, Genetics, 3, 309.
2. Morrison J.W., 1955, Canad.J.Bot., 33, 2, i68.
3. Vazart B., 1955, Rev. cytol.et biol.,veget., 16.
4. Vazart B., 1958, Protoplasmatologia, Wien, 7, 3a, 158.
5. Modilevski G.S., Oksijuk P.F., Khudjak M.O., Dzjubienko A.K., Baylis-Virovaja P.N., 1958, B. Cytoembryology of cereal crops, Ukr.SSR Acad.Sci., 336 (in Russian).
6. Batygina T.B., 1957, Deleg.Congr. All-Union Bot.Soc., 8, 45, (in Russian).
7. Gerassimova-Navashina E.N.,Batygina T.B.,1959, Rep.Ac.Sci. USSR, 124, 223 (in Russian).
8. Batygina T.B., 1959, Rep.Ac.,Sci. USSR, 137, 1, 220 (in Russ.)
9. Batygina T.B., 1962a, Rep.Ac.Sci USSR, 142, 5, 12o5 (in Russ.)
10. Batygina T.B., 1962b, Works Bot.Inst.Ac.Sci.USSR, 7, 5, 260 (in Russian).
11. Batygina T.B., 1966, Bot.J., 51, 10,480 (in Russian).
12. Batygina T.B., 1968, Mat. All-Union Symp.embryol.,23 (in Russian).
13. Batygina T.B., I974, Wheat Embryol.,206 (in Russian).
14. Batygina T.B., Dolgova O.A.,Korobova S.N., 1961, Rep.Ac.Sci. USSR, 136, 6, 1482 (in Russian).
15. Ustinova E.I.,Djakova M.I., 1953, Rep.All-Union Ac.Agric.Sci. 5, 9 (in Russian).
16. Korobova S.N.,1959,Rep.Ac.Sci.USSR, 127, 4, 921 (in Russian).

17. Korobova S.N.,1962, Works Bot.Inst.Ac.Sci.USSR, 6, 5, 294 (in Russian).

18. Tchebotar A.A., 1972, In: Maize Embryol., 384 (in Russian).

19. Khazova I.I., 1969, Bot.J., 54, 4, 557.

20. Erdelska O., 1967, Ann.of Bot.,N.S., 31, 122, 367.

21. Khvedynitch O.A., 1969, Ukr.Bot.J., 26, 5, 120 (in Russian).

22. Khvedynitch O.A., Bannikova V.P., 1970, Cytology & Genetics, 4, 5, 387 (in Russian).

23. Gerassimova-Navashina E.N., 1947, Rep.Ac.Sci.USSR, 57, 4, 395 (in Russian).

24. Gerassimova-Navashina E.N., 1951, Works Bot.Inst.Ac.Sci.USSR 7, 5, 294 (in Russian).

25. Gerassimova-Navashina E.N., 1969, Revue cytologic.et biol.veg., 32, 301.

26. Tatintseva S., 1968, News Ac. Sci.Turkm.SSR, 3, 26 (in Russian).

27. Weatherwax, Bull.Torrey Bot.Club, 46, 73.

28. Poddubnaya-Arnoldi V.A., 1964, General Embryology of Angiosperms, (in Russian).

29. Navashin S.L., 1951, Selected works, Ac.Sci.USSR, 364 (in Russian).

30. Khu-Khan', 1961, Cytology, 3, 189.

31. Simonian E.G., 1955, News Ac.Sci.Arm.SSR, 8, 11, 61 (in Russ.)

32. Pope M.N., 1937, J. Agr.Res., 389.

33. Linskens H.F., 1972, Fertilization Mechanisms in Higher Plants, 189.

Fertilization in Higher Plants, ed. H.F. Linskens.

A CYTOLOGICAL INVESTIGATION ON GAMETES AND FECUNDATION AMONG CEPHALOTAXUS DRUPACEA

M. GIANORDOLI

Laboratoire de Botanique, Université de Reims. 51062 France

Introduction.

The main characteristics of gametes and fertilization among Cephalotaxus drupacea, sketched out in the early XXth century[1, 2, 3], were specified later on[4]; it was advanced that the chondriome (collective name for mitochondria and plastids) of the two sperm cells that are brought by a pollen-tube to an oosphere is jointly responsible, with the female chondriome, for the make-up of the mitochondrial storage of the proembryo. Yet, through light microscopy alone, we can neither tell mitochondria from plastids in sexual cells nor tell male elements from female ones in proembryonary cytoplasm. Moreover, the discovery of plastid and mitochondrial DNA strenthened the view that these organelles are endowed with genetic continuity[5, 6] and get at least a relative autonomy with regard to the nucleus. The results obtained thanks to light microscopy were worth specifying through the techniques of electronic microscopy.

I. Results.

1) The egg cell.

A mature oosphere is a voluminous oblong cell whose nucleus is located in the uppermost third of the archegonial cavity. The ventral canal nucleus makes up an irregular cap pushed aside against the oosphere wall near the archegonial neck : it presents many degenerating features.

The better part of the cytoplasm, like most gymnosperm female gametes, looks like cytoplasmic nodules surrounded with a cupuliform vacuole (fig. 1).

Under the oosphere nucleus, the cytoplasm is arranged in several dense spheres ; a tube of the same texture can be seen around the nucleus (fig. 1). The granular texture of these zones and their similar response to ferric hematoxylin had led investigators to describe[4] them as mitochondrial clusters.

Actually, these zones are made up of the gathering of three kinds of constituents (fig. 2) : lipid globules, components of smooth endoplasmic reticulum, seen in cross section like short tubules or vesicles coalesced and more or less anastomosed, bundles of fine fibrils, flexuous-looking structures nearly parallel to each other more or less densely grouped, frequently in close contact with the tubules and saccules of the endoplasmic reticulum (fig. 2).

During the growth of the central cell, plastids undergo deep changes. In young central cells, leucoplasts can be seen in the shape of rings or cupules according to the angle of the cross section (fig. 3). These shapes spread more and more as the central cell grows. From one organelle, several thinned plastidial layers, keeping linked up with each other through bulged zones, stretch in various directions and fold back on themselves, surrounding large cytoplasmic enclaves that are thus partitioned again and again (fig. 4). Every plastid undergoes those changes but it remains identifiable because of the two lamellae of the plastidial membrane that it keeps all over its surface (fig. 5).

The oosphere contains no identifiable plastid. The plastidial bodies have a dense stroma (fig. 5) and the plastidial membrane presents many gaps. At that stage, it looks as if a number of plastids are being-lysed. Plastidial changes similar to those described here have been observed in the oosphere of two Pinaceae[7].

The oosphere mitochondria, too, undergo deep changes. But the morphological transformations of these organelles come up only with the mitosis of the central cell, that is, much later than for plastids.

The progamete mitochondria, seen in cross-section, look like clusters of 20-30 organelles ; these organelles, poor in cristae, are tied , one to the other, by series of short dense lines about 70 Å thick (fig. 6) ; these lines bind the outer lamellae of two neighbouring mitochondria. In the oosphere, those two outer lamellae cling

---

Methods. Thin sections of material fixed in glutaraldehyde osmium tetroxide were stained with $KMnO_4$ (fig. 2 to 13 and 15-16-18-19), with uranyl acetate and lead citrate (fig. 17), or with procedure of Thierry[8] (fig. 14).
The unit of Lenght used in the plates is the μ.
Key to labelling : AZ, amorphous zones ; BF, bundle of fibrils ; CBD, plastidial bodies ; CLC, concentric lamellar systems ; CN, cytoplasmic nodule ; G, granules ; LG, lipid globule ; M, mitochondria ; MF, myelinic formation ; MR, myelinic ribbon ; N, nucleus ; Nu, nucleolus ; P, plastid ; PL, plastidial layer ; SER, smooth endoplasmic reticulum ; SM, sequestration membrane ; V, vesicles ; WO, oosphere broken wall; ♀ cyt, female cytoplasm; ♂ cyt, male cytoplasm; R, ribosomes
Fig. 1-4. 1. Light microscopy, longitudinal cross section of an oosphere, arrow indicates dense sphere. 2. Dense sphere, arrow indicates close contact of fibrils with smooth endoplasmic reticulum. Inset : fibrils at higher magnification. 3. Plastid of a young central cell. 4. Plastidial transformations.

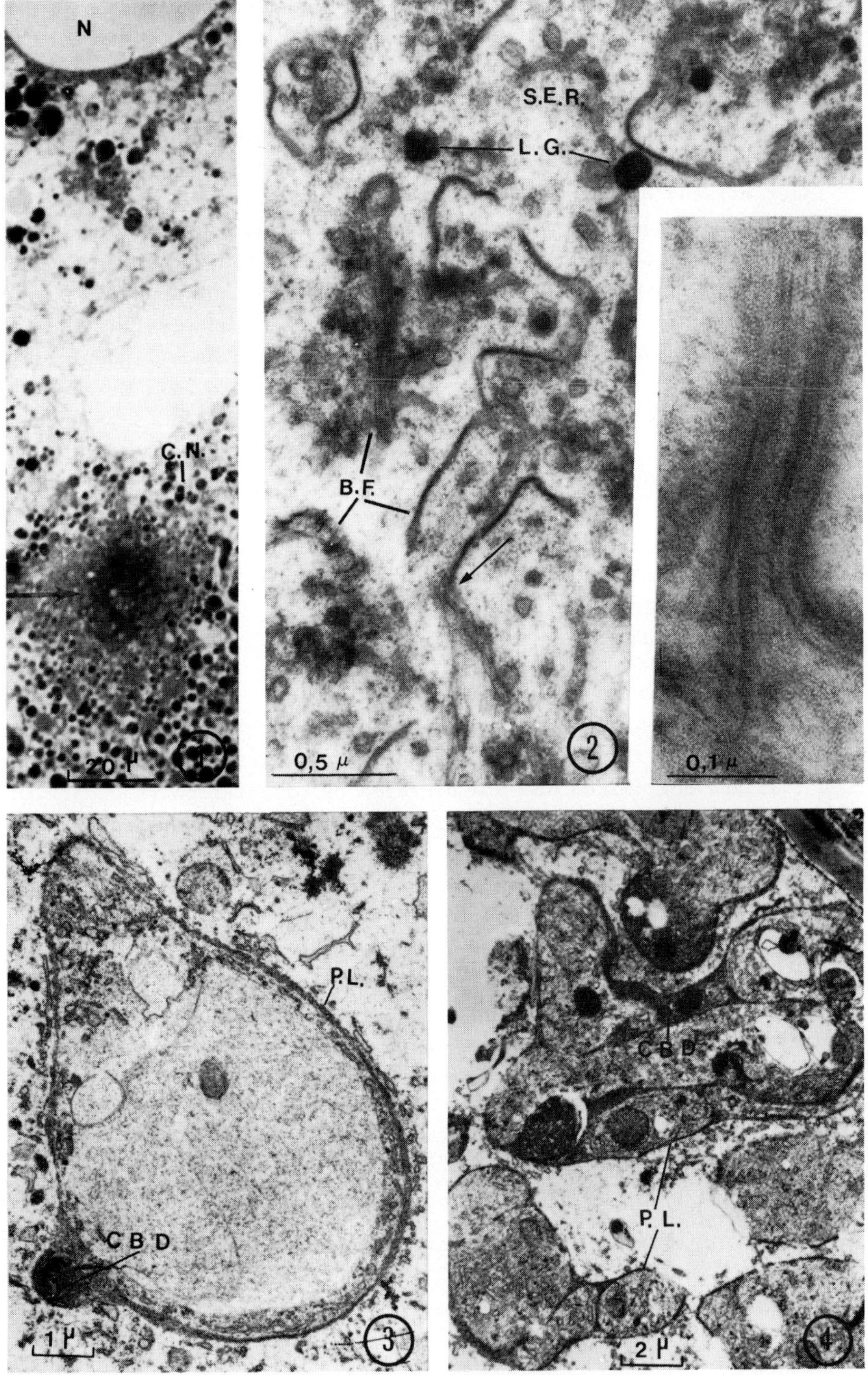
N
C.N.
20 μ
1
S.E.R.
L. G.
B.F.
0,5 μ
2
0,1 μ
P.L.
C B D
1 μ
3
C B D
P. L.
2 μ
4

together and we can no longer tell the one from the other (fig. 7) ; one of the organelles often looks as if it were moulded on the other (fig. 9).

As this "agglutination" of mitochondria goes on, we can observe a proliferation and a swelling of inner cristae which, seen in cross section, seems to re-partition each organelle (fig. 8). The blebbing of inner cristae will then bring into being vacuolised zones in each mitochondrion (fig. 10). Those changes go along with a swelling of mitochondria. When those transformations are over, the oosphere mitochondria still clinging are seen by clusters presenting, in cross-section, 20 to 30 voluminous organelles vesiculated and re-partitioned, this repartitioning coming either from the blebbing of inner cristae or from the close clinging of 2 mitochondria (fig. 9). We came across similar changes among the oosphere mitochondria in Sciadopitys verticillata[9].

When oogenesis is over, every plastid, every mitochondrion in the female cell has undergone a deep change and will thus be easily identifiable during fecundation and proembryogenesis ; on the other hand, we interpret these transformations as an early process of degeneration which goes on during proembryogenesis[10].

II. The male gamete.

An archegonium about to be fecundated is topped with a pollen-tube containing 2 large hemispheric spermatozoids of equal size. Both spermatozoids are far from being parted because of irregular rows of vesicles that are not joined and are deprived of parietal polysaccharidic fibrils. The main characteristic of sperm cytoplasm is its wealth of little differentiated plastids and mitochondria as well as of polyribosomes always clearly condensed in clusters in a medium cytoplasmic zone ; peripheral and perinuclear cytoplasmic zones reveal vacuolar profiles, golgi bodies near vesicules clusters that come from them, as well as a few RER parallel lamellae[11]. The cytoplasm of mature spermatozoids shows an actual topographic segregation between plastids, mitochondria and polyribosomes on the one hand, and the other cytoplasmic components on the other hand.

Fig. 5-9. 5. Plastids in mature oosphere. Arrow indicates gaps in plastidial membrane. Inset : Double membrane of plastids. 6. Neighbouring mitochondria of the central cell. Arrow indicates the short dense lines. 7. Mitochondria with two outer lamellae cling together. 8. Repartition of a mitochondrion by inner cristae. 9. Mitochondria of mature oosphere.

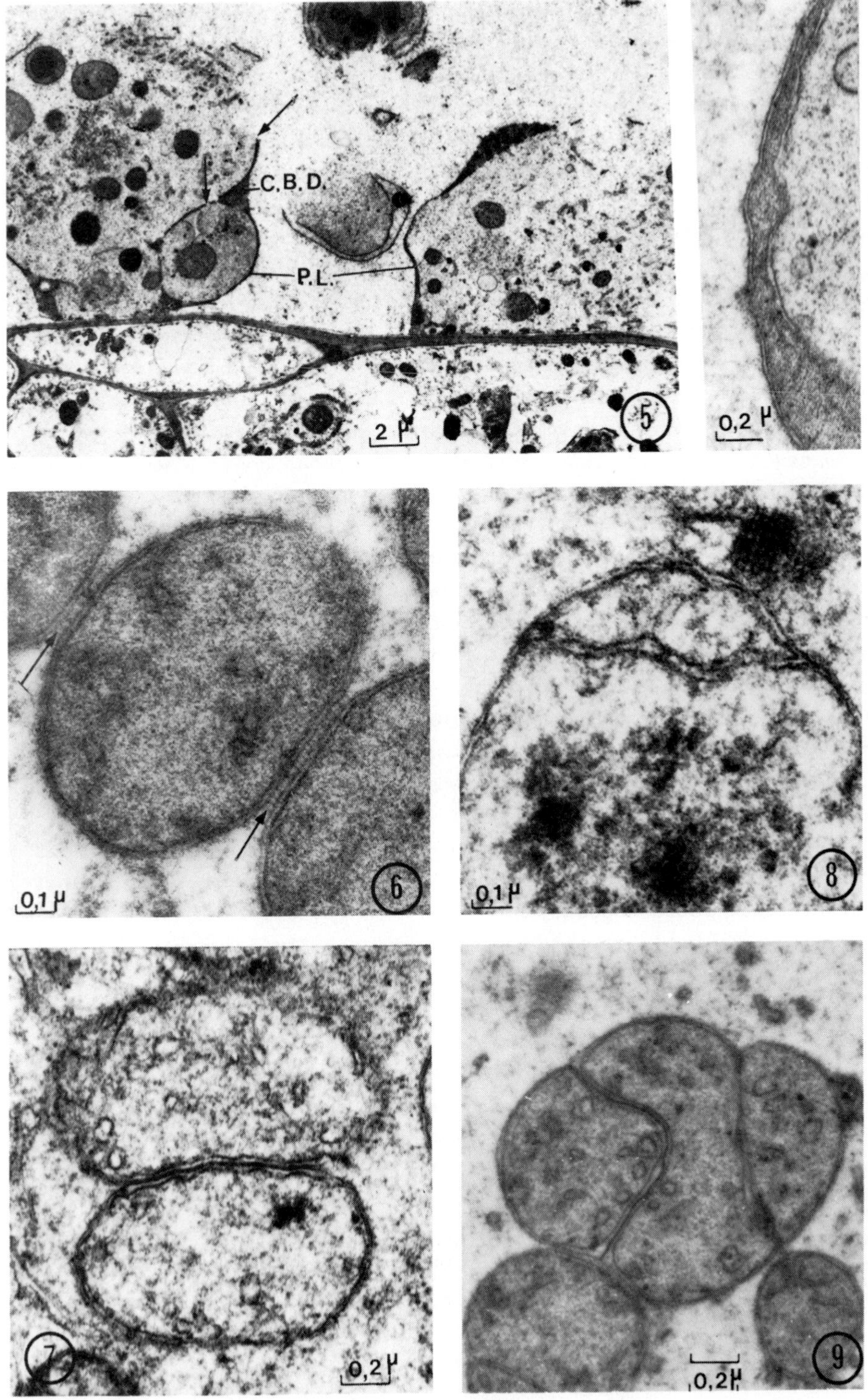
C.B.D.
P.L.
2 μ
5
0,2 μ
0,1 μ
6
0,1 μ
8
7
0,2 μ
0,2 μ
9

III. Penetration of the male gamete into the oosphere and fertilization.

a) Penetration of the male gamete.

As the spermatozoid penetrates the oosphere, the spermatic cytoplasm that has not yet entered the archegonial cavity is seen as studded with dense clusters made up of coils of membranes that look like concentric lamellated systems (fig. 11). These cytoplasmic zones outside the oosphere are deprived of plastids and mitochondria contrary to the cytoplasm already inside the oosphere, which is rich in organelles and presents few concentric lamellated systems (fig. 12).

Concentric lamellated systems show 3 main aspects (fig. 13) : 1) Typical concentric lamellated systems made up of parallel membranes that are more often than not coiled up and go by twos. 2) Amorphous looking zones, irregularly studded with granules, with rudiments or remnants of parallel lamellae ; these amorphous zones always lie inside multilamellar formations. 3) Thicker myelinic ribbons contained in vacuolised-looking zones often adjoining multilamellar formations.

After watching numerous photos and comparing them with similar formations described in materials allowing the use of cytoenzymological tests[12, 13, 14], we suggest the following remarks as to the origin and evolution of these myelinic formations. We can first watch the genesis of sequestration-membranes (fig. 14) that may stem from coalescing vesicles ; then, these sequestration-membranes isolate a cytoplasmic enclave which may sometimes look like a hernia in a cupuliform vacuole if the 2 lamellae of the sequestration-membrane open up (fig. 15). Inside the zone thus isolated we can watch a disappearence of the granular structure and an appearance of amorphous zones studded with tiny granules (fig. I6). From those amorphous zones multilamellar myelinic bodies appear and, later on the thickening of joined lamellae -may be in relation to phenomena of lipid overstorage- lead to the emergence of myelinic ribbons. All these morphological features might represent the various stages of a cellular autophagy process concerning the whole spermatic cytoplasm poor in plastids and mitochondria that has not yet entered the archegonial cavity.

The male cytoplasm already in contact with the female one or down in the space demarcated by the oosphere broken wall is dense because of its wealth of ribosomes. Male mitochondria are numerous in this

---

Fig. 10-12. 10. Degenerated mitochondria of mature oosphere. 11. Penetration of the fecundating sperm in archegonial cavity. Arrow indicates Myelinic figures. Double arrow indicates male cytoplasm without myelinic figures. 12. Male cytoplasm inside the oosphere, in contact with the female one Inset. Mitochondrion at higher magnification.

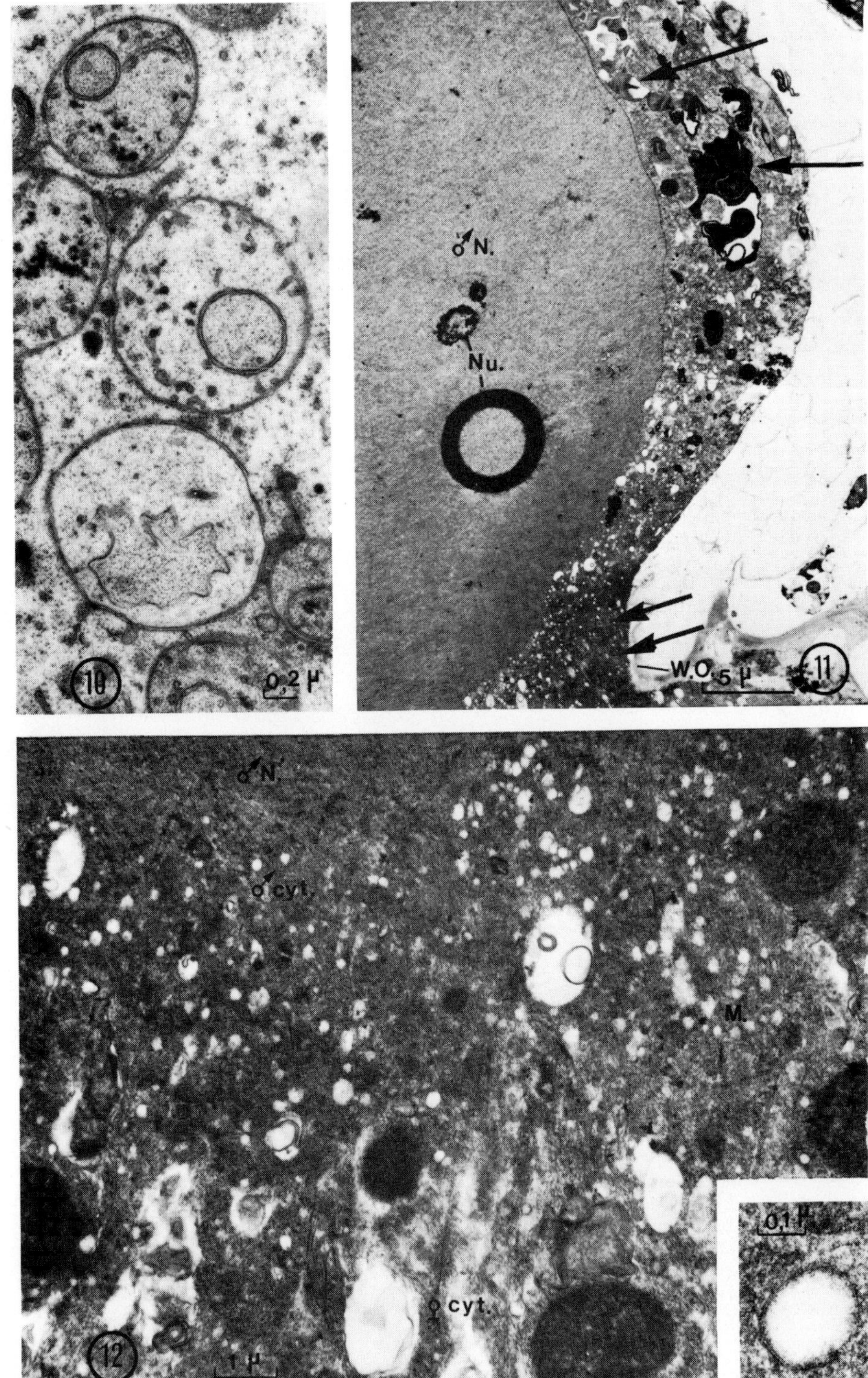
10
0,2 μ
♂N.
Nu.
W.O.
5 μ
11
♂N.
♂cyt.
M.
♀cyt.
12
1 μ
0,1 μ

zone and they get a large clear center (fig. 12). In return, we came across few profiles which could assuredly be spotted as the leucoplasts of the spermatozoid for it is likely the density of their stroma makes them hardly identifiable. So, we see that a functional segregation occurs in the spermatic cytoplasm during the penetration of the spermatozoid into the archegonial cell. Zones that are poor in plastids and mitochondria are lysed whereas zones where these organelles, accompanied by ribosomes, are densely grouped enter the oosphere without being degraded. This functional segregation combines with the topographical segregation observed among gametes that are still confined in the pollen-tube.

b) Fertilization and cenocytic proembryo.

Once in contact with the oosphere nucleus, the male nucleus is always accompanied by the spermatic cytoplasm,easily identified because its wealth of ribosomes (fig. 17). These cytoplasmic enclaves do not fuse with female cytoplasm and their only constituents are ribosomes, amyloplastids (fig. 17) and mitochondria, excluding any other kind of organelles such as RER, vesicles of various sizes, which were in male gametes still confined in the pollen-tube. A few myelinic formations, probably residual, can be found in this cytoplasm. The sperm cytoplasm moulds itself around the female nucleus which grows into the zygote after karyogamy (fig. 18).

The upper part of the zygote always presents a large nucleus which stems from the second spermatozoid confined in the fecundating pollen-tube. This compulsory penetration of the second sperm nucleus into the oosphere is associated with the fact that inside the pollen-tube both spermatozoids depend on each other because there is no actual wall between them. This second male nucleus is accompanied by no male cytoplasm ; it is in direct contact with the female cytoplasm being lysed. Plastids, mitochondria and ribosomes in the second spermatozoid may likely have increased the stock of organelles previously brought in to the zygote by the fecundating spermatozoid[4].

Yet, after watching the importance of lysing phenomena concerning the cytoplasm of fecundating spermatozoid, as it penetrates the oosphere, any conclusion about what the plastids and mitochondria of the second spermatozoid might become is questionable as long as it is not scientifically observed.

Fig. 13-16. 13. Myelinic formation : Various stages of evolution. 14. sequestration-membranes isolate a cytoplasmic enclave . 15. Vacuoles surrounding a cytoplasmic enclave. 16. Amorphous looking zones and concentric lamellated system

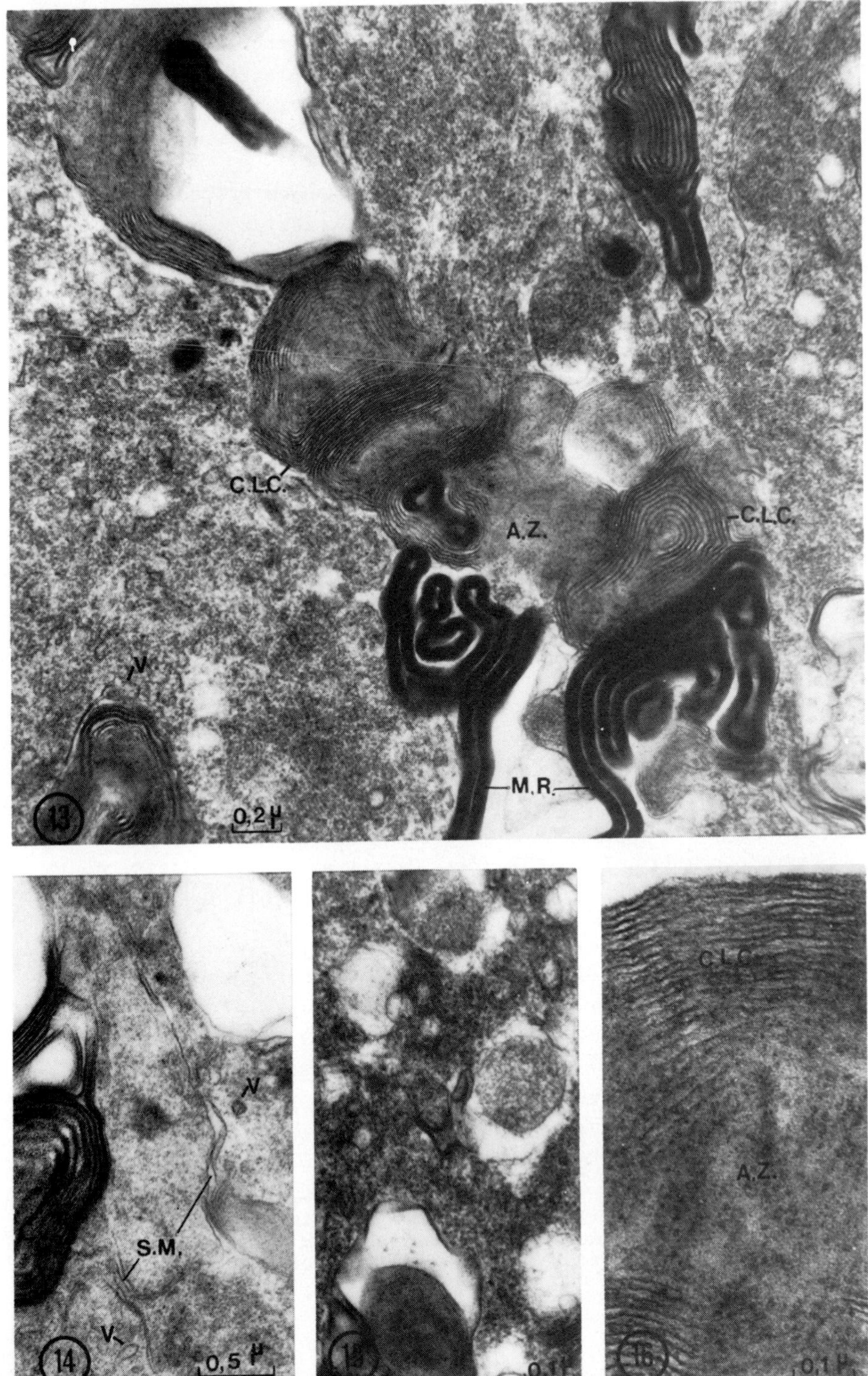
C.L.C.
A.Z.
C.L.C.
V
M.R.
13
0,2 µ
V
S.M.
V
14
0,5 µ
15
0,1 µ
C.L.C.
A.Z.
16
0,1 µ

The 2 then 4 nuclei resulting from the division of the zygote nucleus settle down at the bottom of the oosphere. In the proembryonic cytoplasm surrounding them we can find only male plastids and mitochondria still easily identifiable at this stage (fig. 19).

Conclusions.

After demonstrating the morphological changes preceding the degeneration of the oosphere mitochondria and plastids, then the lysis of the zones of spermatic cytoplasm deprived of these organelles, we can state that all the plastids and mitochondria of the proembryo of *Cephalotaxus drupacea* as well as the better part of its ribosomal RNA are of a male origin.

Among some gymnosperms, the male origin of at least a part of the proembryo plastids was demonstrated in the early XXth century[15]. More recent investigations proved that, according to the genus considered, the male origin of plastids and mitochondria may be either complete and exclusive[9, 10, 16], largely prevailing[17], or partial[7].

This quite unusual phenomenon in sexual reproduction is therefore, to a certain extent, a general feature among gymnosperms and it is probably linked up with the possibility of a non-Mendelian heredity, whose genetic demonstration was recently made among *Cryptomeria japonica*[18].

References

1. Arnoldi, W., 1900, Flora 87, 43.
2. Coker, W.C., 1907, Bot. Gaz. 43, 1.
3. Lawson, A.A., 1907, Ann. Bot. 21, 1.
4. Favre-Duchartre, M., 1957, Rev. Cytol. et Biol. Vég. 18, 4, 1.
5. Stabbe, W., 1971, Origin and continuity of cell Organelles (Springer Verlag, Berlin) 65.
6. Baxter, R., 1971, Origin and continuity of cell Organelles (Springer Verlag, Berlin) 46.
7. Camefort, H., 1968, Bull. Soc. Bot. Fr. 115, 137.
8. Thierry, J.P., 1967, J. Microscopie 6, 987.
9. Gianordoli, M., 1973, Caryologia 25, 1, 135.
10. Gianordoli, M., Personal observation unpublished.
11. Gianordoli, M., 1974, C.R. Acad. Sci. Paris 278, 2368.
12. Coulomb, P., 1968, C.R. Acad. Sci. Paris 267, 1373.

Fig. 17-19. 17. Fertilization : sperm cytoplasm surround the egg nucleus. Inset : Amyloplastid in sperm cytoplasm. 18. Zygote nucleus surrounded by sperm cytoplasm. 19. Cytoplasm of the tetranucleoted cenocytic proembryo.

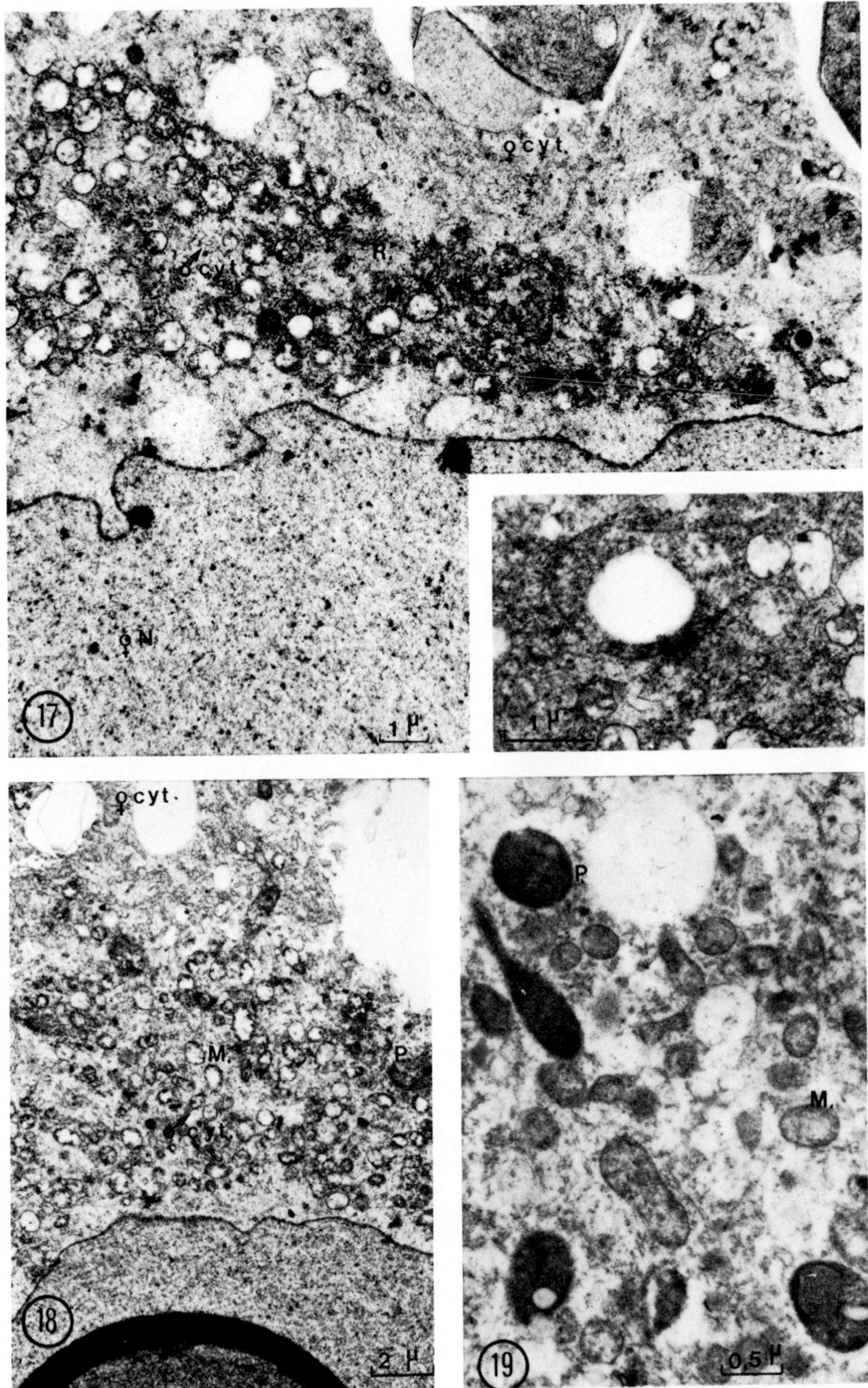
♀cyt.
R
♀cyt.
♀N
17
1 μ
1 μ
♀cyt.
M.
P
♀cyt.
18
2 μ
P
M.
19
0,5 μ

13. Hebant, CH., 1969, C.R. Acad. Sci. Paris 269, 1951.
14. Coulomb, Cl., 1972, Thèse 3ème Cycle, Marseille.
15. Vazart, B., 1958, Protoplasmatologia VII, 60.61.62.
16. Gianordoli, M., 1964, C.R. Acad. Sci. Paris 259, 3327.
17. Chesnoy, L., 1973, Caryologia 25, 1, 223.
18. Ohba, K., Iwakawa, M., Okada, Y. and Murai, M., 1971, Silvae genetica 20, 101.

Fertilization in Higher Plants, ed. H.F. Linskens.

SOME PHYSICO-CHEMICAL FACTORS IN THE OVULE DURING EMBRYOGENESIS

M. Ryczkowski

Department of Plant Physiology, Jagellonian University, Cracow

1. Introduction

The present paper summarizes the results of researches carried out by the author aiming at explaining the physico-chemical and physiological properties of the liquid /central vacuolar sap/ and solid /endosperm tissue/ environment of the developing embryo /during proembryo and proper embryo stages/, and partly the embryo itself.

These researches concerned: 1. osmotic value /osmotic gradients/ [1,2], 2. concentrations and composition of free amino acids[3,4], 3. oxygen tension /pO_2/[5], and 4. respiration rate /Qo_2/ gradients[6] in basic constituent tissues of the developing ovule.

For a few reasons it seemed to be appropriate to follow these properties in the developing ovule: the first is the lack of such data in the literature[7,8,9,10], the second is the usefulness of their knowledge for the embryo and endosperm tissue cultures in vitro /particularly the normal and abortive proembryos/, and the third they make it possible to compare the embryogenesis in the plant and animal kingdom and possibly find a common mechanism controling this process.

2. Material and methods

Ovules of Haemanthus Katharinae Bak. were used as experimental material. The number of days counted from the day the perianth wilt to the day of sampling, and the sizes of ovules and embryos were the adopted criteria of the age of ovules and the embryos.

The technique of coat /integuments+nucellus/, endosperm tissue and embryo preparation, their separation into the micropylar and chalazal parts was given in the previous paper[2]. The coat from the micropylar part of the ovule is denoted by Mpc /micropylar part of the coat/ and that from the chalazal part - Chpc /chalazal part of the coat/, and the endosperm tissue and embryo correspondingly - Mpen and Chpen resp. Mpe /micropylar part of the embryo with radicle/ and Chpe /chalazal part of the embryo with shoot apex/.

The osmotic value was determined by means of the thermoelectric method[1], the concentrations of free amino acids - micro column amino acid analyser[11], the oxygen tension /pO_2/- physiological gas analyser[5], and the respiration rate /Qo_2/ gradients - Warburgś apparatus.[12]

The results shown in fig.1 and fig.3A-B are means of 2-3 measurements. The results of Qo_2 are multiplied by 1000.

3. Results

Osmotic gradients. a/ At the proembryo and proper embryo stages there was a distinct/chalaza ⟶ micropyle/ osmotic gradient in the coat and endosperm tissue. An analogous gradient was found in the embryo during its development, fig.1. b/ The osmotic value of the sap from chalazal part of each of the examined tissues /coat, endosperm and embryo/ was always higher than that of the micropylar one of the same tissue. c/ The proembryo was characterized by the osmotic value almost equal to the osmotic value of the central vacuolar sap and changed during its development, fig.1, curves I,II. d/ The beginning of the differentiation of the proper embryo occurred at low osmotic value of its environment. e/ The elongation of the embryo proceedsin the direction opposite to the osmotic gradients in the coat, endosperm tissue and embryo itself.

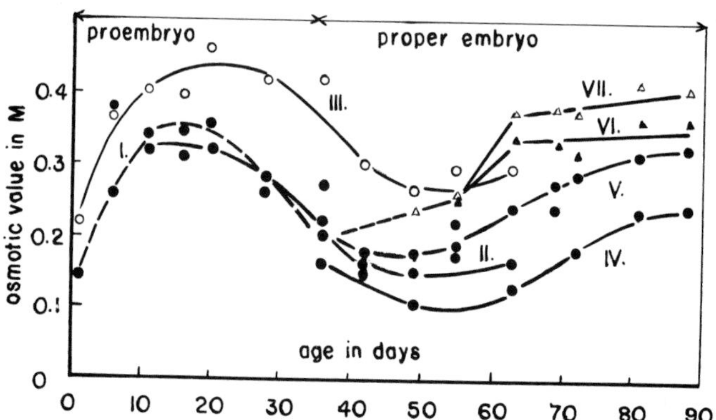

Fig.1. Osmotic /chalaza ⟶ micropyle/ gradient in the coat, endosperm tissue and embryo; abscissae: age of the ovules in days counted from the perianth wilt to the day of sampling. Curve I- osmotic value of the central vacuolar sap, II- osmotic value of the sap from Mpc, III- osmotic value of the sap from Chpc, IV- osmotic value of the sap from Mpen, V- osmotic value of the sap from Chpen, VI- osmotic value of the sap from Mpe, VII- osmotic value of the sap from Chpe; abbreviations as in the text.

Table

Mean concentrations and compositions of free amino acids in the liquid /central vacuolar sap, proembryo stage/ resp. solid /endosperm tissue, proper embryo stage/ environment of the embryo and the embryo itself. The number after the line indicates the number of stages in which analyses were carried out and the determined amino acids were found.

No	Component				
	Age of ovules in days	9–18	28–33	46–82	60–82
	Sizes of embryos in mm	0,13x0,10 - 0,20x0,20	0,45x0,40 - 0,56x0,54	2,21x1,14 - 9,82x2,26	6,20x1,06 - 9,82x2,26
		central vacuolar sap		endosperm	proper embryo
		nmoles/ml sap		resp. g tissue	
1	MetSO	+	+	+	+
2	Asp	1057,7/3	1288,5/2	4900,0/3	3302,0/2
3	T+S+A+G	1799,7/3	2609,5/2	8775,3/3	11451,0/2
4	Glu	344,3/3	487,0/2	2142,3/3	6429,5/2
5	Pro	1453,3/3	+ /2	248,0/3	355,0/2
6	Cit	-	-	+ /1	+ /1
7	Pen	-	-	+ /1	-
8	Gly	363,7/3	89,5/2	215,3/3	218,5/2
9	Ala	3268,3/3	769,5/2	3538,0/3	8927,5/2
10	Aaba	27,0/2	-	37,7/3	99,5/2
11	$GlucNH_2$	-	-	28,0/3	-
12	Val	791,7/3	98,5/2	274,3/3	304,5/2
13	Cys	33,0/1	+ /1	-	79,0/2
14	Met	278,7/3	47,0/2	18,5/3	+ /2
15	Ileu	226,0/3	106,5/2	733,0/3	109,0/2
16	Leu	292,0/3	141,5/2	70,1/3	85,0/2
17	Tyr	77,3/3	63,0/2	81,7/3	87,0/2
18	Phe	2058,7/3	427,0/2	69,7/2	44,0/2
19	$EtNH_2$	194,3/3	76,0/2	363,0/3	1330,0/2
20	Gaba	185,3/3	125,0/2	186,0/3	215,0/2
21	Orn	+ /3	+ /2	+ /3	+ /2
22	Lys	768,7/3	355,5/2	541,7/3	2554,0/2
23	Try	189,7/3	282,5/2	91,0/1	-
24	His	261,3/3	254,0/2	119,3/3	179,0/2
25	Arg	1106,0/3	790,0/2	1380,7/3	12579,0/2
	Total	14803,7	8010,5	23153,9	48351,5
	NH_3	++ /3	3541,0/2	2900,0/3	5750,0/2

The very low and high concentrations of some amino acids and ammonia were denoted in table by + resp. ++, T+S+A+G = threonine+serine+asparagine+glutamine.

Free amino acids. a/ The differentiation of the proper embryo began during the low global concentration of free amino acids, table. b/ Since the same free amino acids /21-24/ occurred in the liquid and solid environments and proper embryo /table/ it is probable that a similar complex of free amino acids is characteristic of the proembryo. c/ In the environment of the proembryo and proper embryo high concentrations of ammonia were found, table.

Oxygen tension /pO_2/. a/ In young ovules /proembryo stage/ the pO_2 rapidly decreased to a minimum value /0-5%/ and in older ones /proper embryo stage/ it slightly increased, fig.2. b/The endosperm tissue and embryo could respire in an anaerobic way in a certain period of their development. c/ The begining of the differentiation of the proper embryo occurred during the minimum value of pO_2,fig.2. d/ Probably the changes of pO_2 /in the ovule/ are accompanied by concomitant but reverse changes of the pCO_2.

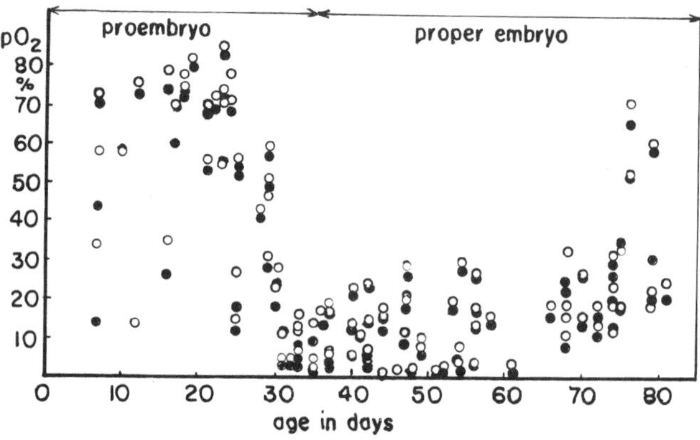

Fig.2. Changes of the oxygen tension /pO_2/ inside the ovule; abscissae: age of the ovules - see fig.1. White dots - pO_2 values measured 30 sec after the micro electrode was inserted into the ovule; black dots - values of pO_2 measured after 1 min. pO_2 is expressed in % of mm Hg/pO_2 of oxygen tension in water measured before each measurement of this value in the ovule to eliminate changes of atmospheric pressure and temperature.

Respiration rate /Qo_2/ gradients in the coat and endosperm tissue. a/ The Qo_2 of the chalazal part of the ovule /coat resp. endosperm tissue/ was generally higher than the corresponding value found in these tissues taken from its micropylar part, fig.3A-B. b/ The Qo_2 in the coat /mean values/ was 4-8 times higher than the analogous values found for the endosperm tissue in the investigated ovules. c/ In the coat and endosperm tissues the Qo_2 gradients overlapped the osmotic gradients. d/ The elongation of the embryo proceeded in the direction opposite to that of the decreasing Qo_2 in the coat and endosperm tissue.

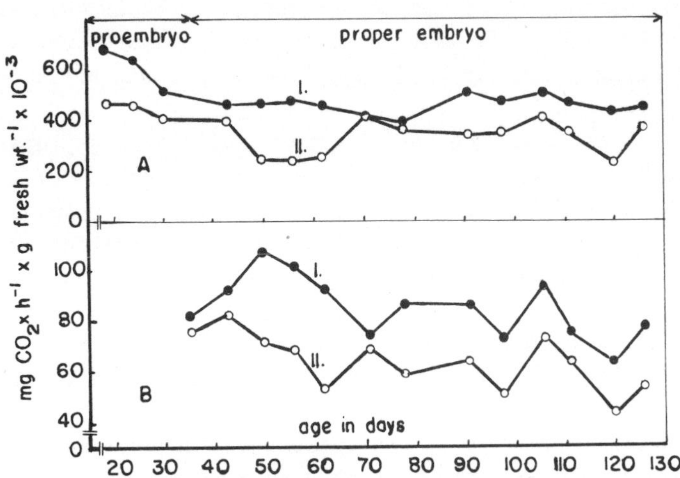

Fig.3A-B. Respiration rate /Qo_2 in mg CO_2/h/g fresh wt./ gradients in the coat and endosperm tissues; abscissae: age of the ovules - see fig.1. A, curve I- Qo_2 in the coat from Chpc, II- Qo_2 in the coat from Mpc. B, I- Qo_2 in the endosperm tissue from Chpen, II- Qo_2 in the endosperm tissue from Mpen; abbreviations as in the text.

4. Discussion

The osmotic gradients in the coat, endosperm and embryo tissues on one hand and the differences in the osmotic values and concentrations of free amino acids between the embryo and endosperm tissues on the other one, could be ascribed to the following causes: a/ A different origin of the embryo /2n chromosomes/ and endosperm tissues /3n chromosomes/ and specificity of the fusion of gametic nuclei[8,9,10]. This probably conditions the differences in the metabolism in both these tissues. b/ Shifting the developmental and biochemical processes in relation to each other[2,3] in the endosperm and embryo tissues. The exponential phase of the embryo growth occurred during the end of the exponential phase of ovule growth[1,2,13]. In this case the synthesis of starch and proteins from the compounds of low molecular weight would be more intensive in the endosperm tissue than in the embryo. In turn this would lead to a lower osmotic value and concentration of free amino acids in the endosperm tissue as compared with these values in the embryo[2,13,14]. c/ It was established that the nutrient compounds were supplied to the ovule by means of a vascular strend which usually end in the chalaza[9]. It is evident that their concentrations will decrease from the chalaza to the micropyle because of being gradually used up by the developing tissue of the ovule.

It could be assumed that the differentiation of the proper embryo is influenced not only by the concentration gradients[2,8] of low molecular compounds but also by the proper /low/ osmotic value of these compounds[1,2] and changes in the composition and concentration in such groups of compounds as sugars[14] and amino acids[3,4]. It is suggested that almost all amino acids occurring in the ovule are supplied to it by vegetative organs[15]. But in the case of green embryos /H.Katharinae/ which are capable of photosynthesis[16] the possibility of the production of free amino acids in situ[17] cannot be excluded.

The decrease of pO_2 inside the ovule could be ascribed to the following factors: 1.The numerous cuticular membranes restricting the penetration of oxygen inside the ovule[18] and, thus, the intensity of the respiration of the inner part of the ovule. They occur on the outer and inner surfaces of the integuments[9]. 2. The second factor is the absorption by the coat of a certain amount of oxygen diffusing inside the ovule. Bils et al.[19] found a higher Qo_2 shown by the soybean coats resp. mitochondria obtained from them than for the whole seeds resp. the cotyledons of their embryos during the development. It should be stressed that coats of young ovules are their basic part[20] and probably play a decisive role in respiration[18,19]. The development of the endosperm tissue probably also contributes to lowering the level of pO_2 inside the ovule. A small increase of pO_2 in older ovules /34-88 days old/ could be connected with a lower consumption of oxygen by their coats and endosperm tissues which could be conditioned by the changes in the ultrastructure of mitochondria and partial inactivation of their enzymes[21].

Recent opinions concerning the biochemistry of respiration of the tissues of the developing ovule are not concordant. Stanly[22], Forman et al.[23] claimedthat respiration of the haploid endosperm tissue /Pinus lambertana/ resp. the embryo /Gossypium hirsutum/ is of aerobic character. On the other hand Johri et al.[24] admit the possibility of anaerobic respiration of seed /endosperm and embryo, Zephyranthes lancasteri/ in a determined developmental stage. This opinion is in agreement with the data obtained by Butrose[25] and Opik[26]. They found that mitochondria in wheat endosperm resp. the pea cotyledons are poorly elaborated in early developmental stages of seed development. Thus it is probable that endosperm tissue resp. embryo of the developing ovule can respire in an anaerobic way depending on the species, the size of the ovule and its developmental stage.

The pO_2 /pCO_2/ and NH_4^+ can play the same important role in plant embryogenesis in situ as they do in animal embryogenesis[27] resp. in embryogenesis of carrot from its tissue in vitro[28].

The results referring to the Qo_2 gradients are in agreement with the authors' hypothesis assuming the existance of Qo_2 gradient[29] and data concerning the osmotic gradients in the ovule[2] resp. the free amino acids gradient in the endosperm tissue[29]. The marked physiological and biochemical relation observed between the embryo and endosperm tissues during their development[7,8,9] and the occurence of Qo_2 gradient in the latter one showed some similarities with animal embryos in which analogous gradients are found[30]. The gradients of Qo_2 in animal embryos overlapped the gradients of nucleic acids and proteins synthesis[30]. The gradients of Qo_2 in the coat and endosperm tissues in ovules of H. Katharinae supported the authors' hypothesis referring to the gradients of nucleic acids and proteins synthesis in it[29]. This would be in accordance with the data obtained for animal embryos[30] and for the endosperm tissue in ovules of Iris pseudoacorus[31].

Distinct differences observed in the Qo_2 between the coat and endosperm tissues on one hand, and the different parts - chalaza and micropyle - of the same tissue on the other hand may be conditioned by the following factors: a/ different number of mitochondria present in these tissues[19,23], b/ differences in their ultrastructure[23,26] and enzymatic activity[19,21]. Perhaps these differences could be connected with the physico-chemical gradients of low molecular compounds in the endosperm tissue and coat[2,29].

Based upon the authors' results and data obtained by Jensen et al.[32] and Forman et al.[23] some similarities were found in animal and plant embryogenesis. The first similarity concerns the mechanism of fertilization[32], the second - respiration of the embryo[23] and Qo_2 gradients in the ovule[6], the third physico-chemical gradients[2,29], and fourth - the role played by pO_2 and possibly pCO_2 in the interior organism[5]. These similarities suggest a possibility of a common basic mechanism controlling the embryogenesis in animal and plant kingdoms.

5. References

1. Ryczkowski,M., 1969, Z.Pflanzenphysiol.,61,422.
2. ---- 1967, Acta Soc.Bot.Pol.,36,627.
3. ---- ibid., 40,475.
4. ----, Ryczkowska,H.,1973, Bull.Acad.Polon.Sci.,Ser.Sci.Biol.,21, 759
5. ---- 1973, ibid.,21,303.
6. ---- 1974, ibid.,in press.
7. Maheshwari,P.,1950, An introduction to the embryology of angiosperms /McGraw-Hill Book Company, INC. New York Toronto London/.
8. Wardlaw,C.W.,1955, Embryogenesis in plants /London: Methuen and Co. LTD; New York: John Wiley and Sons, INC/.
9. Zinger,N.V.,1958, The seed, its development and physiological properties /Moscow/.
10. Wardlaw,C.W.,1965, in: Encyclopedia of plant physiology,vol.15/I eds. W.Rhuland /Berlin, Heidelberg, New York/ p.844.
11. Linskens,H.F.,Tupy,J.,1966,Der Züchter, 26,151.
12. Ryczkowski,M.,Szewczyk,E.,1974, Bull.Acad.Polon.Sci.,Ser.Sci. Biol., in press.
13. ---- 1972, ibid.,20,345.
14. ---- 1962, Acta Soc.Bot.Pol.,31,53.
15. Baptist,N.C.,1963, J.Exptl.,14,29.
16. Ryczkowski,M.,Szewczyk,E.,1973, Bull.Acad.Polon.Sci.,Ser.Sci. Biol.,21,659.
17. Bassham,J.A. and Calvin,M.,1962, The path of carbon in photosynthesis /PWRiL, Warszawa/.
18. Ohmura,T.,Howell,R.W.,1962, Physiol.Plantarum, 15,341.
19. Bils,R.F.,Howell,R.W.,1963, Crop Science, 3,304.
20. Rijven,A.H.G.C.,Banbury,C.A.,1960, 188,546.
21. Kollöffel,C.,1970, Planta /Berl./, 91,321.
22. Stanly,R.G.,1957, Plant Physiol.,32,409.
23. Forman,M. and Jensen,W.A.,1965, Planta /Berl./, 40,765.
24. Johri,M.M.,Maheshwari,S.C.,1966, Plant and Cell Physiol.,7,49.
25. Butrose,M.S.,1963, Austral.J.Biol.Sci.,16,305.
26. Opik,H.,1968, J.Exp.Bot.,19,64.
27. Loomis,W.F.,1959, in: Cell, organism and milieu, eds. D. Rudnic /Ronald Press Company. New York/ p.253.
28. Halperin,W.,Wetherell,D.F.,1965, Nature, 205,519.
29. Ryczkowski,M.,1971, Bull.Acad.Polon.Sci.,Ser.Sci.Biol.,19,801.
30. Brachet,J.,1964, The biochemistry of development /PWN,Warszawa/.
31. Konopska,L.,1972, Acta Soc.Bot.Pol.,41,369.
32. Jensen,W.A.,Fischer,D.B.,1968, Planta /Berl./, 78,158.

PHYLOGENETIC ASPECTS OF FERTILIZATION

Fertilization in Higher Plants, ed. H.F. Linskens.
© 1974, North-Holland Publishing Company – Amsterdam, the Netherlands.

PHYLOGENETIC ASPECTS OF THE SPERMAPHYTES'DOUBLE FERTILIZATION

M. FAVRE-DUCHARTRE

Faculté des Sciences de Reims
B.P. 347, 51062 Reims-Cédex, France

SUMMARY: With the siphonogamous ovulated plants, the pollen tube leads up to the female gametophyte two sperm nuceli which may or may not be united. The female gametophyte may include a unique or multiple egg cells, either distant from one to the another or contiguous, being integrated to similar or different structures. The said case appears most frequently found with the Angiosperms and allows the formation of two different organisms, the embryo and the endosperm.

1. INTRODUCTION

Some botanists[1, 2] consider the angiospermous double fertilization so original a phenomenon that they take argument to conclude to the monophyletism of Angiosperms.

In order to make an opinion on the matter, we shall analyse ♂ and ♀ gametogenesis processes as well as the fertilization types they allow in gymnospermous and angiospermous Spermaphytes[3].

With those plants, which are all siphonogamous, we shall term "double fertilization" the formation of two zygotes into a unique gametophyte reached a unique pollen tube. So, we are dealing with a wider conception as compared to the usual term of "double fertilization" stricto sensu, in which the "Angiospermous" adjective is unexpressed.

The haploid structures of figures 1, 2, 3 and 4 do not imply the least phylogenetic filiation of the taxa which they represent. This suggests that those reproductive gametophytic structures of the different phyla can be compared with ladders, the crosspieces of which are less and less numerous and raised one beside the other. However, in the author's mind, those degrees of decreasing gametophytic organization mark that to which evolution might have been leading, what Angiosperms now are showing us... as small ladders, representing angiospermous gametophytic structures, which may be obtained from progressively shortened ones.

As all the cells of ♂ and ♀ gametophytes are not always individualized, we will consider the numbers, the positions, the relationships and the functions of the nuclei within the pollen tubes of various types and in the gymnospermous ♀ prothalli and angiospermous embryo sacs.

2. WHERE ARE THE ♂ AND THE ♀ GAMETES FORMED?

It is well known that the Thallophytes form their ♂ as well as ♀ gametes from a protoplasm which is separated from the outside only by the cell-wall of the gametocyte (that of the spermatocyte around sperm-cells, fig. 1a: oocyte around egg cell, fig. 2a).

In the Cormophytes, on the contrary, an envelope constituted of several or, at least one cell, generally integrates the gametes into gametangia (♂ antheridia, fig. 1 b-e; ♀ archegonia, fig. 2 b-e).

In Siphonogamous plants, the antheridial unicellular envelope increases greatly toward the ♀ gametes and for that reason, is called the "tube-cell". The latter protects a number of sexual nuclei (fig. 1c, 1d) limited to never more

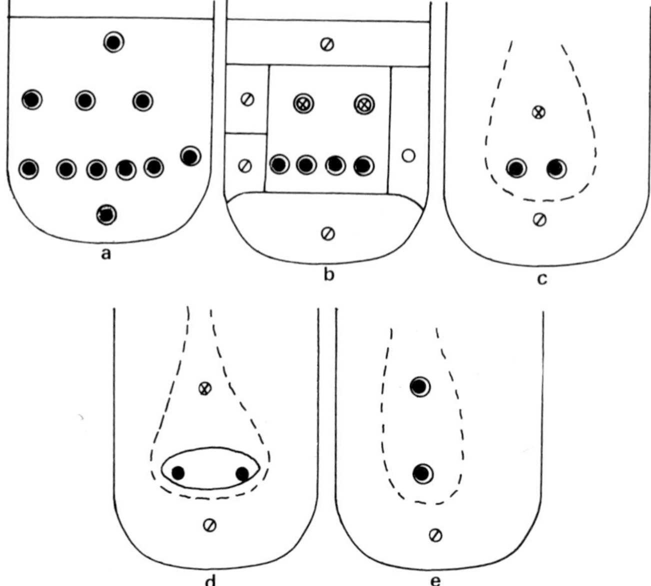

Fig.1. The ♂ gametes are formed: a) Immediately under the spermatocyte cell wall in Thallophytes (in Sphaeroplea, Chlorophyceae, for example[4]).
In a general way, in all the figures illustrating this article, sexual nuclei, ♂ as well as ♀, are represented black. b) Under an antheridial pluricellular envelope, in Pteridophytes [Azolla, for example[5]: "The spermatids' mother-cell normally forms 8 spermatids, but often the last horizontal division fails in a group of cells: then 4 spermatids of normal size and 2 larger "double" ones"] can be counted. In the schematized special case, the two deepest spermatogene nuclei (crossed) have not divided. The antheridial envelope cell nuclei are barred once. c, d, e) Under a unicellular anthiridial envelope, called tube-cell, in Spermaphytes, with the following organization simplification: c) in the Taxodiaceae and the Cupressaceae (Gymnosperms) a sterile spermatogene nucleus can be seen, called a stalked nucleus (crossed), and of two independent sperm cells; d) in the Pinaceae, the sperm nuclei are in a common cytoplasm; e) in Gnetum, Welwitschia and the Angiosperms, the equivalent of stalk nucleus and of the mother nucleus of the ♂ nuclei of Pinaceae, Taxodiaceae, Cupressaceae play the sperm nuclei part.

than one sterile spermatogenous nucleus called the "stalk nucleus" (absent in Gnetum, Welwitschia, and Angiosperms, fig. 2e) and two sperm nuclei. These are united (in Pinaceae, for example, fig. 1d) or incorporated to cells independent of one other (in the Cupressaceae, fig. 1c, the Angiosperms, fig. 1e, for example).

In the ♀ gametangium too, the envelope of sterile cells that protects the egg cell becomes less and less important in the course of evolution: according to the different phylogenetic level (fig. 2b-2e) the egg cell is then separated from the outside by a decreasing number of cells, so that it is finally found naked (fig. 2f).

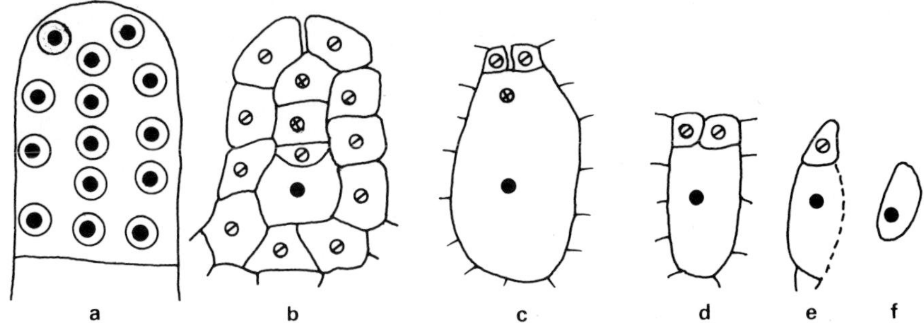

Fig. 2. The ♀ gamets are formed: a) Immediately under the oocyte cell wall, in Thallophytes (in Sphaeroplea, Chlorophyceae, for example[4]). b) Under an archegonial pluricellular envelope, in Pteridophytes. The egg cell is covered by a ventral canal cell and two canal nuclei (crossed). c, d, e) In archegonia which are simpler in their structure when one considers the Taxodiaceae, the Cupressaceae (c); Taxus, Oenothera (d); the majority of Angiosperms (e) in which each synergid would represent a unicellular neck covering a ♀ gametic central nucleus (cf. fig. 5). f) In a marginal naked cell, in archegonium initial position, in Gnetum, Welwitschia and the great majority of Angiosperms (cf. fig. 5).

In Pinus radiata, Torreya taxifolia, Dicraea, Apinagia, the gametophyte produces only one egg cell (fig. 3a-d). Instead, in the great majority of Spermaphytes taxa, several egg cells are differentiated, generally disposed at the micropylar pole, distant from one another (fig. 4a and c) or contiguous (fig. 4b, d and e).

In all cases, egg cells are not fertilizable for a long time. In archaic taxa, such as Pinaceae, the different egg cells of a same gametophyte are formed simultaneously, so that they all degenerate at the same time and the gametophyte remains fertilizable only as log as if it contains a single archegonium. On the contrary, in genera such as Cephalotaxus and Taxus (fig. 4c), archegonia ripen one after the other[3] so that the gametophytes bearing them are fertilizable longer than in the first case. In Angiosperms, the ♀ gametophyte is called "embryo sac".

Since an egg cell is a cell, which, being fertilized by a sperm nucleus will produce a zygote, we realise that most often (fig. 5), egg cells integrated at two different levels of organization coexist in those haploid organisms: 1) each central sexual nucleus situates an egg cell pertaining, in the author's point of view, to one archegonium the neck of which is represented by one synergid (fig. 2e, 5) [if two (fig. 4e, 5) or more than two (fig. 4d) central egg cells are not individualized in the same number of gametes separated from each other by cell walls, that is due, in the author's opinion, to the fact that the ♀ gametophyte is fertilizable before it has reached the centripetal partitioning which is accomplishes in Gymnosperms (fig. 6B1). Resulting from that, central sexual nuclei fuse before or during fertilizing caryogamy1] ; 2) the mariginal egg cell (fig. 2f and 5) occupies the position of initial archegonium and therefore represents a juvenile structure as compared to the central egg cells integrated to bi- or tri-cellular archegonia (fig. 2d, e, 4d).

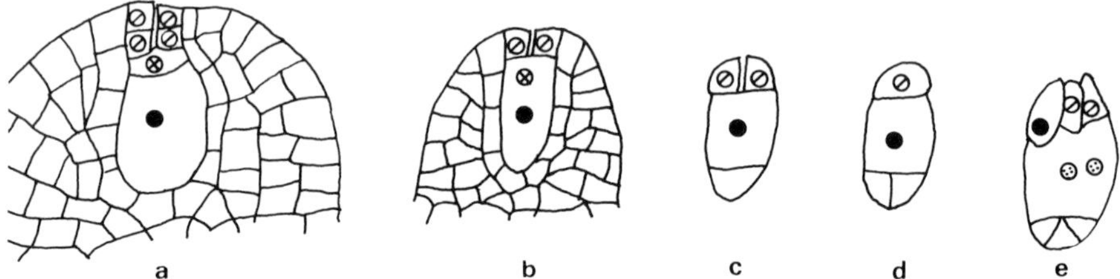

Fig. 3. ♀ gametophytes producing but one egg cell incorporated to more and more simple archegonium structures: a) Pinus radiata; b) Torreya taxifolia; c) Dicraea; d) Apinagia; e) some monandrae orchidaceae in which the central nuclei (dotted) have lost their sexual character, the unique marginal egg cell, assimilable to an initial archegonium are fertilizable[6].
For the sake of clarity, in that embryo sac drawing as well as in those of figures 4d, 6A3, 6C1, the marginal egg cell is represented in the same plane as both synergids, though it usually stands behind or in fron of them. (cf. fig. 5).

In some Orchidaceae of the subfamily monandrae, the marginal egg cell represents only the unique fertilizable ♀ gamete, for the other two ones, integrated to the bicellular archegonia, have fallen into desuetude and are nc longer reached by the second sperm nucleus or, in case they are, the zygote thus formed does not proliferate[6] (fig. 3e): in consequence of that, the embryo sac of monandrae Orchidaceae is drawn as in the one egg cell ♀ gametophyte category.

Exceptionally, one or several marginal egg cells may differentiate in the synergid or antipod positions.

As early as a939, Joshi[8] inventied more than 17 species, the embryo sacs of which presented "egg-like synergidae" and among 7 of those species is observed the development of embryos that appear to be "due to the fertilization of egg-like synergidae". Instead concluding with Joshi: "The synergidae therefore do not differ fundamentally from the egg and should be regarded as of the same nature" the author thinks it more logical to admit that what is called "egg-like synergidae" are true supernumerary egg cells exceptionally differentiated at the place of synergids (cf. fig. 4e).

Figures 3c, d, e, 4d, e illustrate the diversity of the angiospermous ♀ gametophyte organization. In fact, this one is due much more to bispory, tetraspory and the nuclei fusion which occurs in some taxa. However, in 70% of the species, the embryo sacs are of the *Polygonum* type characterized by one marginal cell and two central egg cells. Although, among a single species some variability has been depicted[9] regarding the cell disposition of those haploid organisms which so are poorly developed and parasitic, they keep ability to modify their organization.

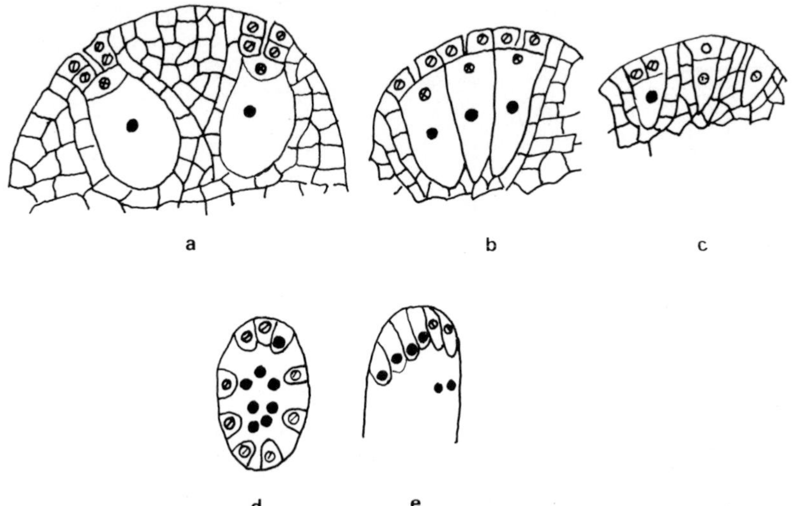

Fig. 4. ♀ gametophytes producing more than one egg cell incorporated to more and more simple structures. a) *Pinus silvestris*; b) Taxodiaceae, Cupressaceae; c) *Taxus*, in which a gradual sexual maturation is observed. The dots symbolise the immature character of the nuclei of the initial archegonium and of the central cell of the unachieved archegonium; d) *Peperomia pellucida*; e) *Crepis capillaris*, teratoligical case[7].

3. DIVERS TYPES OF FERTILIZATION IN SIPHONOGAMS

The essentials of the above statements are summarized in figure 6 which expresses moreover the results of the different types of gametic confrontation.

So one may realise that:

The ♂ gametophytes-pollen tubes always produce two sperm nuclei.

When they are joined, both penetrate into one archegonium cavity: one of them fertilizes the egg nucleus, the other degenerates or, in some genera such as *Cephalotaxus*, *Taxus*, multiples[3] (fig. 6A1 and 2). That last eventuality led to the misinterpretation of intra-archegonial double fertilization (especially in *Ephedra*), the ventral canal nucleus then being supposed to play a gamete's part[10].

In taxa where only one egg cell differentiates per ♀ gametophyte (fig. 3), only one fertilization may occur producing only one embryo.

When both sperm nuclei are integrated to two independent cells, they may either penetrate into one archegonium, which applies to cases just envisaged (fig. 6A), or fertilize two contiguous egg cells. Those may possess the same structure (each being integrated to a pluricellular archegonium, as in Taxodiaceae and Cupressaceae (fig. 4b, 6B1 and 7) or being marginal (fig. 6B2) as in Gnetum, Welwitschia and some teratologic embryo sacs (fig. 4e); then fertilization may be double, giving birth to two similar and competitive embryos (fig. 6B).

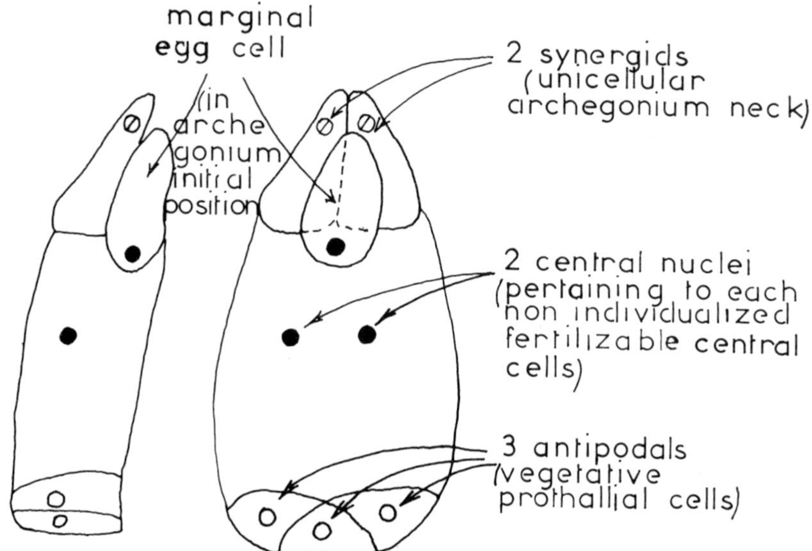

Fig. 5. Embryo sac of the Polygonum and its interpretation by the author. On the left is the half view of an embryo sac cut perpendicularly to the presentation on the right.

In the case of Callitris (fig. 7), each of the twin zygotes thus formed gives rise to four proembryos. Baird[12] writes, p. 282: "where three or four embryos have long straight suspensors reaching to the same level, all may grow to an advanced stage, almost up to the formation of cotyledons, before one becomes dominant" and p. 280: "The mature embryo almost fills the seed, both the prothallus and the nucellus being reduced to thin layers". So, in the author's opinion (fig. 7c), the collapsed brother embryos absorbed by the successfull one play the part and are the homologs of angiospermous endosperm.

Finally, when contiguous egg cells are integrated to two different types of organization (fig. 7C1, 2, 3), the one pertaining to the most evoluated structure, i.e., the most simplified one, gives rise to an embryo; whereas the one (or those) covered by a neck and whose dimension and cytological characters confer a more archaic character give(s) rise to an endosperm. That may be compared to a Gymnosperm proembryo in its cencytic or indifferentiated cellular first phase of development.

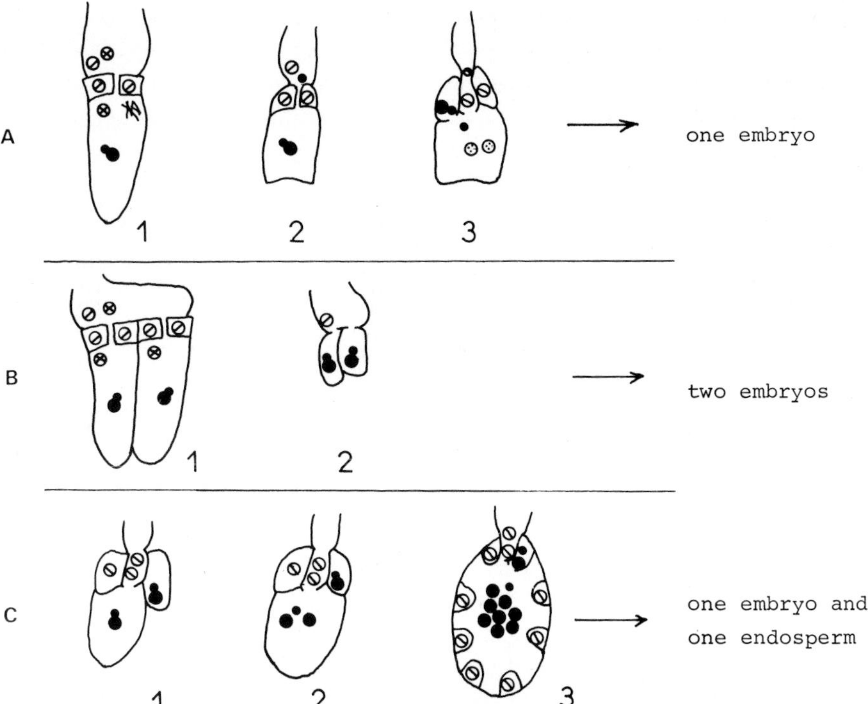

Fig. 6. Three fertilization types in Siphonogams. A) Only one egg cell is fertilized; 1) in a Gymnosperm such as Cephalotaxus[3]. The ventral canal nucleus (crossed) is not fertilized and the second sperm nucleus may proliferate into the archegonium cavity; 2) with Taxus and Apinagia, the fertlized egg is still covered by a neck; 3) with some monandrae Orchids, the sole marginal egg is fertilized. In those three cases, the zygote produces an organized embryo without any concurrence. B) Two contiguous and similar egg cells are fertilized and produce two concurrent embryos one of which usually aborts. 1) With the Taxodiaceae and the Cupressaceae, the egg cells are incorporated in archegonia with a ventral canal nucleus and a neck. 2) With Gnetum[11] and some teratological embryo sacs, the egg cells are marginal sexual cells, interpretable as archegonium initials. We have pointed out cases of embryos developed from "egg like synergids" that we consider as true supernumerary marginal egg cells (cf. fig. 4e). C) Two types of contiguous egg cells integrated into different structures are fertilized and produce, the marginal one an embryo, the central one(s) an endosperm; 1) with the Oenotheraceae, the central egg possesses only one haploid nucleus; 2) with the Polygonum type there are two central eggs (cf. fig. 5); 3) with Peperomia and other genera, more than two.

So poorly organized as it is, the endosperm must be considered as a true organism and not as a "food stuff tissue", for it draws its origine from a zygote and the xenia phenomenon demonstrates that the paternal genome still expresses itself in a mature endosperm (in Zea mays, for instance). The fact that the endosperm zygote is most often triploid is not sufficient to explain the low differentiation degree amid the nutritive organism for which it produces on the one hand, triploid endosperms to be which are known perfectly constituted and, on the other hand, diploid endosperms (that of Oenothera, for example) which do not possess organs. This precocious interruption in the organization makes the endosperms stagnate in a kind of larval state comparable to that at which orhids embryos are dispersed.

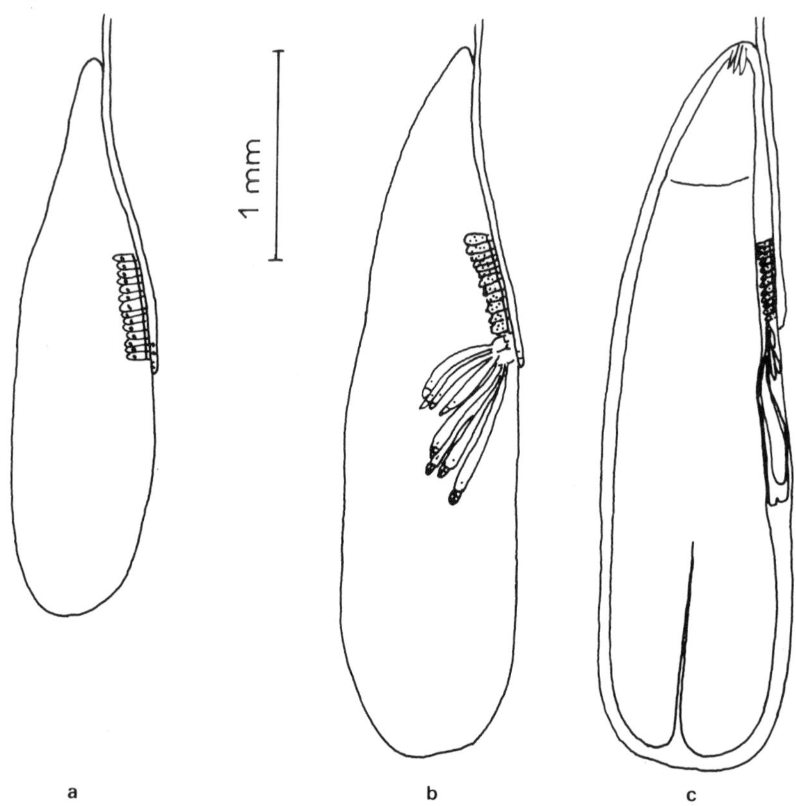

Fig. 7. Double fertilization in Callitris; drawings after Baird[12], and quotations taken out of his own publication: a) "cellular prothallus with archegonia against the pollen tube" (for details of unfertilized archegonia, see fig. 4b); b) "two adjacent archegonia are fertilized by each pollen tube, normally two at or very near the lower end of the group; (for details of this kind of double fertilization, see fig. 6B1). Each zygote produces four proembryos. c) "The mature embryo almost fills the seed...."

4. CONCLUSION

So, some Gymnosperms[11, 12] and a few Angiosperms with a teratological embryo sac present a kind of double fertilization allowing the start of more than one embryo; other Angiosperms possess only a simple fertilization[6]. Then the typical angiospermous double fertilization appears to be the generalization of a

♂ and ♀ gametic confrontation process which is, of course, a special case (cf. fig. 6), but it could have been attained along various phyla.

In the same way, conformations presented by plants able to endure long lack of water may be much similar, in far related taxa.

Though these considerations do not represent proof of the polyphyletic origin of Angiosperms, they seem to invalidate the argument in favor of monophyletism enunciated at the beginning of that article[1, 2].

However, one realises that the angiospermous adelphophagy of the embryo regarding to the endosperm may be phylogenetically released: in Orchids it is an endophytic fungus which plays the part of the nutritive organism stimulating the embryo development... but the presence of symbiotic fungi do not represent a criterion to relate all the taxa manifesting it!

The ideas presented above have, in a way, an original character which may be unexpected in a sphere where reflection is in action since Navaschin in Russia, and Guignard in France, independent dicovered the angiospermous double fertilization three quarters of a century ago.

Nevertheless, it appears that botanists have not yet acquired a consensus regarding the interpretation of that important phenomenon.

Every objection, criticism, reticence, and enquiry for explanations addressed to the author will be welcome.

REFERENCES

1. HUI-LIN LI, 1960.- A theroy on the ancestry of Angiosperms. Acta Biotheoretica, **13**, 185-202.

2. TAKHTAJAN A., 1969.- Flowering plants. Oliver and Boyd, Edinburgh, 310 p.

3. FAVRE-DUCHARTRE M., 1970.- Des ovules aux graines.Aspects morphologiques de la reproduction sexuée chez les plantes supérieures. Masson, Paris, 136 p.

4. CHADEFAUD M., 1960.- Traité de Botanique systématique. Les Végétaux non vasculaires. Masson, Paris, 1018 p.

5. BONNET A., 1957.- Contribution à l'étude des Hydroptéridées. III. Recherches sur Azolla filiculoides Lamk. Rev. Cyt. et Biol. Vég., **18**, 1-88, 1 pl.

6. PODDUBNAYA-ARNOLDI V., 1960.- Study of fertilization on the living material of some Angiosperms.
Phytomorph., 10, 185-198.

7. GERASSIMOVA H., 1933.- Fertilization in Crepis capillaris L. WALL
La Cellule, 42, 103-148.

8. JOSHI A.C., 1939.- Morphology of Tinospora cordifolia, with some observations on the origin of the single integument, nature of synergidae, and affinities of the menispermaceae.
Am. J. Bot., 26, 433-439.

9. RUTISHAUSER A., 1969.- Embryologie und Fortpflanzungsbiologie der Angiospermen. Eine Einführung.
Springer-Verlag-Wien, 163 p.

10. HAUSTEIN E., 1967.- Befruchtung der Archegoniaten und Blutenpflanzen. Sexualität, Fortpflanzung, Generationwechsel.
Handbuch der Pflanzenphysiologie, 18, Spinger-Verlag-Berlin, 407-446

11. VASIL V., 1959.- Morphology and embryology of Gnetum ula Brongn.
Phytomorph., 9, 167-215.

12. BAIRD A., 1953.- The life history of Callitris.
Phytomorph., 3, 258-284.

Fertilization in Higher Plants, ed. H.F. Linskens.

GAMETOGENESIS, EMBRYO SAC AND POLLEN GRAIN
(Contribution to the Origin of Angiospermae)

M.S.Yakovlev

Laboratory of Embryology, Komarov Botanical Institute
Academy of Sciences of the USSR, Leningrad USSR

The idea of Gametogenesis is connected with the concept of gametophyte. During the process of fertilization the male and female gametes provide the formation of zygotes. The latter give rise to a new generation.

Gametes are the source of the accumulation of hereditary information. They are the basic link of the sexual process, having their own ontogeny and their characteristic features in different groups of plants .

The study of gametogenesis is of great importance for understanding the phylogeny of higher plants particularly for the solution of problem concerning the origin of Angiospermae.

It is well known, that gametogenesis is closely connected with the alternation of sexual and asexual generations.

From our point of view the conception concerning the presence of two generations, gametophyte and sporophyte in Cormobionta, requires some critical consideration.

The question about the origin of the embryo sac and pollen grains of Angiospermae remains to be solved. Whether they are homologous with mega and micro gametophytes of other Cormophyta and whether they have sexual elements similar to archegonia and anteridia,are questions that require further study.

According to the theory of Porsch[1] the micropylar sexual apparatus of the gametophyte or embryo sac, which contains two synergids and an egg cell together with one polar nucleus, corresponds to one archegonium of pteridophytes and gymnosperms. Three antipodes and another polar nucleus correspond to the other archegonium as well. Thus, according to Porsch, the embryo sac of Angiospermae is represented by two archegonia in polar arrangment.

The archegonium theory is related to the hypothesis of Schürhoff[2]. However there is now little to support it (Maheshwari)[3]

Favre-Duchartre [4] suggests that in the embryo sac of Angiospermae there is present gametophyte tissue but it is represented only by antipodes: in Graminae - 12, in Polygonum - 3, in Oenothera - 0. As to archegonia, he states that there are three of them. One is reduced to an egg cell whereas the other two are situated on either side of the first one and each one is represented by the synergid and the polar nucleus.

However, we do not agree with this point of view.

Let us turn to the Gnetales theory or the theory of equivalence as quoted by Maheshwari[3].

1. The polar nuclei of the angiosperms are the last remnants of the free nuclei seen in the female gametophyte of Gnetum and in the earlier stages of development of the gametophytes of other gymnosperms.

2. The central vacuole of the angiosperm embryo sac is homologous with the similar temporary or permanent vacuole seen in Gnetum and other gymnosperms.

3. The cells in the angiosperms embryo sac are homologous with the peripheral cells in the gametophyte of Gnetum; the egg is a fertile peripheral cell or an arrested archegonium, and the antipodal cells correspond to the lower nutritive part of the gametophyte of Gnetum.

4. The endosperm of angiosperms is arrested gametophytic tissue which is stimulated to further development through fusion with a male gamete.

The endosperms of Angiospermae cannot be considered as homologous with gametophyte as it is well known that it appears only after fertilization. The endosperm is a sexual formation and, naturally, can not bear any relationship to the haploid gametophyte. Therefore such ontogenetic treatment of endosperm makes doubtful the hypothesis of equivalence.

The suggestions of Fagerland[5] , Gerasimova-Navashina[6,7] support the theory of equivalence.

Hence we see how far are the embryologists from understanding the nature of the embryo sac of Angiospermae.

First of all, it is not clear whether it is homologous with the gametophyte of Gymnospermae and, consequently, whether we can speak about the phylogenetic relationship of Angiospermae with Gymnospermae.

The question of homology of Angiospermae gametophyte proper is very intricate. In some cases the cells of the antipodes are homologous with the gametophyte, in other cases-synergids and the central cell are added to the antipodes. There is even less clarity in the question: what elements of the embryo sac are homologous with the archegonia of Gymnospermae? There exists three contradictory explanations of this problem. In the opinion of some authors, the embryo sac is represented in the form of two archegonia; according to the others - in the form of three; it is believed that the archegones disappeared completely, while the gametophyte has remained. Moreover, the homologue of gymnospermous gametophyte is considered to be the endosperm resulting from the sexual process, while it is quite evident that the gametophyte is the asexual haploid generation. Such is the discord in the understanding of the nature and origin of the embryo sac. There is no clarity in the interpretation of the homology of male gametophyte as well.

What is the reason of this contradictory and extremely confused conception of their nature? Why is there no unity of outlook on the homology of embryo sac and pollen grain elements?

In my earlier work and in a number of papers and reports at the symposia (Yakovlev[8,9,10]) I pointed out my own conception on the nature of the male and female gametophyte of Angiospermae. I have stated that the growth of macrospore is accompanied by a free-nuclear division and the formation of a small quantity of embryo sac nuclei usually equal to 8. These nuclei do not become gametophyte cells, but represent the potential sexual elements specialized in certain functions. There is no cellular gametophyte phase, and, naturally, there are no archegonia. Hence, on the basis of coenocytic state, inherited by the Angiospermae from their far ancestors there appeared their own type of gametogenesis.

The gametogenesis of Angiospermae proceeds in the tissues of nucellus and anther. These morphological formations may be considered as final links of generative shoot growth points, as they have lost the capacity for further growth and for the formation of any new morphological structures.

It is well known that meiocytes are differentiated in the cells of the anther and nucellus in the generative meristem. They differ from other cells by their denser cytoplasm and size. A peculiar type of cellular division - meiosis - is inherent to meiocytes and results in the formation of a tetrad of haploid cells that we have named gametocytes (mega - and micro). They participate directly in the formation of potential gametes, and their differentiation takes place in the embryo sac and pollen grain.

In the presence of such gametogenesis we do not need to refer to female and male gametocytes . There is no need to look for homologues of archegonium and anteridium in the embryo sac and pollen grain.

Now we shall consider briefly the formation of the sexual elements in the embryo sac of Polygonum - type.

As a result of meiosis, the tetrad of gametocytes is formed of a meiocyte; three of them disintegrate and only one of them functions as a sexual coenocytic cell in which the subsequent divisions are of a free-nuclear character.

In the gametocyte the nuclei division is synchronous, its further development proceeds on the basis of a coenocytic structure. Consequently there are no cellular differentiations in this case. At the first division of the gametocyte nucleus a binuclear coenocyte with a well-defined polarity is formed. At the second division, which proceeds synchronously, a four-nuclear coenocyte is formed. Thereupon the eight-nuclear coenocyte is formed. In the most widespread Polygonum-type this completes the further division of nuclei and a multinuclear coenocytic structure is formed, which may be called a mature mega gametocyte corresponding to the embryo sac with 8 potential sexual nuclei.

What happens with these sexual nuclei later on?

So far we have considered the gametocyte as a coenocytic cell, in which the number of nucleiequals 8. All 8 nuclei, being the third generation of the gametocyte nucleus, are closely related together genetically, their development proceeding in a single coenocytic cell. There is full reason to believe that all 8 nuclei are potential gametes of a coenocytic cell.

After the formation of potential gametes there takes place the functional reconstruction from coenocyte structure to cellular structure.

Consequently, in a mature megagametocyte or embryo sac three well differentiated cellular groups appear: the micropylar with an egg cell and two synergid cells; a chalazal one with three antipodal cells and a central binuclear cell.

The above mentioned groups are well distinguished morphologically and functionally. From the eight potential sexual nuclei only one becomes the nucleus of the egg cell; two other nuclei of the central cell preserve their own syngamic properties, being capable of conjugating between themselves and the sperm, while five remaining nuclei loose their sexuality due to their specialization. These are two nuclei of synergids and three nuclei of antipodes. They play an auxiliary role, entering the general complex of the embryo sac sexual elements, which ensures the normal course of the double fertilisation process in Angiospermae.

Irrespective of the type of embryo sac development (the so called mono-, bi- and tetrasporic) in all cases it is a coenocytic structure inherent to gametocyte.

As regards the genesis of male sexual elements we have the same picture. The meiocyte forms a tetrad of microgametocytes - each becoming an initial cell of pollen grain. The gametogenesis here bears a more accelerated character than in the formation of female gametes.

During the first division of the gametocyte nucleus the binuclear coenocyte appears; however, one of coenocyte nuclei ceases its division, while the other continues to divide. The first nucleus accepts the vegetative functions, and the second one forms the sperms. The pollen grain as well as the embryo sac is a very specialized structure, but with an earlier differentiation of gametes and a single auxiliary siphonogamic cell.

Thus from our point of view the source of gametes formation is the derivative of the meiocyte, i.e. the gametocyte.

Hence it becomes evident that in Angiospermae there is no gametophyte as a certain sexual generation which gives the archegonia, antheridia and, finally, gametes. Apparently it should be recognized that in Cormobionta there were different ways and sources of sexual elements formation in the course of evolution, each of them providing its own phylogenetic line of development.

Naturally, the question arises whether in the vegetative world there exist some types of plants, in which gametogenesis is not connected with the gametophyte phase, but proceeds on the basis of gametocyte, as in Angiospermae.

If we direct our attention to the existing phylogenetic patterns we shall easily notice that they are all alike. They are based on the general phylogenetic principle - the presence of gametophyte and sporophyte phases of ontogeny. According to the general opinion the whole progressive evolution of Cormobionta takes its origin from green algae that gave rise to the Psylophyta.

Psylophyta, in their turn, produced new phillums among Pteridophytes, they gave rise to Gymnospermae and Angiospermae. The Psylophyta inherited from the green algae the alternation of gametophyte and sporophyte generations (Takhtajan[11, 12], Zerov [13], Ehrendorfer[14]).

However among Phaeophyta in the order of Fucales there exist species only in diploid (sporophyte) phase, while the gametophyte phase is absent. The meiosis takes place during the formation of gametes. Hence, a question arises: should we not search for the clue to the problem of embryo sac origin in Angiospermae without taking into the consideration the alternation of gametophyte and sporophyte phases?

How does the matter stand with the process of reproduction in Fucales?

According to the data of many authors [15, 16, 17], the representatives of brown algae have no diplo-haplophase cycle, in their ontogenesis. They are represented only by diploid plants. Meiosis precedes the gametogenesis. There is no reproduction of the sexual generation by means of spores.

How does the formation of sexual gametes occur in Fucus? According to Fritsch[18], the oogonia develop in conceptacles from one single initial cell. At first, it divides into external covering and internal basal cells. The latter due to the division of neighbouring cells adjacent to the initial cell, proves to be submerged into a receptacle. The nucleus of the initial cell of oogonium after the first meiotic and second mitotic division forms four nuclei. Then follows one more division, the third one, which finally results in the formation of eight egg cells surrounded by a common cover. Simultaneously, the spermatozoids are formed in the male conceptacles. Fertilization of egg cells takes place in water at the time of their coming out of the conceptacle. The fertilized egg cell ataches itself to the bottom substrate and begins to divide. It should be noted that the embryogenesis of Fucus (Nienburg[19]) bears a great resemblance to the embryogenesis of Angiospermae; it follows the same cellular regularities.

The above statement concerning the genesis of sexual elements and the origin of Angiospermae is of preliminary character and requires further study.

In conclusion we state that:

Gametogenesis of Angiospermae unlike other phyllums of higher plants has its own characteristic features.

The development of gametes proceeds inside the tissue of nucellus and anther.

During the formation of male gametes, meiocyte gives rise to the tetrade of initial cells of microgametocyte.

In the case of female gametes out of four cells of tetrades only one becomes a megagametocyte, while the other three degenerate.

The formation of potential gametes proceeds on the basis of coenocytic structure.

. In the mature megagametocyte potential gametes differentiate into an egg cell and the central two nucleate cell. The nuclei of synergids and of antipodes lose their sexual potentiality. Such functional reconstructions contributes to the process of double fertilization.

Angiospermae have no gametophyte phase. The formation of gametes proceeds according to the scheme: somacyte - meiocyte - gametocyte - gamete.

We suggest that among Protobionta the type Fucales with its diploid ontogenesis could be the source of the origin of the phylogenetic branch: Proangiospermae - Angiospermae.

References

1. Porsch, O., 1907, Versuch einer phylogenetischen Erklärung des Embryosackes und doppelten Befruchtung der Angiospermen (Jena).
2. Schürhoff, P.N., 1926, Die Zytologie der Blütenpflanzen (Stuttgart).
3. Maheshwari, P., 1950, An introduction to the embryology of Angiosperms. Mc Graw-Hill, London, 453.
4. Favre-Duchartre, M., 1971, Phytom., vol.21, N 4.
5. Fagerland, F. , 1947, Arkiv bot., 32A, N 8.
6. Gerasimova-Navashina, E.N., 1958 , Probl.bot.
7. Gerasimova-Navashina, E.N., Phytom., vol.11, N. 1, 12, 139-146.
8. Yakovlev, M.S., 1951, O nekot. charakt.tschertah morphog.vysch. rast. 243-267.
9. Yakovlev, M.S. 1971, Probl.bot. 152-169.
10. Jakovlev, M.S., 1973, Embryol. pokrytosem.rast. (SSSR, Kischinev) 16-24.
11. Takhtajan, A.L. ,1961, Proish.pokrytosem.rast. (SSSR, Moskva)
12. Takhtajan, A.L. , 1966, Sistema i phylog. cvetk.rast.
13. Zerov, D.K., 1972, Otscherk phylog. bessosudist.rast.
14. Ehrendorfer, F., 1972, Symp.Biol.Hung.12, 227-231.

15. Strasburger, E., 1879, Die Angiospermen und die Gymnospermen (Jena).
16. Farmer, J.B. and Williams, J.L., 1898, Phil.Trans.Roy.Soc. London, B, 190, 623-45.
17. Papenfuss, G.F., 1951, Manual of Phycology, ch.7, 119-158.
18. Fritsch,F.E., 1945. The structure and reproduction of the Algae, Vol.2 (Cambridge).
19. Nienburg,W., 1931, Wiss.Meeresuntersuch.Abt.Kiel.21, 49-63,14f.

Fertilization in Higher Plants, ed. H.F. Linskens.

ON THE BEHAVIOUR OF SPERMS IN THE PROCESS OF FERTILIZATION OF HIGHER PLANTS

S.N. Korobova
The Komarov Botanical Institute, the U.S.S.R.
Academy of Sciences, 2, Prof. Popov Street,
Leningrad, U.S.S.R.

The male gametes of Angiospermae, in order to achieve the double fertilization, should make rather a long journey from the stigma to the nuclei of the egg cell and the central cell. The question of how the sperms move along this path has been posing itself before the biologists for a long time and has generated many hypotheses. In this report I shall confine myself only to the motion of sperms inside the pollen tube.

It is understood that, now the subject of this report is in motion, the research on living material is of special interest. By now, a considerable amount of factual data on the sperms behaviour inside the pollen tube has been collected by way of observation of live specimens. These data made the basis for most of the hypotheses or the cause of the motion of male gametes.

One should note that most of the observations deal with the generative cell which moves similarly to sperms.

It is characteristic that the observations of various authors, whatever plants they work with, are strikingly similar, their interpretations, however, being wide apart.

The main question under discussing is whether the sperms move actively or passively. S.G. Navashin[1,2] was the first who suggested the idea that sperms are able to move actively. However, he stressed the fact that this ability was possessed only by those sperm nuclei which have already lost their cytoplasm and only when they, after having got out of the pollen tube, move in the embryo sac towards the female nuclei. The twisted shape of the Compositae and Liliaceae sperm nuclei gave the author the idea that they penetrate the female cells which are being fertilised by way of active wormlike movements. Later having discovered that the sperm nuclei of other plants may be of a roundish shape preventing wormlike movements, S.G. Navashin[3] abandoned this idea completely. Nevertheless, the idea of the active motion of the male gamete became very popular. The original idea of S.G. Navashin of the male sexual nuclei active motion during the definite period of their existence inside the embryo sac has been extended to the whole male gamete (sperm cell) as well as on the mother cell of the sperm-generative cell. There is a series of publications which argue that the sperms and the generative cell can move actively not only in the embryo sac but also in the pollen tube. Nowadays the majority of scientists tend to admit that active motion of the sperms does exist. The main fact on which the adherents of the "activity" base their assumptions is that the sperms and the generative cell move asynchronously and therefore independently of the cytoplasm motion in the pollen tube. This is especially vivid when the generative cell stops in the process of division while the pollen tube cytoplasm continues intensive motion. The reasons for this motion are not clear; some scientists believe that this is chemotaxis. The question of a propelling organ is not clear either, since the sperms and the generative cell do not possess flagellae or ciliates. The amoeboid motion of the sperms described by Steffen[4] is not universal because the generative cells of other plants, e.g. Amaryllidacea, do not possess amoeboidity. At the same time, they spin slowly around their longitudinal axis which, it is believed, imparts them a progressive motion[5]. A resolute opponent of this "active motion" idea is M.S. Navashin[6,7,8]. In his opinion, the shape and position of the generative cell gives evidence in favour of its passive motion. Active motion should blunt the front end as a result of overcoming the medium resistance and according sharpen the rear end, whereas the actual blunting of the rear end and sharpening of the front end prove that the generative is pushed from behind by the cytoplasm current. However, M.S. Navashin is far from the basic, in the spirit of Strasburger[9], interpretation of the passive motion of the gametes by the cytoplasm current since that would imply their circular motion together with cytoplasm from the pollen grain towards the end of the pollen tube and back. Actually, the generative cell moves only towards the apex of the pollen tube and stays there at a rather permanent distance from its end. Considering the generative cell and the sperms as an integral part of the pollen grain - pollen tube system (which was called "gamocyt" by E.N. Gerassimova-Navashina[10]), M.S. Navashin suggested that the motion and localization of the generative cell depend on its selective affinity for the ascending current of the pollen tube cytoplasm (which makes it move progressively) and a relative inertness to the opposed discending current. The author suggests that there exists a zone where both currents equalize each other. Here the assumed affinity of the generative cell for one of the currents is discontinued and, consequently, its progressive motion stops.

It is characteristic that the authors of both hypotheses consider the generative cell and the sperms as the structures which possess highly specific and peculiar features; these are either their ability of active motion or their specific affinity for one of the cytoplasm currents.

In this connenction it is worthwhile to note the behaviour of the vegetative nucleus. Without referring to the functions of the vegetative nucleus (its metabolic activity at a certain stage, the possible role in the division of the generative cell, etc.) we shall consider only its motion during the pollen tube growth. If the vegetative nucleus doet not degenerate into the pollen grain as it does in the case of Compositae, wheat, etc., but emerges into the pollen tube, it behaves, as a rule, exactly like the generatibe cell or the sperms. This is especially well shown by the microfilming of the pollen tube[7,11]. The vegetative nucleus may be localized near the generative cell and later near the sperms or move asynchronously with the pollen tube cytoplasm, stop when the generative cell stops, for example during the division period, etc. One might conclude that the vegetative nucleus has the same specific motion features as the generative cell or the sperms. However, the vegetative nucleus is the actual nucleus of the pollen tube which is nothing but a spread-out vegetative cell. Therefore, it is more likely that it is not the vegetative nucleus which displays the specific features of the generative cell but, quite contrary, the generative cell, and the sperms move along the pollen tube similarly to its nucleus. This depends possibly on the fact that both the generative cell and the sperms as well as the vegetative cell, have dimensions of the same order. The presence of a similar wall of plasma membrane type or some other yet unknown factors may play the important role.

Is there any special difference in the behaviour of the vegetative nucleus as compared to the behaviour of nuclei in other cells? It is quite evident that the position of the nucleus in any cell is not accidental. Localization of the nucleus differs for various types of cells, but it is quite definite and regular for each single type. For instance, the nuclei of the mesistematic cells are placed in the center while they may be arranged eccentrically in many specialized cells. The exact physical and chemical mechanisms of the nucleus localization are not yet known.

Generally, one might assume that the localization of the nucleus as part of the protoplast is the result of the interaction of the nucleus with the rest of the protoplast and, possibly, with the cell wall. The nucleus becomes fixed at the point where all the forces affecting it become resultant. Gerassimova-Navashina[12] called this point a "dynamic center" of the cell. Furthermore it should be noted that the nuclei of many types of cells change their initial position during the ontogenesis. There are a lot of examples confirming this fact.

Thus, during the development, the maize embryo sac[13] (as well as other plants[12]) the nuclei of synergids and egg cells, initially placed in the cell center, move gradually towards the wall. The "ontogenetic" motion of the nuclei during the development of the Graminae microspores is very noticeable[14,15]. Thus, at the definite stage of the microspore development its nucleus shifts from the center towards the wall opposite the pore. After the microspore has been divided the vegetative nucleus moves to the side opposite the local of generative cell and after that the latter moves to the vegetative nucleus (Table 1, Fig. a-i). Our observations of live maize microspores and data by other authors[15,16] show that the localization of the nuclei and their motion in ontogenesis takes place independently of the cytoplasm motion. It is possible to suggest that the change in the shape, volume, physiological state as well as emergence of the one-directional physiological gradient change the character and direction of the intracellular connections which makes the nucleus move to the new dynamic center.

The period of the pollen tube growth is the ontogenesis nucleus in the growing pollen tube is, in our opinion, essentially similar to those of nuclei in other developing cells. While the pollen grain is germinating, the vegetative cell changes its shape and volume. The longitudinal physiological gradient sets up very quickly. Naturally, the intracellular connections get off balance which results in the change of the cellular (vegetative) nucleus position. Its shift towards the growing end of the pollen tube (which might now be called the gamocyt) indicates that a resultant point of all the forces acting on the nucleus (dynamic center) moves in that particular direction (Table 2, Fig. a-c). As the gamocyt grows further it changes its shape, volume, etc., which makes the resultant point continuously shift causing the nucleus motion.

Thus, what is usually called "the motion of the generative cell and the sperms in the pollen tube" is, in our opinion, similar to the regular ontogenetic motion of the pollen tube nucleus due to the one-sided expansion and specific polarization of the gamocyt. This motion is also similar to the motion of other cells which change in the process of growth and developments.

Now from this point of view, let us consider some peculiarities in the behaviour of the vegetative nucleus, generative cell and the sperms observed on the living material; for instance, the motion of the generative cell in the pollen grain and its repeated efforts to leave it for a pollen tube.

It is known that after the pollen grain reaches the stigma, the progressing hydration of its protoplast starts which causes the increasing of the volume and the change in the physiological state of the protoplast. Evidently, the constantly changing situation inside the pollen grain makes the dynamic center of the generative cell shift. This makes both the nucleus and the generative cell move constantly. After the germination starts the dynamic center shift towards the growing pollen tube and therefore the generative cell and the vegetative nucleus move towards the pore. But the generative cell (of Amarillydaceae) is rather large and can penetrate the pore only if one of its end gets into the pore. However, such precision is far from probable. The generative cell may be pressed to the pore subterminally or sideways. As the necessity of its entering the pollen tube gets

---

Fig. 1. (a-j). Zea mays microspore development (from Oryol[15]).
Fig. 2. (a-f). An illustration of the motion of the generative cell (g) and the vegetative nucleus (v) in the pollen tube. (c)- callose plugs.
Fig. 3. (a-d). The generative cell division in the pollen tube (from Litvak et al.[18]).
Fig. 4. (a-e). The generative cell division in the Zea mays pollen grain (from Korobova[17]).

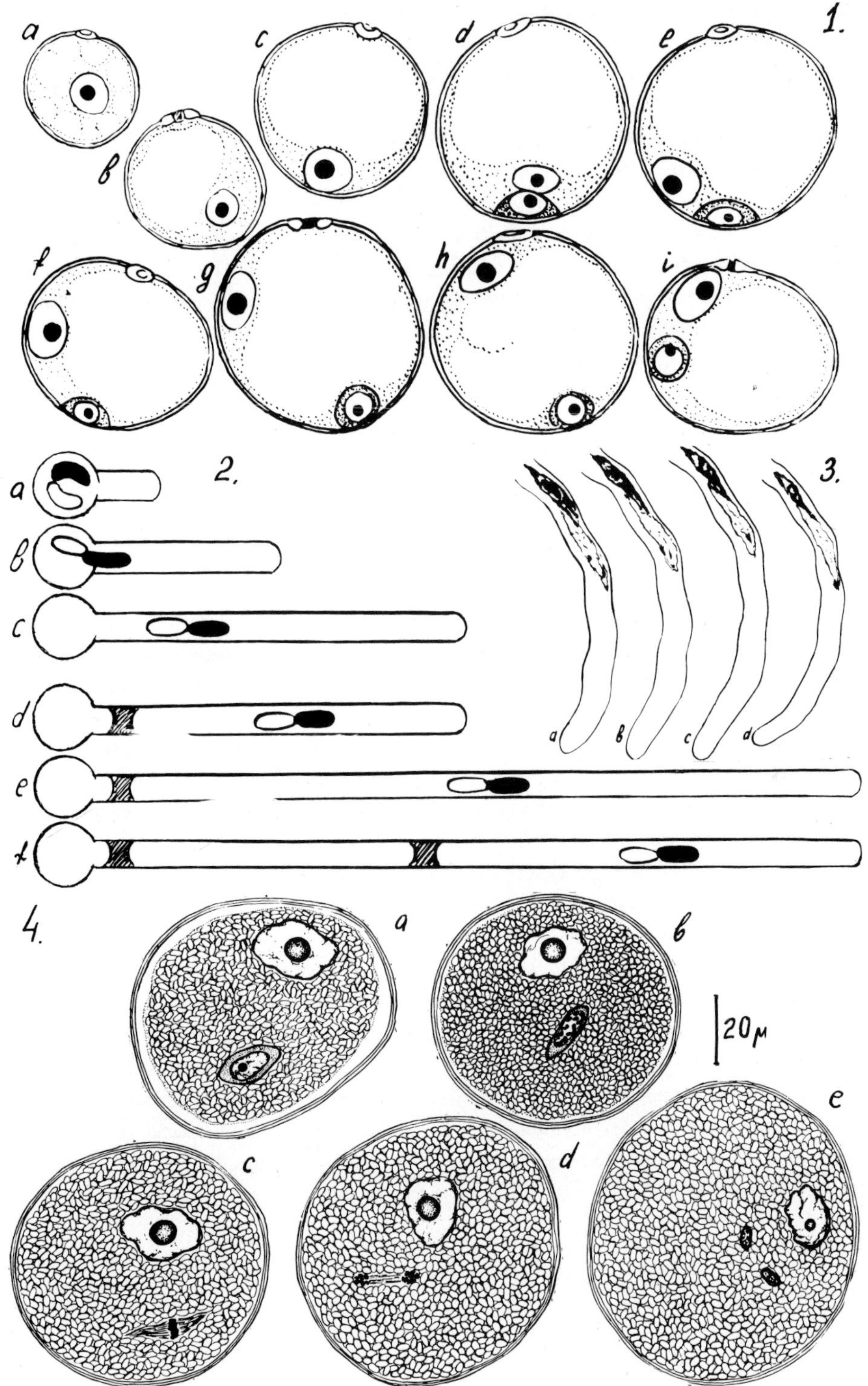
1.
a
b
c
d
e
f
g
h
i
2.
a
b
c
d
e
f
3.
a
b
c
d
4.
a
b
c
d
e
20μ

evermore urgent because of the continuing growth of the gamocyt, the generative cell penetrates finally into the pore by way of a sideways movement caused by the moving cytoplasm and squeezes through it into the pollen tube.

The vegetative nucleus which is similar to the generative cell in shape and volume (in the case of Amarillydaceae) leaves for the pollen tube simultaneously.

Let us, on the example of maize (Table 4, Fig. a-d; Table 5, Fig. a-f), consider the case when the vegetative nucleus is late in leaving for the pollen tube[13,17]. The maize vegetative nucleus in the period of its intensive metabolic activity exceeds considerably the whole of the generative cell. After the sperms have been formed, the nucleus starts decreasing, the nucleolus gradually disappears, resulting in the chromatization of the nucleus in the form of the thin net.

At the moment when the sperms leave for the pollen tube the vegetative nucleus still has the shape and size preventing it from penetrating a rather narrow pore. Only when the transformation is over, during which the nucleus becomes more flexible and can change its shape, is it capable of entering, after several attempts, the pollen tube. Then the vegetative cell catches up with the sperms, that is, as we understand, it is shifted into the dynamic center where the sperms are already found. After that, all of them form the tight group (Table 5, Fig. g). Usually, the sperms or the generative cell and the vegetative nucleus move at a certain, though very close, distance from each other. This may be somehow connected with the individual physical and chemical peculiarities of these structures (one may remember, for instance, the enantiomorphism of the sperms[3].) These peculiarities may cause some disparity in the character of the interaction of the sperms/generative cell and the vegetative nucleus with other gamocyt components. It may be assumed that the differences between the sperms/generative cell and the vegetative nucleus make them occupy their own dynamic center; their similarity determines the territorial proximity of these dynamic centers. The dynamic center of the pollen tube has certain limit. Besides, the interaction between these elements cannot be excluded.

The stop of the generative cell during division described by many authors is possible, in our opinion, only if there is at the moment no considerable change in the gamocyt which would cause the change in the dynamic center localization. This is confirmed by a drawing from the work by Litvak and Kolesnikov[18] where four photographs of the same pollen tube taken at regular intervals within 70 minutes are represented. The dividing generative cell has not moved during that time (Table 3, Fig. a-d). Authors did not notice that the pollen tube itself had not grown at all during this period judging by its tip. Therefore no change in the components interaction took place and the generative cell position remained the same.

Fig. 5. (a-g). The sperms and the vegetative nucleus entering the Zea mays pollen tube.

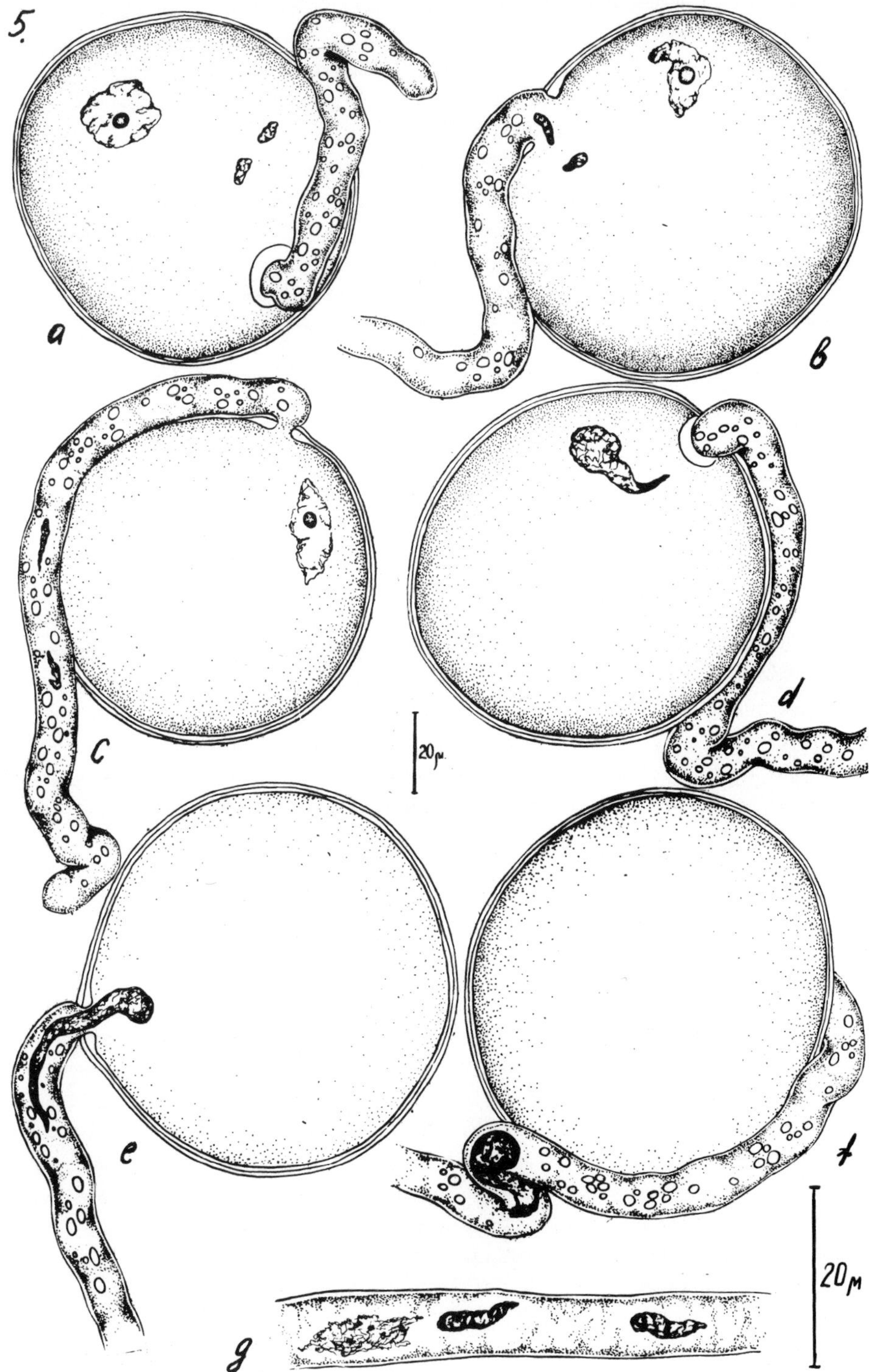
5.
a
b
c
d
20µ
e
f
20µ
g

Let us now consider why the generative cell or the sperms always stay at a small, more or less constant, distance from the tip of the pollen tube although it may be lengthy. The reason for this may be explained as follows. Since Strasburger[19] the callose plugs are known to be formed in the pollen tube. Some of the publications[20,21] demonstrate that these plugs are regularly formed at a certain, specific for each species, distance from the tip of the growing pollen tube. This regularity is noticeable on the drawings by other authors[22,23,24]. The composition of the plugs is similar to that of the pollen tube membrane. Therefore[26], at every given moment the tip of the pollen tube is an independent cell of a rather small size. The generative cell or the sperms and the vegetative nucleus are situated in the dynamic center of such cell. One should not assume that the dynamic center coincides with the geometric center of the cell. More often it is shifted towards the top cell which is, possibly, connected with the presence in it of the longitudinal physiological gradient. There is no common of view on the causes of the callose accumulation in the pollen tubes. Some of the authors believe that it is accidental and causes by the mechanical factors[25,26]. However, reaction to accidental mechanical injuries and damages though it undoubtedly exists, cannot be the main cause for such a regular plug formation. More notable is the point of view by Brink[21] who believed that the callose accumulation depends on the decrease in the protoplast activity expressed in the slowing down of the pollen tube growth. According to his observations, the callose plugs are formed more often when the growth is slow. The data by Litvek and Kolesnikov[18] confirms this. They discovered that in the maize pollen tube an abnormally large number of plugs exists. The tube was slowly growing on the surface of the stylodium making stops at each intercellular duct. At the incompatible hydrizations[27] the large number of plugs is formed in the slowly growing pollen tubes, too. This may be connected with the additional callose accumulation in the older parts of the tube which gradually lose their activity.

If we agree that the callose accumulation really depends on the slowing down of the pollen tube growth, then for the regular formation of, the plugs which cut off the growing apex, the equally regular slowing down of the pollen tube growth is essential. Precisely the same phenomenon is known to be inherent in the pollen tube. Some authors, beginning from M.S. Navashin[6,7] have convincingly demonstrated that the pollen tubes grow rhythmically. Regular stops in the growth, in the opinion of M.S. Navashin, are due to the periods of synthesis in the pollen tube end of the substances essential for the building of the membrane in the next period of growth.

Thus, the gamocyt does not seem to us to be a single cell combining both the pollen grain and the pollen tube. Instead of a single cell we observe a peculiar formation which consist of many "anuclear cells" (not capable of growth and preserving only the remains of the active cytoplasm later degenerating) and one active apical cell capable of the intensive growth and possessing the nucleus and the generative cells or the sperms which, possibly, can somehow replace the actual cell nucleus if it is absent.

On the grounds of the aforesaid, it is possible to visualize the motion of the generative cell and the sperms as follows. When the pollen grain germinates due to the expansion of the forming gamocyt, the generative cell or the sperms and sometimes the vegetative nucleus leave for the pollen tube where they get balanced at a certain point. After the next growth period the generative cell and the vegetative nucleus move to a new dynamic center. The following period of rest causes the formation of the callose plug which cuts off the small apical cell. The therein generative cell and the vegetative nucleus are compelled to move to the newly shifted dynamic center and so forth... As the pollen tube growth and the callose plug formation take some time, the new balance is not set up at once.

All this agreement with the ideas of Gerassimova-Navashina[10] on the gamocyt as a device developed in the process of evolution for the transportation of the sperms into the embryo sac. As we see, this function is connected with the apical cell of the gamocyt. In a sense, this cell can be compared with moving an animal cell of the amoeba-type. The motion of amoeba is known to start with the formation of the pseudopodium in which the whole mass of cytoplasm flows and the nucleus moves. Amoeba drags, if we may put it so, its nucleus with itself.

The apical cell of the gamocyt regularly forms an excrescence in the direction of the ovary, being regularly cut off from the older parts of the pollen tube by the callose plug. An impression is produced that this cell moves along a style carrying with it (much like the amoeba) its own (vegetative) nucleus as well as the generative cell or sperms.

One question remains open - how far is this mechanism universal; do all the Angiospermae from the callose plugs in the pollen tubes? Here, special research is required. Usually, the authors who specially looked for the plugs in the pollen tubes, detected them. Exceptions are the publication by Schoch-Bodmer[28] who did not detect the callose plugs in Fagopyrum esculentum and the publication by Müller-Stoll[26] who established that at cultivating the pollen tubes "in vitro" 10 to 15 per cent of them do not form the callose plugs. In the last case, the possibility of the artificial cultivation affecting the plug formation cannot be excluded.

Nevertheless, if such pollen tubes really exist, it may be assumed that the role similar to those of the callose plugs can be performed by the enormous vacuole filling the older parts of the pollen tube. Still, we consider the formation of the callose plugs to be a more reliable mechanis,.

The idea of the concrete causes for the generative cell and sperm motion in the pollen tube may be formulated only when the causes for localization and "ontogenetic" motions of cell nuclei are elucidated.

REFERENCES

1. Navashin, S.G., 1898, Bull. Acad. Sci. St. Pet. 9,4. 377.

2. Navashin, S.G., 1909, Oestr. Bot. Ztschr. 59, 12, 457.

3. Navashin, S.G., 1927, Sb. pam. I.P. Borodina (SSSR, Leningrad) 94.

4. Steffen, K., 1953, Flora 140, 1, 140.

5. Kostryukova, K.Y., and Chernoyarov, M.V., 1938, Sb. pam. A.V. Fomina (SSSR, Kiev), 302.

6. Navashin, M.S., Bolkhovskikh, Z.V., and Makushenko, L.M., 1959, Mater. sovesch. po cytol. probleman (SSSR, Leningrad), 101.

7. Navashin, M.S., 1968, Mater. Vses. embryol. symp. (SSSR, Kiev), 141.

8. Navashin, M.S., 1969, Rev. Cytol. et Biol. veget., 32, 141, 148.

9. Strasburger, E., 1884, Neue Untersuchungen über den Befruchtungsvorgang bei den Phanerogamen, etc. (Jena).

10. Gerassimova-Navashina, E.N., 1951, Tr. bot. inst. AN SSSR, 2, 294.

11. Polunina, N.N., and Sveshnikov, A.J., 1959, AN SSSR 127, 1, 217.

12. Gerassimova-Navashina, E.N., 1954, Dokt. diss. (SSSR, Leningrad).

13. Korobova, S.N., 1962, kand. diss. (SSSR, Leningrad).

14. Romanov, J.D., 1965, Dokl. AN SSR, 169, 2, 456.

15. Oryol, L.J., 1972, Cytol. muzhsk. cytopl. ster. kukuruzy i dr. kul. rast. SSSR, Leningrad).

16. Alexandrov, V.G., and Alexandrova, O.G., 1952, Tr. Bot. inst. AN SSSR 3, 147.

17. Korobova, S.N., 1961, Dokl. AN SSSR 136, 1, 223.

18. Litvak, A.J. and Kolesnikov, S.M., 1966, Sb. biol. opl. i geteros. kult. rast. (SSSR, Kishinev), 4, 117.

19. Strasburger, E., 1878, Über Befruchtung und Zelltheilung (Jena).

20. Bobolioff-Preisser, W., 1917, Beih. Bot. Centralbl. 1.34.459.

21. Brink, R.A., 1924, Amer. J. Bot. 11, 351.

22. Borthwick, H.A., 1931, Bot. Gaz. 92, 23.

23. Iwanami, Y., 1956, Phytomorphology 6, 288.

24. Poddubnaya-Arnoldi, V.A., 1958, Bot. Zh. SSSR 43, 2, 178.

25. Zinger, N.V. and Petrovskaya-Baranova T.P., 1967, Sh. Physiol. rast. 14, 3, 477.

26. Müller-Stoll, W.R., Lerch, G., 1957, Flora 144, 227.

27. Tupý, I., 1959, Biol. Plant (Praha) 1, 192.

28. Schoch-Bodmer, H., 1945, Schweiz. Bot. Ber. 55, 154.

INCOMPATIBILITY

Fertilization in Higher Plants, ed. H.F. Linskens.

POLLEN WASHING INFLUENCES (IN)COMPATIBILITY IN BRASSICA OLERACEA VARIETIES

H. Roggen

Institute for Horticultural Plant Breeding
Wageningen, the Netherlands

1. Introduction

One of the mechanisms that plant species have developed to prevent inbred degeneration during evolution is Self-Incompatibility (SI). Since its discovery many people have studied the two distinct systems: the gametophytic and the sporophytic. Despite numerous and often excellent efforts, the basic biochemistry of gametophytically controlled SI is still unknown. Also the sporophytic SI system is not yet fully understood, but in recent years our knowledge has been increased significantly (Knox & Heslop-Harrison, 1971a; Roggen, 1972; Knox , 1973; Dickinson & Lewis, 1973; Nasrallah, 1974). Geneticists and plant breeders would like to switch on and off the SI. A successful switching on has never been reported, in contrast with either weakening or switching off of both SI mechanisms.

Concerning breaking sporophytic SI, many attempts were made, especially in cruciferous plants. For the most part, only the successful ones have been reported. These are: changing the nutrient conditions during development (Stout, 1931); mutilation or removal of the stigma (reviewed by Linskens & Kroh, 1967; Roggen & van Dijk, 1972); pollen transplantation (Kroh, 1966); chemical treatment of the stigma (Tatebe, 1968); CO_2 treatment (Nakanishii et al. 1969); high temperature (Gonai and Hinata, 1971); application of an electric potential difference (Roggen et al. 1972) and bud pollination. The last two methods mentioned are the best ones (Roggen & van Dijk, 1973) and are used for hybrid seed production.

For a compatible pollen behaviour with sporophytically determined SI, attachment of the outside of the pollen to the outside of the papilla seems necessary (Christ, 1959; Roggen, 1972; Dickinson and Lewis, 1973). Changing or removing either outside surfaces or both might therefore influence the (in)compatibility. Most of the above mentioned operations to break SI involve both treatment of the outside of the pollen and that of the papilla, except the chemical treatment of the papillae with KOH and ether by Tatebe (1968). No reference has yet been made in the literature to the effect of changing or removing the outside of the pollen and how this influences the self- and cross- (in)compatibility.

For the outside layer of the cruciferous pollen type Dickinson and Lewis (1973) propose the term tryphine. This is the same layer I have described as "the outer layer of the exine" (Roggen, 1972), which should read "the outside layer". Echlin (1971) prefers "Pollen-kitt" for the lypophylic pollen coatings, reserving the term tryphine for a complex mixture of hydrophylic substances. To avoid misunderstanding I will use the term pollen coat (PC).

2. Methods

Ripe anthers were collected, dried in a desiccator for 2h, and the pollen sifted out. About 20 mg was placed on filter paper under vacuum in a 25 ml Büchner funnel. Washing was done by sucking 20 drops of solvent through the pollen. After washing with acetone and chloroform, pollen was no longer sticky; unlike fresh pollen it was dusty and consequently difficult to pollinate with a brush. Therefore pollination with washed pollen was effected by dipping the stigma in the pollen. *In vitro* pollen germination was optimal in 35% raffinose in double distilled water.

3. Results and discussion

The percent of *in vitro* germination was generally low (0-18%) and varied greatly from day to day. No significant differences either in germination or in vital staining was found between untreated and washed pollen; therefore, I consider the pollen alive after treatment.
Table 1 shows that pollen washing with chloroform has an effect on seed yield. The marked decrease mainly occurs in self- and crosscompatible combination with SI plants remaining so. SEM pictures show a complete disappearance of the PC, indicating that the PC plays an important role in successful pollination.

Table 1

The effect on seed production of different Brassica oleracea varieties after pollination with normal and chloroform washed pollen.
BrS: Brussels sprouts (B.oleracea L.var.gemmifera DC);
SaC: Savoy cabbage (B.oleracea L.var. sabauda);
WiC: White cabbage (B.oleracea L.var.alba DC);
*: and reciprocal.

type of pollination	pollen untreated		treated with chloroform	
	number of			
	flowers pollinated	seeds per flower	flowers pollinated	seeds per flower
BrS_1 x self	127	0.13	70	0.06
BrS_2 x self	71	0.00	64	0.11
SaC x self	140	4.01	57	1.12
WiC_1 x self	98	17.67	41	0.78
WiC_2 x self	145	1.63	69	0.04
BrS_1 x BrS_2*	193	6.76	158	1.06
BrS_1 x SaC*	45	15.64	50	1.06
BrS_2 x SaC*	45	14.87	57	0.35
WiC_1 x WiC_2*	82	13.62	139	0.41

To obtain more insight in the function of the PC, I washed pollen with solvents of various polarity. Pollen was killed with alcohol/water mixtures but survived acetone.

Table 2 shows the results after selfing and crossing the pseudocompatible clone 601 with aceton/water washed pollen.

Table 2

Influence of pollen washing on seed production in Brassica oleracea L.var. gemmifera DC. (Brussels sprouts).
* mean number of seeds per pollinated flower.

Pollen washing	601 - self			601 x 566		
	number of flowers pollinated	seed set %	seed* yield	number of flowers pollinated	seed set %	seed* yield
-	87	68	7.4	24	100	20.8
water	80	100	18.7	48	96	22.6
10% acetone	76	93	18.3	35	100	24.5
50% "	89	99	21.8	21	95	21.7
90% "	83	88	7.6	37	92	19.8
99,8% "	84	31	1.3	45	80	8.4
chloroform	57	30	1.1	65	22	1.0

Pollination with self-pollen washed with water, 10 and 50% acetone, results in a 3 fold seed yield as compared with the control. This is partly due to an increased seed set of about 30%. However, even when seed set of the control should be 100%, it still does not explain the increased number of seeds per fruit. Perhaps by washing the pollen, the PC has changed in such a way that attachment to the papilla is improved. With decreasing polarity of the solvent, self seed production decreases rapidly. To a lesser extent the same phenomenon occurs after crossing.

After selfing the SI clone 566 (table 3), seed set remains the same, but after 50 and 90% acetone washings the number of seeds per successful pollination increases up to 10 seeds per pod.

Table 3

Influence of pollen washing on seed production in Brassica oleracea L.var. gemmifera DC.
* mean number of seeds per pollinated flower.

Pollen washing	566 - self			566 x 601		
	number of flowers pollinated	seed set %	seed* yield	number of flowers pollinated	seed set %	seed* yield
-	76	13	0.0	38	97	19.3
water	147	10	0.6	39	100	20.2
10% acetone	126	14	0.8	42	93	19.6
50% "	128	14	1.4	33	97	18.5
90% "	100	14	1.3	37	84	16.5
99,8% "	115	10	0.7	55	53	3.4

Probably these washings are not adequate for increasing seed set. I am searching for other treatments that may increase both.

The results after crossing the SI plant with washed pollen are similar to the pseudocompatible plant. Compare table 2 and 3.

Though chloroform removed all SEM visible PC, the other washings only partially did so. The substances that are washed off from the pollen seem relevant for controlling the SI. Therefore, a rough analysis of the washed off solvent has been carried out (table 4).

Table 4

Composition of the removable PC.
* γ/ml solvent/20 mg pollen.

	water	10% acetone	50% acetone	90% acetone	99,8% acetone	chloroform
reducing sugars*	9	5	32	68	5	0
sudan IV stainable	-	-	-	±	+	+++
Lowry positive* material	25	13	155	55	5	25
protein stain after electrophoresis	-	+	+++	-	-	++

It is clear that with the various washings, different substances are removed from the pollen. It seems as if by (partial) removal of the tapetal "coded" PC, the pollen is "recoded" as far as acetone water mixtures are concerned, and probably "decoded" by aceton and chloroform. The "recognition" is changed respectively removed. If the PC in <u>Brassica</u> is similar to what is called "recognition substances" by Knox and Heslop-Harrison (1971b), at least part of these are acetone and chloroform extractable. The proteinacious character these authors describe for these substances is confirmed by my findings and these substances are likely lipo-proteins.

References

1. Christ, B., 1959, Z. Bot. 47, 88.
2. Dickinson, H.G. and Lewis, D., 1973, Proc. R. Soc. Lond. B. 184, 149.
3. Echlin, P., 1971, in: Heslop-Harrison, J.: Pollen development and physiology, Butterworth (London).
4. Gonai, H. and Hinata, K., 1971, Jap. J. Breed. 21, 195.
5. Khox, R.B., 1973, J. Cell. Sci. 12, 421.
6. Knox, R.B.,and Heslop-Harrison, J., 1971a, J. Cell. Sci. 9, 239.
7. Knox, R.B. and Heslop-Harrison, J., 1971b, Cytobios 4, 49.
8. Kroh, M., 1966, Der Züchter 36, 185.
9. Linskens, H.F. and Kroh, M., 1967, in Handbuch der Pflanzenphysiologie. W. Ruhland ed. XVIII, 506. Springer Verlag, Berlin - Heidelberg - New York.
10. Nakanishii, T., Esashi, Y. ard Hinata, K., 1969, Plant cell Physiol. 10, 925.
11. Nasrallah, M.E., 1974, Genetics, 76, 45.

12.Roggen, H.P., 1972, Euphytica 21, 1.
13.Roggen, H.P. and van Dijk, A.J., 1972, Euphytica 21, 424.
14.Roggen, H.P. and van Dijk, A.J., 1973, Euphytica 22, 260.
15.Roggen, H.P., van Dijk, A.J. and Dorsman, C., 1972, Euphytica 21, 181.
16.Stout, A.B., 1931, Amer. J. Bot. 18, 686.
17.Tatebe, T., 1968, J. Jap. Soc. Hort. Sci. 37, 227.

I am indebted to the late Professor Bob Stanley, University of Florida, Gainesville, U.S.A. for his invaluable encouragement and his reviewing of part of this manuscript. Thanks to Mr. A.J. van Dijk for helpful technical assistance and Mr. D. Visser for supplying the plant material.

Fertilization in Higher Plants, ed. H.F. Linskens.

GENE ACTIVITY AND THE INCOMPATIBILITY REACTION IN PETUNIA

J.A.W.M.van der Donk

Department of Botany, Section
Molecular and Developmental
Biology, University, Nijmegen.

The incompatibility reaction is controlled by the genome. If the S-alleles in pollen and styles are identical, the growth of the pollen tubes is restricted. Therefore, the first step in the incompatibility reaction has to be a recognition of identity or non-identity of the genome of pollen and style. According to the hypothesis of Lewis[1] recognition takes place by dimerisation of the products of identical S-alleles in pollen and style and activation of those parts of the genome, that govern the rejection of these pollen tubes. If no dimerisation occurs, other parts of the genome would be activated.

However, activation of parts of the genome so far had only indirect support from the work of Ascher[2], who by application of inhibitors of RNA synthesis showed the necessity of synthesis of RNA for both compatible and incompatible pollen tube growth.

In the present study, RNA synthesis was measured directly by application of ^{3}H-orotic acid (like all other radioactively labeled precursors purchased from the Radiochemical Centre, Amersham, England). After a pulse labeling of 3 hours, RNA was extracted from unpollinated styles as well as from cross- and self-pollinated styles at different times after pollination. The radioactivity and the amount of RNA were measured and the specific incorporation (dpm/µg RNA) was calculated. The values of pollinated styles were divided by those of unpollinated styles in order to show better the effect of pollination (fig.1A). Also protein synthesis was measured. Therefore, polyribosomes were extracted from styles at different times after pollination and used _in vitro_ for protein synthesis in the presence of ^{14}C-algal protein hydrolysate. In fig.1B the relative protein synthesis is given (pollinated/unpollinated). Both RNA and protein synthesis showed 2 maxima and possibly a third. However, in self-pollinated styles the first maximum occurred earlier than in cross-pollinated styles. From 12 hours after pollination, the patterns of RNA synthesis in cross- and self-pollinated styles were

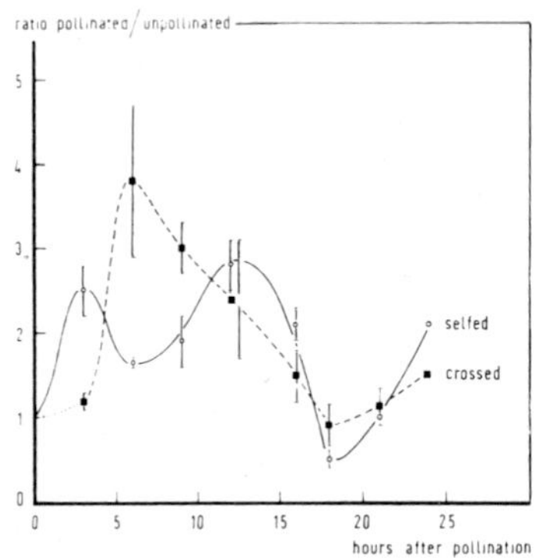

Fig.1A. Relative RNA synthesis in time after cross- and self-pollination

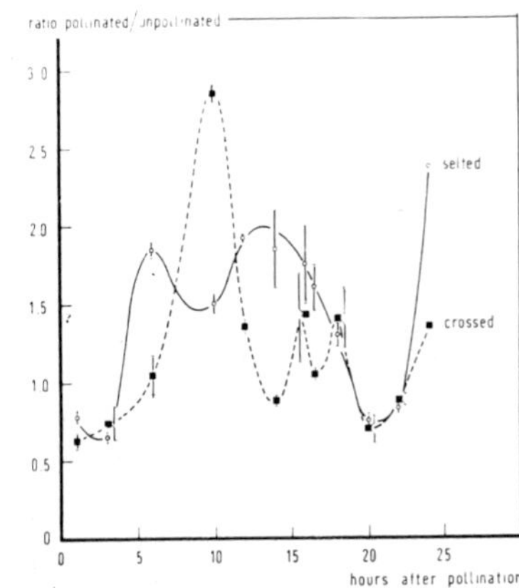

Fig.1B. Relative protein synthesis in time after cross- and self-pollination

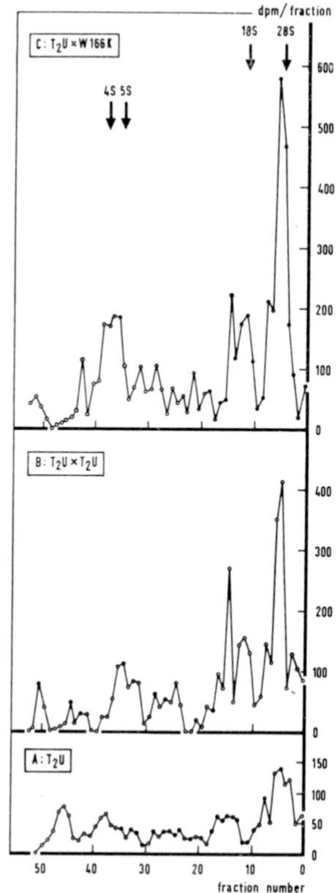

Fig.2. Distribution of labeled RNA after electrophoresis. RNA was extracted from not (A) self(B) and cross(C) pollinated styles

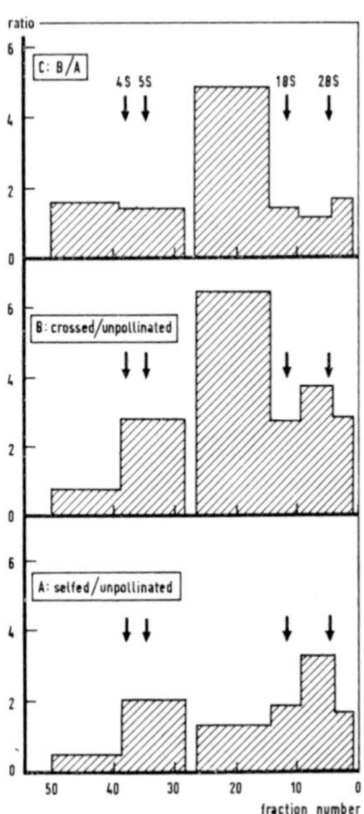

Fig.3. Specific incorporation of 3H-orotic acid in RNA.

similar, whereas the rates of protein synthesis in cross- and self-pollinated styles were similar from 18 hours after pollination. The conclusion from these results, therefore, was that gene activity as a function of time during the first part of the progamic phase is quantitatively different in self- and cross-pollinated styles.[3]

Qualitative analysis of the newly synthesized RNA was carried out to determine if different genes are active in cross- and self-pollinated styles. Therefore, RNA was labeled continuously during 24 hours, extracted and separated electrophoretically in a polyacrylamide tandem gel consisting of an upper gel of 3% and a lower gel of 7.5% acrylamide.[4] In fig.2 the radioactivity per mm of the gel is given for unpollinated (A), self-pollinated (B), and cross-pollinated styles (C). The arrows indicate the place in the gel of ribosomal (28, 18, and 5 S RNA) and transfer RNA (4 S). These data show, that after continuous labeling more radioactivity is found in RNA from cross-pollinated styles than in RNA from self-pollinated ones. The reverse was true after pulse labeling, so that it is concluded that RNA synthesized in cross-pollinated styles is more stable. On the other hand, most of the RNA synthesized after pollination is ribosomal and transfer RNA. However, calculation of the specific incorporation (dpm/µg RNA) showed that the main differences between self- and cross-pollinated styles were to be found in those parts of the gel where no ribosomal or transfer peaks were present (fig.3). To test the messenger activity of this RNA, it was re-extracted from the gel parts and injected into egg-cells of Xenopus levis (a tadpole) together with ^{3}H-leucine.[5] After incubation proteins were extracted and the specific incorporation was calculated as dpm per µg injected RNA. The distribution of the messenger RNA in the gel is given in fig.4:

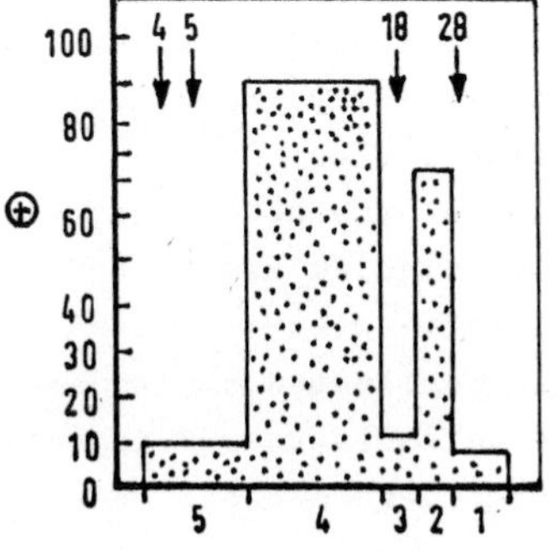

Fig.4. Messenger RNA distribution in polyacrylamide gel

From these data can be concluded that the RNA that is responsible for the main differences between self- and cross-pollinated styles is messenger RNA. The final conclusion from these experiments was that differential gene activity accompanies compatible and incompatible pollen tube growth.

The next step was to investigate the proteins synthesized by the messenger RNA at different stages of pollen tube-style interaction. Therefore, the RNA was injected into egg-cells of Xenopus levis together with ^{3}H-leucine and the proteins were separated by SDS-ureum-polyacrylamide gel electrophoresis. The radioactivity per mm gel was measured and the values of pollinated styles were divided by those of unpollinated ones. By doing this protein synthesized both by Xenopus RNA and by RNA from unpollinated styles was excluded. The remaining bands are plotted in fig.5:

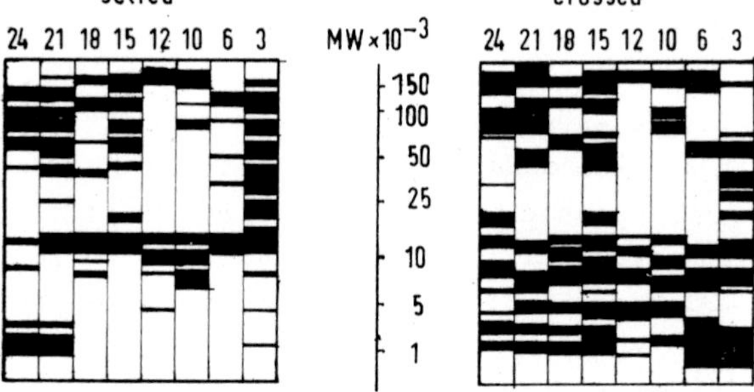

Fig.5. Bands of newly synthesized proteins with RNA extracted from cross- and self-pollinated styles at different times after pollination.

The main differences between self- and cross-pollinated styles in all stages of pollen tube growth were found in the proteins with molecular weights lower than 10,000, which were only found after cross-pollination. On the other hand, the protein patterns were not the same in all stages of pollen tube-style interaction, although some bands were found in all samples. Therefore, it may be concluded that also qualitatively, gene activity is different in cross- and self-pollinated styles.

Presently, the function of the newly synthesized proteins is under investigation. This is carried out by injecting the proteins synthesized in Xenopus egg-cells with RNA extracted from self-pollinated styles, in cross-pollinated styles and vica versa. Preliminary results showed no influence of injection of distilled water, buffer, Xenopus protein and protein made by RNA extracted from unpollinated styles on the growth rates of the pollen tubes. However, injection of protein made by RNA from self-pollinated styles 3 hours after pollination, restricted the length of the compatible pollen to the length of incompatible ones.

The conclusions from the data presented here are:

1. Recognition of self or not-self occurs also in the gametophytic type of incompatibility at the very beginning of pollen tube style contact, since 3 hours after pollination quantitative and qualitative differences in RNA synthesis could be found between self- and cross-pollinated styles. After the first contact, recognition does not take place continuously, but could occur only anothe one or two times during the whole progamic phase.
2. After recognition the style show differential gene activity; quantitative as well as qualitative differences have been found in both RNA and protein synthesis between self- and cross-pollinated styles. During the different stages of pollen tube growth different protein patterns have been obeserved. This indicates that rejection or acceptance of pollen tubes by styles is not a straight forward reaction, but a result of a sequence of activations and inactivations of a number of genes.

Part of the research was made possible by the good cooperation of miss J.Weijers, mr.P.J.Jans, and mr.J.L.W.Cornelissen and by financial support from the Association Euratom-ITAL.

References.

1.Lewis, D.A., in: Genetics to-day (S.J.Geerts ed.) vol 3, p.657 London, Pergamon Press, 1965

2.Ascher, P.D., Theor.Appl.Gen.,41, 75 (1971)

3.Donk, J.A.W.M.van der, not yet published

4.Donk, J.A.W.M.van der, Molec.gen.Genet.,131, 1 (1974)

5.Donk, J.A.W.M.van der, Incomp.Newsletter 4, 30 (1974)

Fertilization in Higher Plants, ed. H.F. Linskens.

TRANSLOCATION PHENOMENA IN THE PETUNIA FLOWER AFTER CROSS- AND SELF-POLLINATION

H.F. Linskens

Department of Botany
Section Molecular Developmental Biology
University, Nijmegen

With the fertilization barrier caused by incompatibility (literature: 4,6) two reactions can be distinguished:

1. the recognition reaction, which takes place on the molecular level during the very early contact period between the male gametophyte (resp. the pollen grains) and the female tissue of the pistil, and
2. the rejection reaction, which includes physiological and biochemical processes as a consequence of the change in metabolic patterns during the progamic phase caused by the recognition reaction. Rejection is, therefore, a series of processes, which results in prevention of normal fusion of the gametes.

Among the processes, which belong to the rejection reaction are differences in enzyme activities (1,8), respiration (2), pollen tube wall structure (7) and many other parameters. Quite regularly plant breeders observe differences in the speed of wilting of ephemeral flower parts depending on the type of pollination, cross or self. Therefore, we assumed that the internal transport system of the flower can be influenced by the pollination process and is an integral part of the rejection reaction.

Recent literature on accumulation and transport of organic compounds in flowers is scarce (see 3). Only the corolla of Ipomoea has attracted some attention: The Zurich group of Matile (9,10,11) has studied carbohydrate and enzyme changes in senescing petals, especially the mobilization of cell wall polysaccharides. It became evident that the capacity of Ipomoea to form an enormous number of flowers is linked with the partial degradation of the cell wall followed by the extraction of sugars, soluble phosphates and ninhydrin positive compounds as well as the mobilization of intracellular compounds.

The above observations concern wilting and senescence of

unpollinated flowers. In connection with the incompatibility reaction, especially the rejection phase, it was important for us to obtain information on the translocation phenomena in Petunia flowers.

To get preliminary information we adapted pulse-chase experiments to our problem. Flowers of Petunia hybrida were gathered 1 day before anthesis, emasculated, and placed in a radioactive solution for a 1 hour pulse. After pollination the flowers were brought into an illuminated, temperature constant environment of 25°C. As known from former experiments (2), after about 22 hours compatible pollen tubes have reached the base of the style and start to enter the ovary, whereas incompatible pollen tubes have ceased to grow downward into the styles about halfway to the ovary. That means that both phases of the incompatibility reaction, recognition and rejection, take place within this period.

After application of a C-14 sugar flower parts were separated after 1,2,4,10,18,22,36 and 48 hours, dryed and the label measured. The results are given in Figure 1 for cross-pollinated flowers and in Figure 2 for self-pollinated flowers. There is not much difference in the accumulation of labelled carbohydrates in various flower organs.

It becomes evident from the graphs that the carbohydrate content of the corolla of self-pollinated flowers remains at a higher level than that of cross-pollinated flowers. This is in good agreement with the crosspollinated stage, in which wilting of the corolla is retarded. The accumulation of carbohydrates in the ovary after the tubes from cross-pollination have reached the base of the style is also quite evident.

Pulse-chase experiment. After application of a mixture of generally labelled amino acids from protein hydrolysate-C^{14} one can distinguish between incorporation in the pool of free amino acids and incorporation into proteins. Results of pulse-chase techniques for flowers after cross-pollination are given in Figure 3 and for self-pollinatedflowers in Figure 4. Differences for all investigated flower parts are striking. While labelling of the calix shows no significant differences in amount of incorporated label between zero and 48 hours after pollination between self- and cross-pollinated flowers, the corolla experiences a strong influx of soluble substances, mainly amino acids, after pollination.

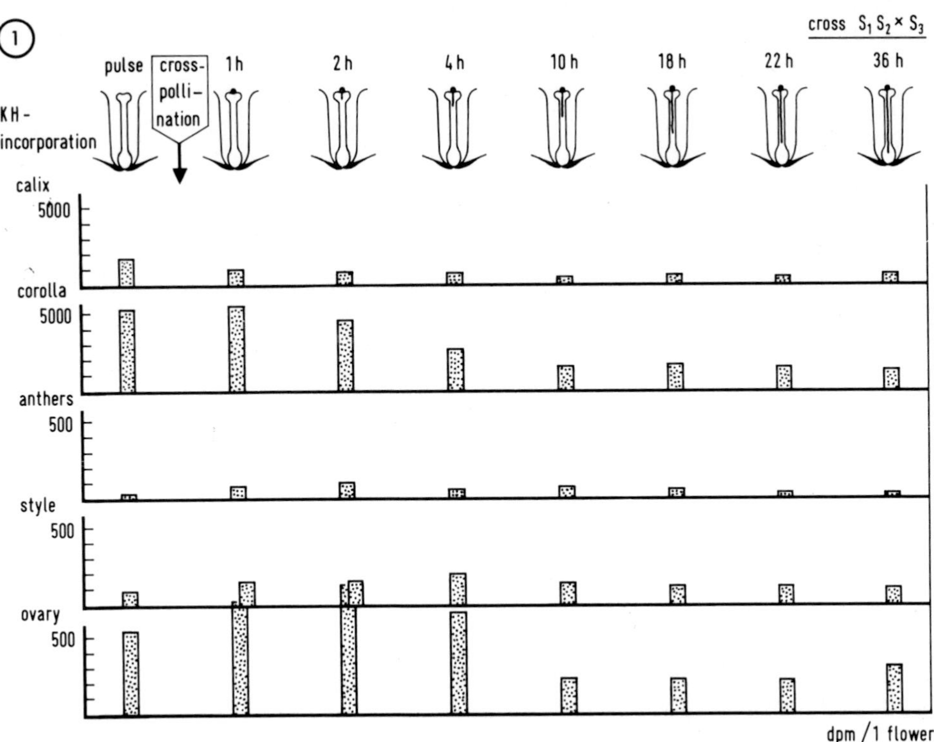

fig. 1

Distribution of radioactivity in the various parts of the Petunia flower after a pulse-chase experiment with radioactive sugar after cross-pollination (S_1S_2 x S_3).

Each result is an average of 2 experiments with 20 flowers each, the corrected values are calculated for 1 flower. Pulse labelling for 1 hour with 3μCi in 10 ml, specific activity of D-glucose-2-C14 52,4 mCi/mmol (Radiochemical Centre, Amersham). The carbohydrate fraction was extracted with 70% ethanol from the fresh material. Counting in a Philips Liquid Scintillation Counter. The material was counted in 10 ml of a scintillation liquid consisting of 800 ml toluene, 200 ml Triton X-100, 4 g PPO and 0,3 g POPOP.

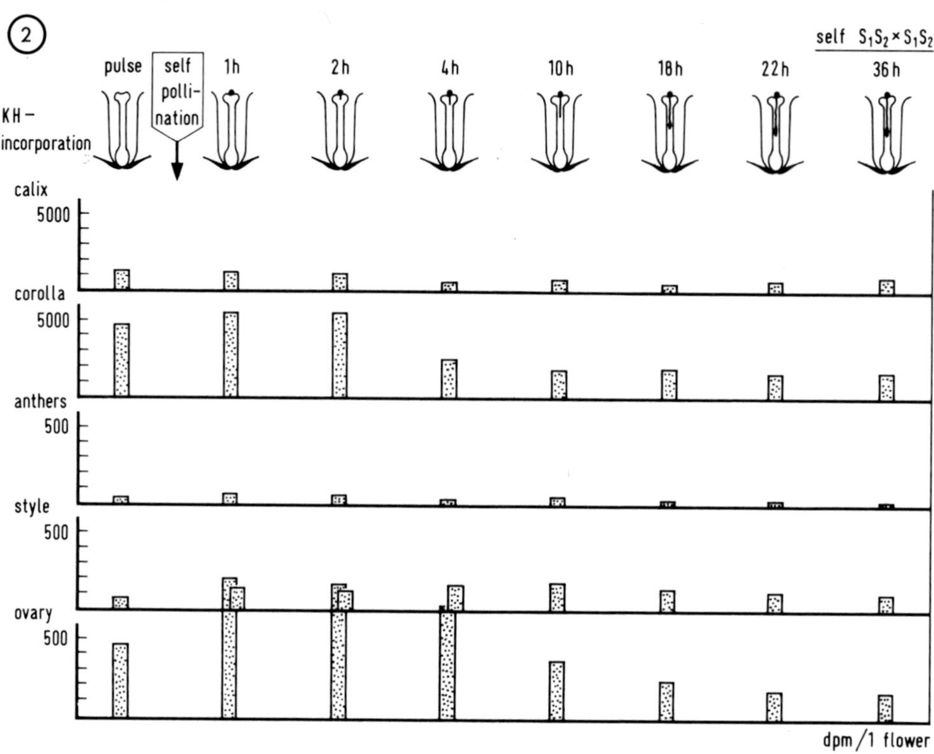

fig. 2

Distribution of radioactivity after a pulse chase experiment with radioactive sugar in various parts of the Petunia flower after self-pollination (S_1S_2 x S_1S_2). Details as in fig. 1.

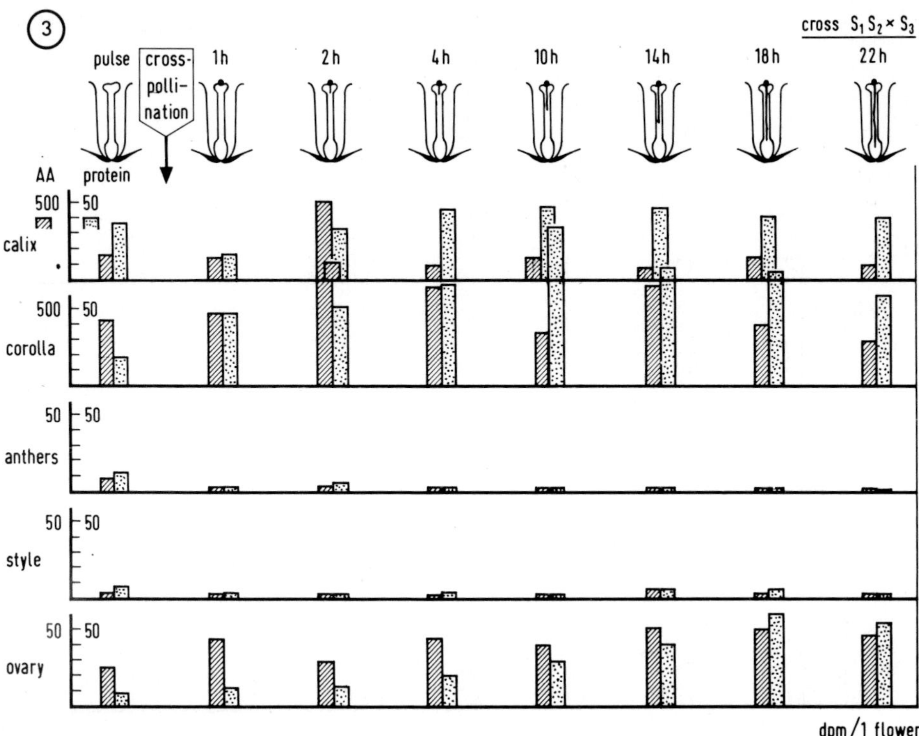

fig. 3

Distribution of the radioactivity in the soluble amino acids and protein fractions after a pulse chase experiment with radioactive protein hydrolysate in various parts of the Petunia flower after cross-pollination (S_1S_2 x S_3).

Each result is an average of 2 experiments with 20 flowers each, the corrected values are calculated for 1 flower. Pulse labelling for 1 hour with 0.75 µCi in 10 ml, specific activity of the protein hydrolysate-C14(u) (Radiochemical Centre, Amersham) 57 mCi/mAtom carbon. The amino acids are extracted with tris-HCl buffer, pH 7.6 and the protein fraction is the precipitate with 5% TCA. Counting in a Philips Scintillation Counter.

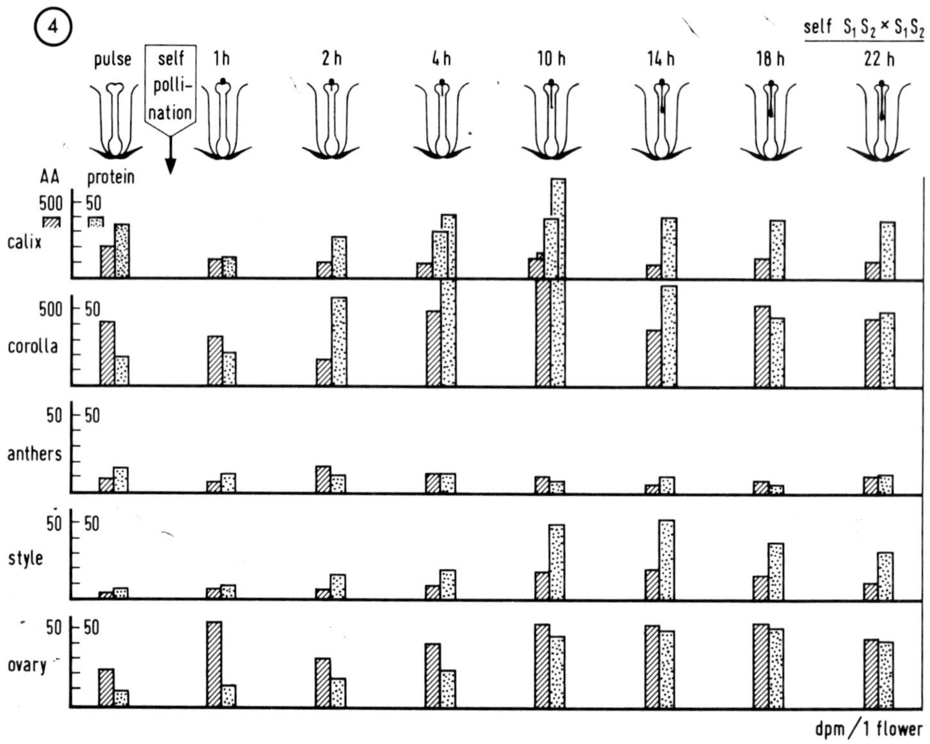

fig. 4

Distribution of radioactivity in the soluble (amino acids) and protein fraction after a pulse chase experiment with radioactive protein hydrolysate in various parts of the Petunia flower after self-pollination (S_1S_2 x S_1S_2). Details as in fig. 3.

Cross-pollination results in a brief, intense labelling of proteins during the first few hours; under selfing conditions the maximum amount of label in the corolla occurs after about 10 hours, the period of maximum strength of the inhibition reaction. Quite evident is the intense labelling of anthers in self-pollinated flowers and the very strong labelling of the self-pollinated style, compared with the cross-pollinated one. In self-pollinated styles strong labelling of the protein fraction takes place between 10 and 18 hours, when the tubes are subjected to the rejection reaction. During the beginning of the penetration of the pollen tubes into the style the ovary is activated in the same way for both pollination types. However, while in self-pollinated styles there is a decrease of the labelling after 18 hours, the labelling continues to increase in cross-pollinated styles.

Considering these results and comparing them with earlier observations on unpollinated flowers (3), one can try to sketch a flow pattern for the translocation of organic substances in the Petunia flower (5). One comes to the following general conclusions:

1. After pollination an overall redistribution of the organic substances takes place between the flower organs.
2. As a consequence of the invasion of the pollen tubes, the style becomes an attraction centre for organic materials, which are translocated from the stamen, the corolla and the green calix.
3. There is a significant difference between the flow pattern in cross- and self-pollinated flowers. While the unpollinated flower remains in a steady state at least for one or 2 days, a strong influx of organic constituents into style and ovary is observed 10 hours after self-pollination, whereas the same tendency in the cross-pollinated styles is less intense.
4. About 18 hours after pollination the cross-pollinated ovary becomes the main sink into which all materials from the corolla, calix and from the vegetative parts of the plant, via the pedicil, are transported. In contrast, the self-pollinated ovary has little influx and the main direction of translocation is no longer observed in the flowers but rather to other plant parts. It seems that the sexual organs of the flowers are now without further function, because the pollen tubes have been stopped by the incompatibility reactions. Thus, the flow diagram reflects, in a convincing way, the altered metabolic state in incompatibility-pollinated flowers.

Translocation phenomena are adequate indicators of the rejection reaction.

References

1. Bredemeijer, G., 1974, Acta Bot. Neerl. 23, 149-158.

2. Linskens, H.F., 1955, Z. Bot. 43, 1-44.

3. Linskens, H.F., 1973, Transact. 3. Symp. Accumulation and Translocation Skierniewice, Prof. Res. Inst. Pomology, ser. E., 3, 91-106.

4. Linskens, H.F., 1974a, Biol. J. Linnean Soc. (Lond.) - in press.

5. Linskens, H.F., 1974b, Proc. Roy. Soc. (Lond.) - in press.

6. Linskens, H.F. and Kroh, M., 1967, Encycl.Plant Physiol., 18, 506-530.

7. Mühlethaler, K. and Linskens, H.F., 1956, Experientia 12, 253-254.

8. Schlösser, K., 1961, Z. Bot. 49, 266-288.

9. Wiemken-Gehrig, V., Wiemken, A. and Matile, Ph., 1974, Planta 115, 297-307.

10. Winckenbach F., 1970, Ber. Schweiz. Bot. Ges. 80, 374-406.

11. Winkenbach, F. and Matile, Ph., 1970, Z. Pfl. Physiol. 63, 292-295

Fertilization in Higher Plants, ed. H.F. Linskens.

EFFECTS OF ACTINOMYCIN D ON LYCOPERSICUM PERUVIANUM POLLEN TUBE GROWTH AND SELF-INCOMPATIBILITY REACTION.

G. Sarfatti, F. Ciampolini, E. Pacini and M. Cresti
Department of Botany, University of Siena (Italy)

1. Introduction

In the course of our researches on the mechanism of self-incompatibility in Lycopersicum peruvianum Mill. we have started to carry out a series of tests on the physiological and submicroscopical effects on pollen tubes of transcription and translation inhibitors. Treatment of pollen "in vitro" and "in vivo" with actinomycin D was found to stimulate pollen tube growth and seems to prevent at least partially the incompatibility reaction. It is these first experiments which we wish to illustrate in this preliminary report.

2. Materials and methods

The self-incompatible, clonal, Lycopersicum peruvianum plants we have used are derived from the original plants supplied by Professors D. de Nettancourt and M. Devreux, of Comitato Nazionale Energia Nucleare (Rome), and already utilized for our previous experiments[1,2].

"In vitro" tests. Lots of pollen harvested from ten flowers (ca. 5 mg) were immediately transferred to Petri dishes containing 20 ml of liquid culture medium of the following composition: H_3BO_3, 100 mg; $Ca(NO_3)_2 \cdot 4H_2O$, 432 mg; KNO_3, 300 mg; $MgSO_4 \cdot 7H_2O$, 408 mg; sucrose, 150 g per liter of bidistilled water. For treatments with actinomycin D part of the water was substituted with a stock solution of actinomycin D in order to reach the following final concentrations of this substance: 4,8 and 16 μg/ml. The actinomycin, supplied by Serva (Heidelberg) - code number 10710, was pure, crystallized. In the course of our experiments two stock solutions were prepared. The Petri dishes were kept at room temperature.

"In vivo" tests. The pollen, immediately after collection, was put in a spoon and covered with the culture medium already described, with or without actinomycin D. Self- and cross-pollinations were then carried out by dipping the stigmas into the spoon. As the wet pollen does not easily stick to the stigma, care was taken to check that pollination had occurred. The pollinated flowers had been isolated with paper bags 48 hrs before pollination.

Optical and electron microscopy. "In vitro" cultured pollen tubes were fixed in alcohol and centrifuged for observation at the optical microscope; for electron microscopy the pollen tubes were fixed in 3% glutaraldehyde in cacodylate buffer 0.066 M, pH 7.2 for 1 hr at room temperature. After a light centrifugation the pollen tubes were embedded in 7% agar, rinsed in the cacodylate buffer, post-fixed in 1% OsO_4 in the same buffer for 1 hr 30′ at room temperature, dehydrated in alcohol and embedded in Epon/Araldite. Pollinated styles were collected 21 hrs 30′ to 22 hrs 30′ after pollination in the first experiments, and 17 hrs 30′ in the second series of experiments. They were fixed in 5% glutaraldehyde in phosphate buffer 0.075 M, pH 6.9, for 3 hrs at 0-4°C; washed in the same buffer at the same temperature; post-fixed in 1% OsO_4 in the phosphate buffer for 3 hrs; dehydrated in alcohol; embedded in Epon/Araldite.

3. Results

"In vitro" tests. Pollen grown in vitro was collected after 45′, 1 hr, 1 hr 45′, 2 hrs 45′, 3 hrs 30′, 4 hrs 30′. In every case pollen tubes from media containing actinomycin D appeared on the average to be longer than the controls (Figs. 1 and 2). The effect of actinomycin concentration, if present, was not great enough to be estimated without precise measurements.

Figs.1 and 2 - Pollen tubes cultured "in vitro" for 4 hrs 30′ without (Fig. 1) or with (Fig. 2) actinomycin D.

Figs.3 and 4 - Electron micrographs of sections of pollen tubes as above cultured without (Fig. 3) or with (Fig. 4) actinomycin D. In the treated tube the cytoplasm and cytoplasmic organelles do not appear to be in quite normal conditions, and numerous small vesicles are present in the outer wall.

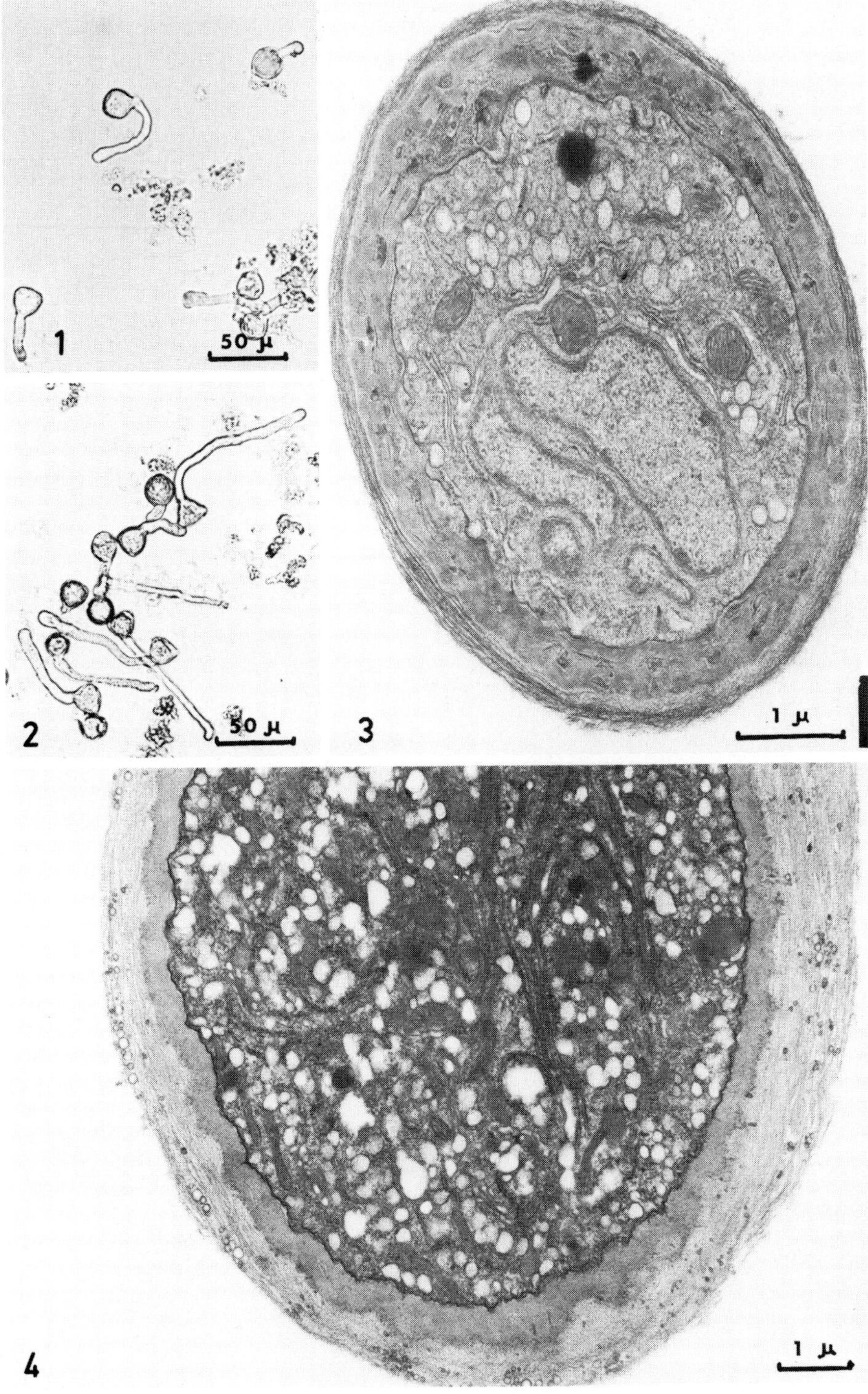

1
50 µ
2
50 µ
3
1 µ
4
1 µ

At the ultrastructural level a comparison between treated and non treated pollen tubes is not easy because sections from pollen tubes taken at random from the same culture liquid can vary noticeably. Some pollen tubes look in good conditions, and some not; the sections can be cut at different points along the lenght of the tube, and so on. On the whole the treated tubes tend to look less "healthy" and less rich in mitochondria; often numerous vesicles are present in the tube wall, especially in the outer pecto-cellulosic layer (Figs. 3 and 4).

"In vivo" tests. Two series of tests have been carried out. In both cases styles were self-or cross-pollinated using pollen soaked in the culture medium with or without actinomycin D.

Styles of the first series were collected 21 hrs 30' or 22 hrs 30' after pollination. Only styles selfed with actinomycin treated incompatible pollen were observed at the electron microscope. Several styles were sectioned in the lowest third, near the ovary, and in all cases numerous pollen tubes were observed some with "normal" cytoplasm, presumably sectioned near the tube apex, and some nearly empty and squashed, presumably sectioned at some distance behind the apex (Figs. 5 and 6).

Styles of the second series of tests were collected 17 hrs 30' after pollination and observed both in the upper third (where incompatible pollen tubes normally cease growing) and lower down at the bottom end of the style.

Also in these cases incompatible pollen tubes derived from grains treated with actinomycin D were present at the lower end of the style near the ovary, while tubes from non treated incompatible grains were absent. Untreated incompatible pollen tubes in sections cut in the upper third (Fig. 7) showed the usual signs of degeneration[1]. In the upper third of styles pollinated with actinomycin treated incompatible grains both tubes showing signs of degeneration (such as the character

---

Figs.5 and 6 - Styles pollinated with actinomycin treated incompatible pollen, sectioned near the ovary.
Some pollen tubes with "normal" cytoplasm, such as the one of Fig. 6, have probably been cut near the apex; others, appearing more empty, have probably been cut at some distance from the apex.

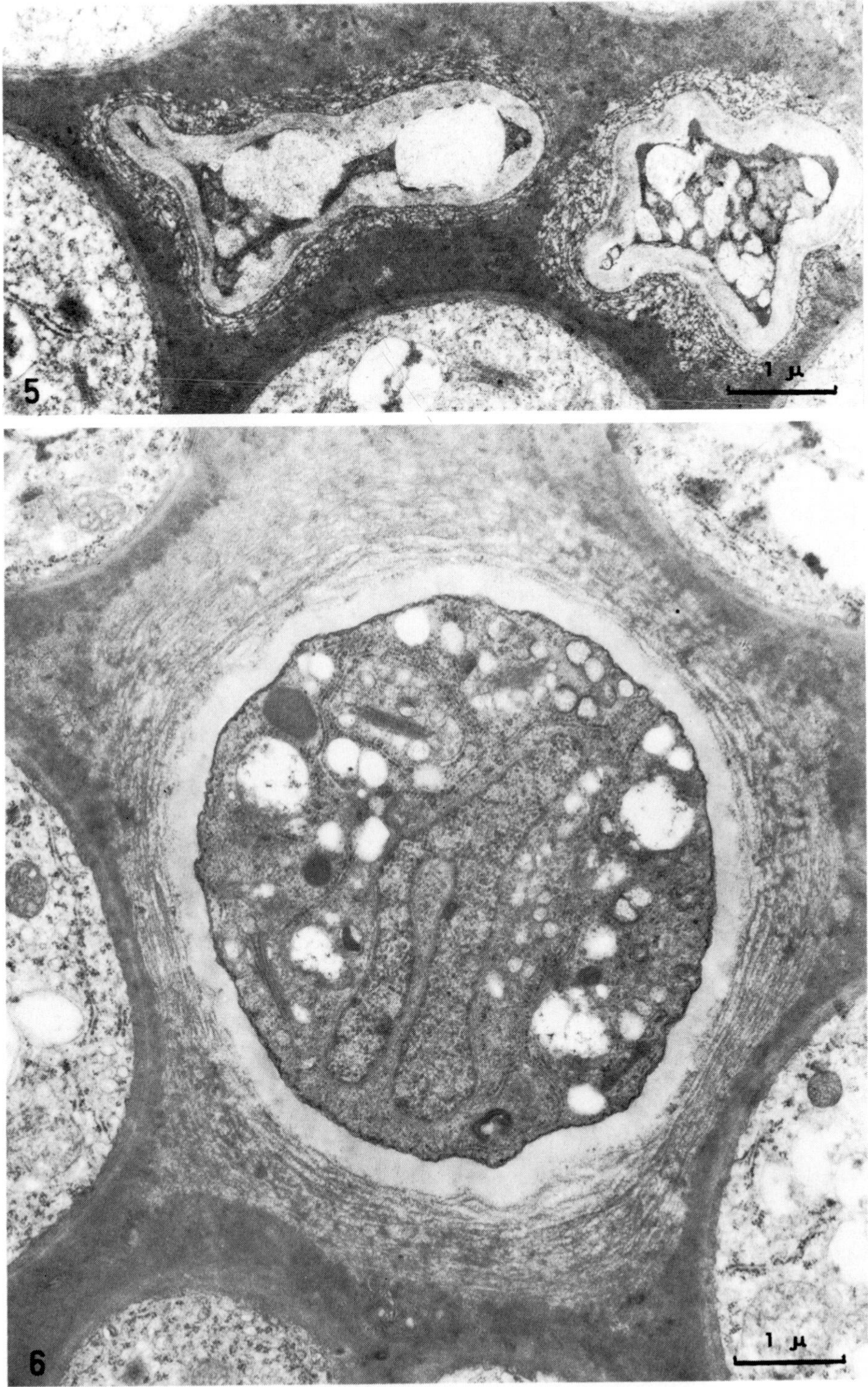
5
1 μ
6
1 μ

istic particles[1]) were present and squashed empty ones which presumably had kept growing further down the style (Fig. 8).

4. Discussion

The data we have obtained so far, even if of a qualitative type, seem to indicate a stimulating effect of actinomycin D on pollen tube growth during the first few hours of culturing and a partial inhibiting effect on the incompatibility reaction in the style.

Other research workers have studied the effect of actinomycin D and, more generally, the rate of RNA and protein synthesis in pollen tubes. From such studies it appears that during the first stage of pollen tube growth no new RNA is synthesised, the RNA necessary for protein synthesis having already been stored in the pollen grain during the process of maturation. This has been confirmed in several species[3-9] and agrees with the older data of Tano and Takahashi[10], and of Steffensen[11]. Consequently it was to be expected that adding actinomycin D to the culture medium should have no effect on pollen tube growth and its substructural features. This appears to be the case for the species studied by Dexheimer[8] and by Sondheimer and Linskens[9].

In Lycopersicum peruvianum instead our data indicate that actinomycin is not inactive. We can not speculate yet on our data, but it must be pointed out that even when no RNA synthesis is revealed by standard techniques this does not mean that synthesis is absolutely absent: a few, indetectable, RNA molecules could still be produced by the nucleus; therefore treatment with actinomycin could prevent the synthesis and arrival to the cytoplasm of these nuclear messages. It must also be borne in mind that there are data recently reviewed by Olszewska[12],

---

Figs. 7 and 8 - Styles pollinated with incompatible untreated (Fig. 7) and treated (Fig. 8) pollen, sectioned near the stigma. All the untreated pollen tubes (Fig. 7) show typical signs of the inhibition reaction, and the intercellular stylar substance is rich with the remains of burst tubes. Some of the treated pollen tubes, instead (Fig. 8; asterisks) have behaved like normal compatible tubes: they show a thick inner callosic wall and appear empty and squashed the active portion of the tube having grown further down in the style.

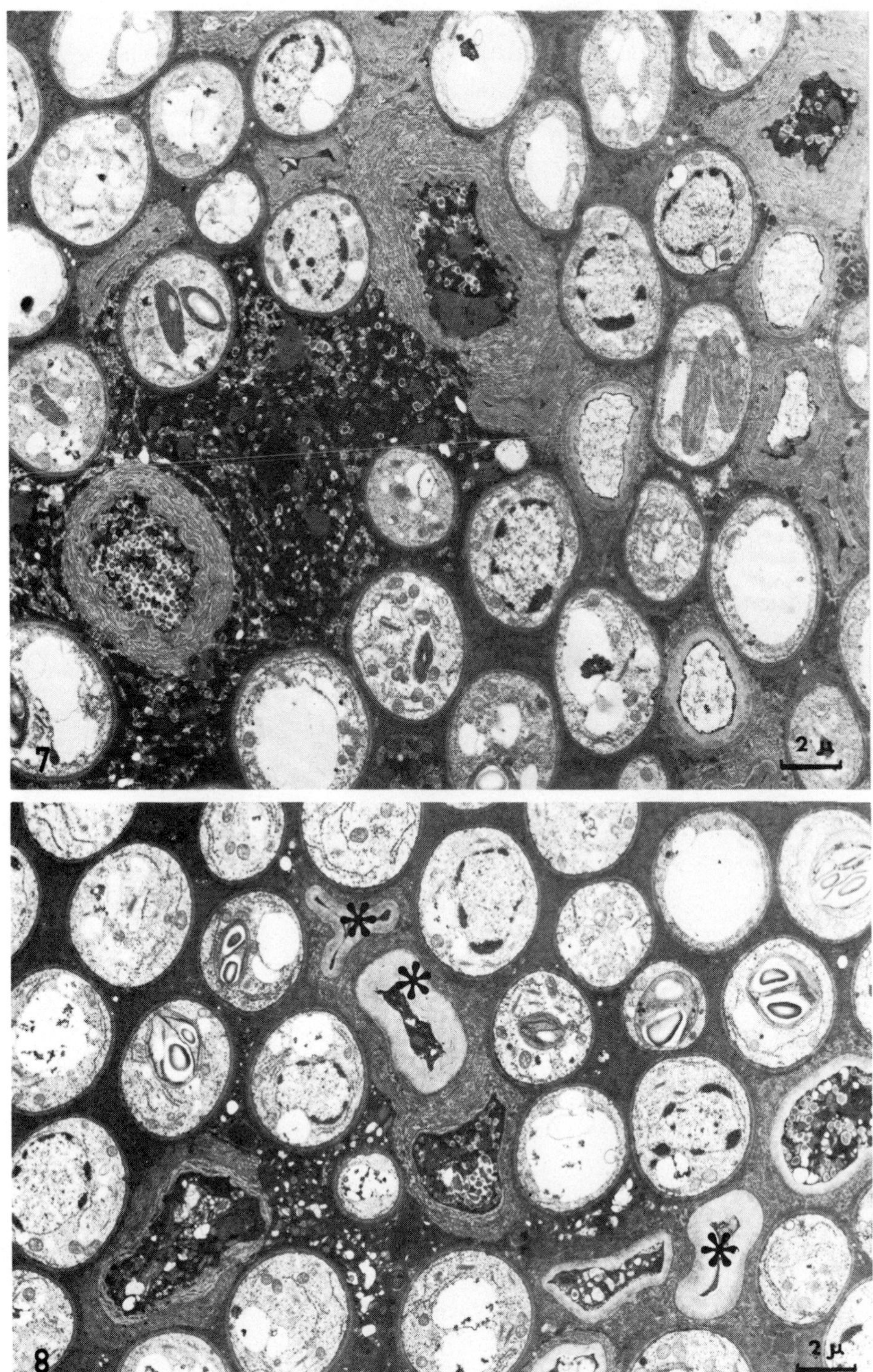
7
2 µ
8
2 µ

suggesting a triggering effect by actinomycin on the synthesis of nuclear and cytoplasmic proteins. This is why it is important to confirm our data using some other inhibitor of the transcription process. Another question that arises immediately is the connection between stimulation of pollen tube growth and a possible partial inhibition of the incompatibility reaction. In view of such possible developments of these researches we feel encouraged to repeat and continue our experiments in the near future.

REFERENCES

1. Nettancourt, D. de, Devreux, M., Bozzini, A., Cresti, M., Pacini, E., and Sarfatti, G., 1973, J. Cell Sci. 12,403.

2. Nettancourt, D. de, Devreux, M., Laneri, U., Pacini, E., Cresti, M. and Sarfatti, G., 1973, Caryologia 25, suppl., 207.

3. Mascharenhas, J.P., 1966, Amer. Jour. Bot. 53, 563.

4. Dexheimer, J., 1968, C.R. Acad. Sci. Paris 267,2126.

5. Mascarenhas, J.P. and Bell, E., 1969, Biochem. Biophys. Acta 179, 199.

6. Mascarenhas, J.P. and Bell, E., 1970, Developmental Biology 21,475.

7. Linskens, H.F., van der Donk, J.A.W.M. and Schrauwen, J., 1971, Planta (Berl.) 97,290.

8. Dexheimer, J., 1972, Rev. Cytol. et Biol. Vég. 35,17.

9. Sondheimer, E. and Linskens, H.F., 1974, Proceed. Koninkl. Nederl. Akad. Van Wetenschappen Ser. C, 77,116.

10. Tano, S. and Takahashi, H., 1964, J. Biochem. 56,578.

11. Steffensen, D.A., 1966, Exptl. Cell Res. 44,1.

12. Olszewska, M.J., 1974, Cytobiologie 3,371.

Fertilization in Higher Plants, ed. H.F. Linskens.

FEATURES OF FERTILIZATION IN THE COURSE OF REMOTE HYBRIDIZATION OF PLANTS

V.P. Bannikova and O.A. Khvedynich
The N.G. Kholodny Institute of Botany of the Academy
of Sciences of the Ukrainian SSR

1. INTRODUCTION

The main problem of remote hybridization is interspecific incompability. It is realized in the course of embryonic processes at all consecutive stages of development: pollen germination and pollen tube growth, fertilization and seed development. The manifestations of incompatibility in the course of fertilization may be studied only in a few combinations of remote crosses: hybridization of soft wheat with the other wheat species, Leymus and Secale (Poddubnaya-Arnoldi, 1939; Khu-Khun, 1959, Batygina, 1966; Kandelaki, 1969, etc.), reciprocal crosses of two Crepis species and cotton (Gerassimova, 1933; Dolgova-Khvedynich, 1967, Beliaeva, 1968).

The present paper is aimed at a detailed comparative study of both the fertilization process of the pollination in the species and remote hybridization, to define similar morphological changes in different combinations of crosses.

2. MATERIALS AND METHODS

Representative of the two families, Poaceae Barnhart and Solanaceae Juss, were used for our investigation. The fertilization process in the pollination of Hordeum vulgare and Nicotiana rustica by their own pollen and the hybridization of barley with rye and N. rustica with the two wild immune species, N. paniculata and N. glutinosa, were examined. Material was temporally fixed by Navashin and Karnua fixer: barley - 10, 20, 30, 40 minutes, then 1, 2, 4, 6, 8, 10, 12, 15, 18, 24 hours, N. rustica - 18, 24, 28, 32, 36, 40, 44, 48, 52, 56, 60, 64, 68, 72 hours after their pollination. The preparations were stained by hematoxilin according to Heidengein. The Feulgen reaction was used to reveal DNA. Localization of both nucleic acids was identified by the Brachet method.

3. RESULTS

Our investigation has shown that irregularities of double fertilization process were common for the studied combinations of crossing. In the degree of their display they may be insignificant or significant so that they may accordingly change the rate of carrying out the process or stop it entirely in a certain percentage of embryo sacs.

The insignificant irregularities are connected with the variations in the rate of fusing and in morphology of nuclei of fusing gametes as compared with the norm. Such changes may also involve syngamy and triple fusion or only one of the processes. In the first case that there is in the combination Hordeum vulgare x Secale cereal (Khvedynich, Bannikova, 1970), correlation between the rates of fusion of sperms with the egg and the polar nucleusis retained while in the second one, that is in the course of interspecific hybridization of Nicotiana, such correlation is broken. During the pollination of N. rustica by its own pollen the triple fusion begins and ends faster than the syngamy (Bannikova, Khvedynich, 1973 a).

In the course of remote hybridization of N. rustica with N. paniculata or N. glutinosa the sperms unite with the nuclei of both fertilized cells in 40 hours synchronously (Fig. 1, 2), or the fusion of sperm with the polar nucleus occurs later than with the egg. In the combination N. rustica x N. paniculata one can trace the zygote for 44 hours after the pollination while the fusion of sperm with the polar nucleus has not yet stopped (Fig. 1, 3). The insignificant deviations manifest themselves when one sperm unites with the egg, and another with only one of the polar nuclei (Fig. 1, 4 - N. rustica x N. glutinosa). Fusion of the fertilized and unfertilized polar nuclei does not occur later on, even though they have come into the mitosis which begins simultaneously with them (Bannikova, Khvedynich, 1973 b).

A morphological picture of fusion of alien sperm with the polar nucleus differs from that of normal fusion too. Chromatin of N. rustica spermium, while loosening, occupies a considerable part of a nucleus (Fig. 1, 1). In the course of remote hybridization it concentrates at the point of sperm contact with the polar nucleus where the sperm chromosomes gradually despiralize (Fig. 1, 3, 4). It is possible that such compact localization of chromatin within the sperm appears to prevent later the fusion of the fertilizated polar nuclei. Despite the above mentioned irregularities the fertilized nuclei proceed to division and the seed formation begins in both combinations: N. rustica x N. paniculata and N. rustica x N. glutinosa in 50-55% and 10-15% of embryo sacs, respectively.

In the case of significant irregularities morphologically similar for different combinations of crossing, fertilization takes place partly or not at all (Bannikova, Khvedynich, 1972). The partial or single fertilization is observed in the normal and anomalous (incomplete) divergence of sperms. As it is displayed

Fig. 1. Fertilization of Nicotania rustica in the course of remote hybridization and pollination inside the species.
Fig. 2. Irregularities during fertilization in the interspecific hybridization of Nicotiana.

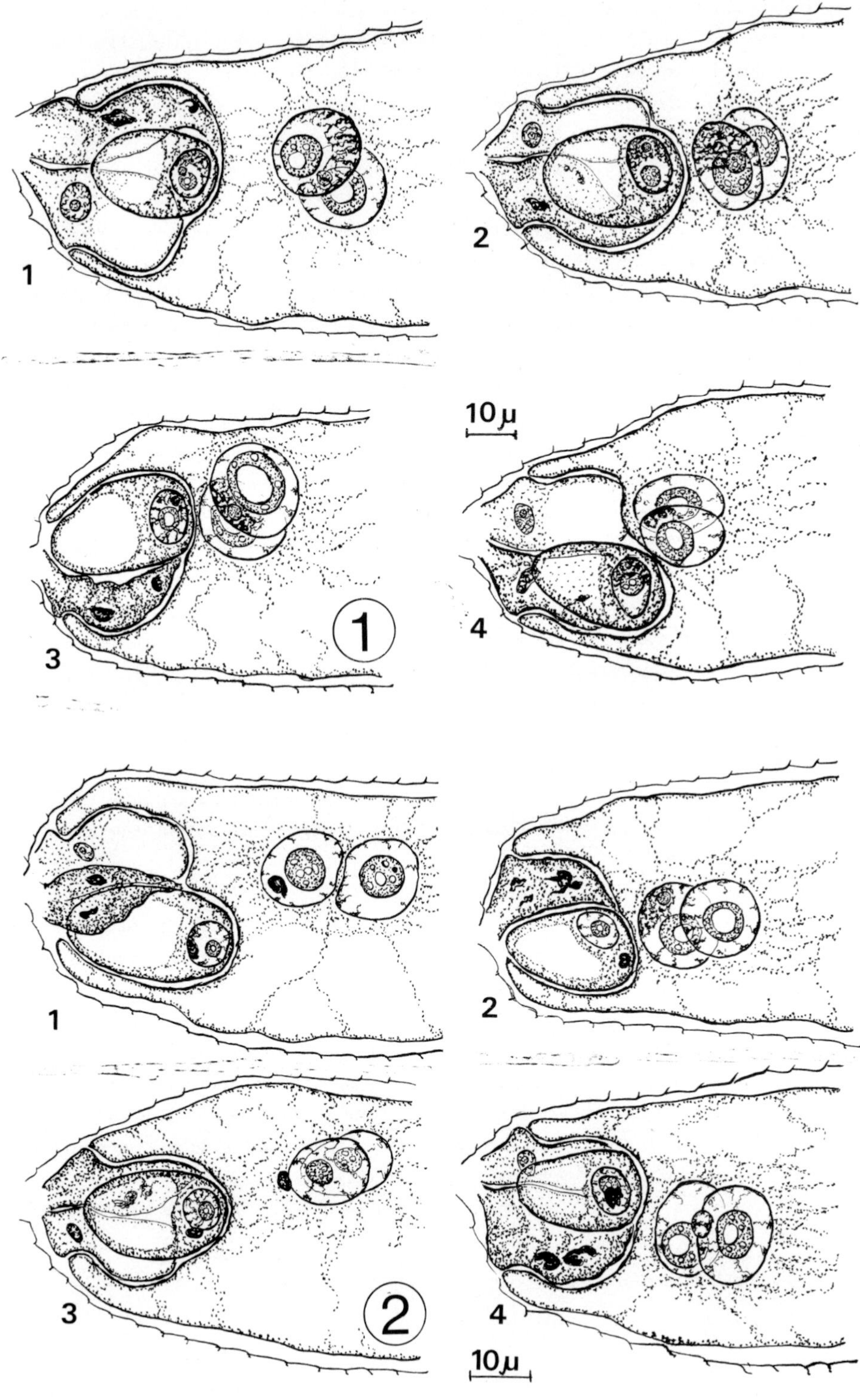

1
2
10 μ
3
1
4
1
2
3
2
4
10 μ

by the combination N. rustica x N. paniculata, one of the sperms unites only with the nucleus of the egg (Fig. 2, 1) or with the polar nucleus (Fig. 2, 1) while another sperm degenrates within the cytoplasm or on the nucleus of the other female cell, in the synergide or space between the female cells, respectively. An absence of fertilization is noticed in the anomalous and normal divergences of sperms or their inundivergence. When the divergence is normal both sperms degenerate either after getting into contact with the nuclei of female cells (Fig. 2, 3 - N. rustica x N. glutinosa) or when in their cytoplasm. But when the divergence is anomalous, sperm stops in the synergide or in the space between the egg and the central cell and the other enters one of the female cells and degenerate either on its nucleus or in the cytoplasm. The whole absence of fertilization occurs when both sperms stop in the synergide (Fig. 3, 1 - Hordeum vulgare x Secale cereale), space between the egg and the central cell (Fig. 3, 3 - N. rustica x N.paniculata, 4 - H. vulgare x S. cereale). The whole or partial absence of the fertilization process is accompanied by the lesion of those natural cyclic changes of nuclei in fusing gametes that are carried out normally (Khvednych, Bannikova, 1973). One can trace it quite well on the sperms. Under normal conditions of pollination in the species in the process of fusion, there is a gradual despiralization of chromosomes in the earlier compact sperms, then the transfer from the telophase into the interphase is observed and the nucleosis form. During the remote hybridization most of alien sperms become much more compact. Without finishing the mitotic cycle they pass to the pycnosis condition (Fig. 4, 1, 2). Chromatin of some sperms coming into contact with the nuclei of fertilized cells is loosened and primarily localized in their periphery. Gradually the sperms become Feulgen-negative (Fig. 4, 3).

Only in a few case do the sperms complete the mitotic cycle and form the interphase nucleus (Fig. 4, 4). However, they also degenerate in 6-8 days after their pollination.

Thus, in the course of remote hybridization in the fertilization process ther there are the irregularities different in their degree of display but morphologically similar for different combinations. They occur at all stages of fertilization: in the synergide, "cleft", fertilized cells. They slow down the rate of the process or stop it at all in a certain part of the embryo sacs. A number of irregularities is different at different stages. The sperms change differently depending on the location in the embryo sac. The sperms are most often left in the synergide and "cleft" whereas the degenerating sperms occur more seldom in the egg and central cell. The common fate for most of sperms which do not participate in fertilization is that they do not end the mitotic cycle and that the transfer from the telophase into the interphase does not take place. In those rare cases

Fig. 3. Degeneration of alien sperms in the embryo sac.
Fig. 4. Fertilization process in the cross Nicotiana rustica x N. glutinosa.

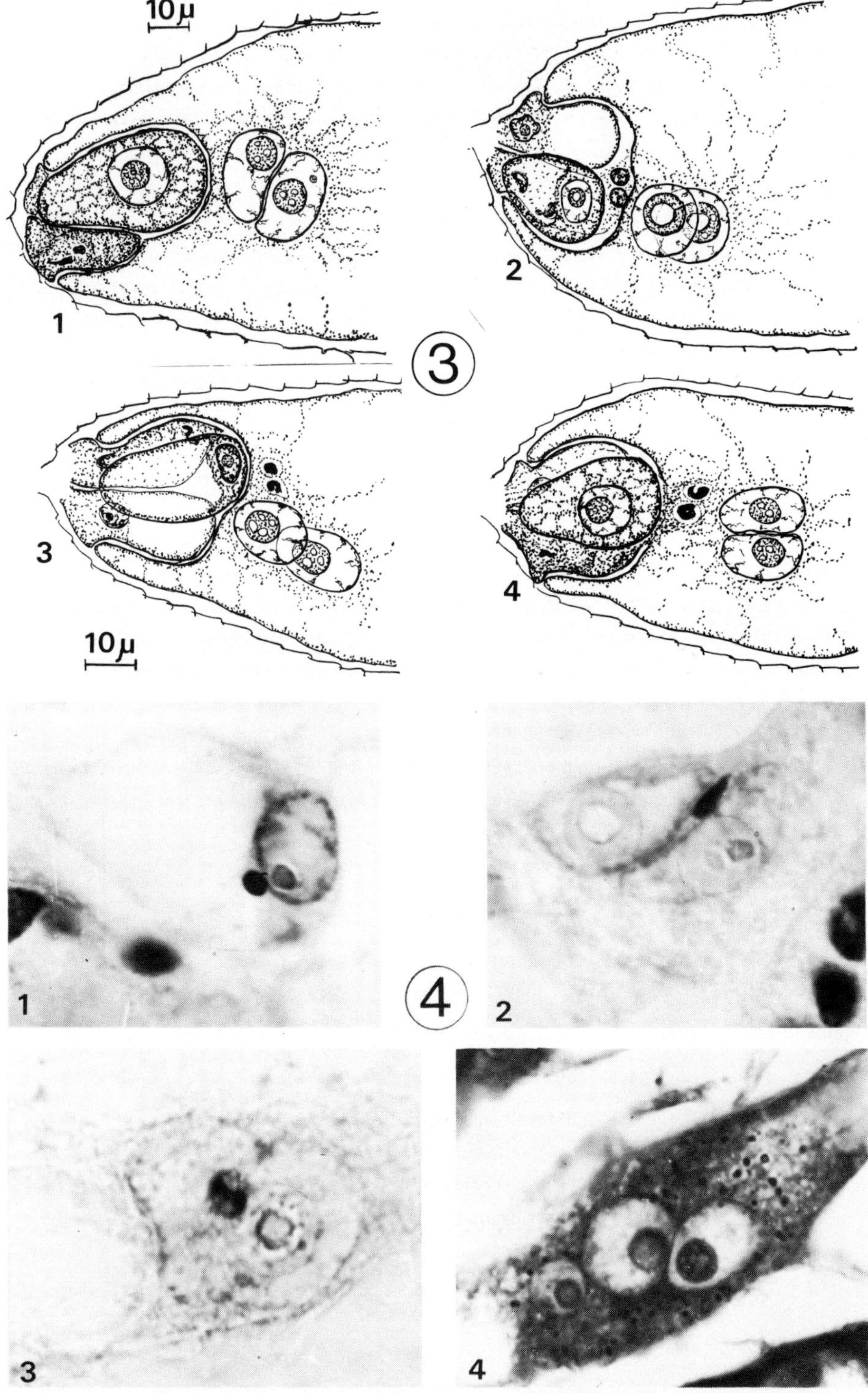
10μ
1
2
3
3
4
10μ
4
1
2
3
4

when the sperms complete the mitotic cycle the succeeding stages of their development connected with the transformation of nuclei in the interphase do not occur. If it is suggested that the initiation of fertilization is mainly or completely conditioned by the influence of female cells on the sperms, the delay of double fertilization in the hybridization of incompatible forms should be considered an inadequacy of this influence because of physiological and genetic remoteness of gametes.

4. CONCLUSION

1. At the stage of fertilization in none of the studied combinations of remote crosses is the development not entirely interrupted, as the fertilization always takes place in a certain part of the embryo sacs. The observed deviations may be insignificant or significant.

2. The insignificant deviations manifest in the delay of rate of fertilization process (Hordeum vulgare x Secale cereale), in the lesion of correlation of rates of syngamy and triple fusion, in the change of nucleus structure of fusing gametes as compared with normal Nicotania rustica x N. paniculata; N. rustica x N. glutinosa).

3. The significant lesions occur in both links of double fertilization or involve one of them. The result is a whole or partial absence of the process.

4. The sperms which do not participate in fertilization undergo the considerable structural transformations: most of them without finishing the mitotic cycle become compact, show an intensive Feulgen reaction and pass to the pycnosis condition; chromatin of some sperms is loosened and they become Feulgen-negative or form the interphase nucleus.

5. The peculiar type of deviation which is characteristic of the interspecific hybridization of Nicotania is the absence of triple fusion when the syngamy is realized successfully.

REFERENCES

1. Poddubnaya-Arnoldi, B.A., 1939, DAN SSSR 24, 5, 380.
2. Khu-Khun, 1969, Tez. koord. sovesh. "Uzlovie voprosy tsitologii", L., 177.
3. Batygina, T.B., 1966, Bot. sh SSSR 51, 1461.
4. Kandelaki, G.V., 1969, Otdalennaya gibridizatsia i ee zakonomernosti. Tbilisi. "Metsniereba", 160.
5. Gerassimova, E.N., 1933, La cellula, 42, 103.
6. Dolgova-Khvedynich, O.A., 1967, Bot. zh. SSSR 52, 759.

7. Beliaeva, N.S., 1968, Izv. A.N. Turkm. SSR., ser. biol., 1, 3.

8. Khvedynich, O.A., Bannikova, V.P., 1970, Bot. zh. SSSR 55, 1111.

9. Bannikova, V.P., 1972, Tez. dokl. 5s'ezda Ukr. bot. ob-va, Uzhgorod, 195.

10. Bannikova, V.P. and Khvedynich, O.A., 1973, Ukr. bot. zh. 30, 670.

11. Bannikova, V.P. and Khvedynich, O.A. 1973 b, Tez. dokl. simp. "Polovoi protsess i embriogenes rastenii" M., 12.

12. Bannikova, V.P. and Khvedynich, O.A., 1972, Tez. dokl. 2 s'ezda VOGIS, M., 18.

13. Khvedynich, O.A. and Bannikova, V.P., 1973, Tez. dokl. simp. "Polovoi protsess i embriogenes rastenii", M., 251.

DISTURBED GAMETE MATURATION AND FERTILIZATION

Fertilization in Higher Plants, ed. H.F. Linskens.

DISTURBANCES IN THE PROCESS OF FERTILIZATION IN ANGIOSPERMS UNDER HEMIGAMY (HEMIGAMY AND ITS MANIFESTATIONS IN PLANTS)

M.P.SOLNTZEVA

Komarov Botanical Institute of the Academy of Sciences of the U.S.S.R., Laboratory of Embryology Leningrad, U.S.S.R.

After the process of double fertilization in Lilium martagon and Fritillaria tenella was discovered in I898, Navashin[I] used a representative of the Rudbeckia genus, namely Rudbeckia speciosa, to prove the universality of the phenomenon of double fertilization. He found that in the family Compositae and, particularly, in Rudbeckia and Helianthus annuus, as well as in Liliaceae, Ranunculaceae and Orchidaceae double fertilization takes place, i.e. one of the sperms fuses with the central nucleus of the embryo sac. This results in formation of an endosperm. The second sperm was observed by Navashin in the egg cell on its way to the female nucleus (plate I-a). Having thus confirmed his discovery, Navashin, unfortunately, made no further or more thorough study of the process of fertilization in Rudbeckia. Meanwhile this process has very many interesting features.

The study of the process of fertilization in the genus Rudbeckia has shown that in a number of cases it has a normal course, and in some cases severe abnormalities are observed.

Under the normal course of the sexual process in the studied Rudbeckia laciniata the pollen tube enters the embryo sac through one of the synergids. In this case the sperms have the form of compact chromatine balls. When the sperms leave the synergids they despiralize and take on the form of elongated spiral bodies (plate I -B). In R.laciniata sperms enter the embryo sac in the upper third of the egg cell and are observed at various distances from female nuclei. However,in I.5 to 2 hours after pollination one of the sperms gets into contact with the central nucleus and then the nuclei join rapidly, producing a small nucleolus. In 6 to 7 hours after pollination a complete fusion of nuclei takes place and only small clots of sperm chromatine remain noticeable. The division of the primary endosperm nucleus occurs 24 hours after pollination (plate I, c).

Thus, the fusion of the sperm with the central nucleus of the embryo sac according to the classification of fertilization types suggested by Gerassimova-Navashina, belongs to the premitotic type.

The second sperm implants itself into the egg cell and moves towards its nucleus. The speed of the sperm movement in the egg cell differs notably from that in the central cell, being much slower.

However, it was possible to observe normal fertilization of the egg cell in Rudbeckia laciniata. In these cases the sperm nucleus contacts the egg cell nucleus; the sperm chromatine gradually despiralizes, and at the same time in the area of chromatine concentration in the zygote nucleus a small nucleolus is formed. The fusion of the sperm with the egg cell nucleus proceeds very slowly, and complete fusion of these nuclei is observed a long time after the division of the endosperm primary nucleus. Such a course of the sexual process in Rudbeckia is observed by far not always. Even in the ovules of the same inflorescence of the very same plant, quite another process has been observed: the process of incomplete fertilization. In this case the fusion of the sperm with the central nucleus takes place in the way described above.

The disturbances of the fertilization process in R. laciniata take place in the egg cell after the sperm has penetra-

---

Plate I. - a Rudbeckia speciosa (From Navashin[I]). One of the plates proving the universality of double fertilisation. One of the sperms is in the egg cell cytoplasm, the other has fused with the central nucleus; b-h Rudbeckia laciniata; b-sperms leave the synergyda in the embryo sac; c-the dissolution of sperm is coming to an end in the zygote nucleus, the primary nucleus of the endosperm is in the metaphase of division; d - the egg cell with a recently penetrated sperm; e - the sperm begins rounding off; f- the egg cell and the sperm nuclei in the prophase of division; the sperm is at a certain distance from the egg cell; g-synchronous division: metaphase of the sperm nucleus and the egg cell nucleus; h - the four-nuclear proembryo two large nuclei are the derivatives of the egg cell, two smaller nuclei in the basal part are the derivatives of the sperm.

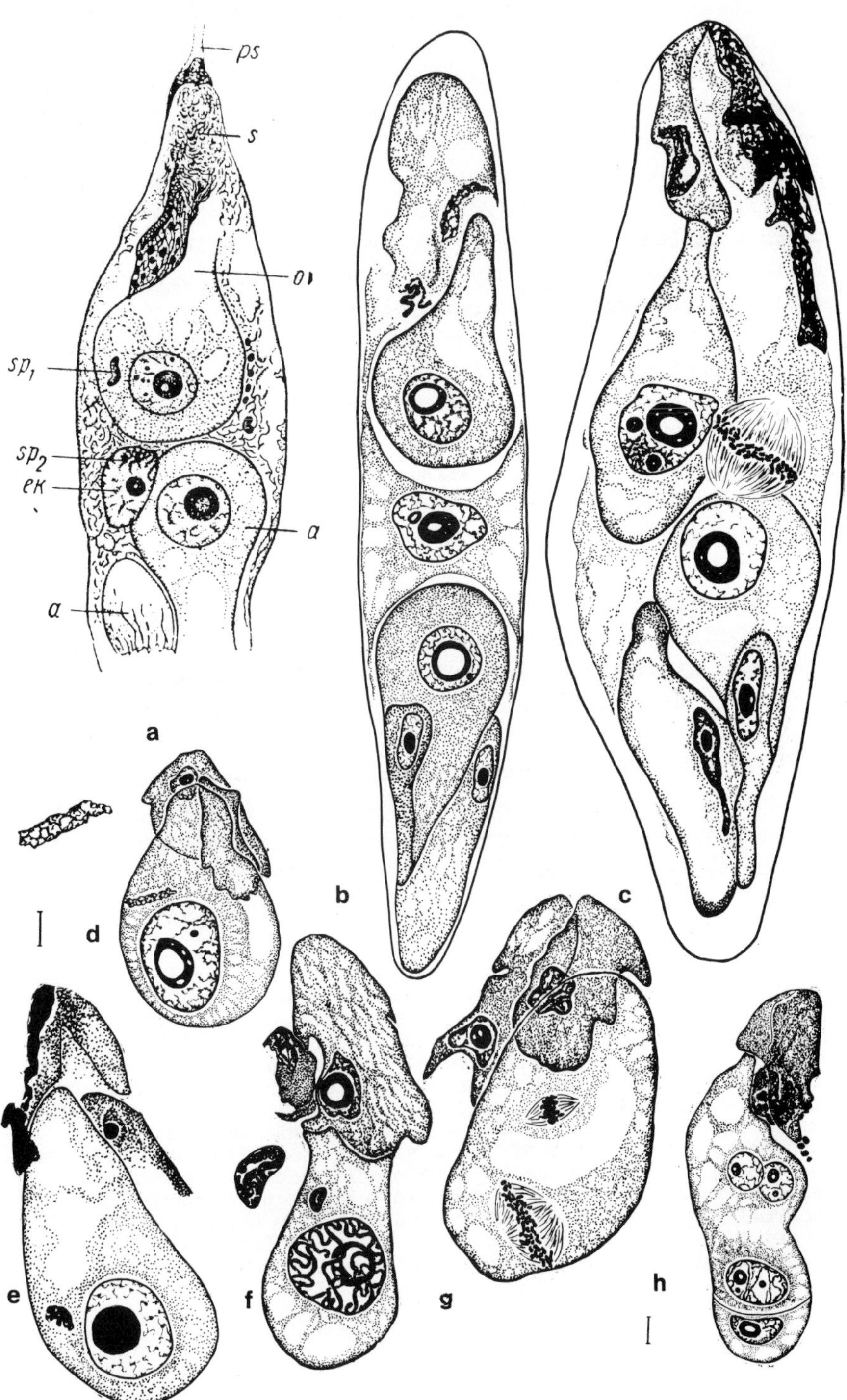
ps
s
oi
sp_1
sp_2
ek
a
a
a
b
c
d
e
f
g
h

ted into its cytoplasm. The sperm does not fuse with the nucleus of the egg cell but remains at a certain distance from it, and is gradually rounding off. The rounded sperm is at the stage of telophase of the mitotic cycle (it shows an intensive Feulgen reaction), and remains in this state as long as 24 hours. Finally, a nucleolus is formed in the sperm, and the latter completes its mitotic cycle. When in an egg cell, the sperm stimulates further development of its nucleus, and the nucleus of the egg cell divides. Simultaneously with the division of the egg cell nucleus, the sperm divides. (Sometimes the division is delayed). The figures of the division both of the sperm and the egg cell greatly differ in size.

The phenomenon of the sperm nucleus penetration into the egg cell without further fusion with its nucleus and its independent division has been called „semigamy" by Battaglia[9-14] who discovered it in 1945.

The term "semigamy" introduced by Battaglia is rather complicated from the linguistic point of view. „Semi" is a word of Latin origin and means „half", whereas „gamos" is a Greek word meaning „marriage". When forming a new term the linguistic laws allow to combine two words of one language. Translated into Greek this term would sound „hemigamy", and in what follows this term will be used.

As a result of autonomous division of the sperm and the egg cell a new four-nuclear embryo is formed (plate I, h). Two of the nuclei are the derivatives of the egg cell and the two others are the derivatives of the sperm. The sizes of the nuclei are different. The nuclei derived from the sperm are small,

---

Plate 2. Rudbeckia laciniata; a-the sperm nucleus is dividing itself synchronously with one of the proembryo nuclei; b - the derivatives of the sperm (small nuclei) have not isolated themselves by a cell wall from the other nuclei of the proembryo; c - a very large nucleus of the proembryo is the result of fusion of a male and a female nuclei; d - scheme of formation of a triploid nucleus during unification of chromosomes at the moment of division; e - a polynuclear cell has come into being as a result of the division of nuclei derived from the sperm; f - in the cells with nuclei derived from the sperm numerous micronuclei come into being as a result of abnormal division; g - synchronous division of nuclei of different sizes derived from the sperm; h - a large nucleus has been formed in the apical part of the proembryo.

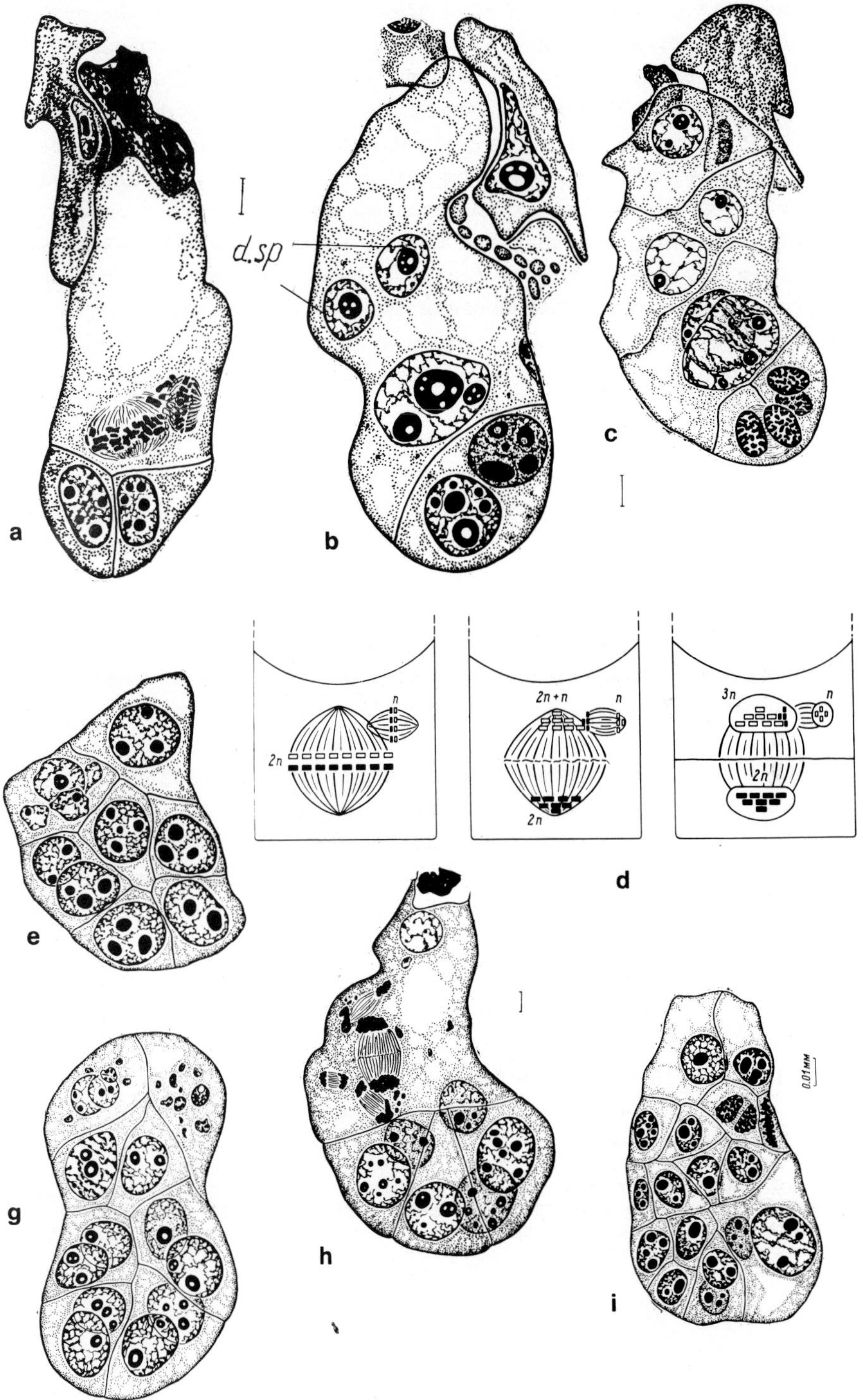
d.sp
a
b
c
n
2n
2n+n
n
2n
3n
n
2n
d
e
g
h
i
0.01мм

haploid (the pollen grains are haploid); whereas the nuclei derived from the egg cell are large, diploid (the embryo sac is not reduced). In the course of division,cellular walls are formed between the female nuclei (plate 2,b), while in most cases no walls are formed between the male or between the male and the female nuclei (plate I,h; 2,b). The division of the nuclei of one cell takes place simultaneously (plate 2,a), and then the fusion of the male nucleus derived from the sperm and the female nucleus derived from the egg cell may occur. This process takes place in the course of the next mitosis when the figures of the division find themselves close enough to one another (plate 2, a, d).

Thus, the embryo of R.laciniata develops after normal fertilization following the premitotic type, or as a result of hemigamy.

If we try to arrange all the known types of fertilization in sequence [7,8] they may appear in following succession: premitotic, intermediate, and postmitotic.

The premitotic type can be considered as the most advanced one, because the process of fertilization itself is more complete. During the development of this type the sexual nuclei lose their autonomy immediately after contact, and even in the prophase of the first mitosis it is impossible to distinguish between the male and the female chromosomes; they behave as chromosomes of a single set.

The intermediate type is the one when the sexual nuclei, being in close contact, do not fuse for a long time. The sperm nucleus becomes somewhat larger and a nucleolus appears in it. The fusion of the male and the female nuclei proceeds very slowly but finally they form a united nucleus and a united metaphase figure, though in the prophase of the zygote it is still possible to discern the chromatine of the sperm and that of the egg cell.

The postmitotic type is the one when the sexual nuclei

Plate 3. - Cooperia (From Coe, 15); H - the sperm nucleus is isolated from the other cells of the embryo by the cell wall; B - F - the sperm nucleus divides twice which is accompanied by cell formation; I - X - the sperm nucleus has divided only once.

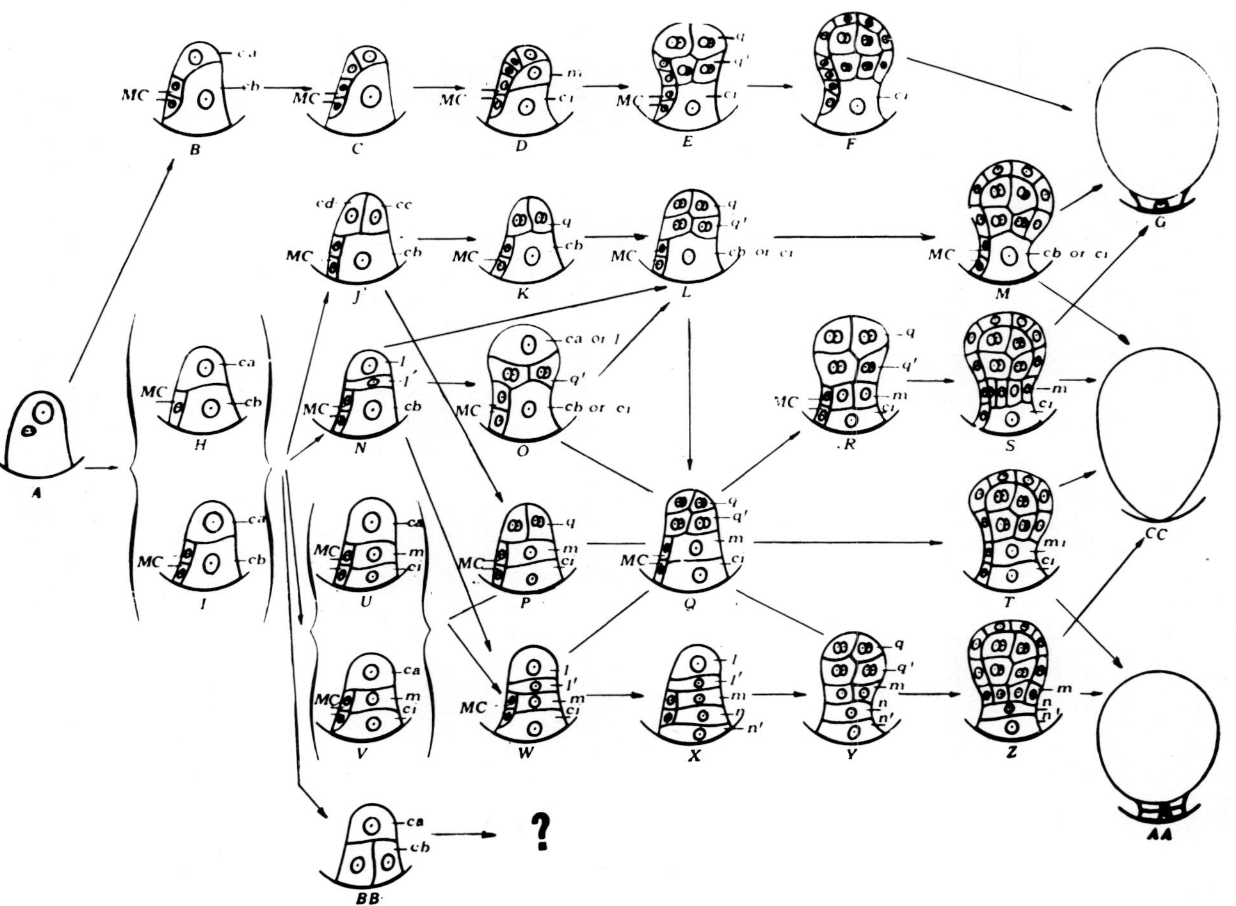
A
B
C
D
E
F
G
H
I
J
K
L
M
N
O
P
Q
R
S
T
U
V
W
X
Y
Z
AA
BB
CC
MC
ca
cb
ci
cc
cd
q
q'
m
n
n'
l
l'
cb or ci
ca or l
?

preserve a certain autonomy of their development for a long time. They develop only in contact with one another: both of them change their forms (the sperm grows considerably larger in size), change their chromatization, and nucleoli appear in both. Each nucleus individually but synchronously enters the prophase and forms its chromosomes. But later a united division spindle is formed, chromosomes of both nuclei make one metaphase plate, and then the autonomous development of the nuclei which existed previously is lost.

This sequence can be continued by hemigamy.

In hemigamy the sexual nuclei preserve the ability of autonomous development even longer. The nuclei of the egg cell and the sperm not only do not fuse, but being isolated in space, form different division figures, and as a result two male and two female nuclei come into being. Further development may lead to the fusion of male and female nuclei in a certain $n^{\underline{th}}$ generation, and in some cells the process of fertilisation will be accomplished. In other words, in hemigamy we observe a longer interval between the sperm's penetration into the egg cell and the fusion of genomes than in the postmitotic type of fertilisation. We find that in the case of eugamy the fusion of genomes takes place at the moment of formation of the initial embryo cell, i.e. zygote, whereas in hemigamy this fusion may occur in the course of further development. At the beginning just one cell (or two cells) will be the bearers of united inheritance, and only afterwards will a number of cells of the embryo bear it. By its ploidy the embryo will be mosaic in character.

At present hemigamy is known in various families, both in the dicotyledons and the monocotyledons. They are 6 species of Rudbeckia in the family of Compositae, 3 species of Zephyranthes genus, and 2 species of Cooperia genus in the family Amaryllidaceae, and Arabidopsis thaliana in the family

---

Plate 4. - Zephyranthes macrosiphon; a - the sperm has penetrated into the egg cell; b - the sperm has come near the egg cell nucleus; c - the egg cell nucleus in the division prophase, the sperm is at a certain distance from it; d - the division telophase of the sperm in proembryo; e - proembryo with small nuclei derived from the sperm in the basal part; f - nuclei derived from the sperm in the lateral of the proembryo; g) a restitutional nucleus has been formed in one of the proembryo cells.

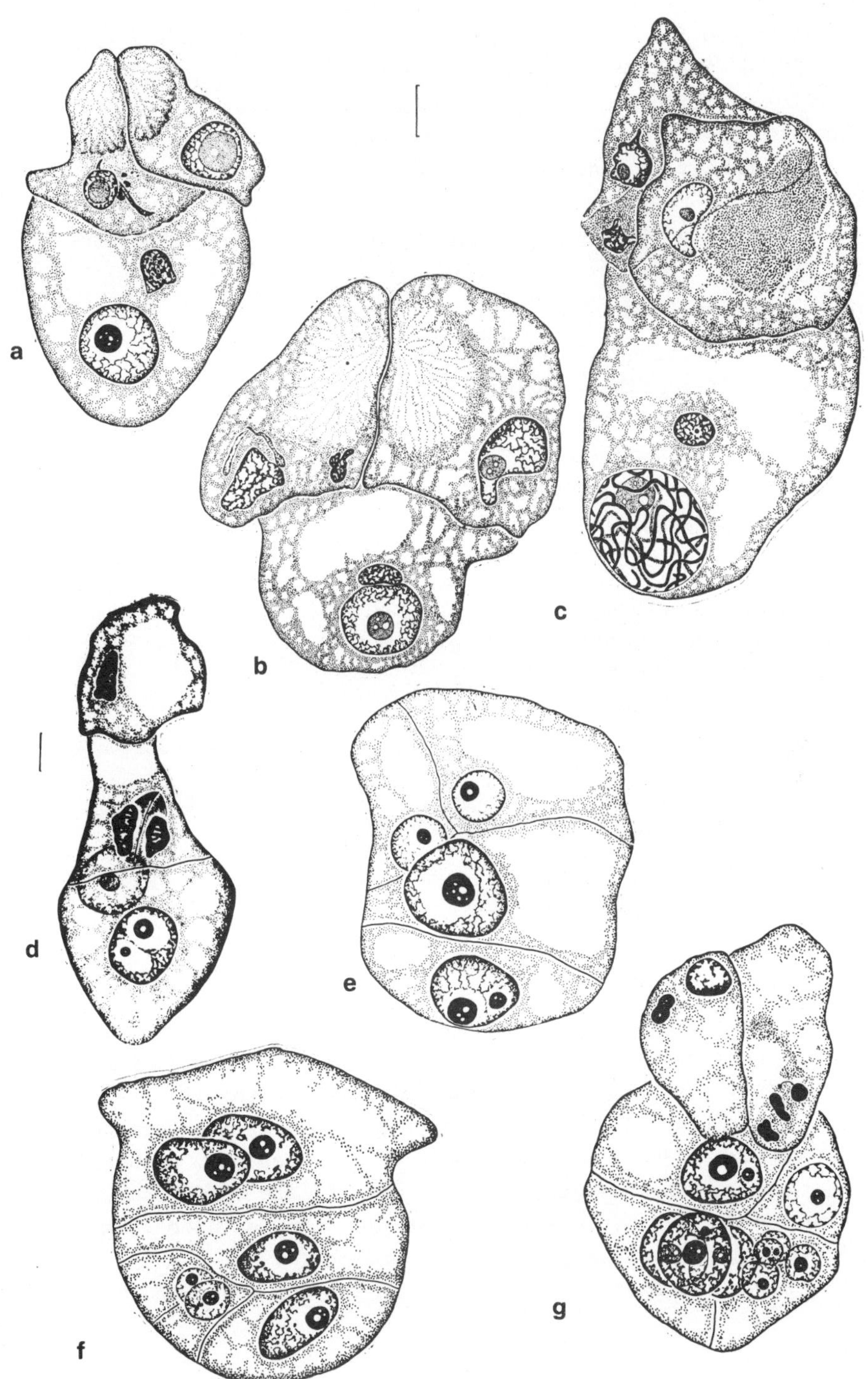
a
b
c
d
e
f
g

Cruciferae (in the experiment the ovules and hence the egg cells of the latter plant were exposed to various dosages of X-ray irradiation). The genetic study proves the presence of this phenomenon in the genus Gossypium of the family Malvacae namely in a double haploid of one of the cotton variety.

The plants in which hemigamy was found are listed below:

Amaryllidaceae

Cooperia drummondii Herb.[I5]
Cooperia pedunculata Herb.[I5]
Zephyranthes candida Herb.[I6]
Zephyranthes macrosiphon Baker[I7]
Zephyranthes texana Greene[I8]

Compositae

Rudbeckia laciniata L.[9]
Rudbeckia speciosa Wender.[II]
Rudbeckia sullivantii Bouton et Bealde[I2]
Rudbeckia maxima Nutt.[I9]
Rudbeckia triloba L.[20,2I]
Rudbeckia hibrida[20,2I]

Cruciferae

Arabidopsis thaliana (L.) Heynh.[22]

Malvaceae

Gossypium barbadense L.[23,24]

The list is certainly not final and is not claimed to be complete. In future it will be probably enlarged.

The results of hemigamy investigations have shown that the phenomenon has a specific character of its own in various objects, although it can take different forms in one and the same plant. All the variety of hemigamy manifestations in various objects can be classified in three main groups:

I. On penetration into the egg cell, the sperm nucleus does not divide but remains active and soon isolates itself by a wall from other parts of the embryo.

II. The sperm nuclei divide in the egg cell, and the

division is accompanied by formation of a cell wall.

III. The sperm nucleus divides in the egg cell and the division is not accompanied by formation of cell walls.

The first case was observed by Coe[I5] in Cooperia drummondii, when on penetration into the egg cell the sperm never divided, but always isolated itself by a cell wall and formed the basal cell of suspensor.

The second case when sperm nuclei divided and formed cell walls, was observed in a number of objects of the family Amaryllidaceae, with some variations:

I. The sperm nucleus divides only once, and the division is accompanied by formation of walls both between the male nuclei and between the male and the female ones. It has been observed in Cooperia pedunculta.[I5]

2. The sperm nucleus undergoes several divisions. During the first division it isolates itself from other cells by a cell wall; then its derivatives divide several times (plate 3) with accompanying cell formation. (In Cooperia pedunculata the male nucleus divides twice[I5]) or without any cell formation as it occures in Zephyranthes macrosiphon and Z.candia (plate 4 a-c) which we studied in colleboration with L.I.Vorsobina[I6,I7]. In case of Z.macrosiphon after the second division there are some abnormalities in the process of mitosis, and micronuclei, aneuploid, and restitutional nuclei come into being (plate 4e).

The third version, when the sperm nucleus penetrats into the egg cell, but does not isolate itself from the rest of the embryo by a cell wall, and its division is not accompanied by formation of a cell wall, is observed in Atomosco texana, in Arabidopsis thaliana, and in various species of Rudbeckia. In this case the behaviour of male nuclei is extremely diverse. In our research[4-6] in Rudbeckia laciniata the first division of male nuclei proceeded normally (Plate I,g,h; 2, b). In the second and the subsequent divisions of male nuclei it was possible to observe abnormalities of the division with the result of formation of micronuclei and aneuploid nuclei (plate 2 e-g). We succeeded in observing synchronous (or nearly synchronous) divisions of nuclei of different sizes in one cell (plate 2 g). In the course of division bridges appear between the nuclear masses, and in some cases a complete divergence of chromosomes to the poles of the spindle does not occur at all, and restitutional and hence diploid nuclei come into being[17] (plate 4 g). Similar evidence was found by Battaglia[11]. As Gerlach-Cruse[29] notes, in Arabidopsis sperm derivatives, when in one cell, can fuse with one another which means that diploidization of male nuclei takes place. And, finally, one or both of the nuclei of sperm derivation can fuse with female nuclei, if they are in the same cell (plate 2 a, c, d). Such fusion takes place when male and female nuclei are close to each other at the moment of the next synchronous mitosis (plate 2 d), and then very big sized triploid nuclei arise (plate 2 c). The location of male nuclei in the embryo as well as the nuclei formed by their fusion varies and depends upon the part of the embryo in which the sperm enters, and on the manner in which further divisions in the mother cell proceed. More often they are observed in the basal part of the proembryo (plate 2 b), and sometimes they are found in the central or even in the apical part (plate 2 h).

Of course, the data on the behaviour of sperms and their derivatives in the embryo are not sufficient, but at this stage it is already possible to trace the trend of diploidization of male nuclei and hence the sufficient longevity of sperm derivatives in the embryo. It is very likely that in some plants their chimeric tissues found already in the proembryo can hold on in the mature seed of an adult plant.

The genetic study of doubled haploids of one of the cotton varieties[23,24] showed formation of quite viable chimera plants. In the experiment the doubled haploid variety with dark-green leaves and oily glandules was pollinated with the pollen of the variety having light-green leaves and no oily glandules. This resulted in formation of chimeric plants some of which had dark-green tissue, and some were light-green; some had oily glandules, and some were deprived of them. One could observe sectors of chimeric tissues. In some of the plants chimerism was more pronouced, in some less pronounced. Chimerism remains in generative organs as well, i.e. in the flowers and in the ovaries.

Comparing all the known cases of hemigamy with one another and with other similar cases observable in a number of plant phenomena, we come to the conclusion that hemigamy is a form of incompatibility between male and female gametes.

Thus, as can be seen from the above disussion, the phenomenon of hemigamy manifests itself in many different, forms and is found in plants of different families of philogenetic classification. Hemigamy has different forms in different objects and manifests itself differently even in one and the same plant, but in all cases the sperm invariably performs the function of stimulating the division of egg cell nuclei and takes part in the building up of the embryo. In course of this process a certain chimerism in tissnes of the embryo appears, and this is often accompanied by different ploidy. Hemigamy is to be considered as a form of male and female incompatibility.

The phenomenon of hemigamy is, in fact, a prolonged and not completed process of fertilization. And it allows us to enlarge our understanding of the fertilization process and of the functions performed by the gametes. Besides the main function of male gametes as bearers of male inheritance factors, there is evidently another function (which is no less important) of activation of the egg cell nucleus, stimulating it to division. In all the cases of normal fertilization these functions are, as it were, combined into one, and that is why they are rather hard to distinguish, and in case of hemigamy the function of stimulation fully reveals itself.

References

I. Navashin, S.G., I898, Bull. de l'Acad.Sci.St. - Petersbourg, v.9, N 4, November, 377.
2. Navashin, S.G., I900, Bull. de l'Acad.Sci. St. - Petersbourg, I3, 335. (in Russian).
3. Navashin, S.G., I900, Berichte der Deutschen Botanischen Gesellschaft. I8, 244.
4. Solntzeva M.P., I968, in: Mater. Vses. Embryol.Symp. SSSR,Kiev, 2II (in Russian).
5. Solnzeva M.P., I97I, Dokl. A.N.SSSR, I97, 234 (in Russian).
6. Solnzeva M.P., I973, Bot.J., 58, I26I (in Russian).
7. Gerasimova-Navashina H.N., I956, in.: Probl. Sovr. Embryol. SSSR, L., 48. (in Russian).
8. Gerasimova-Navashina H., I960, The Nucleus, 3.

9. Battaglia, E., I945, Nuovo Giorn.Bot.Ital., 52, 34.
IO. Battaglia, E., I946, Nuovo Giorn. Bot.Ital., 53, 483.
II. Battaglia, E., I947, Nuovo Giorn. Bot.Ital., 54, 277.
I2. Battaglia, E. I954. VIII, Congr.Int.Bot.Paris Rapp. et Common. Sect. 8, 245.
I3. Battaglia, E., I955, Caryologia 8, I.
I4. Battaglia, E., I963, in: Recent advances in the embryology of Angiosperms. Delhi. 22I.
I5. Coe, G.E., I953, Am.J.Bot., 40, 335.
I6. Vorsobina, L.I., M.P.Solntzeva, I973, in: Sexual Process and Embryogenesis, M. 4I (in Russian).
I7. Solnzeva M.P., L.I.Vorsobina, I972, Dokl. A.N. SSSR, 206, I006, (in Russian).
I8. Pace, L. I9I3, Bot.Gaz., 56, 376.
I9. Movsesian, S.N. I964, Isv. A.N.Arm.SSR, I7, 77 (in Russian).
20. Movsesian, S.N., I968, in: Mater. Vses. embryol. Symp. SSSR, Kiev, I38 (in Russian).
2I. Movsesian, S.N., I970, in: Apomixis and Selection, M., I26 (in Russian).
22. Gerlach-Cruse, D., I970, Biol.Zentralbl., 89, 435.
23. Turcotte, E.L. and C.V.Feaster, I967, J.Heredity, 58, 55.
24. Turcotte, E.L. and C.V.Feaster, I969, Crop. Sci., 9, 653.

Fertilization in Higher Plants, ed. H.F. Linskens.

THE LETHAL POLLEN FACTOR
A TEST FOR THE EARLY DIAGNOSE OF GENETIC DEPRESSION

R. Linder

Université des Sciences de Lille

Laboratoire de
Cytogénétique et d'Ecologie

Villeneuve D'Ascq

The lethal pollen factor has been observed in diverse varieties of cultivated apple trees, in wild pear and apple trees, in maize and tomato, in grapes, in Oenothera, etc. As a result of the lethal gene in the genotype, 50% of the pollen produced is abnormal. This lethal pollen mutation is interesting because its presence is revealed in the products of meiosis of the heterozygous individual +/p, when the factor +, which is the normal condition, is separated from its allele p, which indicates abortion of the grain. This disjunction of the two alleles is transfered to the pollen grain genotype by segregation yielding 50% lethal pollen (Linder, 1961).

The appearance of the mutant p can serve as a tracer of mutability in the perennial individual and especially in a clone, which has been maintained by vegetative propagation during several centuries, as the cultivated grape.

The factor p is so wide-spread as to be spontaneous:

in the collection of apple trees of the I.N.R.A. Clermont-Ferrand, of the 300 varieties in the collection 15 diploids are found to carry the lethal pollen factor (p_1 to p_4) (A. Gagnieu).

The analysis of one thousand wild pear and apple trees in the chain of mountains of the Haut-Rhin reveals the existence of 3 pear and 12 apple trees carrying lethal pollen ($p_1 p_2 p_3$).

In the genus Oenothera, the factor p has been found in the tetraploid species fruticosa and in the diploid species purpuranta of the sub-genus Eu-Oenothera.

The collection of grapes of the Institut Viticole Oberlin of the city of Colmar is comprised of 369 varieties from all of Europe; 23 of these show the manifestation of the factor p.

In the grape vines from Alsace, in the experimental collection of the Institut Oberlin, the observation was carried out on local graft varieties, each on 13 different grafts.

The frequency of mutation p is greater for certain of these, such as the Traminer (11 out of 25).

Certain grafts (125/1 for example) are shown to be more mutagenic.

These observations suggest to us the utilization of p mutability as an early diagnostic test of genetic depression in the cultivated grape where degeneracy is the main concern of the plant breeders. In effect, the aging of the clone should be considered as an accummulation of mutant recessive genes, provoking a depression of hereditary patrimony.

In some cases mutation of the gametophytic factor p is detected immediately; this is not the case for other mutations of sporophytic characters, where the combination of two recessive alleles in the homozygote is lacking.

The frequency of appearence of p supplies a criterion for determining the speed of aging of a clone. It is important to take this into account in the selection of new grape varieties.

REFERENCE

Linder, R., 1961, Z. Vererb.-Lehre 92, 1-7

Fertilization in Higher Plants, ed. H.F. Linskens.

MALE STERILITY AND CYTOKININ ACTION in *Mercurialis annua* L. (2n=16).

B. Durand and J.P. Louis

Department of Botany and Genetics,
University of Orleans 45100 FRANCE.

1. Introduction.

In the monoecious species *Mercurialis ambigua* L. (2n=32 ; 2n=48) where self pollination is frequent, male sterility is widespread and several phenotypes (with abortive pollen, lack of anthers, empty anthers, staminods or carpods) are encountered in natural populations. In the 6x cytotype (2n=48) a cytoplasmic heredity unit is involved in this character ([1]). In the dioecious diploid species, *Mercurialis annua* (2n=16) where biparental reproduction is constant, male sterility is very scarce because the male sterile individuals are eliminated in panmictic crosses.

However, one sterile male "mutant" having a total sterility with abortive sporogenous tissus has been selected from natural populations of the diploid species. It has been cloned and used in different experiments in order to study the physiology of microsporogenesis .

2. Materials and Methods.

I. - The strains used in the different crosses include the following clones : 1/ The asporogenous male sterile mutant SM, 2/ several male fertile clones of *Mercurialis annua* 2n=16, called K^+ (less sensitive), K^{++} (sensitive), K^{+++} (very sensitive), OK_3 (resistant), with respect to their sensitivity to kinetin, a feminizing hormone for this species ([2]), 3/ several semi-sterile strains called st_2, st_3, st_8, st_{10}, st_{14} and some wild fertile ones not selected and called N_1 N_2 etc...). Females with mutant cytoplasm called S_1, S_2, S_3 and one with normal cytoplasm called N.

II. - Artificial feminization : The conversion of sterile or fertile males into females is obtained by sprayings with 1 °/₀₀ Benzylaminopurine solution during 15 days. After fertilization, the seed production is normal ([3]).

III.- *In vitro* cultures of male nodes are grown on synthetic gelose mediur with specific doses of auxins and cytokins ([4]).

3. Results.

I.- Pollen restorating genes.

After artificial feminization, the sterile male mutant strain is crossed with several wild male strains : in this progeny all the females are fertile ; the sterility affects only the male, but the parental total sterile male phenotype does not appear ; this strain behaves therefore as a recessive one.

Since part of these males are full fertile ones, restorator genes exist ; and since the rest are semi-sterile, semi-restorator genes are encountered. Some semi-sterile individuals are cloned and will be used in reciprocal crossings.

Table I

Cross	Progeny
♂ sterile feminized X wild fertile males	- sterile ♂ with reduced anthers and no functional pollen (Photo II) - semi-sterile ♂ with gathered (A) unequal (B) or tetrad (C) pollen (Photo I) - fertile ♂ with normal microsporogenesis (Photo I) - all fertile ♀

Progeny of an artificially feminized male sterile clone pollinated by several wild fertile males.

II.- Interaction of nuclear and cytoplasmic heredity in male sterility.

In order to know if cytoplasmic units are involved in this phenomenon, reciprocal crosses are made between S_2 and S_{14} semi-sterile clones and the N_1 fully fertile wild one ; this produces 349 offspring individuals (table II).

Table II

Crosses	Sterile or semi-sterile ♂	Fertile ♂	Total ♂	Total ♀
S_{14} ♂ (feminized) x N_1 ♂	46	52	98	0
N_1 ♂ (feminized) x S_{14} ♂	13	24	37	16
S_2 ♂ (feminized) x N_1 ♂	79	18 •	160	4
N_1 ♂ (feminized) x S_2 ♂	7	19	26	8

• 97 ♂ only would be analysed for sterility.

Results of reciprocal crosses between two semi-sterile clones (S_2, S_{14}) and a fertile wild one N_1.

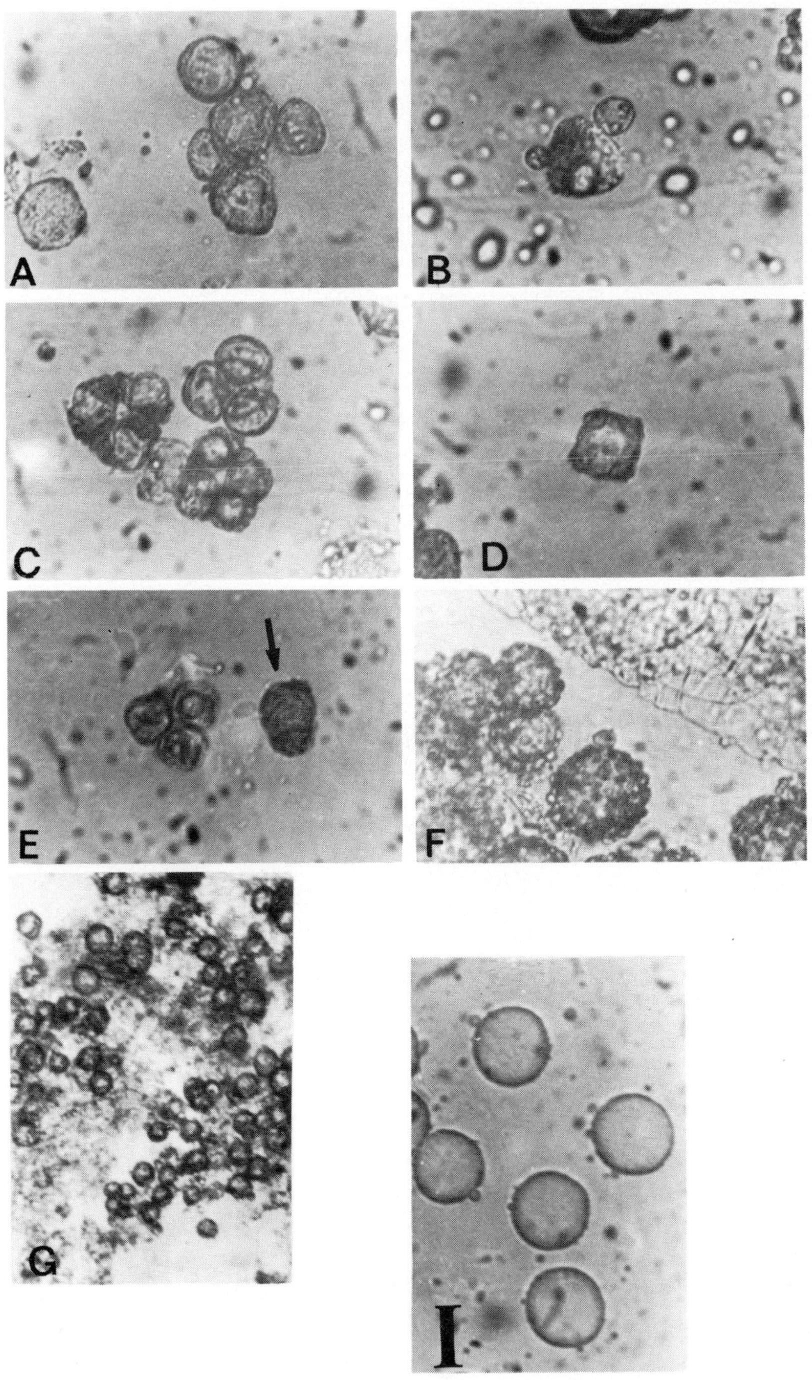
A
B
C
D
E
F
G
I

There is a significant difference in the male sterile segregation as well as in sex segregation in each reciprocal cross : the proportion of sterile males is higher when the semi-sterile clones are used as females. Therefore a cytoplasmic heredity unit is involved. But, since sterile male individuals appear in the "normal cytoplasm", inductor genes exist as well as restorator ones since full fertile males exist in the mutant cytoplasm.

The parental clone SM does not reappear in the progeny : the inductor genes seem to be recessive or hypostatic ones.

All the males used in the preceding crosses behave as heterozygotes for the restorator, semi-restorators or inductor genes.

III.- Genetic system of restoration.

Information on the restoration conditions can be obtained by crossing the SM clone with the selected males whose sensitivity to cytokin is different. Besides, others crosses between these fertile males and some semi-sterile ones will complete these first data:

Table III

	Crosses	Fertile ♂	semi-sterile ♂	Sterile ♂ of Sm type	♀	X^2 for a 69%/30% ratio	X^2 for a 11/5 ratio
Sm	OK_3 (résistant)	22	12		2	0,44	0,25
	K+ (weakly sensitive)	84	30		36	1,12	1,2
	K++ (sensitive)	72	36		32	0,57	0,12
	K+++ (very sensitive)	30	8	4	12	0,04	0,14
St_2	OK_3	106	48			1	0,003
	N1	140	52		8	0,22	1,5
	N2	64	52 •			12,1	9,9
	N3	54	12 ••		8	9	5,2
Total 812 =		562	+ 250			24,29	18,313
Frequency		0,69	0,3		(X^2 of the total)		-0,08
							18,23

• Fit for a 9/7 ratio ($X^2{}_2$= 0,05)
•• Fit for a 13/3 ratio (X^2= 0,012)

Segregation for male sterility : heterogeneity between progeny ratio is obvious ; three types appear : 11/5, 9/7, 13/3, suggesting that a dominant gene (I) induces anther abortion and two other dominant ones (R, R_2) are suppressors of I.

All these fertile males are heterozygote ones for the restorator or semi-restorator genes. The parental SM clone reappears only in the progeny of cytokinin high-sensitive males (K+++) : a relation is established between the induction of

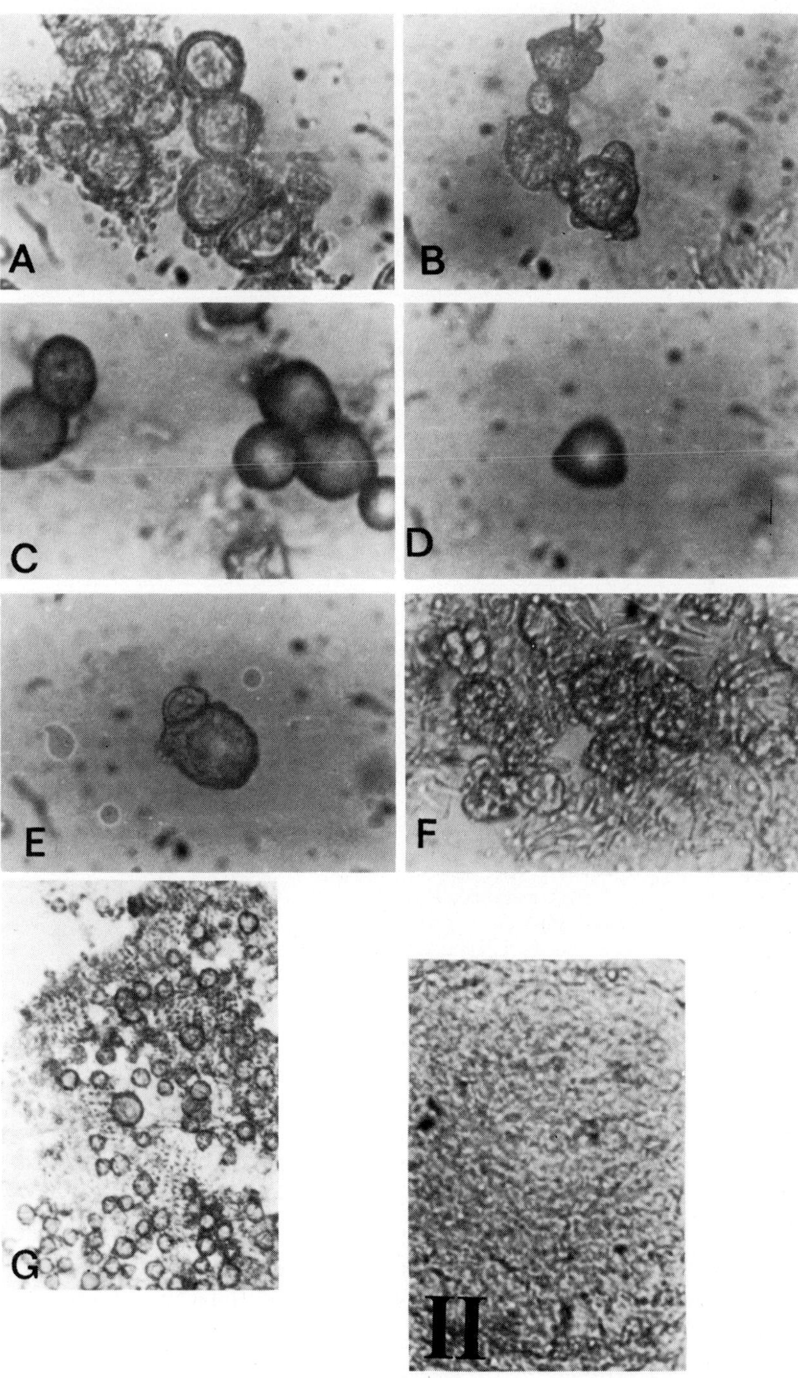
A
B
C
D
E
F
G
II

sterility and cytokinins sensitivity of males.

The two homogeneity test for a 70 %/30% and a 11/5 ratio are negative (table III) : the ratios vary between 11/5, 9/7 and 13/3. Three loci must be considered : one dominant gene inducing sterility (I), two dominant restorator ones (R1, R2) being necessary to inhibit I action. (The genetic formula of the strains could be then : $R_1\ r_1\ r_2\ r_2\ I_2$ for SM clone, $r_1\ r_1\ R_2\ r_2$ Ii for St_2, $R_1\ R_1\ R_2\ r_2$ Ii for N_3 and for the other ones, N_2 excepted).

IV.- Sex segregation and male sterility.

The cytoplasmic mutation is still clearer if the sexes segregation is considered in the reciprocal crosses (table II) : the females disappear or are very few in the mutant cytoplasm and on the contrary, they appear in significant proportion in the wild cytoplasm.

The cytoplasmic mutation alters the sex segregation as is confirmed in the following crosses between males and females having received the mutant cytoplasm.

Table IV

Crosses	♂	♀
S1 ♀ x St_2 ♂	39	45
S4 ♀ x St_2 ♂	21	35
S3 ♀ x St_2 ♂	50	40
S3 ♀ x St 14 ♂	54	4
S3 ♀ x St 8 ♂	6	34
S3 ♀ x St 10 ♂	8	34
S4 ♀ x Fertile restored 0 with mutant cytoplasm	113	81
S2 ♀ x Fertile restored 0 with mutant cytoplasm	72	62
N ♀ x St 14 ♂	7	23
N ♀ x St 2 ♂	0	18

V.- Male sterility physiology.

There is a relation between the induction power of males and their sensitivity to cytokinins : however is this the action of cytokinins on microsporogenesis ? This action is obvious : during the first steps of feminization, there always is a transitory state of male sterility. Then phenocopies of male sterility can be obtained by cultures of male fertile nodes on synthetic medium ([5]) : as sex expression is depending on cytokinins - auxins balances, there always is for all kinds of males,a threshold for the relative concentration of these two hormones for which the male sterility appears simultaneously in all the flowers ([5]).

Moreover the phenocopies of all types of pollen abortion can be reproduced by cytokinin treatments *in vivo* and *in vitro* (Photo I phenotypes, photo II phenocopies). Therefore, the male sterility in *Mercurialis* is dependant on the same kind of hormonal balances controlling the sex expression ([5]).

4. Discussion and conclusions.

The genetic system controlling male sterility in *Mercurialis*, interaction of two pairs of genes with a mutant cytoplasm is analogous to that of many higher plants (*Epilobium*, *Sorghum*, *Beta*, etc...)([5]).

This controlling system interferes with hormone production or hormone receptors : the hypothesis of a partial control of these two metabolic pathways by both nuclear and cytoplasmic units could be proposed.

Alteration of the sexes segregation in mutant cytoplasm (as occurs in *Satureia hortensis* ([6]) ([7]) and *Origanum vulgare* ([8]) ([9]) ([10])) seems to agree with this hypothesis, since the sex expression and male sterility depend on the same hormonal balance. As variations of sex ratio is also frequent in offspring of wild strains, letality alone could not explain these alterations in *Mercurialis*. Male sterility control cannot be disjoined of the general problem of sex expression.

It is likely that nuclear and cytoplasmic units control hormonal metabolism at the stamen primordia level, in the flower meristem rather than by inducing letality at the first step of zygote segmentation, keeping in mind that in Eucaryotes, nuclear cytoplasmic interactions constitute one of the main mechanisms of cellular differentiation ([11]).

References

1. Durand B, 1963, Le complexe *Mercurialis annua* L.s.l. : une étude biosysthématique Ann. Sc. Nat., Bot., 12e s., IV, 579-736.
2. Durand B., 1969, Sélection de génotypes mâles de *Mercurialis annua* L. (2n=16) en fonction de leur sensibilité aux cytokinines, C.R. Ac. Sc., série D, 268, 2049-2051.
3. Durand B., 1966, Action d'une kinetine sur les caractères sexuels de *Mercurialis annua* L. (2n=16). C.R. Ac. Sc., série D, 263, 1309-1311.
4. Champault A., 1972, Effets de quelques régulateurs de la croissance sur des noeuds isolés de *Mercurialis annua* L. 2n=16 cultivés *in vitro*. Bull. Soc. Bot. Fr., 1973, 120, 87-100.
5. Edwarson J.R., 1970, Cytoplasmic male sterility. Bot. Rev., 36, 341-419.
6. Correns C., 1904, Experimentelle Untersuchungen uber die Gynodioecie. Ber. Deut. Bot. Ges., 22, 506-517.
7. Correns C., 1908, Die Rolle der mannlichen Keimzellen bei der Geschlechtsbestimmung der gynodioecischen Pflanzen. Ber. Deut. Bot. Ges., 26 A, 686-707.
8. Appl J., 1929, Weitere Mitteilungen uber die Aufspaltung eines Bastards zwischen *Origanum majorana* L. und *Origanum vulgare* L. in der F_2 und F_3. Generation. Genetica, 11, 519-558.

9. Lewis D. et Crowe L.K., 1952, Male sterility as an outbreeding mechanism in *Origanum vulgare*. Heredity, 6, 136.

10. Lewis D. et Crowe L.K., 1956, The genetics and evolution of gynodioecy. Evolution, 10, 115-125.

11. Brachet J.L. et Formen R.S., 1971, Nucleocytoplasmic interactions in morphogenesis. Proc. Roy. Soc. London, B, 178, 227-243.

Fertilization in Higher Plants, ed. H.F. Linskens.

EXPERIMENTALLY INDUCED HAPLOID PARTHENOGENESIS IN THE POPULUS SECTION LEUCE AFTER LATE INACTIVATION OF THE MALE GAMETE WITH TOLUIDIN-BLUE-O

Z.M. Illies
Federal Research Organization of Forestry and Forest Products,
Institute of Forest Genetics and Tree Breeding,
Schmalenbeck, Federal Republic of Germany

1. INTRODUCTION

In the Genus Populus experiments on the artificial induction of haploid parthenogenesis were carried out to provide haploid seedlings for further use in tree breeding programmes. In the course of this the question arose - at which time prior to the fusion of the ♂ and ♀ nuclei was the parthenogenetic development of the embryo from haploid ♀ gametes initiated. Former experiments indicated that in the genus Populus haploid parthenogeneis occurs spontaneously or can be induced by several means. It had been induced with pollen of weak germinability, with pollen of alien species or pollen from another section of the genus or by irradiated pollen (Kopecki 1960[6], Stettler 1968[9,10], Stettler et al.1971[11], Valentine et al. 1968[12], Winton et al. 1968[13]). The highest frequency of haploids was described by Stettler, who noticed an average of 0.1-1.7% in randomly - picked females of P. trichocarpa. From these results the question arose, whether embryo development in the egg cell was stimulated as early as pollination, thus resulting occasionally in haploid parthenogeneis when the pollen failed to germinate, or if after pollen germination the insertion of the pollen tube into the stigmatic tissue stimulated embryo development, though again fertilization and formation of the zygote failed.

In the present experiments the male gamete was inactivated at different times between pollination and fertilization to find out the period at which embryo development in the female gamete is stimulated by the male gamete prior to fertilization, thus resulting occasionally in haploid parthenogenesis. The inactivation of male gametes with the basic dye Toluidin-blue had been first described by Briggs (1952[3]) and by Edwards (1954[4]), inducing pseudogamy in mice and frogs with inactivated sperm. Rogers and co-workers proved that Toluidin and other Phaenothyacine and Acriditine derivates inactivate the mitosis of the generative nucleus in pollen cultures in vitro of Tradescantia and Vinca rosea (Rogers et al. 1966[8], Gearharts et al. 1969[2]). However, the application of these results to the induction of haploid parthenogenesis in tomato and maize failed (Al-Yasiri 1967[1],

Al-Yasiri et al. 1969[2]), but Winton repeated the method on Populus alba pollen applying a pollen Toluidin suspension on female flowers of P. tremuloides to select 1 haploid seedling (Winton 1970 pers. communication).

2. MATERIAL AND METHODS

The present 3-year study (1970-72) was carried out on female tree of Populus tremula (We 5; We 5; We 61, We 93) and its hybrid P. tremula x tremuloides (Th 1290; J A), and with pollen of P. alba. Only the hybrid Th 1290 had been available during all experiments of the 3-year study. The use of P. alba pollen introduced a marker gene to facilitate the phenotypical selection of haploid seedlings of parthenogenetic origin. The female provenance and the hybrids respectively were known to be homozygous for glabrous leaves, the species alba has pubescent leaves, while the interspecific hybrid with both female species revealed an intermediary leaf character. Thus in the progenies raised from the experiment the haploids of parthenogenetic origin would be known by the matroclinal glabrous leaves, while diploid seedlings originating from zygotes would show the hybrid character. The female poplars were picked randomly among the breeding material the institute, while the alba-pollen was kindly delivered from Italia and Yugoslavia. These pollen samples were used in carefully prepared mixtures.

Toluidin-blue-O was used in an aqueous solution. During the first year, pollen/Toluidin suspensions of 5 ppm, 10 ppm and 15 ppm were applied, according to the method described by Al-Yasiri[1]. In 1971 and 1972 the female flowers were pollinated normally with untreated pollen to be sprayed later with 10 ppm Toluidin at different intervals. The differentiation of the treatment provided the opportunity to determine the time embryo development was stimulated. If a considerable frequency of matroclinal seedlings arose from the first experiment, embryogeny had been stimulated by the actual pollination without regard to the quality of the pollen, as that had been inactivated in the pollen/Toluidin suspension before application to the females (1970). If on the other hand, a higher frequency of matroclinal seedlings arose after the late Toluidin spray of normally pollinated catkins it would be concluded, that the egg cell reacts mainly after pollen germination and the insertion of the pollen tube into the female tissue (1971, 1972). Control pollination with pollen of P. tremula and P.alba without Toluidin, as well as spraying with Toluidin without pollination, proved the females to be non-apomictic. All experiments were carried out on cut branches kept in running water in climatically controlled isolation chambers at a 10 hrs. photoperiod and 18° C temperature.

Independently pollen germination and pollen growth on stigmatic flaps were examined microscopically in the fluorescent light. Both treatments were sampled in 1970 and 1971 (Linskens et al. 1956)[7].

Table 1

Number of matroclinal seedlings of parthenogenetic origin after inactivation of the male gametes with Toluidin-blue

♀	1970 Pollen/Toluidin suspension 10 ppm		1971 Toluidin-spray 10 ppm			1972 Toluidin-spray 10 ppm			hours
	Total no.	No. matroclinals	Total no.	matroclinal seedlings No.	%	Total no.	matroclinal seedlings No.	%	
Th 1290	--	--	2015	179	8.8	14	6	43	12
			--	--	--	44	9	20	18
JA	4	3							
We 5	3	1							
We 93	2	--				376	104	27.7	12
contr.	29	--							
We 1						708	166	23.1	12
We 6						61	8	13.1	12

3. RESULTS AND INTERPRETATION

The phenotypical selection of glabrous matroclinal seedlings originating presumably from haploid parthenogenesis started after the 3rd or 4th leaf evolved 2 months after the seed germinated.

In Table 1 the collected data are summarized separately for each in 3 main columns. Some of the females had been used repeatedly, but only Th 1290 flower branches were available in each year, though here seed set failed entirely after the application of the pollen/Toluidin suspension. However, in two other females 4 and 3 seeds respectively were collected, of which 3 and 1 proved to be matroclinal seedlings. Data from the late application of Toluidin first used in 1971 and repeated in 1972 gave different results. On both occasions the pollen had been of good quality and the late Toluidin spray inactivated the male gametes when the pollen tubes had penetrated into the female tissue. The results were in contrast to both, those in which the pollen/Toluidin suspension was used, and with those from other methods to induce haploid parthenogenesis. It seems that Toluidin occasionally inactivated the male gametes before they had reached the egg cells, thus preventing the subsequent of the and nuclei and consequently the formation of a diploid embryo. However, the different frequency of matroclinal seedlings indicates that the length of the interval between pollination and Toluidin application was critical. In both years no seed had been collected the Toluidin was sprayed 6 hrs after pollination, so probably the male gametes been activated too soon. With one exception normal fertilization was already completed, when the Toluidin had been applied as long as 18 or 24 hrs after pollination. In those series all seedlings showed the intermediary hybrid leaf characterized though in Th 1290 matroclinal seedlings arose in the 12 hrs as well as in the 18 hrs series. In the repetition of the experiment in 1972 the average frequency of matroclinal seedlings ranged from 13,1% to 43%. Though the frequencies in Th 1290 varied markedly from 8.8% in 1971 to 43% in 1972. This may be partly due to the very small number of catkins available in 1972, but it also suggests to numerous exogenous influences during flower and seed development.

Table 2
Fluorescent-microscopical control of pollen germination
and pollen tube growth ♀ Populus tremula
after different applications of Toluidin

♀	Series 70: Pollen/Toluidin Suspension (o.P. alba)														
	5 ppm Tol.			10 ppm Tol.			15 ppm Tol.			H_2O			control		
	lt	st	wt	lt	st	wt	lt	st	wt	lt	st	wt	lt	st	wt
Th 1290	--	1.9	98.1	--	0.06	99.0	--	--	100	--	--	100	42.2	15.0	44.
JA	--	2.4	97.6	--	0.3	99.7	--	--	100	--	0.6	99.4	41.7	2.0	56.
We 5	--	0.6	99.4	--	0.2	99.8	--	0.2	99.8	--	0.6	99.4	66.6	0.3	33.

♀	Series 71: Toluidin-spray after pollination (o.P. alba)										
	Tol/6 hrs			Tol/12 hrs			Tol/18 hrs			Tol/24 hrs		
	lt	st	wt	lt	st	wt	lt	st	wt	lt	st	wt
Th 1290	19.6	14.2	66.2	30.5	21.5	48.0	19.5	14.8	65.8	52.7	47.3	--

In 1970 and 1971 the effect of both treatments on pollen germination and pollen tube growth was compared microscopically in fluorescent light[7]. Table 2 gives the percentage of long and short pollen tubes (lt;st) and ungerminated pollen - without tubes (wt) determined in 3 stigmatic flaps of 6 to 9 catkins in 3 females 24 hrs after the application of the pollen/Toluidin spray respectively. Individual differences between the females are seen from the untreated control in 1970. Particularly the data collected in Th 1290 in both years clearly show the different effect of the treatmenst. Pollen germination was very poor in all concentra-

tions of the pollen/Toluidin suspension. In 5 ppm Toluidin 1.9% of pollen tubes were counted going down to 0.06% in 10 ppm to be none in the 15 ppm treatment.
In 1971, on the contrary, pollen germinated in all series and the pollen tubes penetrated into the stigmatic tissue before the Toluidin spray inhibited further growth. However, pollen tube length and number of germinated pollen grains differed according to the interval between pollination and the Toluiding application. The 6 hrs series gave the poorest results, while pollen had germinated and long tubes grown into the female tissue in the 24 hrs series, thus indicating a successful fertilization. While corresponding to the selection of matroclinal seedlings from 12 as well as 18 hrs series, here again the differences were not distinct in pollen tube growth.

According to the corresponding results in both tests, it may be assumed, that in the application of the pollen/Toluidin suspension Tolluidin reacts at a different phase than it does when sprayed on the female some times after a normal pollination, thus interrupting the sequence of events between pollination to fertilization. In the first case Toluidin inactivated the pollen considerably before it had been applied to the stigma. Consequently the results correspond with other methods aiming at the induction of haploid parthenogenesis in which pollen of low germinability had been used. In contrast to this in the second treatment the pollen started to germinate prior to the inactivation by the late Toluidin spray. Thus, the pollen tube penetrated into the female tissue stimulating embryo development in the egg cell, though the late inactivation of t the male gamete consequently prevented the fusion of the male and female nuclei. Thus eventually the opportunity for the haploid parthenogenesis of an embryo from an unfertilized egg may be possible. However, as haploid parthenogenesis in the Genus Populus has been induced occasionally by pollination with artificially inactivated pollen (6, 9, 10, 12, 13) it may be concluded that the phase in which this essential stimulation acts is quite long lasting. Within this time some egg cells may already be stimulated by mere pollination of the stigma, thus giving rise to haploids of parthenogenetic origin. However, the late application of Toluidin resulted in a higher amount of matroclinal seedlings, thus leading to the assumption, of the early stimulation of the egg cell for embryo development. It was not possible to decide from this study whether Toluidin inactivates the generative nucleus or the haploid mitosis, producing the sperm nuclei.

In about 50% of the selected matroclinal seedlings the chromosome number has been established, ranging from haploid to diploid level, most of them being haploid, 1/3 aneuploid and one diploid plant. In the rest of the plants either mitosis had been too irregular to determine the chromosome number or the plants had been too weak for fixation. The present 3-year old "haploids" revealed a wide variability in characters, numerous recessive genes expressing themselves. For instance growth rate varied from dwarfish growth to almost normal size like diploid plants. However, the induction of haploids of parthenogenetic origin may provide an efficient method to supply haploids for tree breeding programmes with Poplar.

REFERENCES

1. Al-Yasiri, S.A., 1967, Studies on Toluidin blue for inducing haploidy in Lycopersicum esculenta and Zea Mays. Ph.D. Thesis, Univ. of Hampshire.

2. Al-Yasiri, S.A. and Rogers, O.M., 1971, Attempting chemical induction of haploidy using toluidin blue. J. Amer. Soc. Hort. Sci. 96, 126-127.

3. Briggs, R., 1952, An analysis of inactivation of the frog sperm nucleus by toluidin blue. J. Gen. Physiol. 35, 761-780.

4. Edwards, R.G., 1954, The experimental induction of pseudogamy in early mouse embryo. Experimentia 10, 499-500.

5. Gearhart, J.D., and Rogers, O.M., 1969, Suppression of generative nucleus division in Tradescantia paludosa by phenothiazine and acriditine derivative Cytobios 1 A, 17-11.

6. Kopecki, F., 1960, Experimentelle Erzeugung von haploiden Weisspappeln (Populus alba L.) Silvae Genetica 9, 102-109.

7. Linskens, H.F., und Esser, K., Über eine spezische Anfärbung der Pollen schläuche im Griffel und die Zahl der Kallosepfropfen nach Selbstung und Fremdung. 1957, Naturwiss. 44, 16.

8. Rogers, O.M. and Ellis, J.H., 1966, Pollen nuclear division prevented with toluidine blue in Vinca rosen L. Hart. 1966, Hort. Sci. 1, 62-63.

9. Stettler, R.F., Irradiated mentor pollen: its use in remote hybridization Black Cottonwood, 1968, Nature 219, 746-747.

10. Stettler, R.F. Experimental induction of haploid parthenogenesis in Populus trichocarpa. 1968, Genetics 60, 229.

11. Stettler, R.F., and Bawa, K.S., 1971, Experimental induction of haploid parthenogenesis in Black Cottonwood. 1971, Silvae Genetica 20, 15-25.

12. Valentine, F.A. La Bumbard, S. and Fowler, R.G., Selection and identification of monoploid Populus tremuloides Michx. 1968, XVI Northeast. For. Tree Impr. Conf., Quebec 29-34.

13. Winton, L.L. and Einspahr, D., 1968, The use of heat treated pollen for aspect haploid induction. For. Sci. 14, 406-407.

Fertilization in Higher Plants, ed. H.F. Linskens.

APOMIXIS OF BOTHRIOCHLOA ISCHAEMUM L. FLOWERING, POLLINATION, FERTILIZATION.

R.D. Moskova
Agricultural Academy "G.Dimitrov"
Scientific-Educational Department
of Agronomy, Chair of Botany
Sofia Bulgaria

M.S. Yakovlev
V.L. Komarov Botanical Institute,
Academy of Sciences of USSR, Leningrad
USSR

1. Introduction

In genus Bothriochloa and in the related genus Dichanthium and Capillipedium belonging to Gramineae family, apomixis in respect of the embryo sac genesis has a character of apospory[2,3] or, following a more exact interpretation by Battaglia[4] and Solntzeva[5], a character of somatic apospory[6].

Some authors regard the character of apomixis in respect with the embryo sac genesis as probable pseudogamy.[1, 3, 7, 6]. However, the detailed analysis of flowering, pollination and fertilization of this genus had not been carried out and without such an analysis it is not possible to define accurately the type of apomixis. That is why the analysis is indispensible.

2. Material and Method

We have analyzed the representatives of tetraploid population of Bothriochloa ischaemum var. ischaemum.

To trace the process of fertilization, the method of temporal fixation[8] was used. Alcohol - acetic acid (3:1) and chrome-acet-formol after Navashin have been used as a fixator. Schiff's with alcyan blue and light-green as well as procyon dyes had been used for staining.

3. Results and Discussion

The viable three-nucleate pollen grains are formed as the result of the successive meiosis and two mitoses in anthers of the bisexual and male flowers. The aposporous monopolar four-nucleate embryo sacs of Panicum type[4] (Fig. 1), in which mainly two synergides, the egg cell and the only one polar nucleus are differentiated, usually develop in ovules. Sometimes, the normal megasporogenesis takes place in the ovules which terminates in formation of a linear tetrad and development of the bipolar haploid embryo sac of Polygonum type (Fig. 2). It is very seldom that aposporous bipolar embryo sacs of Hieracium type develop in the ovules, diploid nuclei being the only feature differing them from Polygonum type. For analyzed species, development of more than one embryo sac is rather an ordinary phenomenon. All embryo sacs can develop either in one and the same place, namely, in the central part of the nucellus (Fig.3) or in different its parts. Sometimes they are formed even by internal cells of the internal integument (Fig. 4). The above mentioned types of embryo sacs can be developed in one and the same inflorescense or even in one and the same ovule (Figs. 3 and 4). The embryo sacs pf Polygonum type are always located in that part of the nucellus which is nearest to micropyle.

The mature haploid and diploid embryo sacs turn out to be identical in both morphology and arrangement and in their response to coloration. The egg cell is located between the two synergids. The egg cell nucleus is in the central part. The nucleus is Schiff's negative. The central vacuole is not formed in the egg cell. A great amount of starch is observed in the perinuclear space of cytoplasm. When stained with alcyan blue the eggcell wall becomes apparent in its basal part only. That fully agrees with our non-published data on the results of the electron microscope investigations and already numerous reports of other research workers on the absence of the wall in the apical part of the egg cell[9, 10].

Fig. 1. Mature aposporous embryo sac of Panicum type. Fig. 2. Mature haploid embryo sac of Polygonum type. Fig. 3. Three embryo sacs in central part of the nucellus. A-Panicum type, B and C-Hieracium type. Two sperms are seen in the embryo sac A. Fig. 4. Three embryo sacs in one ovule. Central embryo sac A-Polygonum type. Embryo sac B in funicular part of the ovule-Panicum type, autonomous parthenogenesis. Embryo sac C-Hieracium type, formed, formed probably from internal integument cell. Figs. 5-8. Aposporous embryo sacs of Panicum type at different stages of fertilization. Fig. 9. Aposporous embryo sac of Panicum type. Autonomous parthenogenesis. Fig.10. Haploid embryo sac of Polygonum type. Both sperms are already in the central cell and in the egg cell at an equal distance from their nuclei. The bar is 10 microns.
Abreviations: a - antipodes, e - egg cell, m - micropyle , p - polar nucleus, s - sinergid, sp - sperm.

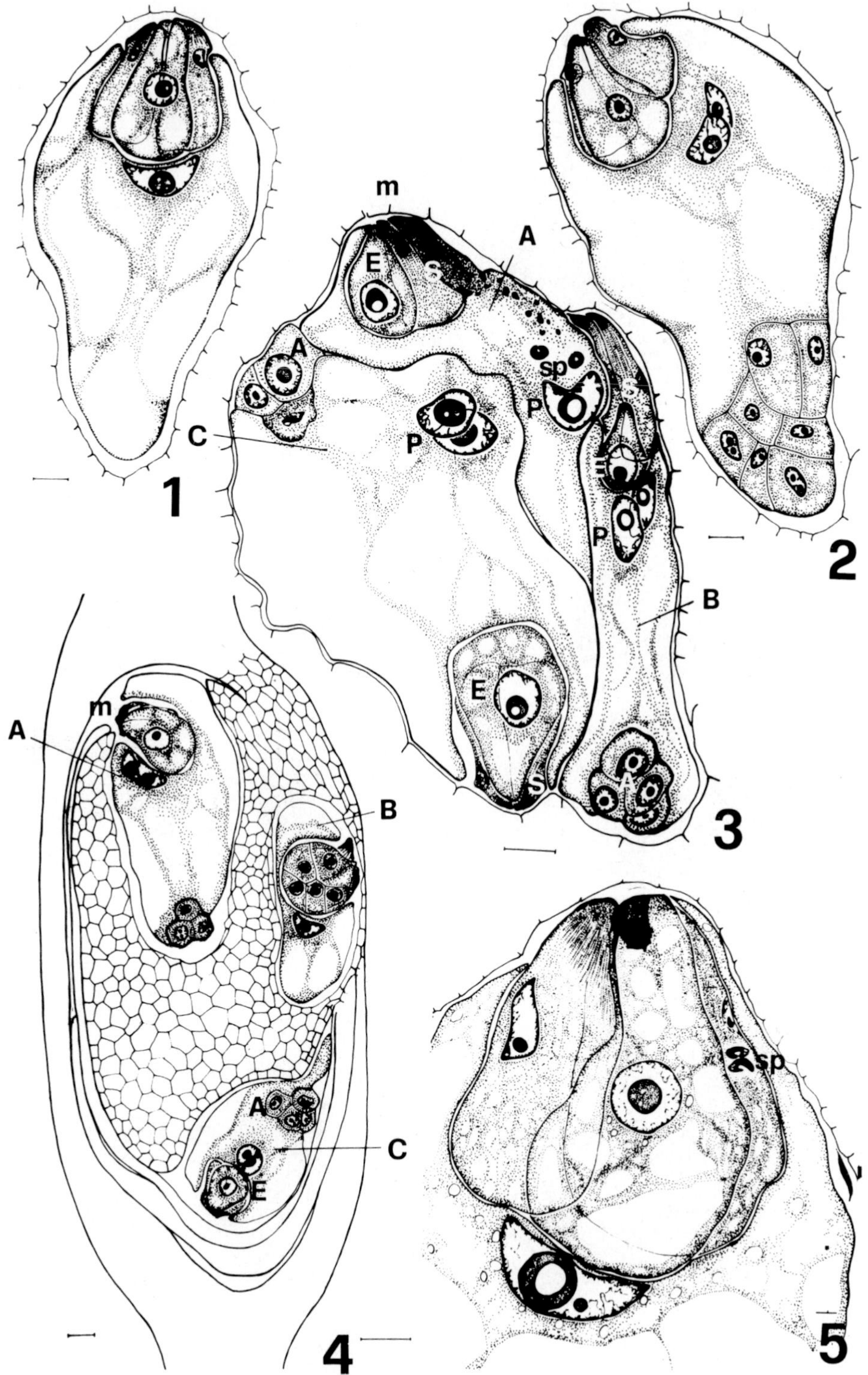
1
2
3
4
5
m
A
E
S
sp
P
C
B
A
m
B
A
C
E
sp

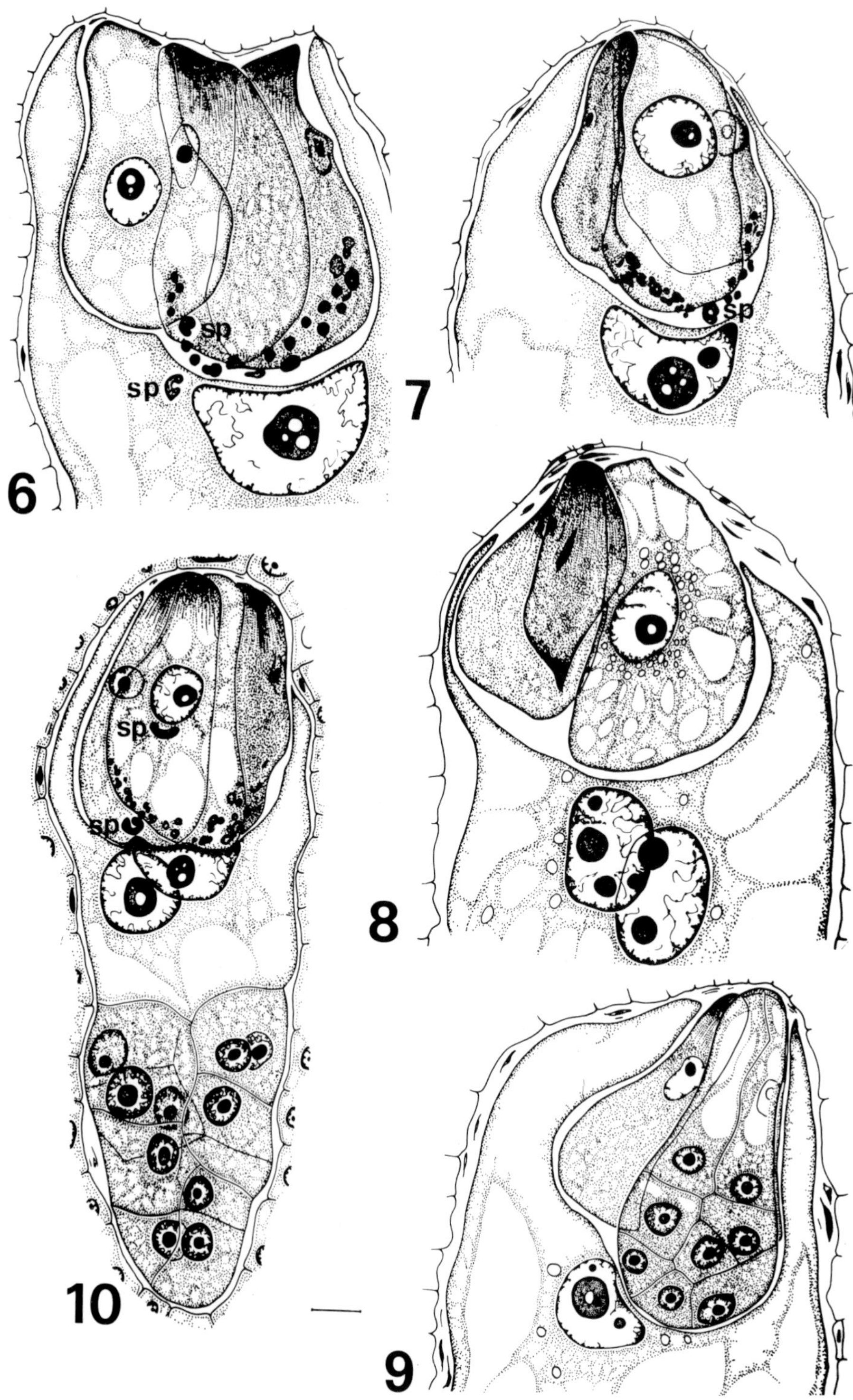
sp
sp
7
6
sp
sp
sp
8
10
9

The cytoplasm of synergides is more dense and has small vacuoles. Starch is not observed in them. Nuclei are arranged near the teeth-like excrescences of synergids. The filiform apparatus is displayed with the help of alcyan blue and procyon dyes. In the apical parts of the synergids a cellular wall is not observed either. The wall of the central cell (excepting the place where it comes into contact with the egg apparatus) is colored very well with alcyan blue and procyon dyes. That enables one to see easily the shape and the size of this gigantic cell. It surrounds the entire egg apparatus and almost reaches microphyle itself, forming the socalled apical pocket[11]. The careful study of slides shows that in mature embryo sacs, and especially in the aposporous embryo sacs of Panicum type, the apical part of the central cell wall from the side of nucellus is thicker. That fully agrees with numerous and large protuberances of the wall observed in the same region (unpublished data). The central cell cytoplasm, with the exception of the polar nucleus part is greatly vacuolated. A great amount of starch (mainly near the polar nuclei) is revealed. The polar nucleus of the embryo sac of Panicum type or polar nuclei of the embryo sacs of Polygonum and Hieracium types are usually arranged close to the egg apparatus, from the side of funiculus. They are Schif's negative. In bipolar embryo sacs (both haploid and diploid ones) the polar nuclei do not fuse till flowering. That interferes with data obtained by Gupta[3] who observes fusing of polar nuclei of B. pertusa before flowering. Nucleoli of polar nuclei are vacuolated. They are the largest in the embryo sac. As regards the analyzed species, availability of micronucleoli is not an unusual phenomenon. Antipodes of bipolar embryo sacs adjoin closely the central cell. Their walls are well colored with alcyan blue, and nuclei are Schif's positive.

The inflorescence of B. ischaemum is composed of two-flower spikelets. One of the flowers is bisexual and the other is male. Flowering of the bisexual flowers is usually chasmogamic. The partial and explosive character of flowering coinciding with the post-meridian time (16-17 p.m.), is the distinctive feature of these flowers. The flower is usually open during one hour.

The central flowers of the inflorescence are the first to blossom. Flowering of the inflorescence continues for a week. The male flowers usually do not blossom during the flowering period of the bisexual flowers of the spikelet. Some of them do blossom several days later but the majority never do. The fresh pollen is viable. It germinates already in five minutes both on the stigma and in artificial cultures. The time and the duration of flowering as well as the time and the duration of pollination and germination of pollen varies with the ambient air temperature and humidity.

With pollen germinating in artifical cultures it was observed that first one sperm comes out into the pollen tube, then another one and finally - the vegetative cell nucleus. With the pollen tube growing up, the vegetative nucleus, all the while intensely elongating, passes by the sperms and outstrips them. With the sperms moving along the pollen tube, their shape varies but the forward end always remains pointed. We share the opinion, that the movement of the sperms in the pollen tube as well as in the embryo sac is a result of interaction between their own movement and the movement of the cytoplasm flow[12]. A great amount of starch is observed both in pollen grain and in the germinating pollen tube. The starch probably represents the material required for the pollen tube to grow. Here, we fully agree with opinion of Ehlers[13], that the pollen tube growth in both the style and the ovary goes on without the absorption of a certain amount of nutriment from outside.

The pollen tube penetration into the embryo sac occurs through one sinergid either via its filiform apparatus (Fig. 7, 10) or by pushing the latter off (Fig. 5). In some cases the pollen tube enters the embryo sac without touching synergids and the latter look viable (as far as it can be seen in the light microscope) during the entire process of fertilization. The contents of the pollen tube gush out, in the form of a droplet - like substance, into the probably slime-filled space between the apical part of the egg cell and the central cell. The sperms are always arranged near the apical part of the egg cell from the side opposite to the destransted synergid. Here, they are in the same telephasal condition as in pollen grains. They are longer as regards the shape, and their chromocenters are clearly revealed when coloured with Schiff's reagent. In embryo sacs of Panicum type, one of the sperms enters the central cell while moving towards the polar nucleus (Fig. 6). Having reached the surface of the latter, the sperm penetrates into it, its nucleolus (Fig. 7) being displayed still in the peripheral part of the polar nucleus. The nucleolus of the sperm gradually moves towards the nucleolus of the polar nucleus and finally is fused with it, that shows that fertilization of the polar nucleus proceedes after the premitotic type in accordance with Gerasimova - Navashina's classification [14, 15]. At the same time, the other sperm is arrested at the boundary of the egg cell (Figs. 6, 7) without penetrating into the egg cell cytoplasm. Soon, it shrinks, becomes more dense and gradually degenerates. Despite this fact, however, the egg cell acquires the appearance of a zygote expressed in certain growth, swelling and peripheral arrangement of smaller vacuoles after the mother endosperm cell comes into its first mitosis. It is kept in that state during the first several divisions of endosperm nuclei (Fig. 8). After that it begins to divide also and forms the embryo. Development of the endosperm before flowering and without fertilization has not been observed.

According to Battaglia[4] this phenomenon should be referred to as pseudogamy. According to Solntzeva it comes nearer to the induced parthenogenesis.

In bipolar embryo sacs of Polygonum type the behaviour of sperms is similar to that already described for other grasses[16, 17]. Here, the sperms enter the egg cell and the central cell correspondingly and move simultaneously towards their nuclei all the while maintaining its equal telophasal appearance (Fig. 10). The fusion of sperms with nuclei goes on in accordance with the premitotic type of fertilization.

Generally, the sperms already get into the space between the egg cell and the central cell in an hour after the pollination. Fusion of the sperm nucleolus with large nucleolus of the central cell nucleus had been observed in two hours after the pollination. The egg cell division starts not until 4 or 6 endosperm nuclei are formed. Further development of the embryo and endosperm goes on rather quickly. The endosperm becoms cellular on the 6th day after the pollination and 9 days afterwards the embryo is already differentiated. It should be taken in to account that the interval between pollination and fertilization varies considerably with the ambient air temperature.

In connection with fertilization it would be interesting to consider the complex of embryo sacs shown in Fig. 3. Here, three embryo sacs have developed in one nucellus, all of them being quite mature. Two sperms have penetrated into embryo sac A, which is the nearest one to microphyle and, having passed by the egg cell, got into the central cell near its polar nucleus and the polar nuclei of the adjacing embryo sac C. It may be assumed, that the central nucleus of embryo sac A shall be fertilized by one sperm while the second sperm, if the central cell walls will not inhibit its penetration the embryo sac C, may fuse with one of the polar nuclei of embryo sac C. In that case, the endosperm may be formed in both embryo sacs which provides a possibility for development of embryos in both embryo sacs and for formation of twins' seeds.

In some cases the beginning of proembryo formation from the diploid egg cell is observed before the flowering (Figs. 9, 4).In embryo sacs distant from microphyle, no fertilization takes place. In the majority of cases, these embryo sacs degenerate. Some times an autonomous development of proembryo takes place in them, but such proembryos degenerate before differentiation, because of the lack of the endosperm. The observed autonomous development of the proembryo fully agrees with parthenogenesis after Battaglia[4]. Other authors [18,5] refer this type of formation of embryos to autonomous parthenogenesis.

Besides somatic apospory, development of diploid embryo sacs of Panicum and Hieracium types and formation of embryo without fertilization, the investigated species demonstrates normal macrosporogenesis, development of embryo sac of Polygonum type and normal fertilization. Having this in mind we may consider it as a facultative apomict. In this respect our data differ from those obtained by Gupta[3] for Bothriochloa pertusa. He determines this species as a facultative apomict but maintains that the viable embryos and the endosperm develop usually in the haploid embryo sacs only. In the aposporous embryo sacs which usually function as accessory ones, the endosperm is not developed, therefore, degeneration of the embryo takes place before its differentiation. For Dichanthium genus, related to Bothriochloa, Reddy and D'Cruz[2] prove that only diploid embryo sacs of Panicum and Hieracium types develop in ovules. They allow for the possibility of development of the haploid embryo sacs but give evidence of fertilization taking place in diploid embryo sacs only.

Judging by the investigated species, we concider diploidness of the egg cell as necessary and decisive factor for transition to formation of embryo without fertilization. The egg cell may enter into that process after its maturing is completed. Development of the egg cell after the beginning of development of the endosperm is a pecularity, which forms the basis of all angiospermous plants.

This pecularity is retained by the majority of apomicts and mainly by those,for example grasses,in which the endosperm is the principal nutrient of the embryo.

References

11. Brown W.V., W.H. Emery, 1957, Bot. Gaz., 118, 246.
2. Reddy P.S., R. D'Cruz, 1969, Stapg. Bot. Gaz., 130, 3., 71.
3. Gupta P.K., 1969-1970. Portug. Acta Biol. A., 11/3-4/, 279.
4. Battaglia E., 1963. Int. Sec. of Pl. Morph. Univ. of Delhi, 8.
5. Solntzeva M.P. 1969. Gen., 5, 8, 20.
6. Moskova R.D., 1974 in press
7. Christov M.A., R.D. Moskova, 1972., Gen. and Pl. Breeding, 5, 1, 71.
8. Gerassimova-Navachina H.N., 1933. La cellule, 42, 1, 101.
9. Jensen W.A., 1965. Amer. J. Bot., 52, 781.
10. Vazart B., J. Vazart, 1966. Revue de Cyt. et biol. vég., 29,251.
11. Diboll A.G. and Larson D.A., 1966. Amer. J. Bot. 53, 391.
12. Steffen K., 1963. Int. Sec. of Pl. Morph-Univ. of Delhi, 8.
13. Ehlers H., 1951, Biol. Zbl. 70, 432.
14. Gerassimova-Navachina H.N., 1951. Tr. BIN, A.N. U.S.S.R., 7, 2, 294.
15. Gerassimova-Navachina H.N., 1960. DAN,U.S.S.R., 131, 3, 688.
16. Gerassimova-Navachina H.N., T.B.Batygina, 1959. DAN, U.S.S.R, 124, 1, 223.
17. Korobova S.N., 1959. DAN,U.S.S.R., 127, 4, 921.
18. Rutishauser A. 1967., Protoplasmatologia, 6, 3.

Fertilization in Higher Plants, ed. H.F. Linskens.

THE INFLUENCE OF THE CARCINOGEN AFLATOXIN B_1 ON THE METABOLISM OF GERMINATING LILY POLLEN

W. V. Dashek and G. C. Llewellyn
Department of Biology
Virginia Commonwealth University
Richmond, Virginia 23284
U.S.A.

1. Introduction

Previously, we[10] reported the use of Lilium longiflorum, cv., 'Ace' pollen as bioassay material for aflatoxin B_1. This compound, a metabolite of Aspergillus flavus, is found on various agricultural products[6]. Aflatoxin B_1, a bifuranocoumarin (fig. 1), is reported to be the most toxic liver carcinogen known[1].

Here, we re-examine the toxin's influence on lily pollen tube elongation and, in addition, report preliminary data on uptake and incorporation of ^{14}C-proline (pro), uptake of ^{14}C-leucine (leu) as well as total protein levels. The reasons for checking aflatoxin B_1 effect's on these metabolic parameters originate from reports in the animal literature that the toxin[11] (as reviewed by Wogan[16],) or its metabolites[13] may interfere with protein synthesis. This synthesis occurs in germinating lily pollen[2]. Also, Sondheimer and Linskens[14] concluded that Petunia hybrida tube extension requires de novo synthesis of proteins.

2. Results and discussion

Pollen tube elongation: Llewellyn and Dashek[10] examined germination and subsequent tube elongation for lily pollen exposed to aflatoxin B_1. They reported a minimal effect on germination at 2 µg/ml (fig. 2a). As the concentration of aflatoxin B_1 was increased from 2 to 16 µg/ml a gradual decrease in percent germination occured. At 18 and 20 µg/ml germination was completely suppressed.

As for pollen tube elongation, it appeared to be stimulated by 2 µg/ml aflatoxin B_1 (fig. 2b). Llewellyn and Dashek[10] also noted that tube lengths for pollen germinated at 4 µg/ml were similar to those of the control. Increasing the concentration from 6 to 16 µg/ml resulted in a gradual decline in tube elongation.

TABLE I. RESPONSE OF POLLEN TUBE ELONGATION TO AFLATOXIN B_1

CONCENTRATION AFLATOXIN B_1 (μg/ml)	TUBE LENGTH (μ)							
	Series 1		Series 2		Series 3		Combination	
	Mean	S. D.	Mean	S. D.	Mean	S. D.	Series Means	S. D. for Means of Each Series
0 (Control A)	—	—	757	269	900	255	828	101*
0 (Control B)	807	298	803	305	792	248	800	8*
5	811	270	791	219	784	275	795	14
10	693	250	767	259	720	254	727	37
15	714	253	793	259	805	274	770	49
20	795	242	807	221	778	188	793	14
25	588	254	626	181	653	282	622	33
30	553	191	516	204	488	176	519	33

*Control (A + B), Series Means = 812, S. D. = 53

Fig. 1 Structure of aflatoxin B_1

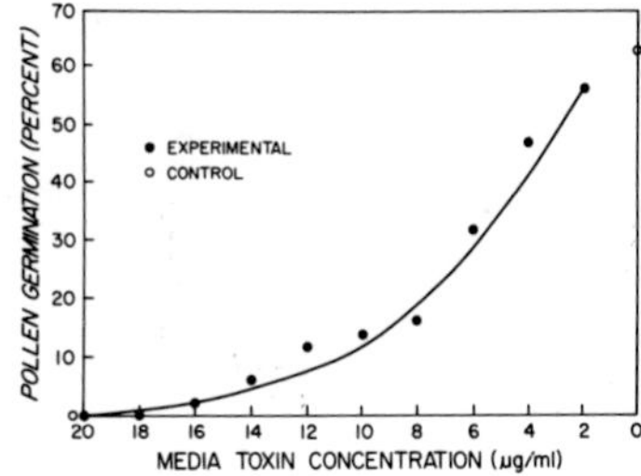

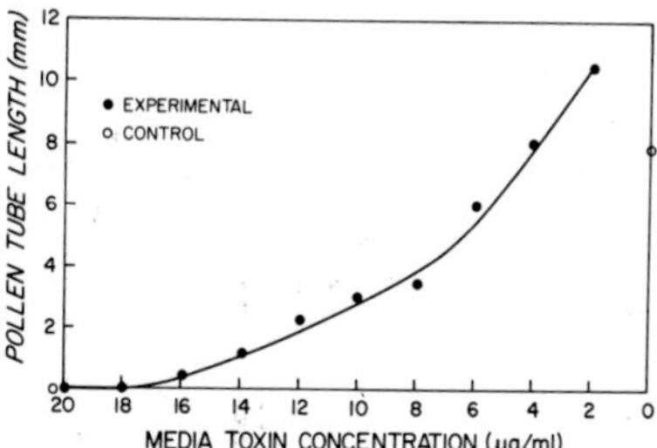

Fig. 2a.; b. Influence of aflatoxin B_1 on percent pollen germination (2a) and tube elongation (2b).

Twenty mg fr. wt. lots of Lilium longiflorum, cv. 'Ace' pollen germinated in 10 ml Dickinson's medium[5], lacking phosphate and tetracycline but containing 2 to 20 µg/ml aflatoxin B_1 (Grade B, dried in situ, Calbiochem, LaJolla, California); concentration of 20 µg/ml aflatoxin B_1 stock confirmed by Virginia Department of Agriculture and Commerce, Mycotoxin Laboratory (Richmond) through use of both quantitative and qualitative test employing several thin layer chromatographic systems and a visual dilution technique sensitive to less than 2 ppb[7]; pollen incubated in sterile, disposable plastic petri dishes for 4 hr. at 27 $\pm$ 2°C under fluorescent light; five replicates made for each toxin concentration; ten replicates in medium lacking aflatoxin B_1 served as controls; pollen tube lengths measured with an ocular micrometer.

Aflatoxin B_1 at 18 and 20 μg/ml totally inhibited tube elongation.

Recently, we (Chancey et al., unpublished) have re-examined the toxin's influence on tube elongation (table 1). A slight inhibiting effect on tube elongation was noted for pollen exposed to aflatoxin B_1 from 5 to 20 μg/ml. Increasing the toxin's concentration to 20, 25 and finally 30 μg/ml resulted in a linear decrease in tube elongation. Extrapolation of the results obtained for 20, 25 and 30 μg/ml indicate that negligible tube elongation would occur at 40 μg/ml aflatoxin B_1. The contrasting results presented in fig. 2b and table 1 probably result from differences in pollen sources, age and storage conditions.

Total protein: In one experiment (fig. 3a), total protein decreased from 2-8 μg/ml aflatoxin B_1 for both 2 and 4 hr. germination and then increased between 8 and 20 μg/ml during the 4 hr. exposure. In contrast, a 2 hr. incubation with aflatoxin B_1 resulted in a leveling of total protein from 8-20 μg/ml. In a subsequent experiment (fig. 3b), exposure of pollen to toxin levels of 2, 8 and 14 μg/ml for 2 hr. yielded a slight increase in total protein and then a decline. A 4 hr. incubation with the toxin resulted in a decrease in total protein between 2 and 8 μg/ml followed by an increase from 8 to 20 μg/ml.

^{14}C-leu uptake: Uptake of ^{14}C-leu was studied as a preliminary to following its incorporation into cytoplasmic and wall-based proteins. This incorporation will serve as a check on aflatoxin B_1 effects on protein synthesis[15] by germinating lily pollen. In the absence of the toxin, ^{14}C-leu uptake increased linearly between 0.25 and 0.5 hr., decreased from 0.5 to 1 and 2 hr. and then was followed by a second increase between 2 and 4 hr. (fig. 4). At 2, 8 and 14 μg/ml aflatoxin B_1 ^{14}C-leu uptake rose during the first hr. of germination and then declined over the second hr. While an enhancement in ^{14}C-leu uptake was noted from 2-4 hr. for toxin levels of 2 and 14 μg/ml, a decrease was seen at 8 and 20 μg/ml during that period. Uptake of ^{14}C-leu at 2, 8, 14 and 20 μg/ml aflatoxin B_1 was higher than that of the control for all time periods tested. This suggested that for this single experiment aflatoxin B_1 at all concentrations

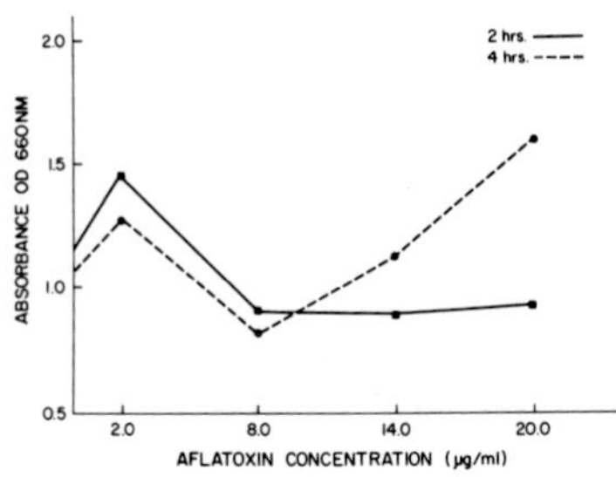

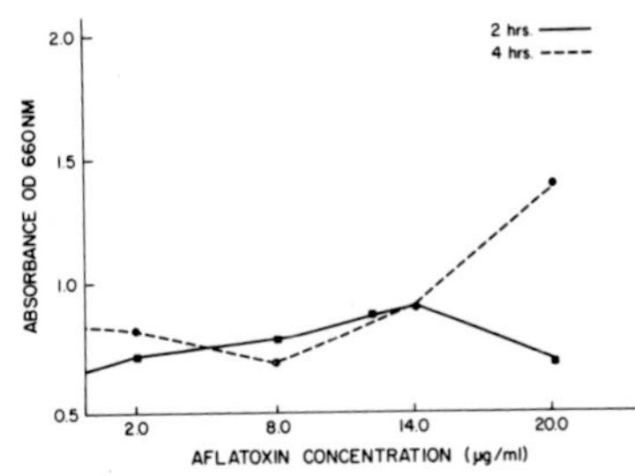

Fig. 3a.; b. Effect of aflatoxin B_1 on total protein levels for two separate experiments.

Germination of pollen as in fig. 2a and b except that phosphate was added to the medium; the aflatoxin B_1 concentrations were 2, 8, 14, and 20 µg/ml and the germination times were 2 and 4 hr.; prior to harvesting germinated pollen was stored for a minimum of 1 hr. and a maximum of 1 night at 4°C; following storage pollen harvested by gentle vacuum filtration onto 0.45µ Millipore filters; pollen on filters washed with 10 ml Dickinson's medium lacking aflatoxin; pollen removed from filter by washing with 10 ml aliquot of H_2O into 30 ml beaker; pollen sonicated, for 1 min., at setting No. 80 (Brownwill, Biosonik III) with a flat probe; sonicated pollen stored overnight at 4°C and then centrifuged at 500 xg for 5 min.; supernatant made to 5% TCA (by addition of an equivalent volume of 10% TCA) and kept at 4°C for 1 hr. at a minimum and 24 hr. for a maximum; centrifuged TCA-supernatant mixture at 1,000 xg. for 30 min.; re-suspended pollen in 5% TCA and centrifuged at 1,000 xg. for 30 min.; pellet suspended in 5 ml 0.5N NaOH; suspension assayed for protein by the Lowry et al.[12], procedure using bovine serum albumin as a standard.

Fig. 4 ^{14}C-leucine uptake as influenced by aflatoxin B_1

Pollen germinated as in fig. 2a and b with the following exceptions: To each 20 mg fr. wt. lot pollen - 10 ml aliquot of Dickinson's medium (containing phosphate) was added 1 µc ^{14}C-leu (specific activity, 270 millicuries/millimole New England Nuclear); germination times 0.5, 1, 2, and 4 hr.; at each of these times pollen placed in cold room to prevent further tube elongation; pollen collected either on nucleopore filters (0.5 and 20 hr. samples) or Whatman No. 1 filters (remaining samples) by gentle vacuum filtration; pollen washed with 10 ml Dickinson's medium lacking ^{14}C-leu; pollen scraped off filter and added to a scintillation vial 2/3 pre-filled with Cab-o-sil and 10 ml aquasol; samples counted in a Beckman LS-250 liquid scintillation counter. Filters from 0.5 and 20 hr. placed in vials and then removed.

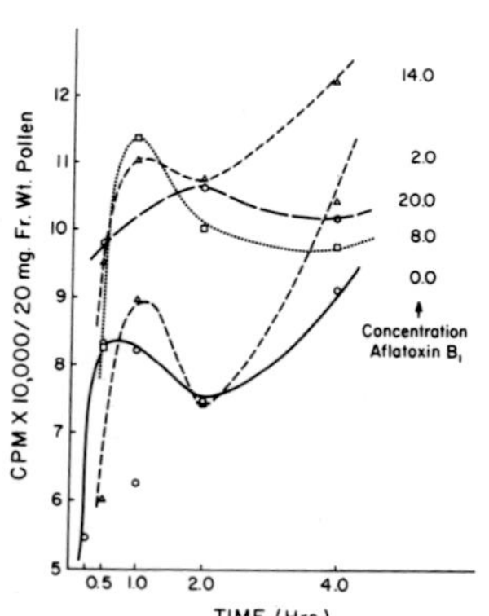

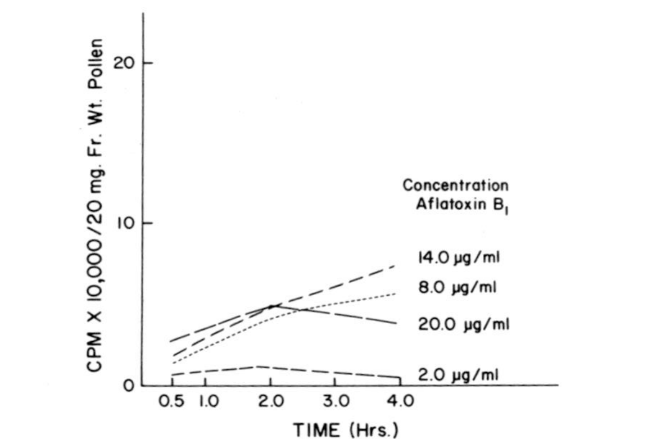

Fig. 5 ^{14}C-pro uptake as affected by aflatoxin B_1

The data for two separate experiments are illustrated here. Germinated pollen as in fig. 2a and b except that each 20 mg fr. wt. lot pollen - 10 ml aliquot of Dickinson's medium contained 1μc ^{14}C-pro (Specific Activity 255 millicuries/millimole-New England Nuclear), germination times 0.5, 1, 2, and 4 hr.; at each of these times pollen placed in cold room to stop tube elongation; pollen collected by gentle vacuum filtration onto 0.45 Millipore filters; pollen washed with Dickinson's medium lacking ^{14}C-pro; pollen counted as in fig. 4.

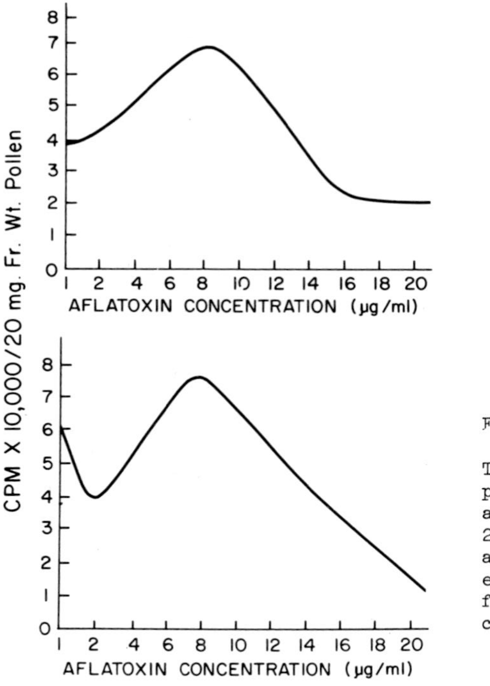

Fig. 6a.; b. ^{14}C-pro incorporation into pollen wall fractions in the absence and presence of aflatoxin B_1.

Pollen germinated as in fig. 5a and b except germination time 4 hr.; pollen harvested, ruptured and centrifuged to yield cell walls as in fig. 3a and b; walls washed 10X with 1 M NaCl and 5X with H_2O on Millipore filters; salt-H_2O washed walls on Millipore filter added to scintillation vial and counted.

tested stimulated ^{14}C-leu uptake. Additional experiments will be required to either affirm or negate this point.

<u>^{14}C-pro uptake</u>: To determine whether aflatoxin B_1 alters the synthesis of a specific protein, i.e., "extensin" (a wall-bound, hydroxyproline-containing glycoprotein[9]), we analyzed the toxin's influence on both uptake and incorporation of ^{14}C-pro (the normal precursor to peptide-bound hydroxyproline[8]). Dashek *et al*.[3], and Dashek and Harwood[4] have presented evidence, derived from labeling germinating pollen with radioactive pro followed by gel filtration of cytoplasm and enzymic-digests of walls, for the existence of "extensin" in germinating lily pollen. Markedly different results were observed for ^{14}C-pro uptake in two experiments. In one of these experiments (fig. 5), the shapes of the curves for pollen exposed to aflatoxin B_1 partially resembled that for pollen grown in the toxin's absence[4]. The latter pollen exhibited a 30 min. lag in ^{14}C-pro uptake and then a linear increase between 30 min. and 5 hr. At 2 and 20 μg/ml aflatoxin B_1 ^{14}C-pro uptake increased between 0.5 and 2 hr. and then decreased from 2 to 4 hr. Uptake of ^{14}C-pro approached linearity between 8 and 14 μg/ml aflatoxin B_1.

<u>^{14}C-pro incorporation</u>: For one experiment this incorporation into purified, wall fractions obtained from 4 hr. germinated pollen increased over that of the control between 2 and 8 μg/ml aflatoxin B_1 and then gradually declined to below the control level as the toxin's concentration was raised to 16 μg/ml (fig. 6a). This figure also reveals that the incorporation remained constant between 16 and 20 μg/ml.

In a repeat experiment (fig. 6b), ^{14}C-pro incorporation was less than the control at 2 μg/ml and 4 μg/ml aflatoxin B_1, the same as the control at 6 μg/ml and higher than the control at 8 μg/ml. As the toxin's concentration was raised to 20 μg/ml, ^{14}C-pro incorporation into walls obtained from germinated pollen decreased linearly. Although some differences between fig. 5a and b are apparent, the overall similarity between the two curves suggests a trend. An aflatoxin concentration of 8 μg/ml and perhaps even those below that may stimulate ^{14}C-pro incorporation. In contrast, higher toxin concentration (14 through 20 μg/ml) may inhibit such incorporation.

Whether the ^{14}C-pro, which was incorporated in the presence of aflatoxin B_1, was converted to hydroxyproline is unknown at the present time.

Future research includes following the metabolic fate of radioactive aflatoxin B_1 as well as examining the effects of aflatoxin B_1 on the respiratory activity and ultrastructure of germinating pollen. Also, the ability of polysomes isolated from pollen germinated in the presence of aflatoxin B_1 to incorporate labeled amino acids will be examined.

Lastly, we have extended this work to the economically important crop plant soybeans (Young _et al_., unpublished).

References

1. Butler, W. H., 1965. Liver injury and aflatoxins. In: G. N. Wogan (Ed.), Mycotoxins In Foodstuffs pp. 175-186, MIT Press, Cambridge.

2. Dashek, W. V., 1966. The lily pollen tube: Aspects of chemistry and nutrition in relation to fine structure. Ph. D. Dissertation, Marquette University, Milwaukee, Wisc., U.S.A.

3. Dashek, W. V., H. I. Harwood, and W. G. Rosen, 1971. The significance of a wall-bound, hydroxyproline-containing glycopeptide in lily pollen tube elongation. In: J. Heslop-Harrison (Ed.) Pollen Development and Physiology pp. 194-200, Butterworths, London.

4. Dashek, W. V., and H. I. Harwood, 1974. Proline, hydroxyproline and lily pollen tube elongation. Ann. Bot. (In press).

5. Dickinson, D. B. 1965. Germination of lily pollen: Respiration and tube growth. Science 150: 1818-1819.

6. Golumbic, C. and M. Kulik, 1969. Fungal spoilage on stored crops and its control. In: L. A. Goldblatt (Ed.), Aflatoxin - Scientific Background, Control and Implications pp. 307-327, Academic Press, New York.

7. Horwitz, W., 1972. (Ed.) Aflatoxins. Official methods of analysis of the association of official analytical chemists. Section 26, 020-26061 p. 429, Washington, D.C.

8. Lamport, D. T. A., 1969. The isolation and partial characterization of hydroxyproline-rich glycopeptides obtained by enzymic degradation of primary cell walls. Biochemistry 8: 1155-1169.

9. Lamport, D. T. A., 1970. Cell wall metabolism. A. Rev. Pl. Physiol. 21: 235-270.

10. Llewellyn, G. C. and W. V. Dashek, 1973. The influence of the hepatocarcinogen aflatoxin B_1 on lily pollen germination and tube elongation. Incompatibility Newsletter 3: 18-22.

11. Llewellyn, G. C., W. W. Carlton, J. E. Robbers, and W. G. Hansen, 1974. The response of the Syrian hamster (Mesocricetus auratus) to chronic administration of aflatoxin B_1 and 17 β-estradiol. Dev. Ind. Microbiol. 15: 358-367.

12. Lowry, O. H., N. J. Rosebrough, A. L. Farr, and R. J. Randall, 1951. Protein measurement with the folin phenol reagent. J. bio. Chem. 193: 265-275.

13. Sarasin, A. and Y. Moulè, 1973. Inhibition of in vitro protein synthesis by aflatoxin B_1 derivatives. FEBS Letters 32: 347-350.

14. Sondheimer, E. and H. F. Linskens, 1974. Control of in vitro germination and tube extension of Petunia hybrida pollen. Koninkl. Nederl. Akademic Van Wetenschappen-Amsterdam Proceedings, Series C, 77: 116-124.

15. Truelove, B., D. E. Davis and O. C. Thompson, 1970. The effects of aflatoxin B_1 on protein synthesis by cucumber cotyledon discs. Can. J. Bot. 48: 485-491.

16. Wogan, G. N., 1968. Biochemical responses to aflatoxin. Cancer Res. 28: 2282-2287.

Acknowledgements

We express our thanks to Drs. D. Dickinson (University of Illinois) and F. Loewus (State University of New York) for pollen supplies. We thank Mr. T. Eadie of the Virginia Department of Agriculture and Commerce for confirming the concentration of our aflatoxin B_1 stocks.

Appreciation is extended to F. Bolton, R. Harden, J. Lalor, J. Lassiter, S. R. Lewis, C. Mills, P. Sheretz, G. Weingart, and J. W. Young who contributed to this work. Special thanks is given to J. C. Chancey, Jr. for his contribution. Mr. R. H. Johnson is thanked for technical advice. We are grateful to Ms. Pat Neweceral for typing. The financial support of Virginia Commonwealth University is acknowledged.

AUTHOR INDEX

SUBJECT INDEX

—